Dynamic Modelling
Edited by Alisson V. Brito

Republished by InTech
Janeza Trdine 9, 51000 Rijeka, Croatia

Technical Editor Teodora Smiljanic

Additional hard copies can be obtained from orders@intechopen.com

Dynamic Modelling, Edited by Alisson V. Brito
p. cm.
ISBN 978-953-7619-68-8

For EU product safety concerns:
IN TECH d.o.o., Prolaz Marije Krucifikse Kozulić 3, 51000 Rijeka, Croatia,
info@intechopen.com or visit our website at intechopen.com.

Meet the editor

Alisson Brito currently works at the Centro de Informática, Universidade Federal da Paraíba, Brazil. Alisson does research in Computer Engineering. His current main project is 'Development of Safe and Efficient Solutions using UAVs.'

Preface

Dynamic modelling means modelling processes or systems, which are formed by attributes changing over time. Such dynamic aspect can make these processes and systems extremely complex. Vehicles transmission and engines, reconfigurable microchips, earthquakes and the effect of diseases in organisms are some examples of complex dynamic systems modeled and presented in this book.

When talking about modelling it is natural to talk about simulation. Simulation is the imitation of the operation of a real-world process or system over time. The objective is to generate a history of the model and the observation of that history help us to know deeply how the real-world system works, not necessarily involving the real-world into this process.

A system (or process) model takes the form of a set of assumptions concerning its operation. In a model mathematical and logical assumptions are considered, and entities and their relationship are delimited. The objective of a model - and its respective simulation - is to answer a vast number of "what-if" questions. When a kid ask his father, for example, what happens if he puts his hand on fire, the father must never answers really putting the hand of his kid on fire. He probably - the sane fathers, at least - will use an abstraction to teach him. He can say: "If you do it, you will burn and hurt your hand". But often a "what-if" question is not able to be answered just with words, and need a more sophisticated abstraction, preferably an executable abstraction - a simulation model - capable to run a huge number of possibilities in order generate a considerable number of histories, and then answer all necessary questions.

Some questions answered in this book are: What if the power distribution system does not work as expected? What if the produced ships were not able to transport all the demanded containers through the Yangtze River in China? And, what if an installed wind farm does not produces the expected energy amount? Answering these questions without a dynamic simulation model could be extremely expensive or even impossible in some cases.

The first two chapters present the dynamic modelling applied to automotive industry. In Chapter 1, *An Electric Simulator of a Vehicle Transmission Chain Coupled to a Vehicle Dynamic Model,* a vehicle transmission simulator is coupled to a vehicle dynamic model to reduce the cost and the time of the development phases of vehicles. In Chapter 2, *Modelling and Design of a Mechatronic Actuator Chain Application to a Motorized Tailgate,* the aim is to evaluate the performances of SimPowerSys (MATLAB) tool through a motorized tailgate application.

In Chapter 3, *Modelling and Simulation of Partially Reconfigurable Systems,* the dynamic modelling is presented to model an innovative kind of circuit systems, the Partially and Dynamically Reconfigurable Systems, which basically are hardware systems that can have their behavior set in runtime, giving them a flexibility before just available for software systems.

The forth Chapter, *Dynamic Modelling and Control Design of Advanced Energy Storage for Power System Applications,* presents how the dynamic behavior of Distributed Energy Storage

(DES) units in advanced energy storage systems over the frequency range from DC electricity to several thousand Hertz can be modeled with sufficient accuracy, something extremely important to power systems applications.

A military application is presented in Chapter 5, *Improving the Kill Chain for Prosecution of Time Sensitive Targets*. An executable dynamic model of human interaction and tasks were developed and presented in this chapter. It models and simulates the kill chain during live exercises without human-in-the-loop, a mix of game theory, Social Network Analysis (SNA) and Artificial Intelligence (AI).

The next chapter, *Investment in Container Ships for the Yangtze River: A System Dynamics Model*, presents a dynamic method to simulate the pattern of the container ships growing on Yangtze River in China after making investment decisions. An important system which models how decisions about can affect the economy and the life of all population involved.

A novel challenge for dynamic modelling of regional agricultural production is presented in Chapter 7, *Integrating Economic and Ecological Impact Modelling: Dynamic Processes in Regional Agriculture under Structural Change*. This work provides a consistent picture of agricultural changes with respect to overall markets and policies, and a major platform for integrated economic-ecological modelling of nutrient leaching impacts and for analysis how both agricultural production and nutrient leaching are impacted by agricultural and agri-environmental policies at regional scales.

Chapter 8, *Advanced Simulation for Semi-Autogenous Mill Systems: A Simplified Models Approach*, bases on a conventional non-stationary population balance approach to develop the necessary dynamic model of the semi-autogenous mill operation, in order to predict the time-evolution of product flow rate, level charge, power-draw, load position and others as functions of mill rotational speed and fresh feed characteristics.

An ecology study is presented in Chapter 9, *Dynamic Modelling Predictions of Airborne Acidification of Polish Terrestrial Ecosystems*. It uses a dynamic model to know how ecosystems respond to changes in atmospheric acid deposition. A number of dynamic models to simulate acidification of soils and surface waters have been developed, tested and applied to specific integrated monitoring ecosystems in various parts of Europe.

The dynamic modelling of an earthquake rupture on a fault surface is extremely challenging not only from a merely numerical point of view, but also because of the lack of knowledge of the state of the Earth crust and of the law which describes the earthquake physics. Thinking on that, Chapter 10, *Toward the Formulation of a Realistic Fault Governing Law in Dynamic Models of Earthquake Ruptures*, analyzes all possible chemical–physical mechanisms that can affect the fault weakening and indicates how they can be incorporated in a realistic governing model for earthquake analysis.

Another dynamic modelling with implications to ecology and power distribution is presented in *Dynamic Modelling of a Wind Farm and Analysis of Its Impact on a Weak Power System*, which models and simulates the voltage fluctuations caused by a wind farm in a weak power system. A model for dynamic performance of wind farms was developed. Both the dynamic behavior of an individual wind turbine and the aggregation effect of a complete wind farm were taken into account.

Chapter 12, *Optimal Design of a Multifunctional Reactor for Catalytic Oxidation of Glucose with Fast Catalyst Deactivation*, presents optimization of continuous stirred tank reactor (CSTR) and gas-lift reactor (GLR) productivity through the gas feed modulation to model the catalytic oxidation of glucose for industrial applications and solving chemical-engineering problems.

Through an advanced three-dimensional (3D), Chapter 13, *Adiabatic Shear: Pre- and Post-critical Dynamic Plasticity Modelling and Study of Impact Penetration. Heat Generation in this Context*, describes the post-critical behavior of a high strength metallic material in the presence of the ASB related evolution. And finally Chapter 14 presents the influence of the effect of treatment of diseases related to bone remodeling by dynamic loading.

First line works are presented in this book and I am sure that a vast knowledge about Dynamic Modelling can be captured from each chapter. I hope you enjoy as much I did!

Editor

Alisson V. Brito

Center of Applied Sciences and Education (CCAE)
Exact Science Department (DCE) Leader
Federal University of Paraiba (UFPB)
Brazil

Contents

Preface VII

1. An Electric Simulator of a Vehicle Transmission Chain Coupled to a Vehicle Dynamic Model 001
A. Chaibet, C. Larouci and M. Boukhnifer

2. Modelling and Design of a Mechatronic Actuator Chain Application to a Motorized Tailgate 015
K. Ejjabraoui, C. Larouci, P. Lefranc, C. Marchand, B. Barbedette and P. Cuvelier

3. A Methodology for Modelling and Simulation of Dynamic and Partially Reconfigurable Systems 029
Alisson Vasconcelos Brito, George Silveira and Elmar Uwe Kurt Melcher

4. Dynamic Modelling and Control Design of Advanced Energy Storage for Power System Applications 049
Marcelo Gustavo Molina

5. Improving the Kill Chain for Prosecution of Time Sensitive Targets 093
Edward H. S. Lo and T. Andrew Au

6. Investment in Container Ships for the Yangtze River: A System Dynamics Model 111
Yan Jin

7. Integrating Economic and Ecological Impact Modelling: Dynamic Processes in Regional Agriculture under Structural Change 125
Heikki Lehtonen

8. Advanced Simulation for Semi-Autogenous Mill Systems: A Simplified Models Approach 145
José Luis Salazar, Héctor Valdés-González and Francisco Cubillos

9. Dynamic Modelling Predictions of Airborne Acidification of Polish Terrestrial Ecosystems 157
Wojciech Mill

10. Toward the Formulation of a Realistic Fault Governing Law in Dynamic Models of Earthquake Ruptures 167
Andrea Bizzarri

11. Dynamic Modelling of a Wind Farm and Analysis of Its Impact on a Weak Power System 189
Gastón Orlando Suvire and Pedro Enrique Mercado

12. Optimal Design of a Multifunctional Reactor for Catalytic Oxidation of Glucose with Fast Catalyst Deactivation 209
Zuzana Gogová, Jiří Hanika and Jozef Markoš

13. Adiabatic Shear: Pre- and Post-critical Dynamic Plasticity Modelling and Study of Impact Penetration. Heat Generation in this Context 233
Patrice Longère and André Dragon

14. Influencing the Effect of Treatment of Diseases Related to Bone Remodelling by Dynamic Loading 263
Václav Klika, František Maršík and Ivo Mařík

1

An Electric Simulator of a Vehicle Transmission Chain Coupled to a Vehicle Dynamic Model

A. Chaibet, C. Larouci and M. Boukhnifer
Laboratoire Commande et Systèmes,
ESTACA, 34-36 rue Victor Hugo, 92 300 Levallois-Perret,
France

1. Introduction

During the two past decades, important vehicle simulators have been developed. The evolution of these simulation tools has attracted the attention of several industrials. The aim of the concept is to seek about effective methods and accurate models which allow to reach this objective and to minimize the cost and the time devoted to the development phases of vehicle systems (Kiencke & Nielsen, 2005), (Pill-Soo, 2003), (Deuszkiewicz & Radkowski, 2003).

With the vehicle simulators, the users can simulate the driving vehicle or new vehicle safety component. It offers several benefits for a designing and comprehension of the vehicle behaviours in order to improve the passenger's safety. Also the interaction of the driver, vehicle and road (environment) is studied with the help of vehicle simulators (Donghoon & Kyongsu, 2006), (Larouci et al, 2006), (Larouci et al, 2007).

The aim of this chapter is to present a method to carry out a vehicle transmission simulator coupled to a vehicle dynamic model. The transmission simulator uses electric actuators with dedicated control laws to reproduce the mechanical characteristic of the real vehicle transmission chain. The vehicle dynamic model takes into account the longitudinal, the vertical and the pitch motions. The coupled electric simulator validates the theoretical studies (automatic gearbox, test of heat engine, dynamic behaviour, passenger comfort, automated driving...) by measurements without need to the real transmission system and the real environment of the vehicle. Such a method allows to reduce significantly the cost and the time of the development phases of vehicles.

The present work is organized as follows. In the first part, a vehicle transmission simulator and vehicle dynamic model are developed. The second part focuses on the decoupled transmission simulator and the vehicle dynamic. Then a coupling approach of the previous models will be shown. The control performances of the electric simulator part depend on the electric actuator parameters which can be change under the vehicle environmental constraints (temperature, vibration…). In order to overcome these drawbacks and to improve the control law robustness of the electric simulator a sliding mode control will be proposed.

Finally, a comparison between the vehicle dynamic performances obtained using the coupled and decoupled models will be presented and discussed

2. The vehicle transmission system simulator

The electric simulator of the vehicle transmission chain simulates the mechanical characteristic of the transmission system. This simulator uses two electric actuators controlled with dedicated control laws. The first one reproduces the dynamic driving torque developed by the heat engine and available at the output of the bridge, while the second one simulates the resisting torque imposed by the vehicle load (the whole resisting efforts to the vehicle advance plus inertias).

2.1 Modeling of the real vehicle transmission system

Figure 1 illustrates the various forces applied to a vehicle during its motion on a road with a slope of angle α. These forces include the driving force and the mean resisting forces.

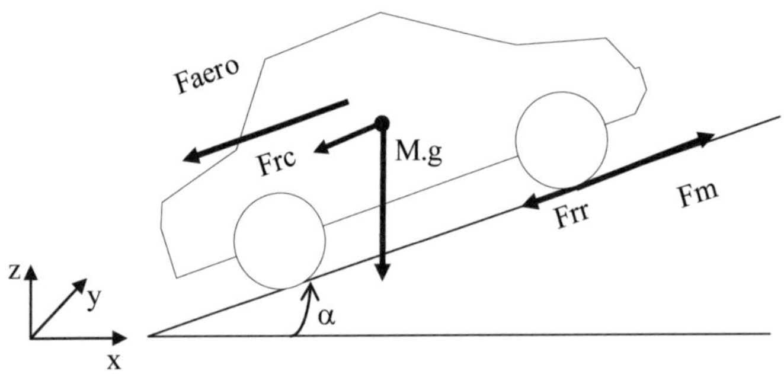

Fig. 1. Forces applied to a vehicle in a slope

Fm, Faero, Frr and Frc are, respectively, the driving force, the aerodynamics force, the rolling friction force and the resisting force in a slope, (Bauer, 2005), (Minakawa et al., 1999). To model the real vehicle transmission system, we suppose that the transmission losses are neglected (the efficiency of clutch and gear box reaches 1) and only longitudinal forces are considered (Liang et al., 2003), (Nakamura et al., 2003), (Sawas et al., 1999), (Krick, 1976). Using these assumptions, the following equations can be written:

2.1.1 According to the heat engine

$$\left(J_{th} + J_{eb}\right) \cdot \frac{d\Omega_{th}}{dt} = C_{m\_th} - C_{r\_eb} \tag{1}$$

J_{th} and J_{eb} are, respectively, the inertias of the heat engine and the input shaft of the gearbox. Ω_{th} is the angular speed of the heat engine. C_{m_th} and C_{r_eb} are, respectively, the heat engine torque and the resisting torque (the resisting torque at the input of the gearbox seen by the heat engine) (see figure 2).

2.1.2 According to the bridge

$$\left(J_{sp} + J_{roues}\right) \cdot \frac{d\Omega_{sp}}{dt} = C_{m\_sp} - C_{r\_roues} \tag{2}$$

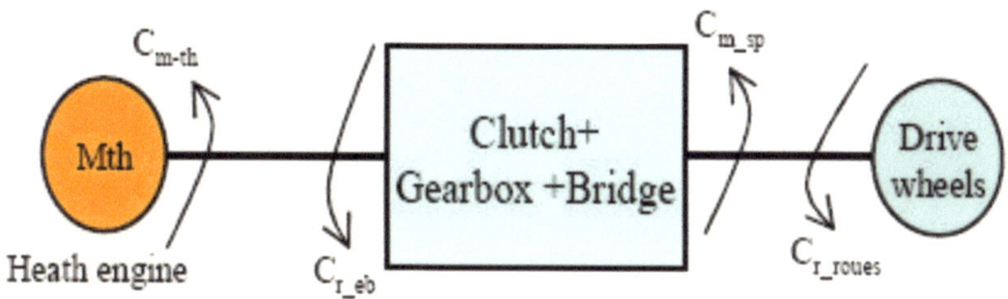

Fig. 2. Simplified transmission system

J_{sp} and J_{roues} are, respectively, the inertia at the output of the bridge and the inertia of the wheels. Ω_{sp} is the angular speed at the output of the bridge. C_{m_sp} and C_{r_roues} are, respectively, the torque at the output of the bridge and the resisting torque at the wheels.

2.1.3 According to the centre of gravity of the vehicle

$$M \cdot \frac{dV}{dt} = F_m - F_{aero} - F_{rr} - F_{rc} \tag{3}$$

$$\begin{cases} F_{aero} = \frac{1}{2} \cdot \rho \cdot C_x \cdot S_f \cdot V^2 \\ F_{rr} = f_{rr} \cdot M \cdot g \cdot \cos(\alpha) \\ F_{rc} = M \cdot g \cdot \sin(\alpha) \\ \Omega_{th} = \Omega_{sp} \cdot R_t \\ V = \Omega_{sp} \cdot R_{sc} \end{cases}$$

M	the total vehicle mass	kg
V	the vehicle longitudinal speed	m/s
ρ	density of the air	kg/m^3
C_x	the drag coefficient	
S_f	the frontal (transverse) section of the vehicle	m^2
f_{rr}	the coefficient of rolling friction	
g	the acceleration of gravity	$9.81\ m/s^2$
α	the slope angle	rad
R_{sc}	loaded radius (ray of the driving wheel)	m
$R_t=R_b.R_p$	total reduction ratio	
R_b	the gearbox ratio	
R_p	the bridge ratio	

Table 1. Nomenclature

The transmission is supposed without losses. So:

$$C_{r\_roues} = F_m \cdot R_{sc}$$

$$C_{m\_sp} = C_{r\_eb} \cdot R_t$$

From the equation 3, we deduce that:

$$\left(J_{sp} + J_{roues} + M \cdot R_{sc}^2\right) \cdot \frac{d\Omega_{sp}}{dt} = C_{m\_sp} - C_{sr\_sp} \quad (4)$$

Where:
$C_{sr\text{-}sp}$ is the total resisting torque in the steady state at the output of the bridge (5):

$$C_{sr\_sp} = \frac{1}{2} \cdot \rho \cdot C_x \cdot S_f \cdot R_{sc}^3 \cdot \Omega_{sp}^2 + M \cdot g \cdot R_{sc} \cdot \left[\sin(\alpha) + f_{rr} \cdot \cos(\alpha)\right] \quad (5)$$

2.2 Modeling of the equivalent system

In order to reproduce the behavior of the real vehicle transmission chain, an equivalent model using two electric actuators is considered (figure 3). In this model, the electric actuator M1 simulates the heat engine, while the second actuator (M2) simulates the resisting forces.

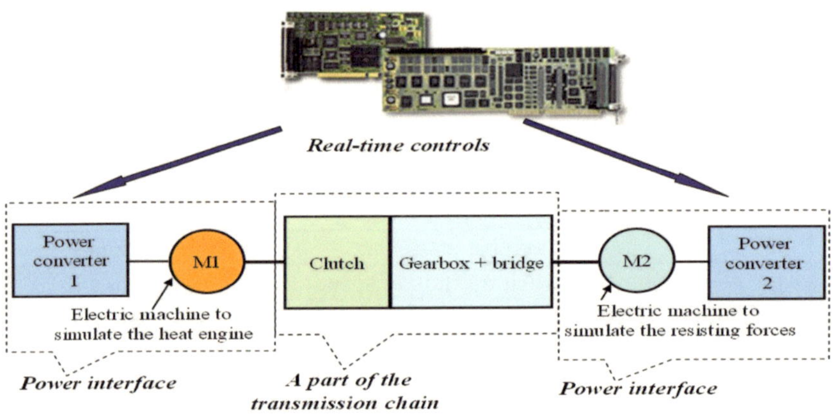

Fig. 3. A first equivalent model

In order to work in a reduced torque scale and to validate the coupling of a transmission model to a vehicle dynamic one, the previous configuration (figure 3) is reduced to the configuration presented in figure 4 where the actuator M2 simulates the whole resisting torque due to aerodynamic frictions, rolling frictions, resisting torque in a slope and inertia with a torque reduction factor (fc2). However, the electric actuator M1 simulates both the heat engine and the gearbox with a torque reduction factor (fc1).

This model can be used to test control strategies of automatic gearbox and to study the influence of these strategies on the vehicle dynamic behavior in order to improve the passenger comfort for example.

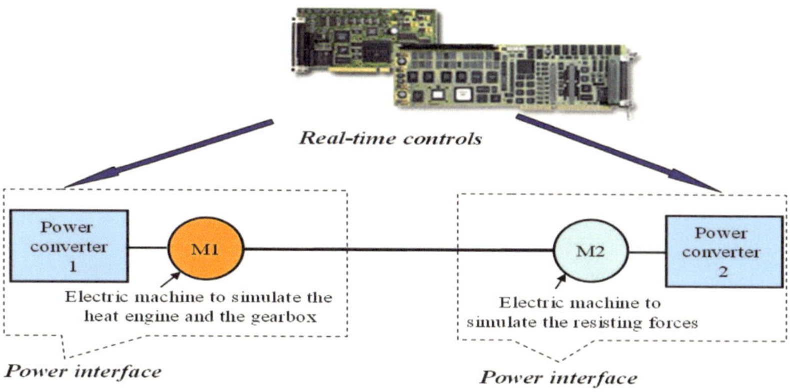

Fig. 4. A second equivalent model

Considering fc2 = fc1= fc yields:

$$\Omega_1 = \Omega_2 = \Omega_{sp} = \frac{\Omega_{th}}{R_t} \text{ and } \quad C_{m\_1} = \frac{C_{m-sp}}{fc}$$

Ω_1 and Ω_2 are the angular velocities of the electric actuators M1 and M2. Therefore, the equation 2 can be written as follows:

$$(J_{sp} + J_{roues}) \cdot \frac{1}{fc} \cdot \frac{d\Omega_1}{dt} = C_{m\_1} - \frac{1}{fc} \cdot C_{r\_roues} \tag{6}$$

The mechanical equation on the common tree of the two electric actuators is:

$$(J_1 + J_2) \cdot \frac{d\Omega_1}{dt} = C_{m\_1} - C_{r\_2} \tag{7}$$

Where:

J_1 and J_2 are the moment of inertia of the actuators M1 and M2. C_{m_1} and C_{r_2} are the torques of the actuators M1 and M2 respectively.

2.3 Torque control laws of the electric actuators

The resisting torque which must be developed by the actuator M2 (C_{r_2}) is deduced from equations (6) and (7). So:

$$C_{r\_2} = \frac{1}{fc} \cdot C_{r\_roues} + \left[\left(J_{sp} + J_{roues}\right) \cdot \frac{1}{fc} - (J_1 + J_2) \right] \cdot \frac{d\Omega_1}{dt} \tag{8}$$

Where:

$$C_{r\_roues} = M \cdot R_{sc}^2 \cdot \frac{d\Omega_{sp}}{dt} + C_{sr\_sp} = M \cdot R_{sc}^2 \cdot \frac{d\Omega_1}{dt} + C_{sr\_sp}$$

$C_{sr\text{-}sp}$ is the total resisting torque in the steady state given by equation 5. So:

$$C_{r\_2}=\frac{1}{fc}\cdot\left[\frac{1}{2}\cdot\rho\cdot C_x\cdot S_f\cdot R_{sc}^3\cdot\Omega_1^2+M\cdot g\cdot R_{sc}\cdot(\sin(\alpha)+\cos(\alpha))\right]+ \\ +\left[\left(J_{sp}+J_{roues}+M\cdot R_{sc}^2\right)\cdot\frac{1}{fc}-(J_1+J_2)\right]\cdot\frac{d\Omega_1}{dt} \tag{9}$$

In the same way, the torque which must be developed by the actuator M1 (C_{m_1}) is deduced from equations (1) and (7). So:

$$C_{m\_1}=\frac{R_t}{fc}\cdot\left[C_{m\_th}-R_t\cdot\left(J_{th}+J_{eb}\right)\cdot\frac{d\Omega_1}{dt}\right] \tag{10}$$

As a result the torque control laws of the actuators M1 and M2 ($C_{m\_1\_ref}$ and $C_{r\_2\_ref}$) are expressed as follows:

$$C_{m\_1\_ref}=\frac{R_t}{fc}\cdot\left[C_{m\_th}-R_t\cdot\left(J_{th}+J_{eb}\right)\cdot\frac{d\Omega_1}{dt}\right]+f_{v1}\cdot\Omega_1+C_{s1} \tag{11}$$

$$C_{r\_2\_ref}=\frac{1}{fc}\cdot\left[\frac{1}{2}\cdot\rho\cdot C_x\cdot S_f\cdot R_{sc}^3\cdot\Omega_1^2+M\cdot g\cdot R_{sc}\cdot(\sin(\alpha)+\cos(\alpha))\right] \\ +\left[\left(J_{sp}+J_{roues}+M\cdot R_{sc}^2\right)\cdot\frac{1}{fc}-(J_1+J_2)\right]\cdot\frac{d\Omega_1}{dt}-f_{v2}\cdot\Omega_1-C_{s2} \tag{12}$$

f_{v1} and f_{v2} are the viscous friction coefficients of the actuators M1 and M2.
Cs_1 and Cs_2 are the torques induced by the dry frictions of the two electric actuators.
These control laws compensate the losses induced by viscous and dry frictions of the two electric actuators.

2.4 Simulation results

A speed regulator is included in the simulation model. It determines the position of the accelerator pedal which allows to track a desired speed.
A vehicle starting test is carried out to validate the modeling of the equivalent transmission chain. It consists to evaluate the time necessary to reach a vehicle desired speed of 90 km/h (figure 5).

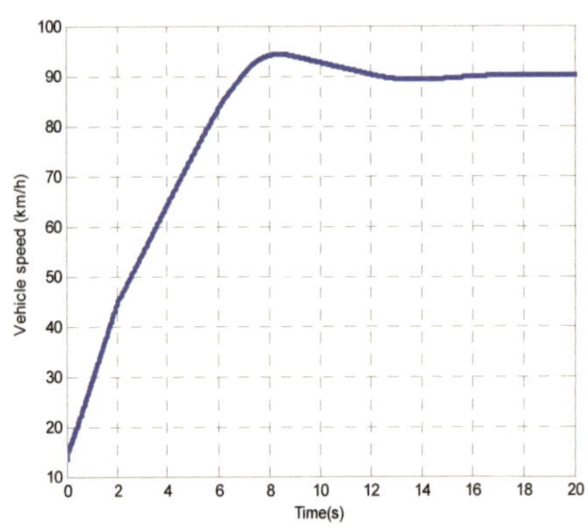

Fig. 5. A vehicle starting test

The regulator parameters are adjusted to obtain a vehicle starting time (12s in figure 5) close to the starting time given by the manufacturer (11.6s), (Grunn & Pham, 2007).
Figure 6 presents the desired torque and the real one developed by the electric actuator M1 in a case of a road profile characterized by different slopes (figure 7). This torque is the image of the torque available at the output of the bridge (with a reduction coefficient fc = 100). As a result, the real torque is very close to the desired one. Moreover, this torque is more important at the vehicle starting and in front of slopes to overcome the vehicle inertia and the resisting torque caused by these slopes.

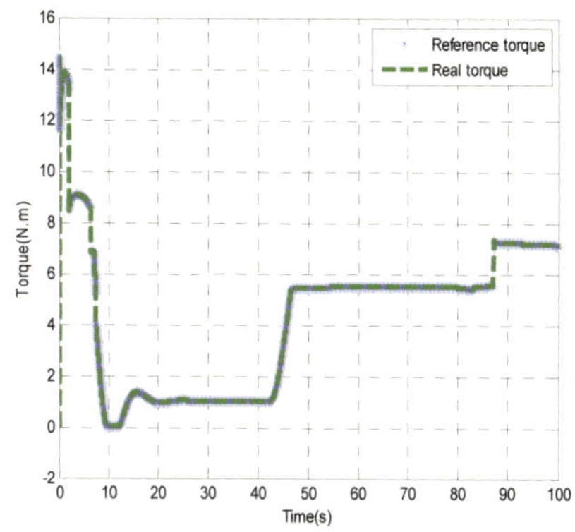

Fig. 6. Real and reference (desired) torques of the machine M1

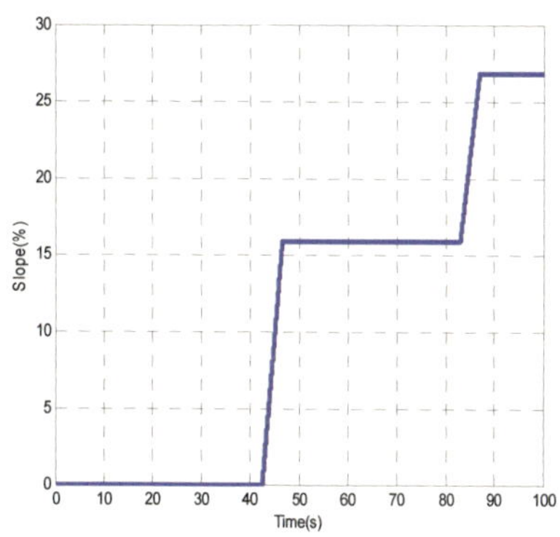

Fig. 7. Slopes of the considered road profile

3. The vehicle dynamic model

In this part a three degree-of-freedom vehicle dynamic model is presented. It takes into account the longitudinal, the vertical and the pitch motions of a vehicle. In this model, the yaw, the roll and the transversal motions are ignored. Only translations according to the longitudinal (x) and vertical (z) directions and the pitch rotation are considered.
Under these assumptions, the overall motion of the vehicle can be described by three equations (13). The first one characterizes the longitudinal dynamic. The second one represents the dynamics of the vertical motion and the latest describes the pitch motion, (Grunn & Pham, 2007).

$$\begin{cases} \dot{V} = \dfrac{F_x - m \cdot h \cdot \ddot{\varphi}}{M} \\ \ddot{Z} = \dfrac{F_z}{m} \\ \ddot{\phi} = \dfrac{M \cdot M_y - m \cdot h \cdot F_x}{M \cdot (I_y + m \cdot h^2) - (m \cdot h)^2} \end{cases} \tag{13}$$

where:
M: the total vehicle mass
m: the sprung mass
h: the vertical distance between the vehicle centre gravity and the pitch centre
I_y: the moment of inertia according to the y-axis
In this model, the resulting forces F_x controls the longitudinal dynamics, (Pacejka, 2005). The vertical motion is controlled by a resulting force F_z and the pitch motion is controlled by the pitch moment M_y. In this vehicle dynamic model (decoupled model), the transmission system is modeled by a gain and the driving torque is supposed proportional to the position of the accelerator pedal.

4. Coupling of the transmission of the simulator to the vehicle dynamic model

The coupled model (figure8) associates the transmission simulator and the vehicle dynamic model by replacing the transmission part of the vehicle dynamic model by the transmission simulator presented in second part. In this case, the resisting torque which must be developed by the actuator M2 takes into account the pitch effect. This torque is the same one calculated in the vehicle dynamic model plus the viscous and dry frictions of the actuator M2.

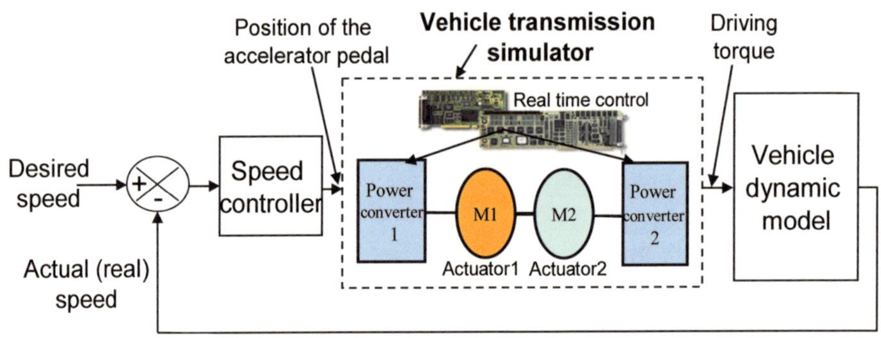

Fig. 8. Block diagram of the coupled model

The control performances of the electric simulator depend on the electric actuator parameters which can be change under the vehicle environmental constraints (temperature, vibration…). In order to eliminate this problem and to improve the control law robustness of the electric simulator a sliding mode control is used.

4.1 Sliding mode control law

In this part we develop a first sliding mode control law. The DC machine is described by the following equation:

$$U(t) = L\frac{dI(t)}{dt} + RI(t) + K_m\Omega(t) \tag{14}$$

U is the supply voltage. L,R,K_m and Ω are respectively the inductance, the resistance the torque coefficient and the velocity of the DC machine.
First, the sliding surface S is chosen as follows:

$$S = \xi_1 + c_1\int_0^t \xi_1 d\tau \tag{15}$$

c_1 is a control parameter.
ξ_1 is the error between the real courant (I) and the desired one (I_{des}):

$$\xi_1 = I - I_{des} \tag{16}$$

The equivalent control input is first computed from $\dot{S} = 0$.

$$\dot{S} = -\frac{R}{L}I - \frac{E}{L} + \frac{1}{L}U + c_1\xi_1 - \dot{I}_{des} = G + BU \tag{17}$$

Where:

$$\begin{cases} G = -\frac{R}{L}I - \frac{E}{L} + c_1\xi - \dot{I}_{des} \\ B = \frac{1}{L} \end{cases}$$

The equivalent control input is thus (U_{eq}):

$$U_{eq} = -\frac{G}{B}$$

By choosing a constant and proportional approach, we finally obtains:

$$U = U_{eq} - K_1 sign(S) - K_2(S) \tag{18}$$

$$sign(S) = \begin{cases} 1 & if\ S > 0 \\ -1 & if\ S < 0 \\ 0 & if\ S = 0 \end{cases}$$

K_1 and K_2 are control parameters. When the system is far from the sliding manifold, the behaviour is dominated by K_2 term, however K_1 term becomes dominant when approaching the manifold. A good choice of K_1 and K_2 will allows to reduce both the convergence time and the well-known chattering phenomena near the sliding manifold (Chaibet et al, 2004). In our case K_1=0.05, K_2=1.

4.2 Simulation results

Different simulations are presented to compare the dynamic performances of the coupled model and the decoupled one for a vehicle desired speed vdes = 60km/h on a straight road. The figures 9 and 10 show the vehicle speed and the longitudinal acceleration for the both models (coupled and decoupled models).

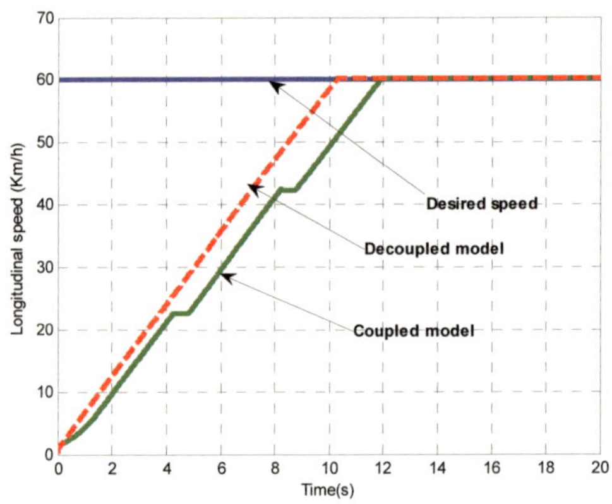

Fig. 9. Longitudinal vehicle speed

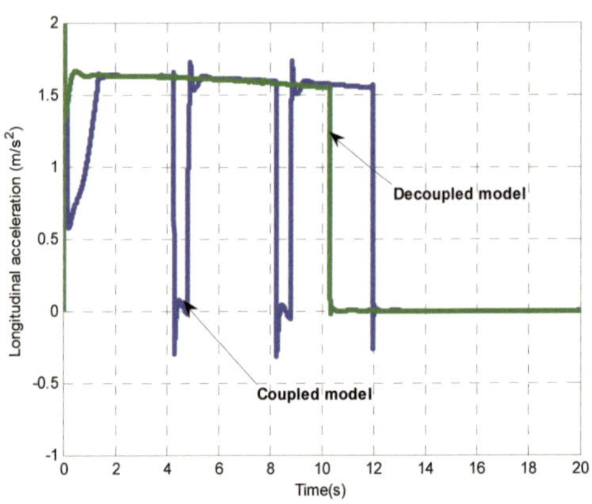

Fig. 10. Longitudinal acceleration

As results, the desired speed is reached more quickly in the case of the decoupled model. This difference is due to the time delay caused by the change of the commuted speeds. In addition and for the same reason, important variations on the longitudinal acceleration of the coupled model are detected.

Note that these variations (-0.3m/s^2 to 2m/s^2) respect the passenger comfort limits (Chaibet et al, 2005), (Nouveliere & Mammar, 2003), (Huang & Renal, 1999).
The figures 11, 12 and 13 show respectively, the vertical acceleration of the sprung mass, its vertical movement and the pitch motion.
We note that the important variations obtained in the case of the coupled model are induced by the change of the commuted speeds.
Through these results, we can deduce that the integrating of the transmission chain simulator in the vehicle dynamic model allows to detect more dynamic variations and to reflect the vehicle dynamic behavior with high accuracy.

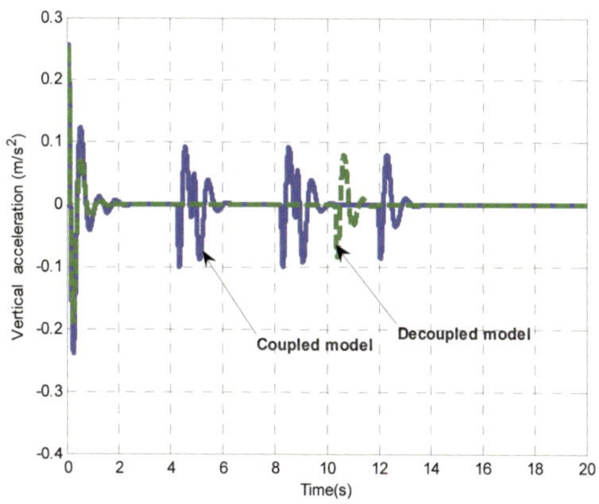

Fig. 11. Vertical acceleration of the sprung mass

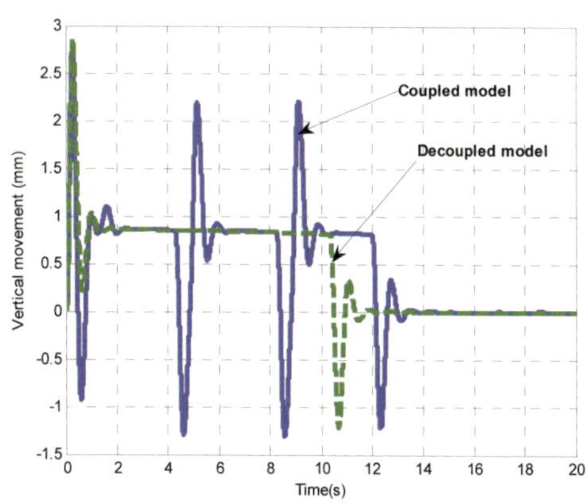

Fig. 12. Vertical movement of the sprung mass

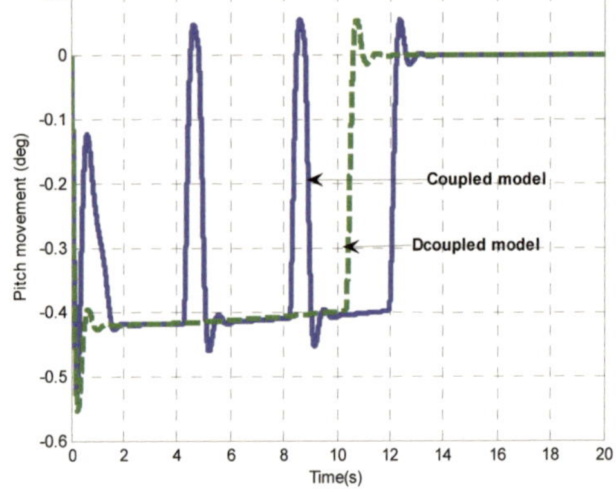

Fig. 13. Pitch movement

5. Conclusion

An electric simulator of the vehicle transmission chain coupled with a vehicle dynamic model is presented in this chapter. The transmission simulator uses two electric actuators with speed and torque control. The first actuator simulates both the heat engine and the gearbox. The second one simulates the forces resisting to the vehicle advance as well as the inertias.

The dynamic vehicle model includes longitudinal, vertical and pitch motions. The coupled model represents the vehicle dynamic behavior with high accuracy. This model is an interesting solution to carry out studies on transmission and vehicle dynamic aspects (development of control strategies of automatic gearbox by taking into account the dynamic behavior, improvement of safety and passenger comfort, test of intelligent vehicle...) without need to the real transmission system and the real environment of the vehicle. Therefore, it allows to reduce significantly the time and the cost of the development phases of the transmission and dynamic behavior systems.

6. References

Kiencke, U.; Nielsen, L. (2005). *Automotive Control Systems For Engine, Driveline and Vehicle*, Springer, ISBN 3-540-23139-0, Berlin

Pill-Soo, K. (2003). Cost modeling of battery electric vehicle and hybrid electric vehicle based on major parts cost, *Power Electronics and Drive Systems, PEDS 2003*, pp. 1295- 1300, ISBN 0-7803-7885-7, Singapore, 17-20 Nov. 2003

Deuszkiewicz, P.; Radkowski, S. (2003). On-line condition monitoring of a power transmission unit of a rail vehicle, *Mechanical Systems and Signal Processing journal*, Vol., 17, No., 6, (November 2003), page numbers (1321-1334)

Donghoon, H.; Kyongsu, Y. (2006). Evaluation of Adaptive Cruise Control Algorithms on a Virtual Test Track, *Proceedings of American control conference,* pp. 5849-5854, ISBN 1-4244-0209-3, Minneapolis, Minnesota, USA, June 14-16, 2006

Larouci, C.; Feld, G & Didier, Jp. (2006). Modeling and control of the vehicle transmission chain using electric actuators, *IEEE Industrial Electronics, IECON 2006,*pp. 4066-4071, ISBN 1-4244-0390-1, Paris, France, November 7-10-2006

Larouci, C.; Dehondt, E.; Harakat, A & Feld, G. (2007). Modeling and Control of the Vehicle Transmission System Using Electric Actuators; Integration of a Clutch, *IEEE International Symposium on Industrial Electronics ISIE,* pp. 2202-2207, ISBN 978-1-4244-0755-2, Vigo, Spain, June 04-07, 2007

Bauer, S. (2005). *Mémento de technologie automobile,* Bosch Edition, page numbers (1-961), ISBN 3934584195, 9783934584198, Germany

Minakawa, M.; Nakahara, J.; Ninomiya, J & Orimoto, Y. (1999). Method for measuring force transmitted from road surface to tires and its applications, *JSAE Review,* Vol., 20, No., 4, (October 1999), page numbers (479-485)

Liang, H.; To Chong, K.; Soo No, T & Yi, S.Y. (2003).Vehicle longitudinal brake control using variable parameter sliding control, *Control Engineering Practice,* Vol.,11, No., 4, (April 2003), page numbers (403-411)

Nakamura, K.; Kosaka, H.; Kadota, K.; & Shimizu, K. (2003). Development of a motor-assisted 4WD system for small front-wheel-drive vehicles, *JSAE Review,* Vol., 24, No., 4, (October 2003), page numbers (417-424)

Sawase, K.; Sano, Y. (1999). Application of active yaw control to vehicle dynamics by utilizing driving/breaking force, *JSAE Review,* Vol.,20, No.,2, (April 1999), page numbers (289-295)

Krick,G .(1973). Behaviour of tyres driven in soft ground with side slip, *Journal of Terramechanics,* Vol., 9, No., 4, (1973), page numbers (9-30)

Grunn,E.; Pham,A .(2007). A 0 D Modelling for Automotive Dynamic, *Journal Européen des Systèmes Automatisés JESA,* Vol., 41, No., 1, (2007), page numbers (30 - 70), France

Pacejka, H.B. (2005). *Tyre and vehicle dynamics,* Publisher Butterworth-Heinemann, page numbers (1-672), ISBN-13/EAN: 9780750669184

Chaibet,A.; Nouveliere,L. ; Netoo .M & Mammar,S. (2004). Sliding mode Control for vehicle following at Low Speed, *IEEE International French-Speaking Conference on Automatics (CIFA),* Douz, Tunisia, November 2004

Chaibet, A.; Nouveliere, L.; Mammar, S.; Netto, M & Labayrade, R. (2005). Backstepping control synthesis for both longitudinal and lateral automated vehicle, *IEEE Intelligent Vehicle Symposium,* pp:42-47, ISBN 0-7803-8961-1, Las Vegas, USA 6 - 8 June 2005

Nouvelière,L.; Mammar,S.(2003). Experimental vehicle longitudinal control using second order sliding modes, *American control conference,* pp.4705-4710, ISBN 0-7803-7896-2, Denver, Colorado USA, June 4 -6, 2003

Huang,S. Ren,W.(1999). Use of neural fuzzy networks with mixed genetic/ gradient algorithm in automated vehicle control, *IEEE TRANSACTIONS ON INDUSTRIAL ELECTRONICS*, Vol., 46, No., 6, page numbers (1090–1102), ISSN 0278-0046

2

Modelling and Design of a Mechatronic Actuator Chain Application to a Motorized Tailgate

K. Ejjabraoui[1], C. Larouci[1], P. Lefranc[2], C. Marchand[3], B. Barbedette[1] and P. Cuvelier[1]
[1]*Ecole Supérieure des Techniques Aéronautiques et de Construction Automobile,*
[2]*SUPELEC Energie,*
[3]*Laboratoire de Génie Electrique de Paris*
France

1. Introduction

Recently, several mechatronic systems are integrated in automotive applications (motorized tailgate, electrical seats…) (Su and al., 2005) (R. Juchem and B.Knorr, 2003) (Mutoh and al., 2005) (Joshi and al., 2008). The modelling of these applications needs to take into account multi-physic aspects (mechanical, electrical, control …) in order to consider the coupling effects between these domains. However, the existing tools are not well adapted to this multi-physic modelling because they are rather mono-field, less libraries are available, modelling levels (0D-1D and 2D-3D) are generally not possible in the same tool, the mechanical and electrical aspects are not modelled with the same accuracy, high difficulties to manage multi-time scale…. The close association of some potential existing tools (G. Remy and al., 2009) appears most favorable to achieve the needed mechatronic environment. The aim of this work is to evaluate the performances of MATLAB/SIMULINK/SimPowerSys tool through a motorized tailgate application.
Firstly, a description of the studied mechatronic application will be given. Secondly, different models are developed for each part (battery, dc-dc converter, electrical machine, gearbox, ball-screw and mechanical joints). In this context, dynamic, friction and losses models will be presented. Then, they are implemented and simulated using MATLAB/SIMULINK/SimPowerSys tool. Simulation results in transition and steady states will be discussed. Finally, the performances of this tool will be listed and its mains advantages and disadvantages will be presented.

2. The studied application: motorized tailgate

The figure 1 presents a synopsis of the motorized tailgate application. It's a system providing an autonomous opening and closing of some recent car trunk which uses two electromechanical actuators. In this system, three main parts can be distinguished: electrical part (battery, LC filter, dc-dc converter, and electromechanical actuator), mechanical part (gearbox, mechanical actuator with ball-screw, car tailgate) and control part (master-slave controller with position and current loops).

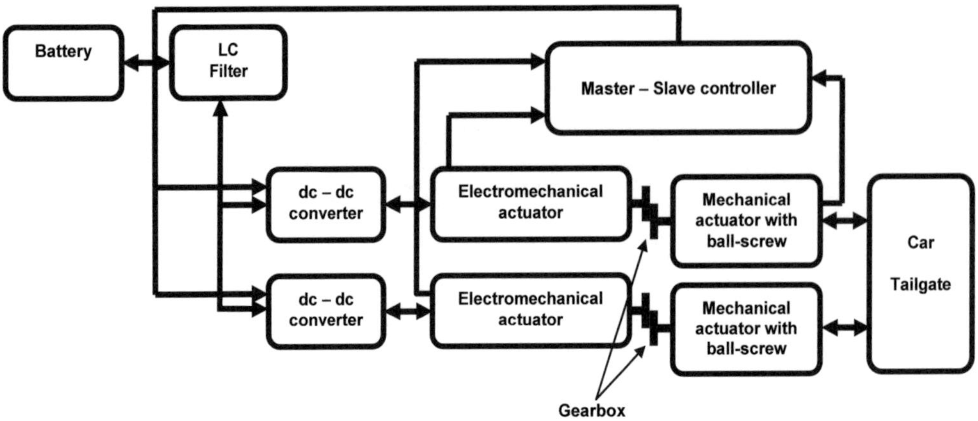

Fig. 1. Synopsis of the motorized tailgate

2.1 Description of the electrical part

The principle of the electrical part for the studied application is given by the figure 2. In fact, two electromechanical actuators (MCC 1 and MCC 2) are used to control two mechanical actuators with ball-screw. These two electromechanical actuators are associated to two dc-dc converters which are connected to a battery. To eliminate the disturbances induced by the switching frequency of the semiconductors, a LC filter is used.

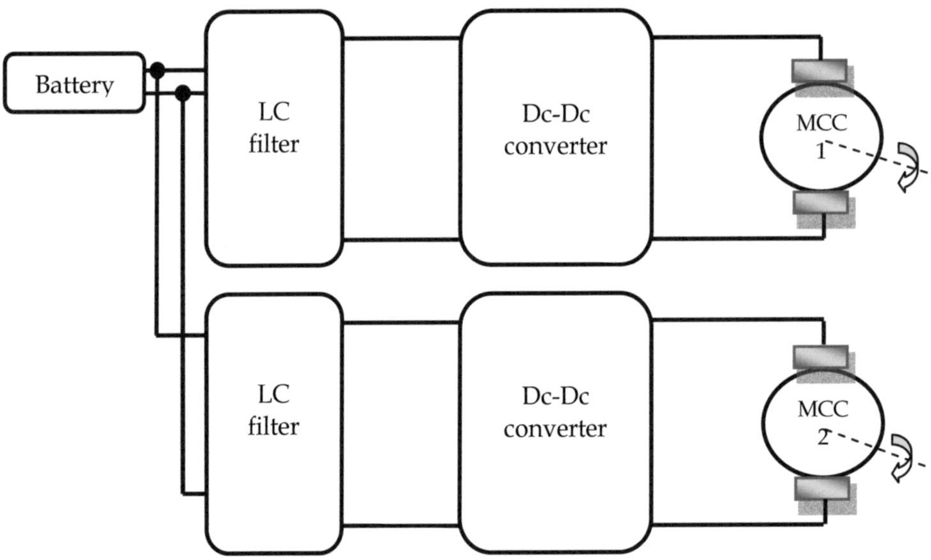

Fig. 2. The principle of the electrical part

2.1.1 Battery

The battery is modelled by a DC voltage source with a resistance representing the losses in the connections between the battery and the LC filter (figure 3).

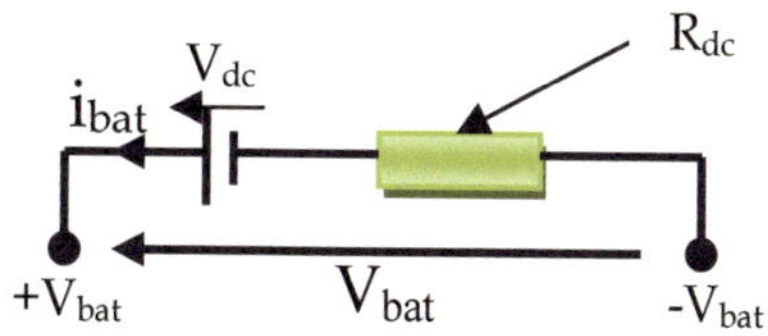

Fig. 3. Simplified model of the battery

2.1.2 LC filter

To eliminate the disturbances induced by the switching frequency of the semi-conductors, a LC filter (figure 4).

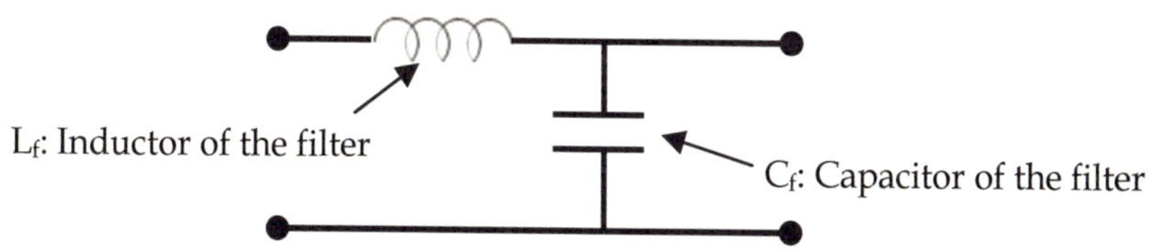

Fig. 4. The input filter scheme

2.1.3 DC-DC converter

The dc-dc converter is used to adapt the energetic exchange between two continuous sources. According to the specifications of the mechanical load (reversibility in torque and in speed) and of the battery (dc voltage source), the chosen converter for the studied application is a four-quadrant dc-dc converter which is composed of four controlled switches and four anti-parallel diodes. The figure 5 shows the architecture of this converter.

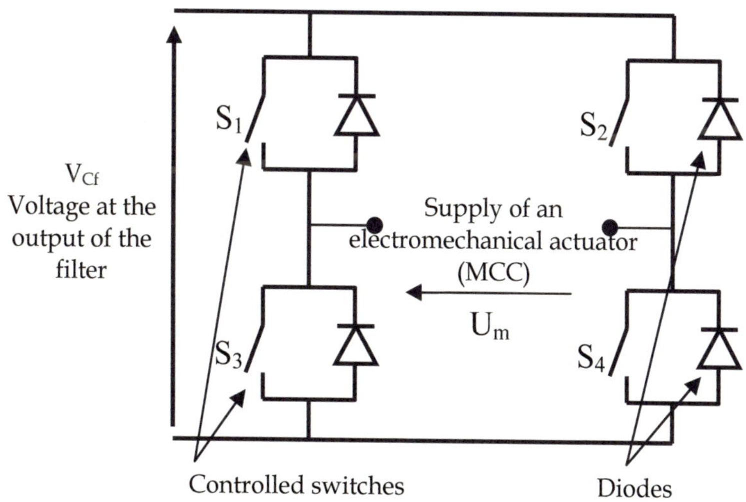

Fig. 5. Architecture of the dc-dc converter

2.1.4 Electromechanical actuator

The electromechanical actuator is used to convert electrical energy to a mechanical energy and reciprocally. It is a dispositive which is reversible in torque (current) and in speed (voltage) allowing to have two modes of operating: motor mode (transform electrical energy to a mechanical energy) and generator mode (transform mechanical energy to an electrical energy). It is composed of a fixed part (stator) and a mobile part (rotor) as shown in (figure 6.a). The figure 6.b gives the electro-mechanical scheme for this actuator. For the studied application, two electromechanical actuators are used to control two mechanical actuators with a screw-ball through gearboxes.

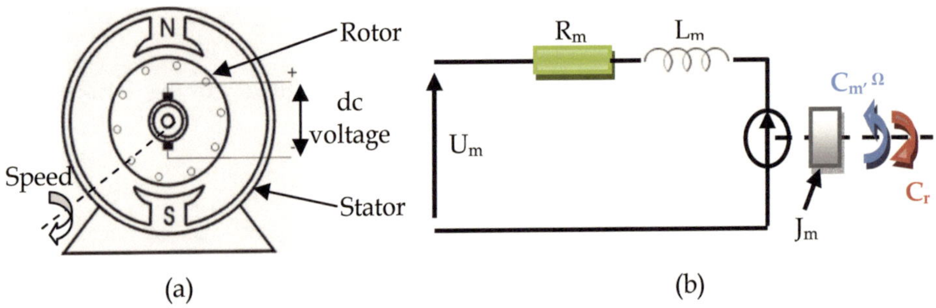

Fig. 6. (a) Physical scheme (b) Electromechanical scheme

U_m is the input voltage of the machine, R_m and L_m are respectively the resistance and the inductance of the armature (stator), C_m is the electromechanical torque of the machine, Ω is the speed angular of the rotor, J_m is the moment of inertia and C_r is the resisting torque due to load and frictions.

2.2 Description of the mechanical part

The mechanical part of the studied application is represented by a mechanical load (car body) which is actuated by two motorized mechanical actuators allowing the autonomous opening and closing of the car tailgate. To adapt the speed between the electrical machine and this mechanical actuator, a gearbox is placed between them.

The kinematics of the tailgate is ensured by hinges that we will approximate to a pivot link between the car body and the tailgate on its upper part and ball joint at lower part of the mechanical actuator.

2.2.1 Car tailgate

The car tailgate is represented by a masse (M) which is centred approximately in the centre of masse of the tailgate in closed position. The tailgate is considered a flexible body by taking into account its first torsion mode. The figure 7 shows the placement of the tailgate masse compared to two mechanical actuators and the car body in the plan (XY).

2.2.2 Motorized mechanical actuator

The motorized mechanical actuators are composed of a body and a stem. A sliding pivot link allows connect these two solids. The extremities of each actuator are connected to the body and the tailgate with a ball joint. During our study, the body of the mechanical actuator is imposed by the industrial partners and it is composed of the electrometrical actuator (DC motor), the gearbox, the spring and the ball screw. The figure 8 presents the composition of the mechanical actuators.

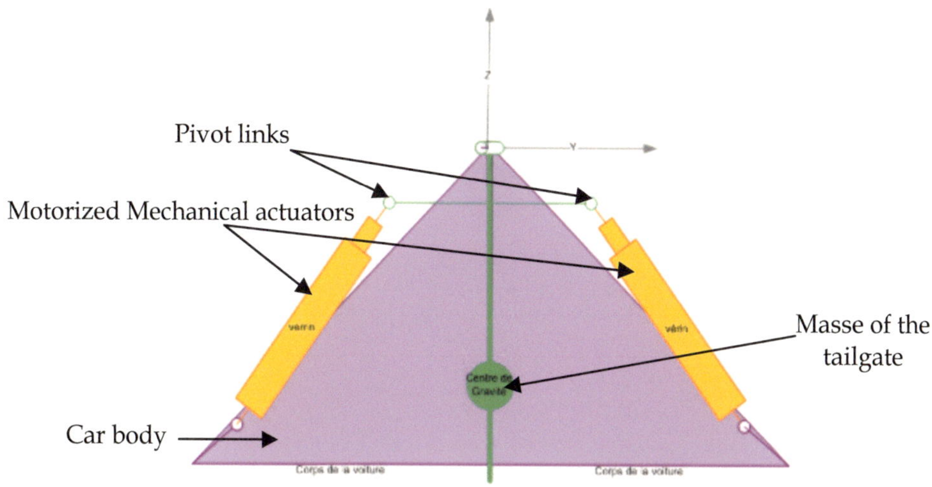

Fig. 7. Placement of the tailgate masse

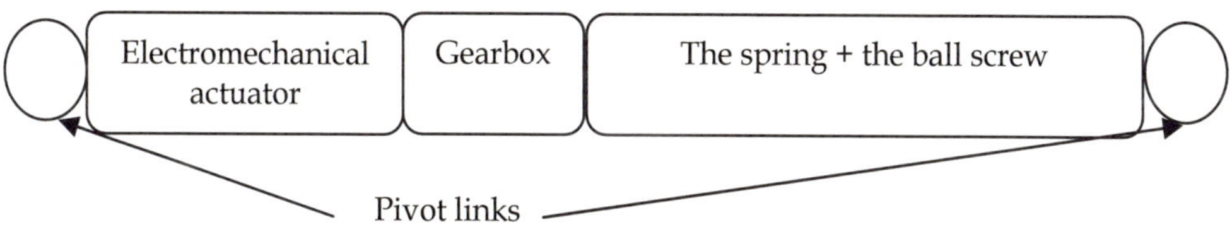

Fig. 8. Composition of the mechanical actuators

2.3 Description of the control part

To ensure the desired performances at the system outputs, a controller is adapted (master - slave controller) and associated to two dc-dc converters. The control strategy is based on a cascade correction. To perform this control aspect, the right mechanical actuator (figure 7) is called slave actuator and the left one is called the master actuator. The primary control (extern loop) is based on the position of the tailgate and the secondary control (intern loop) based on the induced current in the electrical machine. In the intern control loop, the reference current of the slave actuator is measured in the master actuator. For the extern loop, the reference of the tailgate angular position is obtained by integration of the tailgate angular velocity given in figure 9.

The figure 10 shows the principle of the cascade correction adopted for our application.

Com1 and Com2 present the control signals of converters 1 and 2 associated to the master and slave actuators.

A PI corrector is used to the intern loop (current loop) of each machine, while a PID corrector is used for the extern loop (position loop).

3. Modelling

The objective of modeling is to propose models to simulate the motorized tailgate on an open-close cycle. Physical equations governing the operation of the motorized tailgate are

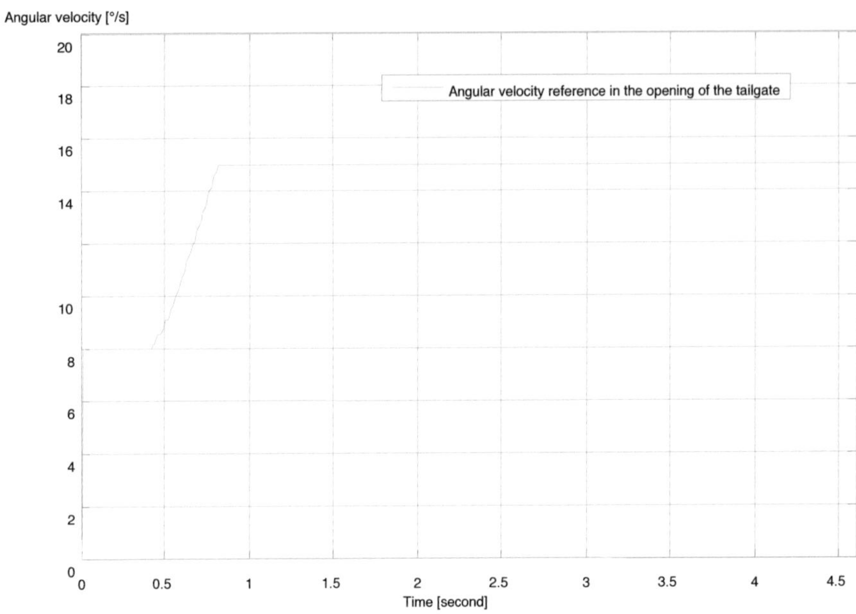

Fig. 9. Angular velocity profile in the opening phase

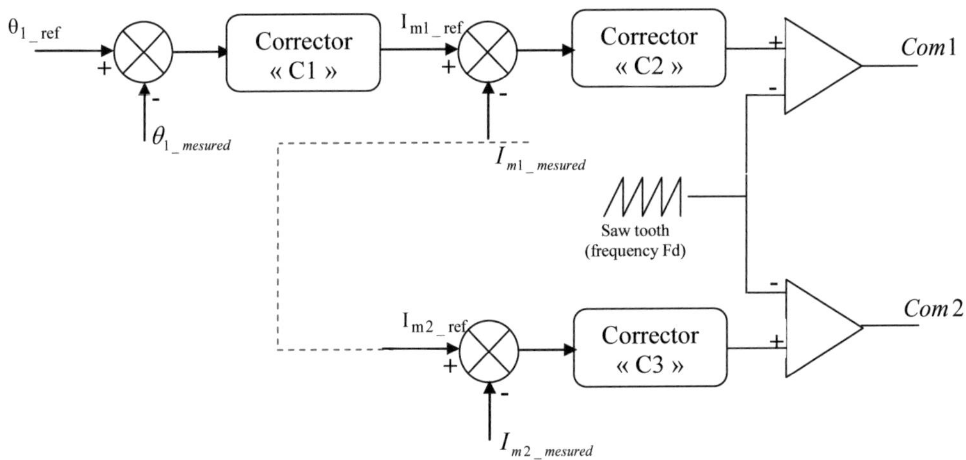

Fig. 10. the principle of the cascade correction

developed. In the electrical part, the electromechanical actuator is modeled by its electrical and mechanical equations. The battery and the LC filter are modeled respectively as shown in figures 3 and 4. In the mechanical part, the motorized tailgate car operation is modeled by differential equations resulting from the application of the kinetic moment theorem.

3.1 Models related to the mechanical part (car tailgate, mechanical actuator, and gearbox)

In order to determine the angular position according to the force developed by the mechanical actuator, we apply the theorem of the kinetic moment to each actuator with the tailgate. We obtain the system of differential equations translating the equations of motion of the tailgate:

$$\left(\frac{J}{2}+\frac{m}{2}R_{XZ}^{2}\right)\ddot{\theta}_g = R_{XZ}\frac{m}{2}g\cos\gamma_h - r_{XZ}F_{Vg}\cos\gamma_g + K\left(\theta_g-\theta_d\right) \tag{1}$$

$$\left(\frac{J}{2}+\frac{m}{2}R_{XZ}^{2}\right)\ddot{\theta}_d = R_{XZ}\frac{m}{2}g\cos\gamma_h - r_{XZ}F_{Vd}\cos\gamma_d + K\left(\theta_d-\theta_g\right) \tag{2}$$

$$\begin{cases}\gamma_{h_d} = \theta_0+\theta_d-\gamma_0-\gamma_{ref}\\ \gamma_{h_g} = \theta_0+\theta_g-\gamma_0-\gamma_{ref}\end{cases} \tag{3}$$

$$\begin{cases}\gamma_g = \sin^{-1}\left(\dfrac{D_{XZ}^2-L_{g_{XZ}}^2-r_{XZ}^2}{-2L_{g_{XZ}}.r_{XZ}}\right)\\ \gamma_d = \sin^{-1}\left(\dfrac{D_{XZ}^2-L_{d_{XZ}}^2-r_{XZ}^2}{-2L_{d_{XZ}}.r_{XZ}}\right)\end{cases} \tag{4}$$

J is the inertia of the tailgate
m is the masse of the tailgate
R_{XZ} is the distance between the center of the pivot link and the center of mass in the XZ plane.
g is the gravity
D_{XZ} is the distance between (O: center) and (B_d: attachment point between the left mechanical actuator and the car body or Bg: attachment point between the right mechanical actuator left and the car body) projected in the XZ plane
L_d is the length of the left mechanical actuator projected in the XZ plane
L_g is the length of the right mechanical actuator projected in the XZ plane
r_{XZ} is the distance between (O : center) and (C_d: attachment point between the left mechanical actuator and the tailgate or C_g : attachment point between the right mechanical actuator and the tailgate) projected in the XZ plane
θ_0 is the Angle projected in the XZ plane between axes (OB) and (OC) in the closed position
θ_d is the left angle opening of the tailgate
θ_g is the right angle opening of the tailgate
F_{Vd} is the force developed by the left mechanical actuator
F_{Vg} is the force developed by the right mechanical actuator
K is is the torsion coefficient of the tailgate
γ_h is the angle projected in the XZ plane between axes (OX) and (OG)
γ_0 is the angle projected in the XZ plane between axes (OX) and (OB)
γ_{ref} is the Angle projected in the XZ plane between axes (OC) and (OG)

3.2 Models related to the electrical part

In this part, the electro-mechanical actuator is modeled by its electrical, mechanical and coupling equations.

The electrical equation is given according to the operating mode of the machine:

- Motor mode:

$$U_m = k_m \cdot \Omega_m + R_m \cdot I_m + L_m \cdot \frac{dI_m}{dt} \tag{5}$$

- Generator mode:

$$U_m = k_m \cdot \Omega_m - R_m \cdot I_m - L_m \cdot \frac{dI_m}{dt} \tag{6}$$

The mechanical equations with the electromechanical coupling are given by the following formulas:

$$\begin{aligned} & C_{em} - C_{rch} - C_{fv} - C_{fs} = J_{mt} \cdot \frac{d\Omega_m}{dt} \\ & C_{em} = k_m \cdot I_m \end{aligned} \tag{7}$$

C_{em} is the electromechanical torque
C_{rch} is the resisting torque imposed by the load
C_{fv} is the viscous friction torque
C_{fs} is the dry friction torque
J_{mt} is the total moment of inertia
Ω_m is the angular speed of the machine
U_m is the armature voltage
R_m and L_m are respectively the resistance and the inductance of the machine armature
K_m is the electromechanical coupling coefficient
I_m is the current in the machine armature
To have compromise between simulation time and precision of the desired performances for the tailgate, the modeling of the dc-dc converter is performed by using three levels:

- **First level**

The converter is considered as a perfect controlled voltage source $V = (2 \cdot \alpha - 1) \cdot V_{bat}$. This level of modeling allows to quickly validate the system without taking into account the switching of semiconductors.
α: is the duty cycle associated with the converter control
V_{bat} is the voltage of the battery

- **Second level**

In this case, an average model of the converter is used by replacing the switching-on semiconductors during $\alpha \cdot T_d$ (or $(1-\alpha) \cdot T_d$) by a current source with a value $\alpha \cdot I_m$ (or $(1-\alpha) \cdot I_m$) and the switching-off semiconductors during $\alpha \cdot T_d$ (or $(1-\alpha) \cdot T_d$) by a voltage source with a value $\alpha \cdot V_{bus}$ (or $(1-\alpha) \cdot V_{bus}$).
T_d is the switching period
V_{bus} is the input voltage of the converter

- **Third level**

In this case, the semiconductors of the converter are modeled by controllable switches and anti-parallel diodes. This level allows considering other physical aspects (thermal, CEM...). The figure 11 below summarizes the four possible configurations for this switch and its associated equivalent scheme.

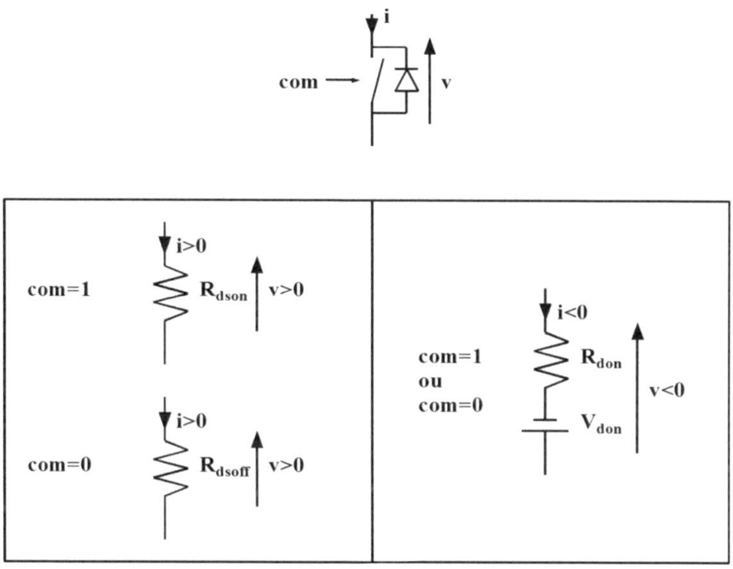

Fig. 11. the principal configurations of the elementary switch

- com: control signal of switch (com= 1: closed switch, com = 0: open Switch)
- Rd_{son}: resistance of the switch in on state (dynamic resistance of the switch).
- Rd_{soff}: resistance of the switch in off state
- Rd_{on}: resistance of the diode in the conducting state (dynamic resistance of diode)
- V_{don}: voltage drop of the diode in the conducting state

4. Implementation in MATLAB/SIMULINK/SimPowerSys

Figure 12 shows the principal of the motorized tailgate implementation in MATLAB/SIMULINK/SimPowerSys. In this work, the implementation is based on a combination between diagram blocks (by respecting the bond graph formalism (effort-flow) allowing a-causal modeling and avoid algebraic loops) in simulink and components of available organs in libraries (in matlab-simulink/SimPowerSystems). In our case, the control part is implemented by using transfer function representing the current controller (PI controller) and the position controller (PID controller). The LC filter is implemented by available organs in libraries (inductance and capacitance). The dc-dc converter is modeled by block diagram in the first level and available organs for the second and the third level. In addition, the electromechanical actuator is modeled by transfer functions representing the electrical and the mechanical aspect (formulas 5, 6 and 7) and by considering the electromechanical coupling. According to the differential equations given by the formulas 1, 2, 3 and 4 previously expressed and the other equations related to the ball screw and the tailgate, the tailgate car is implemented by using diagram blocks.

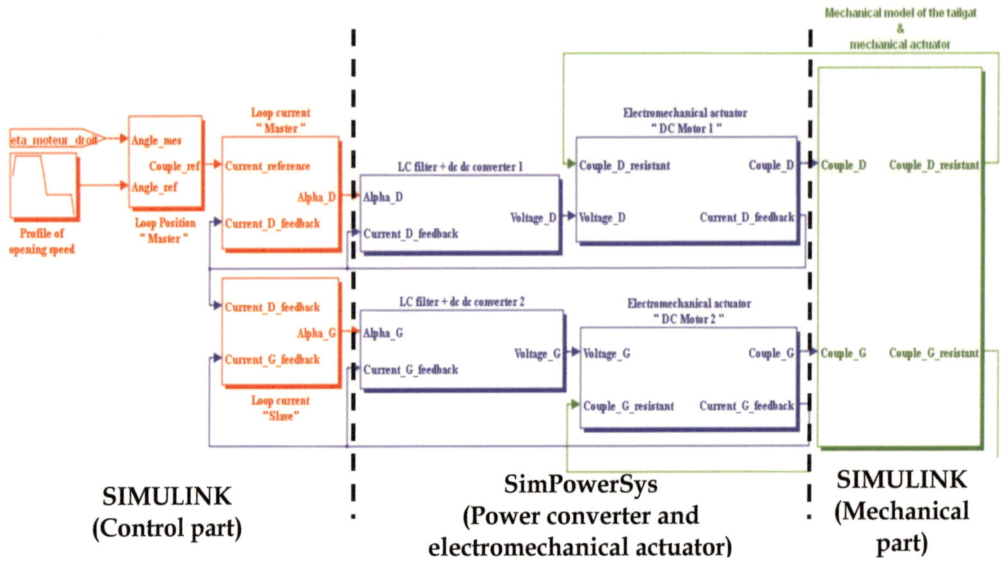

Fig. 12. Implementation in MATLAB / SIMULINK / SimPowerSys

5. Simulation results

The figures 13, 14 and 15 show respectively the tailgate opening angles, the electric machine currents and the mechanical actuator forces related to the master and slave actuators during the opening phase of the tailgate.

To carry out these simulations:

- The initial conditions for the opening angle, the length of the mechanical actuator and the spring force has been taken equal to final values of the closing cycle
- The initial conditions for the closing angle, the length of the mechanical actuator and the spring force has been taken equal to final values of the opening cycle.
- The alimentation of electrical machine (electromechanical actuator) has been stopped at the end of the opening phase and was restored early in the closing phase.
- The integrators of the controllers have been reset in the early closing phase.

Note that the third level of modeling for dc-dc converter is performed in the MATLAB/SIMULINK/SimPowerSys by multi-time scale. In fact, this aspect allows to separate the different time constants in the system which has a mechanical time constant (mechanical load) very slow that the electrical time constant corresponding to the switching frequency of the converter (20 kHz).

As results, the master and slave actuators have the same behaviour. In addition, the opening angle reference is well respected which validate the control aspect (cascade correction) used in this application.

At the beginning of the opening phase, an important torque is delivered by the electrical machine (high absorbed current) to overcome the static frictions. Then, the mechanical actuator ensures the opening with a small contribution of the electrical machine. At the end of the opening phase, the absorbed current increases in order to help the mechanical actuator to establish the tailgate at its final opening position. Note that the ripples observed in the current and a force curves are related to the semi-conductor switching of the dc-dc converter.

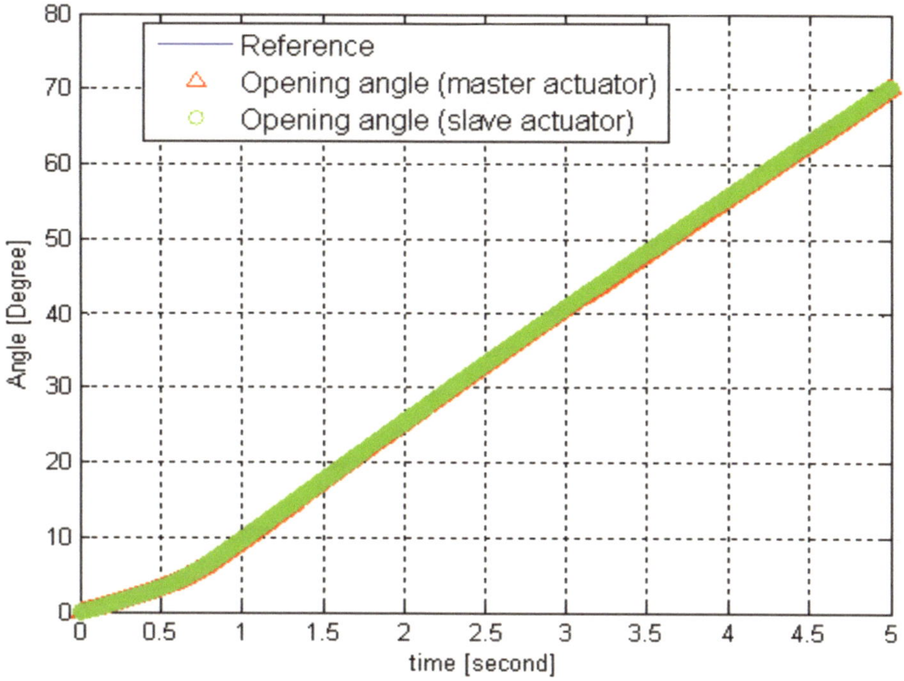

Fig. 13. Opening angles of the tailgate

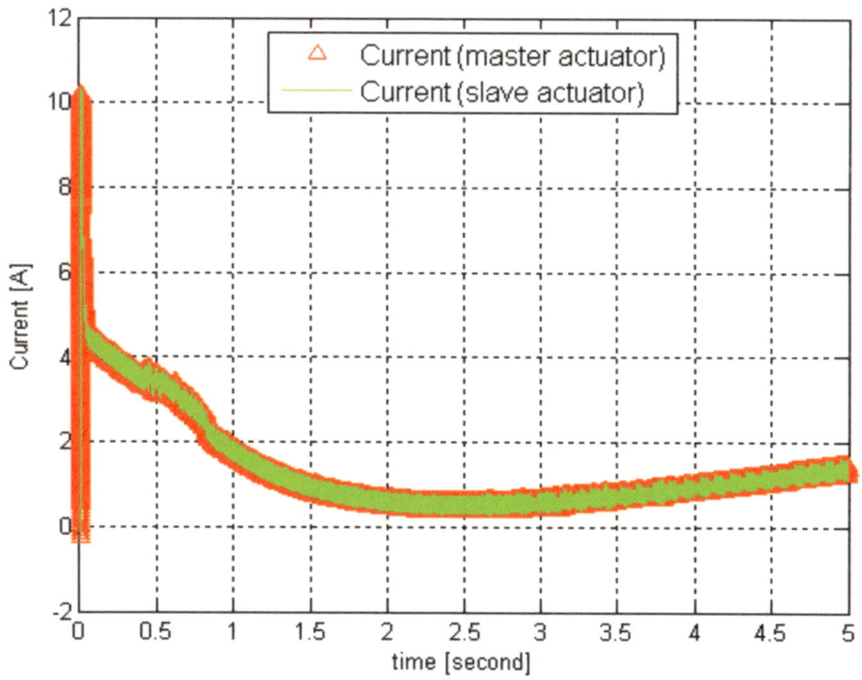

Fig. 14. Currents of the electric machines

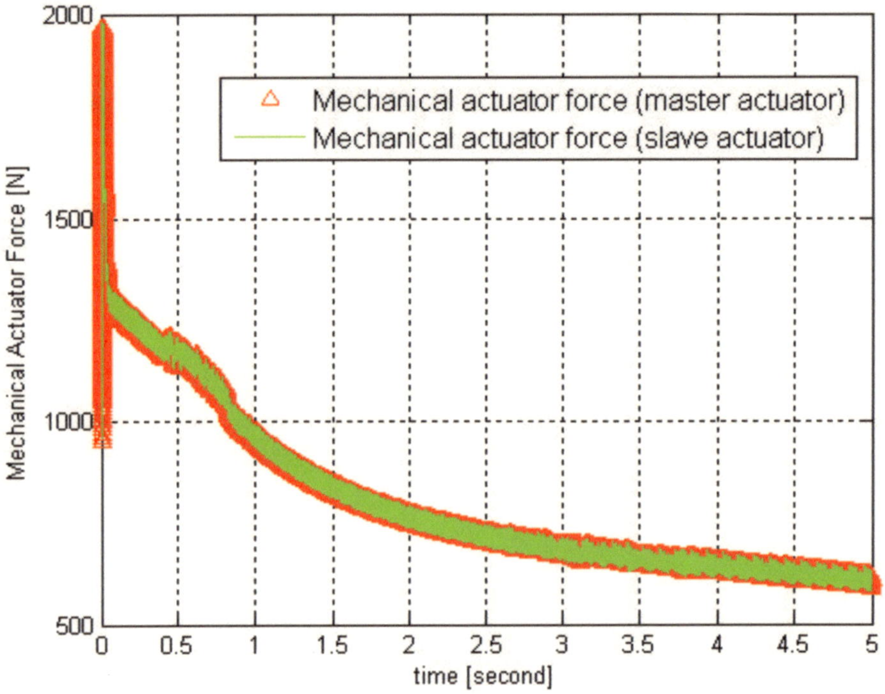

Fig. 15. Mechanic actuator forces

The results presented in figures 13, 14 and 15 are obtained by using the third level modeling for the dc-dc converters. Concerning the first and de the second levels modeling we have the same behavior but without oscillations. In addition, the imposed angular position in these levels is respected. The difference points between these three levels are concentrated on the simulation time which is increasing from first to third level and precision obtained on the outputs of system in order to reach its real behavior.

All simulations are performed using the same settings for different blocks of the system. The objective of these simulations is to test MATLAB/SIMULINK/SimPowerSys to model a mechatronic system type (motorized tailgate) and extract these different performances.

6. Performances analysis

The motorized tailgate is chosen to evaluate the performances of MALAB/SIMULINK/SimPowerSys and to test this tool to simulate a mechatronic system. To perform this analysis, some criteria's are considered (management of the multi-time scale, friction modelling and mechanical modelling in SIMULINK, electrical modelling using SimPowerSys, models implementation difficulties and time simulation of the opening phase...).

According to the implementation of the different part of the system and the all simulations carried out during this work, the table 1 summarizes the analysis of the criteria's defined previously.

The table 2 gives main advantages and disadvantages resulting from the modelling and simulation of the motorized tailgate in MALAB / SIMULINK / SimPowerSys.

Criteria's	Analysis
Management of the multi-time scale	This aspect is well treated in MALAB/SIMULINK, we can easily separate the different time constant of all the system to make the simulation faster
Frictions and mechanical modeling in SIMULINK	These frictions are well modeled using block diagram with a condition to have all the physical equations. The disadvantage is that the mechanical model produces undesirable algebraic loop which increase considerably the simulation time.
Electrical modelling using SimPowerSys	This part of the system is well implemented by using the different components available in SimPowerSys library. Some model parameters are not explicit. Some models require information of many parameters which makes them unusable
Models implementation difficulties	Easy implementation of the different models using the block diagram of simulink with a condition to eliminate any algebraic loops. To model the electrical system with organ available in the library, we must have knowledge of the different parameters to inform, we must have an explicit instructions on the use of each organ and also their domain of validity. Knowledge related to the choice of the solver and its settings are needed to properly simulate the system in good conditions.
Time simulation of opening phase	The simulation is very faster when using the first and the second level of modelling for dc-dc converter. In the third level, the simulation is slower (existence of different time constants in the system) but it is improved by using multi-time scale and an accelerator mode of the used solver. *For indication* **First level :** 47.83 s (without accelerator) and 17.33 s (with accelerator) **Second level :** 49.84 s (without accelerator) and 17.21 s (with accelerator) **Third level :** 273.2 s (without accelerator) and 159.9 s (with accelerator) *Characteristics of the used PC* Dell Precision 390, Core 2 CPU 6400, 2.13 GHz, 2 Go RAM

Table 1. Analysis of the criteria's

Advantages	Disadvantages
- Management of multi-time scale - Using models of electrical components (semiconductors, passive components, electrical machine) available in the SimPowerSystem library - Locating errors - We can inform about the component settings using script (. m)	- Requires some decline on the implementation in block diagram in order to avoid algebraic loops - Not management of causality - Require the implementation of the mechanical part (components not available) - Setting difficult to some electrical components

Table 2. Main advantages and disadvantages of MALAB / SIMULINK / SimPowerSys

7. Conclusion

In this work, a mechatronic application (motorized tailgate) is studied to evaluate the simulation performances of MATLAB/SIMULINK/SimPowerSys. Firstly, the principle of this application is given and explained. Secondly, each part (electrical, mechanical and control) of this application are detailed. Then, the models representing the operation of each part are developed. A modeling in three levels of a dc-dc converter is proposed which allowed compromise between the simulation time and the simulation results accuracy. An implementation of the different parts by using block diagram in simulink and by using the available components in SimPowerSys library is carried out. The simulation results show that the imposed angular position of the tailgate is respected which validate the proposed cascade correction. Analyses of some performances of MATLAB / SIMULINK / SimPowerSys are given and the main advantages and disadvantage resulting from the implementation and simulation of the motorized tailgate are listed. It has been shown that the SimPowerSys suits well to simulate the electrical part of the tailgate. However, the modeling of the mechanical part by block diagram is not the best approach because it generates algebraic loops and the friction modeling is very hard. To overcome these difficulties, specific toolboxes of MATLAB/SIMULINK can be used (SimScape, SimMechanics).

8. References

R. Juchem, B.Knorr, (2003) "*Complete automotive electrical system design*", Vehicular Technology Conference. VTC 2003-fall. 2003 IEEE 58th, 6-9 Oct, Volume 5, pp 3262 – 3266.

Su, G.-J. Peng, F.Z. (*2005*) "*A low cost, triple-voltage bus DC-DC converter for automotive applications*", twentieth Annual IEEE, APEC. 6-10 March 2005, on page(s): 1015-1021, Vol. 2.

Mutoh, N. Nakanishi, M. Kanesaki, M. Nakashima, (2005) "*Control methods for EMI noises appearing in electric vehicle drive systems*", twentieth Annual IEEE, APEC. 6-10 March 2005, on page(s): 1022-1028 Vol. 2.

Joshi, R.P. Deshmukh, A.P. (2008) "*Vector Control: A New Control Technique for Latest Automotive Applications (EV)*", ICETET '08, 16-18 July, on page(s): 911-916.

G. Remy, K. Ejjabraoui, C. Larouci, F. Mhenni, R. Sehab, P. Lefranc, B. Barbedette, S.A. Raka, C. Combastel, S. Cannou, F. Cardon, P. Cuvelier, C. Marchand, D. Barbier (2009)"*Modeling guidelines and tools comparison for electromechanical system design in automotive applications*", EMM 2009, 7th European Mechatronics Meeting. CIUP, Paris, France, June 24 & 25

3

A Methodology for Modelling and Simulation of Dynamic and Partially Reconfigurable Systems

Alisson Vasconcelos Brito[1], George Silveira[2] and Elmar Uwe Kurt Melcher[2]
[1]Federal University of Paraiba (UFPB),
[2]Federal University of Campina Grande (UFCG)
Brazil

1. Introduction

In the present day, partial reconfiguration is a reality (Becker & Hartenstein, 2003). There are many industries investing as well in fine-grain (like FPGAs (Huebner et al., 2004)) as in coarse grain solutions (eg. XPP (Becker & Vorbach, 2003)). This capability enables the necessary configuration area to decrease and the development of lower cost and more energy efficient systems, where timing is the main concern.

The main contribution of this work is to enable the engineers to discover earlier during the design-flow the best cost-benefit relationship between configuration time and saved chip area.

Such relationship is generally obtained only after the prototyping phase during the hardware verification. Once the dynamic reconfiguration simulation is possible in a simple way, the concrete benefits of such simulations can be checked in a simple way.

The innovative technique presented here allows the modeling and simulation of such systems by enabling new functions to module blocking and resuming in the simulator kernel. This enables the dynamic behavior to be foreseen before the synthesis on the target configuration (like FPGA). Furthermore, systems evaluation is possible even before their hardware description using a Hardware Description Language. Papers were published (Brito et al., 2006; Brito et al., 2007) presenting how the partial reconfiguration can be practically simulated.

In this work a novel methodology for simulate partial and dynamic reconfigurable system is presented. This methodology can be applied to any hardware simulator which uses an event scheduler. The main idea is to register each block that is not configured on a chip at a given moment in simulated time. Modifying the simulator scheduler, it is programmed to not execute those blocked modules. We prove in this work that this approach covers every partial and dynamic reconfigurable system situation. SystemC is used as a case of study and several systems were simulated using our methodology.

The section 2 presents what a simulator should implement to be considered able to simulate partial and dynamic systems. The methodology is presented on section 3 and section 4 presents how we applied it to SystemC. A particular strategy was adopted to log the chip area usage enabling the investigation of the benefits of dynamic reconfigurations in each application. This logging strategy is presented on section 5. Section 6 proves that the partial and dynamic reconfiguration can be really modeled and simulated using our methodology in practice with SystemC. Section 8 brings some consideration on the simulator performance after its adaptation and section 9 reports some further works using this methodology applying it to other targets.

2. Simulation of partial and dynamic reconfiguration

Before presenting the novel methodology for simulating partial and dynamic reconfiguration, it is necessary to characterize what in fact can be considered a simulator for dynamic reconfiguration. In (Lysaght & Dunlop, 1993) is described partial reconfiguration as the execution of a tasks sequence by hardware modules scheduled on time. In (Zhang & Ng, 2000) is affirmed that in order to simulate the operation of a Dynamically Reconfigurable FPGA (or DR-FPGA) a simulator must be able to simultaneously model any active static circuit and the switching of dynamic circuits along the time.

In (Dorairaj et al., 2005) is presented best practices for modelling partial reconfiguration using the PlanAhead simulation tool. It mainly recommends the utilization of bus macros among candidate modules for replacement. During the module substitution the original module is deactivated in order to activate the replacing one. The deactivation and activation of modules are the two basic operations for partial reconfiguration simulation.

Meanwhile, Pleis et. al. defend that a dynamically reconfigurable system is formed by different interchangeable functionalities (Pleis & Ogami, 2007).

Based on those interpretations of simulation of partial and dynamic, we can summarize that all simulators should be complete if it can model three operations:

- Module removing;
- Module switching;
- Module partitioning.

These basic operations are presented here. Fig. 1 presents a Module C being removed to give place to another module of same area of smaller.

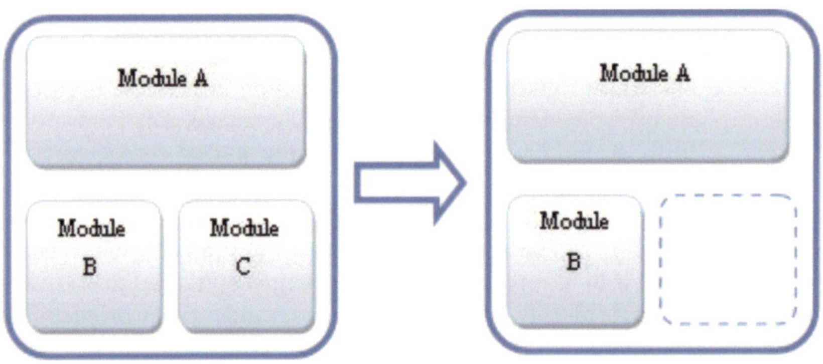

Fig. 1. Module removing of Module C.

Fig. 2 presents the second dynamic reconfiguration case, which can be seen as a logical continuation of module removing, when the Module C, after being removed, is replaced by a different module (Module D) on the same area.

Module partitioning is the third type of reconfiguration and is presented in Fig. 3. On this illustration the Module A is separated into three different modules, which together execute the same functionality of Module A, but by separated modules at different moments.

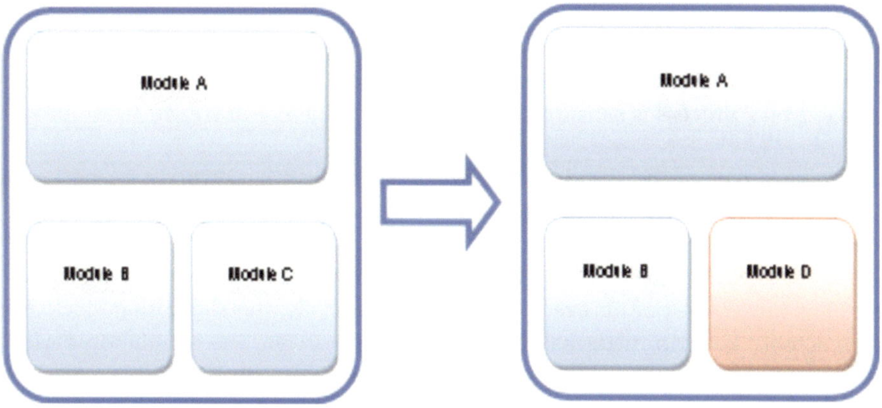

Fig. 2. Switching from Module C to Module D.

The two first reconfiguration types are important because they map the chip modification to save area (module removing) and to change functionality (module switching). The module partitioning is important to enable the same functionality be partitioned into different modules scheduled on time. In this way, we have the three basic benefits from partial and dynamic reconfiguration, save area, change functionality and time partitioning, other benefits are consequences of these.

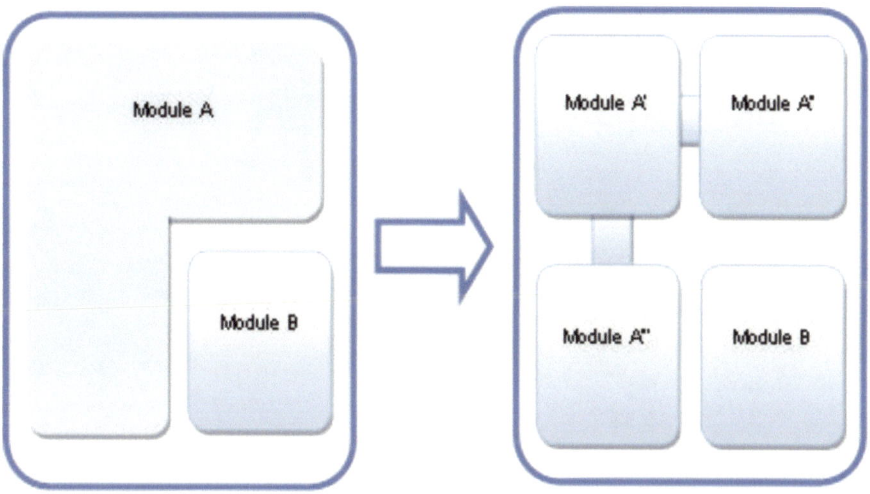

Fig. 3. Module partitioning into three different modules of same functionality.

3. The methodology

The methodology created to simulate dynamic reconfiguration is based on changing the execution mechanism of discrete-event simulators. The simulator must check every module before executing it, verifying if they were deactivated before. In the affirmative case the module must not be executed.

Fig. 4 presents a general simulator module based on events and organized in modules and processes, used mainly for digital hardware systems simulation. Each module can implement one or more processes, which execute the task. The processes have a sensitivity

list each, indicating which events they are sensitive to. A process is executed on a simulation cycle if one event registered on its sensitivity list occurs during that specific cycle.
In the example of Fig. 4, the event E3 could represent the clock signal modification, and as we can see, every process is sensitive to it; each clock signal will trigger every processes to be executed.
The scheduler is part of the simulator kernel, and decides the execution sequence for each cycle. If event E1 is scheduled, for example, it will be searched on the processes sensitivity lists, and be found on processes 1 and 3, which belong to modules A and B, respectively.
The simulated time is formed by a sequence of simulation cycles. At each cycle, one or more events can occur. In case of no event occurs during a cycle, the simulation clock advances and none activity is performed, making the simulation faster. The simulation performance depends directly on sensitivity lists. The more events the lists have, more probable is a process to be executed and new cycles to be created, which costs hardware processing.
Back to dynamic reconfiguration, a not configured module can be defined as a never-executed module, not depending on occurred events, neither on its sensitivity list. On the same way, not configured modules can be reconfigured during simulation just by allowing its normal execution based on events.
Our methodology lies on the interception of the execution signals generated from the simulator to the modules, making that not configured modules never receive those signals. Conceptually, we adopted the module blocking instead of process blocking, as a module normally represents a hardware functionality unit.

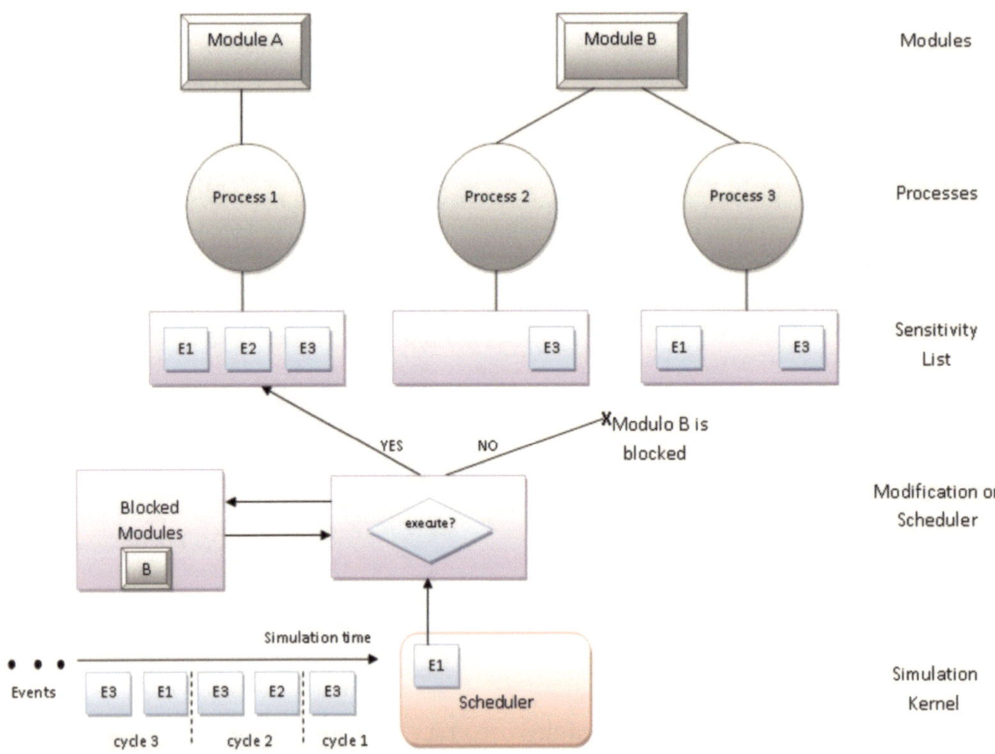

Fig. 4. Modified simulator to block modules not more configured on system.

Fig. 4 presents the modification that should be done aiming at interception of execution signals to not configured modules. Our strategy was implemented by creating a blocked modules list. Instead of immediately executing the processes sensitive to an event we propose the blocked modules list to be checked before its execution. The process will be executed only if the module which it belongs to does not appears in the list. For example, on Fig. 4, the Module B was found on blocked modules list. For that reason, the Process 3 was not executed, although it is sensitive to event E1.
Using our methodology the implementation of dynamic reconfiguration on a simulator can be performed just by managing the blocked modules list, adding some kind of reference to the modules that should not be configured and removing it to reconfigure the module.

4. Adding dynamic reconfiguration simulation to SystemC

In order to implement the methodology using a functional simulator, SystemC was selected. We adopted a bottom-up approach adding functions to activate and deactivate modules by the programmer during simulation. SystemC is open-source, free and enables the modeling and simulation at TLM and RTL using Object-Orientation concepts (Grotker et al., 2002). It does not allow deactivation of modules during simulation, but as an open-source tool, it is a great candidate for our methodology application. The Adriatic project (Qu et al., 2004) also uses SystemC at transaction level (TLM), but it does not simulate the dynamic behaviour of the modules during simulation. On the other hand the OSSS+R project (Schallenberg et al., 2006) simulates the dynamic reconfiguration of SystemC modules using heritage and polymorphism. It implements a SystemC language extension which allows the switching of modules inherited from the same super class. This top-down approach does not allow the simulation of RTL systems, neither its application to other not Object-Oriented simulators.
The strategy is implementing two special functions for activating and deactivating modules during simulation named *dr_sc_turn_on* and *dr_sc_turn_off*, respectively. Both were written modifying the SystemC kernel source code. Figure 6 presents the added functions declarations in the *sc_simcontext.h* SystemC header file. The two routines *dr_add_constraint* are used to store modules attributes, like the chip area occupation by the module and the reconfiguration delay, always present when a module is configured on chip. The *extern* key-word indicates that the routine can be called outside the *sc_context* class. In other words, those functions can be called by user code on regular simulations.

```
extern void dr_sc_turn_off(std::string module_name);
extern void dr_add_constraint(std::string module_name, int area);
extern void dr_add_constraint(std::string module_name, int area,
                              sc_time reconfDelay);
extern void dr_sc_turn_on(std::string module_name);
```

Fig. 5. Main routines added to SystemC library (sc_simcontext.h)

In Fig. 6 is presented how the functions were implemented in sc_simcontext.cpp SystemC kernel file. A linked list is used to store the names of the modules that must be not executed (not configured). The routine *dr_sc_turn_off* add the module name to the list, while the *dr_sc_turn_on* remove the module from the list, allowing it to be executed (reconfigured). Another list is keep to store the modules constraints (chip area and reconfiguration delay). This list is required when the *dr_add_constraint* function is called. In this case, constraints are added to the list and cannot be removed, just overwritten. The chip area of each module is used for chip occupation analysis normally performed after simulation. Such analysis is important to figure out how effective the application of dynamic reconfiguration on chip was.

```
void dr_sc_turn_off(std::string module_name){
    sc_get_curr_simcontext()->dr_add_config(module_name);
}

void dr_sc_turn_on(std::string module_name){
    sc_get_curr_simcontext()->dr_remove_config(module_name);
}

void dr_add_constraint(std::string module_name, int area){
    sc_get_curr_simcontext()->dr_addConstraint(module_name,area);
}

void dr_add_constraint(std::string module_name, int area, sc_time delay){
    sc_get_curr_simcontext()->dr_addConstraint(module_name,area,delay);
}
```

Fig. 6. The added routines from Figure 6 implemented in sc_simcontext.cpp file.

The details of the routines to manipulate the linked lists are presented on Fig. 7. Adding a module name into the configuration list (*dr_add_config* function) is not a problem. The module name is simply added into the list. But, the *dr_remove_config* just remove the module name from the list if the reconfiguration delay for that module has expired, and the first call of this function is considered just a removing request. Therefore, before removing the module name, the delay is compared with the elapsed time since the removing request.

```
void sc_simcontext::dr_add_config(std::string module_name){
    configList->addConfig(module_name,m_curr_time,0,
                          constraintList->getReconfDelay(module_name));
}

void sc_simcontext::dr_remove_config(std::string module_name){
    sc_time delay = configList->getReconfDelay(module_name);
    if(delay > sc_time(0,SC_NS)){
       configList->setActionTime(module_name,delay + m_curr_time);
       configList->request_remove(module_name, true);
    }
     else
       configList->removeConfig(module_name);
    }

void sc_simcontext::dr_addConstraint(std::string module_name, int area){
    constraintList->addConfig(module_name,m_curr_time,area);
}

void sc_simcontext::dr_addConstraint(std::string module_name, int area,
                                     sc_time reconfDelay){
    constraintList->addConfig(module_name,m_curr_time,area,reconfDelay);
}
```

Fig. 7. Implementation of the new routines.

Now the SystemC execution properly can be performed. This execution is made at *sc_simcontext* class by the *crunch* method. The modified code can be seen on Fig. 8. Initially in line 3 the method *pop_runnable_method* returns the *sc_method_handle* to the next method to be executed at simulation. The modifications aim at the execution avoidance of methods from *ConfigList* and store the execution history of each module in a logging file. The *fout* object is responsible to print every event on log file. The blocked modules are represented in log file with and "X" (lines 18 and 20), and when the module is executed, the module area is printed on file instead (lines 15 and 28).
The three conditionals on lines 10, 11 and 12, check whether the module should be executed or not. Initially is checked whether module name is on *ConfigList* (line 10), and then whether the *request_remove* was called for the module (line 11), finishing the verification checking whether the reconfiguration delay was already elapsed (line 12). If all verifications are true, the module is removed from *ConfigList* (line 13) and finally executed (line 14). Following the process, the module area is printed on log file (line 15). Case any conditional returns false, a "X" is printed on log file representing execution blocking.

```
1. while( true ) {
2.   // execute method processes
3.   sc_method_handle method_h = pop_runnable_method();
4.   while( method_h != 0 ) {
5.     try {
6.       if(m_curr_time > sc_time(0,SC_NS)){
7.           str += get_method_name(method_h);
8.           str += ";";
9.       }

10       if(configList->exists(get_method_name(method_h))){
11           if(configList->isOff(get_method_name(method_h)))
12               if(configList->getActionTime(get_method_name(method_h)) <= m_curr_time){
13                 configList->removeConfig(get_method_name(method_h));
14                 method_h->execute();
15                 fout << constraintList->getArea(get_method_name(method_h)) << ";";
16               }
17               else
18                 fout << "X;";
19           else
20             fout << "X;";
21           }
22       else{
23           method_h->execute();
24           fout << constraintList->getArea(get_method_name(method_h)) << ";";
25       }
26   }
27   catch( const sc_report& ex ) {
28       ::std::cout << "\n" << ex.what() << ::std::endl;
29       m_error = true;
30       return;
31   }
32   method_h = pop_runnable_method();
33 }
```

Fig. 8. SystemC crunch routine, responsible for executing every module in simulation.

4. Execution logging

As detailed before, every simulation cycle is logged on a file. A fragment of the log file is presented on Figure 10. Each line on the log file stores the simulation cycle timestamp, the modules occupation area and the respective module names. If a module is not configured at that time, and "X" is stored instead of its chip area. All information is stored on CSV format (*Comma-separated values*).

```
'Log of Dynamically Reconfigured Modules in Simulation'

Time;Module Name;Status

0 s;1;1;1;X;X;X;X;1;1;
5 ns;1;1;1;X;X;X;X;1;1;{1};top.bus;top.config_manager;top.master_d0;top.master_d1;
10 ns;1;1;X;X;X;X;1;1;{0};top.config_manager;top.master_d0;top.master_d1;top.maste
15 ns;1;1;1;X;X;X;X;1;1;{1};top.bus;top.config_manager;top.master_d0;top.master_d1
20 ns;1;1;X;X;X;X;1;1;{0};top.config_manager;top.master_d0;top.master_d1;top.maste
25 ns;1;1;1;X;X;X;X;1;1;{1};top.bus;top.config_manager;top.master_d0;top.master_d1
30 ns;1;1;X;X;X;X;1;1;{0};top.config_manager;top.master_d0;top.master_d1;top.maste
35 ns;1;1;1;X;X;X;X;1;1;{1};top.bus;top.config_manager;top.master_d0;top.master_d1
40 ns;1;1;4;X;X;X;1;1;{0};top.config_manager;top.master_d0;top.master_d1;top.maste
45 ns;1;1;1;4;X;X;X;1;1;{1};top.bus;top.config_manager;top.master_d0;top.master_d1
50 ns;1;1;4;X;X;X;1;1;{0};top.config_manager;top.master_d0;top.master_d1;top.maste
55 ns;1;1;1;4;X;X;X;1;1;{1};top.bus;top.config_manager;top.master_d0;top.master_d1
60 ns;1;1;4;X;X;X;1;1;{0};top.config_manager;top.master_d0;top.master_d1;top.maste
65 ns;1;1;1;4;X;X;X;1;1;{1};top.bus;top.config_manager;top.master_d0;top.master_d1
70 ns;1;1;4;X;X;X;1;1;{0};top.config_manager;top.master_d0;top.master_d1;top.maste
75 ns;1;1;1;4;X;X;X;1;1;{1};top.bus;top.config_manager;top.master_d0;top.master_d1
80 ns;1;1;4;X;X;X;1;1;{0};top.config_manager;top.master_d0;top.master_d1;top.maste
85 ns;1;1;1;4;X;X;X;1;1;{1};top.bus;top.config_manager;top.master_d0;top.master_d1
90 ns;1;1;4;X;X;X;1;1;{0};top.config_manager;top.master_d0;top.master_d1;top.maste
95 ns;1;1;1;4;X;X;X;1;1;{1};top.bus;top.config_manager;top.master_d0;top.master_d1
100 ns;1;1;4;X;X;X;1;1;{0};top.config_manager;top.master_d0;top.master_d1;top.mast
105 ns;1;1;1;4;X;X;X;1;1;{1};top.bus;top.config_manager;top.master_d0;top.master_d
110 ns;1;1;4;X;X;X;1;1;{0};top.config_manager;top.master_d0;top.master_d1;top.mast
115 ns;1;1;1;4;X;X;X;1;1;{1};top.bus;top.config_manager;top.master_d0;top.master_d
120 ns;1;1;4;X;X;X;1;1;{0};top.config_manager;top.master_d0;top.master_d1;top.mast
125 ns;1;1;1;4;X;X;X;1;1;{1};top.bus;top.config_manager;top.master_d0;top.master_d
130 ns;1;1;4;X;X;X;1;1;{0};top.config_manager;top.master_d0;top.master_d1;top.mast
135 ns;1;1;1;4;X;X;X;1;1;{1};top.bus;top.config_manager;top.master_d0;top.master_d
```

Fig. 9. A fragment from an execution log file.

The log file can easily be exported to calculations softwares and the system behavior can be seen in table format, furthermore, graphics can be made. Fig. 10 presents an example of a graphic representing the chip area utilization over the time. On this example, some modules are not configured during some time intervals, making the total chip area varying from 7 to 12 area units (hypothetical unit).

Using this strategy, conventional systems can also have their execution log analyzed and candidate modules for partial reconfiguration can be detected. Therefore, the log analysis can be used as the first step for system behavior study.

5. Experiments and results

In order to apply our methodology to model and simulate dynamically reconfigurable hardware systems, two case studies were developed.

The first work was the modelling and simulation of a research project for Daimler-Crysler in collaboration with the University of Karlsruhe in Germany (Becker & Vorbach, 2003). The objective is to simulate a dynamically reconfigurable hardware, which controls some eight

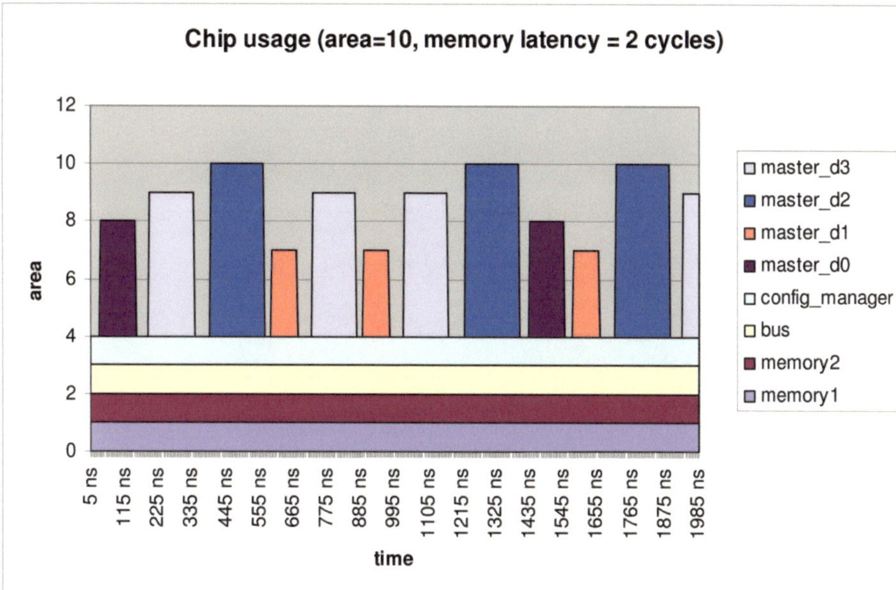

Fig. 10. Chip area usage generated from an execution log file.

inner cabin devices on-demand, four windows, two seats, one internal mirror and one controller for the lights. If the user requests a certain service, the corresponding hardware unit is configured and initialized in an unoccupied slot within the dynamic reconfigurable area of the FPGA system (see Fig. 11). The results of this work were published in *IEEE Computer Society Annual Symposium on Emerging VLSI Technologies and Architectures (ISVLSI'2007)* in Porto Alegre (Brito et al., 2007).

In this example, a maximum number of four applications can be executed in parallel. This hardware constraint enables the reduction of the number of different electronic hardware control units within a car, hence saves space, power consumption and costs. The justification of hardware implementation can be easily demonstrated, when considering heavy CAN traffic, where traditional microprocessor based systems reach their limits.

The example application is implemented on a Xilinx Virtex-II FPGA (XC2V3000). To get an overview of the complete system, Fig. 11 shows a block schematic containing all main integrated components. A MicroBlaze Soft-IP controller from Xilinx is used. A detailed description of the run-time system and the tasks of the MicroBlaze controller can be found in (Huebner et al., 2004).

The FPGA of the Virtex-II series also provides an internal configuration access port (ICAP) that allows reconfiguration without the need of external wiring. The partial bitstreams for the modules are stored in an external flash memory. The run-time system accesses them by sending start address and end address to a decompressor module on demand. A further start command enables the decompressor, which reads the compressed bitstream from the flash memory in order to write the configuration code through the ICAP interface to the internal configuration memory of the FPGA.

While it is being processed, the controller and all other modules are able to continue the execution of their tasks. A signal from the decompressor reports the end of the configuration process, which indicates that the service is ready for use. The complete system is connected via a CAN interface to its environment.

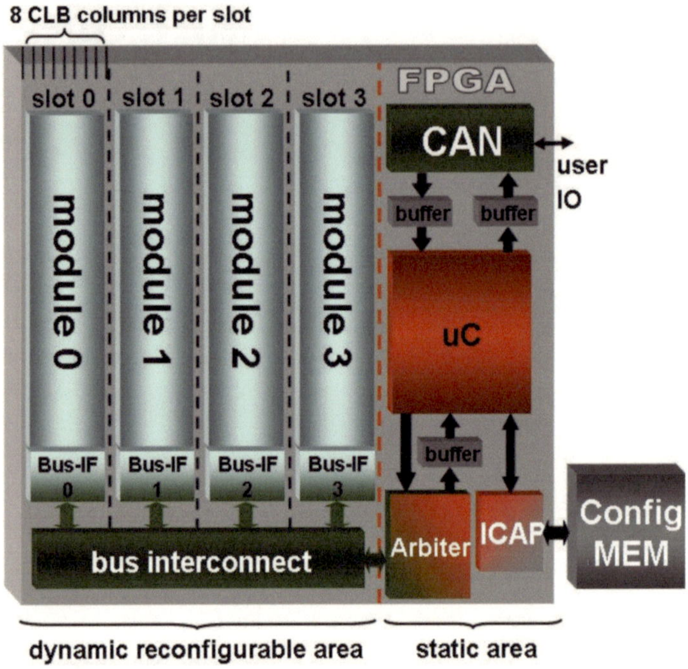

Fig. 11. Architecture of the automotive system.

The experiments show that if the FPGA's dynamic area is constrained to 8 CLB columns which are equal to 1 application slot, the average response time is about 1000 times larger than the client timing constraint, which is 100ms. On the contrary, a system owning 64 CLB columns, where all eight applications can be configured at the same time, the average response time satisfies the timing constraint. However, the area usage is far from being reasonable or efficient.

Actually the real hardware implementation (as represented by Fig. 11) uses 32 CLB columns. In this case, the simulations show that the system's average response time is shorter than 100ms if the request rate is set to maximum 1 per second. A larger rate implies a system stall for a specific period of time. The problem arises mostly after the fifth request, when no slot is temporarily available.

The response time with 32 configurable columns satisfies most use cases, although with 24 columns (which mean 3 applications per time) it may be sufficient for non-critical applications. It could not respond instantly, for example, if a window were closed with somebody having his hand in between.

The second example implements a general purpose simulator for processors, called PReProS (A General Purpose Partially Reconfigurable Processor Simulator), whereas this technique supports run-time reconfiguration (Brito et al., 2007). Such technique uses high-level representations to model and simulate the reconfiguration, giving the opportunity to designers to foresee the dynamic behavior of your system before the hardware is going to be implemented for the target architecture, or even before the system specification in HDL, if desired.

Considering the simulation of dynamic and partially reconfigurable systems, a couple of steps should be done, like the target architecture specification, the definition of necessary hardware resources and the designing of the applications. The presented approach aims at writing a reusable parametrizable SystemC program able to model and simulate real target processor architectures. For example, coarse-grained like XPP (Becker et al., 2003) which consists of configurable ALUs communicating via a packet oriented, automatically synchronized communication network. Further, fine-grained architectures, like standalone FPGAs and embedded FPGAs, which have the well known FPGA behavior, or any other processor, running any kind of application.

The goal is to parameterize the individual processor's characteristics in such a general way that all kind of processing element can be fully described using this set of parameters. The main features that have to be considered here are the clock frequency, properties of the data and configuration ports, and the number of chip area available on chip. In the same way, the applications' properties can be set by the frequency, needed ports, data width and number of configured area units. When using this simulator the designer just have to set the parameters and implement its own blocks to configure the applications and exchange data with the PReProS.

On Fig. 12 it is possible to see the amount of used resources of the XPP simulated chip when five different applications were scheduled. XPP was simulated containing 144 ALUs. In this way more parallel configurations could be simulated. The free area is marked by the darker area in the figure. By investigating these results, the best parallel performance and hence the best processing power and efficiency of the simulated processor area can be achieved. It helps the designer to reevaluate his/her algorithms and implementation strategy, or if the selected architecture should be changed to better target his needs.

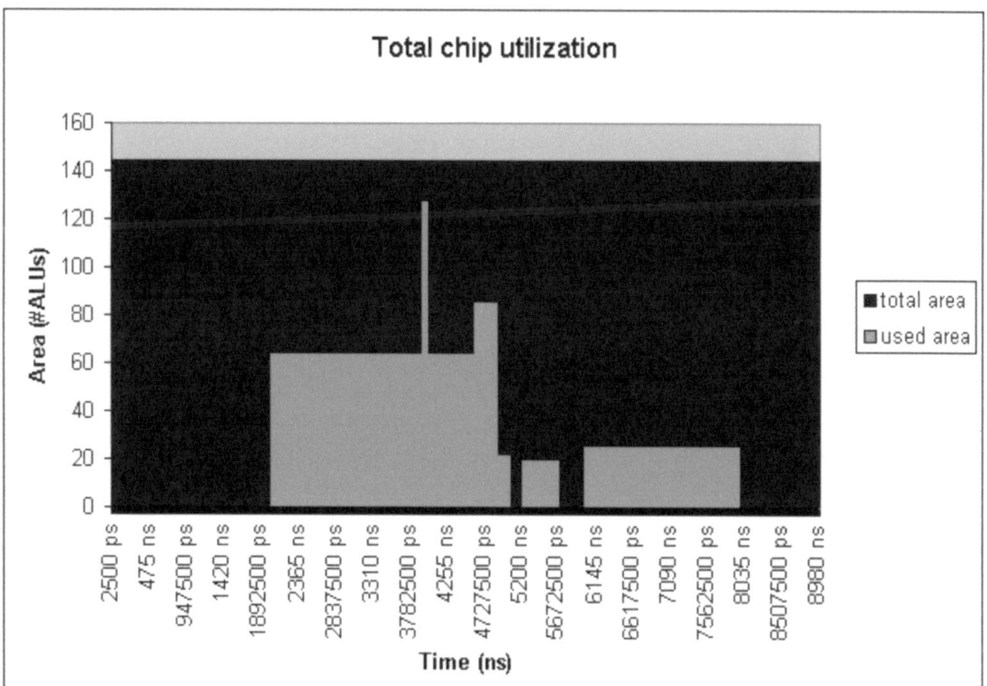

Fig. 12. Total chip area utilization by PRePros

6. New design-flow with partial and dynamic reconfiguration

An important aspect is the integration of this modeling and simulation technique into the design flow. It is desired to achieve this in a plug and play manner. To provide such lightweight integration, the SystemC (www.systemc.org) description language is used. The capabilities are presented as an easy to use API and can be applied to any system, which is described in SystemC. Fig. 13 presents a typical SystemC based design flow. Usually, the same approach is used twice, to develop both, statically and dynamically reconfigurable systems. The absence of specific techniques and tools would turn such development into an arduous and costly task.

During hardware verification, it is quite common to iterate several times within the design cycle, thus returning to the TLM and RTL model. Our technique aims at reducing these verification cycles and, as a result, decreasing development time.

There are other efforts to provide similar functionalities using SystemC. However, they are mostly TLM-based (like OSSS+R project (Schallenberg et al., 2004)) including operation restrictions, or do not focus on simulation (like Adriatic project (Qu et al., 2004)). The presented approach attacks the same problem in a more general way. Any module can be removed, added or switched at simulation-time.

Aiming at decreasing design time, an extension of the common SystemC based design flow is proposed. The modeling and simulation of dynamic and partial reconfiguration is aggregated, resulting in a modified design flow, as shown in Fig. 13.

The dynamic behavior at TLM or RTL is performed by specific instructions. The designer decides about a proper location in his code. An interesting way is an implementation in one or more separated models, which centralizes the dynamic behavior of the system. These modules can then be realized as dedicated blocks that control and schedule run-time configuration.

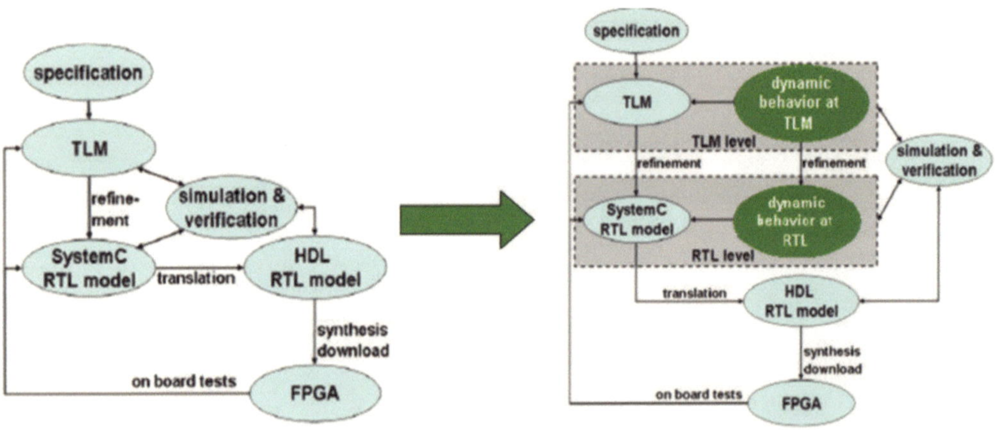

Fig. 13. Typical design-flow using SystemC adapted for dynamic reconfiguration.

7. Proof of concept

In order to validate the methodology, we should proof that all three types of dynamic reconfiguration operations defined on Section 2 can be modeled and simulated by our SystemC modified version. In general, the strategy used to model partial reconfigurable system with SystemC is based on, first declares and connects all modules that will be part of the system at some time. Fig. 14 shows how the module substitution should be done. It replaces the *sc_module_C* by the *sc_module_D*. Initially both modules are present in the system, but just the module C is configured. At the second moment, the module C is deactivated by calling *dr_sc_turn_off ("moduleC")* and the module D is configured by calling *dr_sc_turn_on ("moduleD")*.

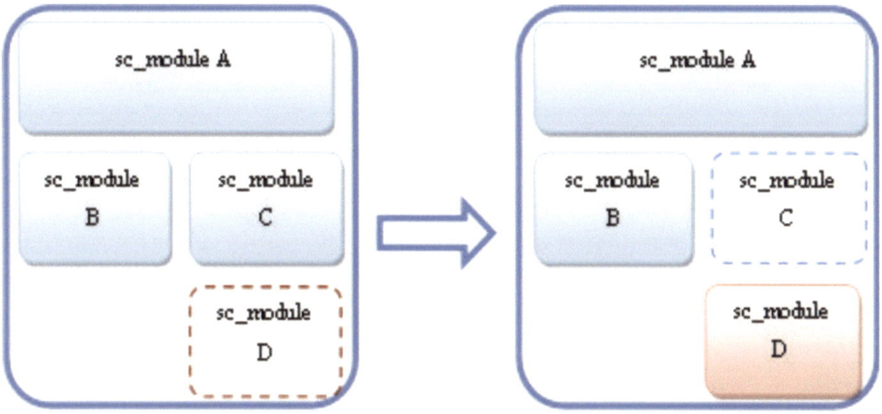

Fig. 14. Implementation of the first dynamic reconfiguration type (switching).

On the second type of reconfiguration operation, a module should be removed from the system. As can be seen on Fig. 15, at the first step every modules were instantiated on simulation, and at the second the module C was deactivated by calling *dr_sc_turn_off ("moduleC")*.

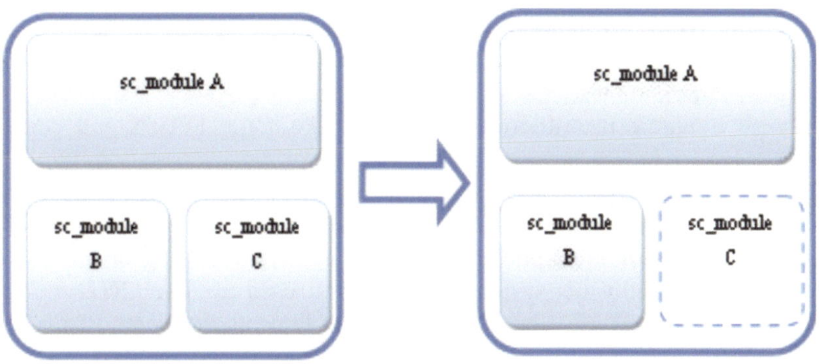

Fig. 15. Implementation of the second dynamic reconfiguration type (removing).

For the third partial reconfiguration operation (see Fig. 16) is necessary instantiate the complete module (*sc_module A*) at the same time with all the sub modules (modules A', A'' and A''') that execute the module A functionality partitioned in time. The sub-modules are deactivated at the first time and at the second moment the module A is deactivated and the sub modules are configured.

These three demonstrations show that using the methodology is possible to simulate the three basic dynamic reconfiguration operations, the module switching, removing and partitioning. We believe that each simulator able to simulate these three operations is able to simulate any dynamically (and partially) reconfigurable system.

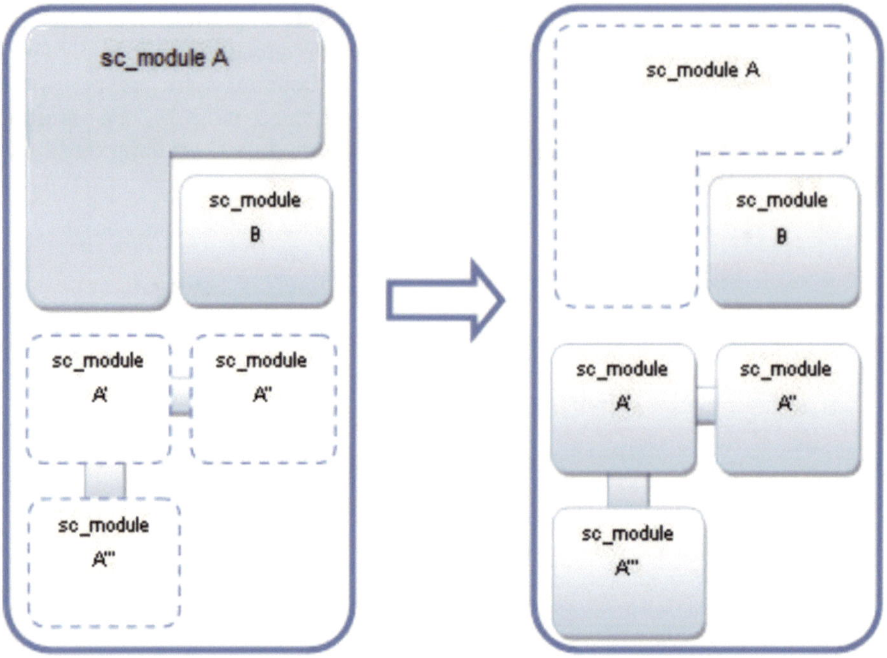

Fig. 16. Implementing the third type of reconfiguration (partitioning).

8. Simulator performance

The feasibility of the methodology was demonstrated for the first time in (Brito et al., 2006). In (Brito et al., 2007) an automotive application was simulated and the dynamic reconfiguration benefits could be visualized using the logging feature. In (Brito et al., 2007) a general purpose simulator was created using the modified SystemC, in order to simulate processors with dynamic reconfiguration features like some FPGAs and coarse-grained chips.

These works were designed at TLM, so the performance of using the modified SystemC was not significantly low. Our experiments demonstrated some performance limitations with RTL simulations. The simulator performance was tested simulating an MPEG-4 decoder (Rocha et al., 2006). Initially the system was modeled used SystemC RTL and brought to chip synthesis and silicon fabrication. The decoder implements the *Simple Profile Level 0* from MPEG-4. The decoder architecture contains the project of a personalized hardware to the bitstream decoding, *Variable Length Code* (VLC), texture decoding, movement compensation and color spaces conversion. The experiments on hardware demonstrate that 30 frames per second were decoded (Rocha et al., 2006).

A 16 frames video was simulated in two different runs. For the first run the original SystemC version 2.1.1 without modification was used. For the second run the modified SystemC of the same version was used. In both cases, no dynamic reconfiguration was used. The results show that the modified simulator presented a three times slower simulation than the SystemC without modification (see Table 1).

Using the modified SystemC, the Config List is checked at each simulation cycle. This checking causes a negative impact to the simulation time, as the list is completely analyzed at each cycle. We believe that the simulation time increase is tolerable considering the advantage to be able to simulate dynamic reconfiguration both at RTL and TL abstraction level.

Simulator	Simulation time
Traditional SystemC	12m56.630s
Modified SystemC	36m34.334s

Table 1. Performance of the modified SystemC in RTL (MPEG-4 decoder example).

9. Methodology extension

In general, the methodology principles applied in partial reconfiguration consists in turning off a sub-module "A" before of configuration of the sub-module "B" in the area previously occupied by "A" and then turning on the sub-module "B". Analyzing the turning on and off principles of the sub-modules, these principles are similar to those adopted by the technique of power gate, differentiating which in technique power gate turning on and off the same module. This section will be shows the work based on reusability of the methodology to modify the SystemC simulator, the purpose is to simulate power gate design in RTL (Silveira et al., 2009).

9.1 Overview power-gate

Power gate strategy is based on adding mechanisms to turn off blocks within the SoC that are not being used, the act of turning off and on the block is accomplished in appropriate time to achieve power saving while minimizing performance impact (Keating et al., 2007).
When the event of turning off happens, the energy savings is not instantaneous due to thermal issues of the previous activity and the nature of technology is not ideal for power gate. In the event of turning on the block requires some time that cannot be ignored by the system designer for the block to retake the activity (Keating et al., 2007). Fig. 17 shows an example of the activity of a block with power gate implemented.

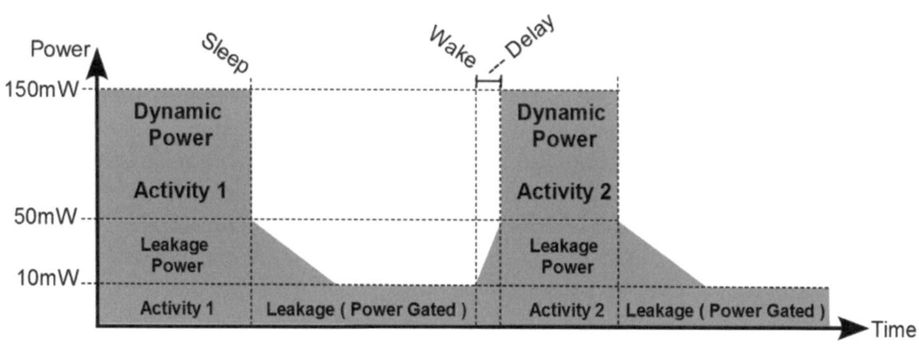

Fig. 17. Profile with Power Gating (Keating et al., 2007)

Differently of a block that is always active, a power-gate block is powered by a power-switching network that will supply VDD or VSS power gate block, the CMOS (Complementary Metal-Oxide-Semiconductor) switches are distributed within or around the block. Control of CMOS switches is accomplished by a power gating controller. In some cases it is necessary to retain the state of the block during the turned off period to restore the state when it is turned on. This restraint is implemented using special flip-flops. Figure 18 shows the diagram with the structure of the SoC with power gate.

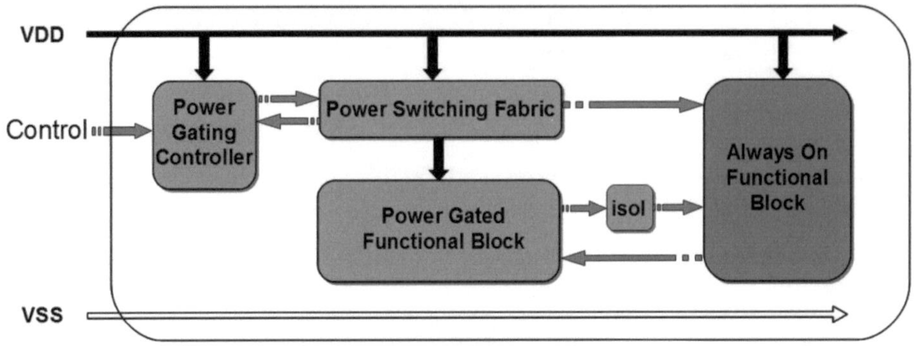

Fig. 18. Block Diagram of a SoC with Power Gating (Keating et al., 2007)

9.2 Simulator implementation

In order to implement the functional verification of low power design using a functional simulator, a similar approach developed to simulate partial and dynamic reconfiguration (Brito et al., 2006; Brito et al., 2007) was selected. This is a bottom-up approach adding functions to activate and deactivate modules by the programmer.

The strategy implements two new special functions for turning on and off modules during simulation named *sc_lp_turn_on* and *sc_lp_turn_off*, respectively. These functions were written modifying the SystemC kernel source-code. The routine *sc_lp_add_constraint* was also created and is used to store modules attributes about their energy consumption and the turn-on delay, always present when a module is re-activated on chip. Table 2 presents how the functions signatures in sc_simcontext.h SystemC kernel file.

extern void sc_lp_turn_on(std::string module_name);
extern void sc_lp_turn_off(std::string module_name);
extern void sc_lp_add_constraint(std::string module_name, sc_time wakedelay);

Table 2. Functions declarations

A linked list is used to store the names of the modules that must be not executed (turn-off). The routine sc_lp_turn_off adds the module name to the list, while sc_lp_turn_on removes the module from the list, allowing it to be executed (activity). Another list is kept to store the module constraints (wake delay and energy consumption). This list is required when the sc_lp_add_constraint function is called. In this case, constraints are added to the list and cannot be removed, just overwritten. The extern key-word indicates that the routine can be called outside the sc_context class. In other words, those functions can be called by user code on regular simulations.

9.3 Functional verification

VeriSC methodology adopts projects with hierarchy concept, therefore a project can be divided into parts to be implemented and verified (Silva & Melcher, 2005). BVE-Cover library was chosen to accomplish the functional verification with coverage of the design. Several simulations were performed with different versions of SystemC simulator and design:

- **SC + DV1:** At this stage were used the original SystemC version 2.2.0 and the first implementation of the design.
- **SC-LP + DV1:** At this stage were used the new SystemC-LP functions added and the first implementation of the design.
- **SC-LP + DV2:** At this stage were used the new SystemC-LP version and the second implementation containing the power gate design.

9.4 Results

Several results were extracted (Silveira et al., 2009), but with respect to reusability of the methodology we can highlight, (1) was possible to simulate low power design in RTL, and during the simulation we can verify the power gate principles operating; (2) the simulator performance loss, which a negative point, fact occurred due to the adoption of the strategy used in the dynamic reconfiguration simulator. Fig. 19 shows a graphic with the different simulators performance. The first simulation time was measured using regular SystemC (SC) and the first design (DV1), which does not use the new functions. It took 0.32 seconds. The next experiment achieved 0.75 seconds to simulate the first design (DV1) using SystemC modified for low power (SC-LP). The third and worst result was achieved when simulated using low power and using in design the new implemented functions (DV2).

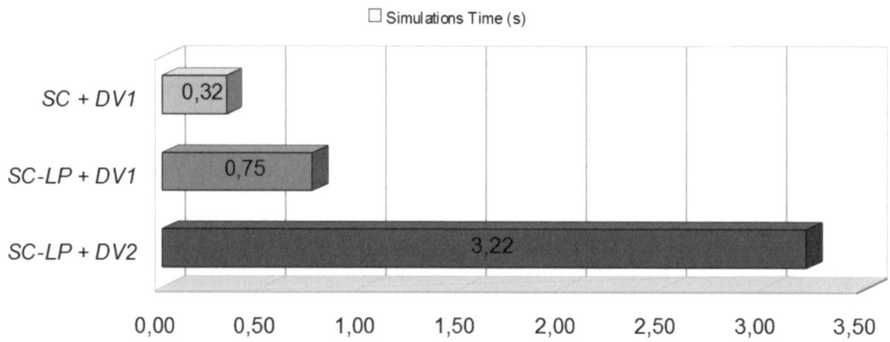

Fig. 19. Simulators performance

10. Simulator improvement

Due to simulator performance loss around 1000% compared with original SystemC, improvements were accomplished. This section presents that improvement to SystemC simulator with support for the functional verification of designs containing the principles of power gate design implemented in RTL. To demonstrate that the new modifications improved the performance of the simulator, the same techniques adopted in (Silveira et al., 2009) will be used.

10.1 Simulator optimization

The optimization of the simulator (Silveira et al., 2009) was accomplished based on the profiling of the running simulator, which demonstrated an excessive number of accesses to linked lists added to SystemC simulator kernel. A linked list is used to store the names of the modules that must not be executed. The routine *sc_lp_turn_off* adds the module name to the list, while *sc_lp_turn_on* removes the module from the list, allowing it to be executed. Another list is kept to store the module constraints (wake delay). This list is required when the *sc_lp_add_constraint* function is called. In this case, constraints are added to the list and cannot be removed, only overwritten.

Based on profiling information, an asymptotic and semantic analysis of data structures used to implement the simulator kernel was performed. That consists of: (1) a new data structure to store information about which modules are turned off and the delay needed to retake full activity after its reactivation, (2) the data structure must provide information access at a very short and constant time interval.

The new functions were rewritten using a hash map to replace the linked list. Each hash map element represents a design module and is composed two variables (a boolean and a time). The boolean variable is responsible for identifying whether the module is activated or not, the time variable is responsible for storing the necessary time delay to re-activate the module. The elements are accessed using a key, which is the name of the module. The functions signatures have been altered, *sc_lp_add_constraint* was removed and its function was added to the routine *sc_lp_turn_on* and attributes are now passed to hash map. Table 3 shows how the functions signatures currently in *sc_simcontext.h* SystemC kernel file.

extern void sc_lp_turn_on (const char* module_name, sc_time wakedelay);
extern void sc_lp_turn_off (const char* module_name);

Table 3. Functions Declarations

10.2 Results

Among the simulations results, the preservation of the semantics and performance enhancement of the new simulator compared to the version shows in (Silveira et al., 2009) can be highlighted.

The improvement in simulator performance can be seen in Fig. 20. It can be seen that the design simulations (DV1) using the improved simulator (SC-LP-V2) presents an increasing of 4% in simulation time and simulations of power gate design (DV2) the increase of 8% in comparison with the original SystemC simulator.

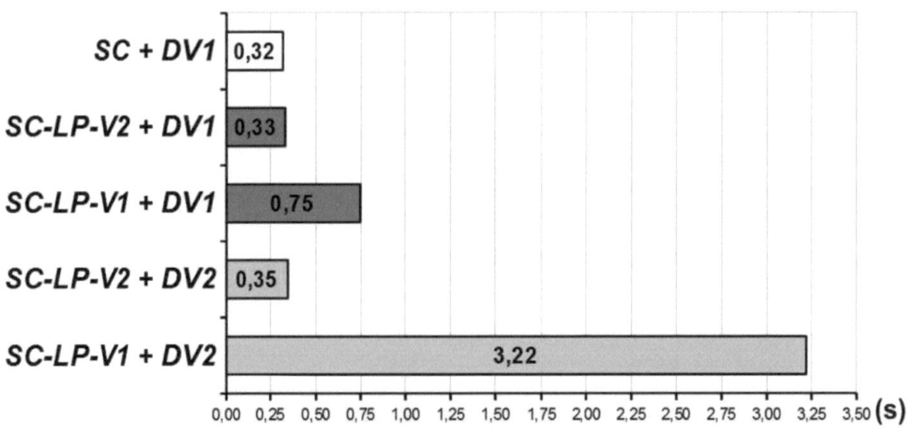

Fig. 20. Simulators performance

Comparing the two SC-LP simulators, the gains were significant. The SC-LP-V2 simulator achieved a performance increase of 224% in the execution of design without power gate design and 925% simulating power gate design. These performance gains were reached by eliminating the costs of elements addition and removal from linked lists and increasing the speed for accessing information through the use of hash map structure.

12. Final considerations

The innovative methodology presented here allows the modelling and simulation partially and dynamically reconfigurable hardware systems, enabling new functions to module blocking and resuming in the simulator kernel. This enables the dynamic behaviour to be foreseen before the synthesis on the target hardware (like FPGA). Furthermore, systems evaluation is possible even before their hardware description using a Hardware Description Language.

Even further, the same approach is being used to model and simulate low power hardware systems through power gate technique. The results prove that as dynamic reconfiguration, as low power systems can be simulated using the identical simulators. This opens new opportunities for both areas, enabling the tool exchanging for both proposes.

Our innovative methodology can be applied to any hardware simulator which uses an event scheduler. The main idea is to register each block that is not configured on a chip at a given moment during simulation. The simulator scheduler is programmed to not execute those blocked modules. We prove in this work that this approach covers every partial reconfigurable system situation. A particular strategy is also adopted to log the chip area usage enabling the investigation of the benefits of partial reconfigurations for each application.

13. References

Becker, J. & Hartenstein, R. (2003). Configware and morphware going mainstream. *Journal of Systems Architecture*. Vol. 49, No. 4-6, p. 127-142, September, 2003.

Becker, J., Vorbach, M. (2003). Architecture, Memory and Interface Technology Integration of an Industrial/Academic Configurable System-on-Chip (CSoC)", IEEE COMPUTER SOCIETY. ANNUAL Symposium ON VLSI, Tampa, Florida, February 20-21, 2003.

Becker, J.; Huebner, M. & Ullmann, M. (2003). Power Estimation and Power Measurement of Xilinx Virtex FPGAs: Trade-offs and Limitations". *Proceedings of the 16nd Annual Symposium on Integrated Circuits and System Design (SBCCI03)*, Sao Paulo, Brazil, September, 2003.

Brito, A. V.; Rosas, W. & Melcher, E. U. K. (2006). An open-source tool for simulation of partially reconfigurable systems using SystemC. *Proceedings of IEEE Computer Society Annual Symposium on VLSI (ISVLSI 2006)*, Karlsruhe, Germany, 2006.

Brito, A. V.; Kuehnle, M.; Huebner, M.; Becker, J. & Melcher, E. U. K. (2007). A General Purpose Partially Reconfigurable Processor Simulator (PReProS)" *Proceedings of 15th Reconfigurable Architecture Workshop (RAW'2007), 2007, Long Beach. 21st International Parallel & Distributed Processing Symposium*. Piscataway, New Jersey: IEEE, 2007.

Brito, A. V.; Kuehnle, M.; Huebner, M.; Becker, J. & Melcher, E. U. K. (2007). Modelling and Simulation of Dynamic and Partially Reconfigurable Systems using SystemC".

Proceedings of IEEE Computer Society Annual Symposium on Emerging VLSI Technologies and Architectures, (ISVLSI'2007), Porto Alegre. IEEE Computer Society Piscataway, Vol. 1. p.200 - 203. New Jersey: IEEE 2007

Dorairaj, N.; Shiflet, E. & Goosman, M. (2005), PlanAhead Software as a Platform for Partial Reconfiguration. *Xcell Journal*. Xilinx, Inc. December 2005.

Grotker, T.; Liao, S.; Martin, G. & Swan, S. (2002). System Design with SystemC. Kluwer Academic Publishers, 2002.

Huebner, M.; Becker, T. & Becker, J. (2004). Real-Time LUT-Based Network Topologies for Dynamic and Partial FPGA Self-Reconfiguration. *Proceedings of the 16nd Annual Symposium on Integrated Circuits and System Design (SBCCI03)*. Recife, Brazil, September, 2004.

Keating, M.; Flynn, D.; Aitken, R. & Gibbons, A., Shi, K. (2007). Low Power Methodology Manual, For System-on-Chip Design, Series: Series on Integrated Circuits and Systems 2007, XVI, 304 p., Hardcover, ISBN: 978-0-387-71818-7

Keating, M.; Flynn, D.; Aitken, R.; Gibbons, A. & Shi, K. *Low Power Methodology Manual, For System-on-Chip Design*, Series: Series on Integrated Circuits and Systems 2007, XVI, 304 p., Hardcover, ISBN: 978-0-387-71818-7

Lysaght, P., Dunlop, J. (1993). Dynamic Reconfiguration of Field Programmable Gate Arrays. *Proceedings of the 1993 International Workshop on Field-Programmable Logic and Applications*. Oxford, England: Abingdom EE&CS Books, p. 82-94, 1993.

Pleis, M. A. & Ogami, K. Y. (2007). Dynamic reconfiguration interrupt system and method. *Cypress Semiconductor Corporation*, San Jose, CA, US. 2007.

Qu, Y.; Tiensyrja, K. & Masselos, K. (2004), System-Level Modeling of Dynamically Reconfigurable Co-Processors. *Proceedings of International Conference on Field Programmable Logic and Applications*, Antwerp, Belgium, August-September, 2004.

Qu, Y.; Tiensyrja, K. & Masselos, K. (2004). System-Level Modeling of Dynamically Reconfigurable Co-Processors", International Conference on Field Programmable Logic and Applications, Antwerp, Belgium, August-September 2004.

Rocha, A. K.; Lira, P., Ju, Y. Y., Barros, E.; Melcher, E. U. K. & Araujo, G. (2006). Silicon Validated, IP Cores Designed by The Brasil-IP Network". *Proceedings of IP/SOC Conference*, Grenoble, França, 2006.

Schallenberg, A.; Oppenheimer, F. & Nebel, W. (2004). Designing for Dynamic and Partially Reconfigurable FPGAs with SystemC and OSSS, *Proceedings of Forum on Specification and Design Languages (FDL '04)*, Lille, France, September, 2004.

Schallenberg, A.; Oppenheimer, F. & Nebel, W. (2006). OSSS+R: Modelling and Simulating Self-Reconfigurable Systems. *Proceedings of the International Conference on Field Programmable Logic and Applications*, p. 177–182, August 2006.

Silva, K. R. G. & Melcher, E. U. K. (2005). A methodology aimed at better integration of functional verification and RTL design, *Design Automation for Embedded Systems*, Vol. 10, No. 4, p. 285-298.

Silveira, G. S.; Brito, A. V. & Melcher, E. U. (2009). Functional verification of power gate design in SystemC RTL. *Proceedings of the 22nd Annual Symposium on Integrated Circuits and System Design: Chip on the Dunes*, Natal, Brazil, August, 2009, SBC, Porto Alegre.

Zhang, X. & Ng, K. W. (2000). A review of high-level synthesis for dynamically reconfigurable FPGAs". *Microprocessors and Microsystems*, Vol. 24, No. 4, p. 199-211. August 2000.

4

Dynamic Modelling and Control Design of Advanced Energy Storage for Power System Applications

Marcelo Gustavo Molina
CONICET, Instituto de Energía Eléctrica, Universidad Nacional de San Juan
Argentina

1. Introduction

In general, a large percentage of the electric power produced is generated in huge generation centres far from the consumption, and with centralized transmission and distribution systems, where the weak point of this scheme is the efficiency with high energy losses in the form of heat. This problem has been increased in the last years due to the significant growth of electric energy demand and in the case of structures of weakly meshed electrical grids, due to the high vulnerability in cases of faults that can originate frequently severe transient and dynamic problems that lead to the reduction of the system security (Dail et al., 2007). Many large blackouts that happened worldwide in the last decade are a clear example of the consequences of this model of electric power. These problems, far from finding effective solutions, are continuously increasing, even more impelled by energy factors (oil crisis), ecological (climatic change) and by financial and regulatory restrictions of wholesale markets, which causes the necessity of technological alternatives to assure, on one hand the appropriate supply and quality of the electric power and on the other one, the saving and the efficient use of the natural resources preserving the environment.

An alternative technological solution to this problem is using small generation units and integrating them into the distribution network as near as possible of the consumption site, making this way diminishing the dependence of the local electrical demand, of the energy transmission power system. This solution is known as in-situ, distributed or dispersed generation (DG) and represents a change in the paradigm of the traditional centralized electric power generation (El-Khattam & Salama, 2004). In this way, the distribution grid usually passive is transformed into active one, in the sense that decision making and control is distributed and the power flows bidirectionally. Here it is consolidated the idea of using clean non-conventional technologies of generation that use renewable energy sources (RESs) that do not cause environmental pollution, such as wind, photovoltaic (PV), hydraulic, biomass among others (Rahman, 2003).

At present, perhaps the most promising novel network structure that would allow obtaining a better use of the distributed generation resources is the electrical microgrid (MG) (Kroposki et al., 2008). This new paradigm tackles the distributed generation as a subsystem formed by distributed energy resources (DERs), including DG, RESs and distributed energy storage (DES) and controllable demand response (DR), also offering significant control capacities on its operation. This grid is designed to be managed as a group with a predictable unit of generation and demand, and can be operated as much interconnected to the main power system as isolated. In this way, the coordinated control of DERs and DR would allow maximizing the benefits for the owners of the microgrid, giving an attractive remuneration, as well as for the users, providing the thermal and electric demands with lesser energy costs and meeting the local requirements of security and dependability (Katiraei et al., 2008).

In recent years, due mainly to the technology innovation, cost reduction, and government policy stimulus there has been an extensive growth and rapid development in the exploitation of renewable energies, particularly wind and photovoltaic solar ones. However, the power provided by these RESs frequently changes and is hardly predictable, especially for the case of wind generation. Today, there exists an increasing penetration of large-scale wind farms (WF) and PV solar power plants into the electric power system all over the world (Battaglini et al., 2009). This situation can lead to severe problems that affect the micro grid security dramatically, particularly in a weak grid, i.e. system frequency oscillations due to insufficient system damping, and/or violations of transmission capability margin due to severe fluctuations of tie-line power flow, among others (Slootweg & Kling, 2003; Pourbeik et al., 2006). Even more, as presently deregulated power markets are taking place, generation and transmission resources are being utilized at higher efficiency rates, leading to a tighter control of the spare generation capacity of the system (Pourbeik et al., 2006a).

In order to overcome these problems, energy storage systems (ESS) advanced solutions can be utilized as an effective DES device with the ability of quickly exchanging the exceeding energy stored during off-peak load periods and thus providing a bridge in meeting the power and energy requirements of the microgrid. By combining the technology of energy storage with a recent type of power electronic equipments, such as flexible alternating current transmission systems (FACTS) (Song & Johns, 1999; Hingorani & Gyugyi, 2000), the power system can take advantage of the flexibility benefits provided by the advanced ESSs and the high controllability provided by power electronics. This allows enhancing the electrical grid performance, providing the enough flexibility to adapt to the specific conditions of the microgrid including intermittent RESs and operating in an autonomous fashion. There are many advanced technologies available in the market for energy storage with high potential of being applied in electrical microgrids. Such modern devices include super (or ultra) capacitors (SCES or UCES, respectively), superconducting magnetic energy storage (SMES), flywheels (FES) and advanced batteries (ABESS) among others. These ESSs can play a crucial, multi-functional role since storage facilities are designed to excel in a dynamic environment. Some factors driving the incorporation of these novel storage technologies include reduced environmental impact, rapid response, high power, high efficiency, and four-quadrant control, solving many of the challenges regarding the increased use of renewable energy sources, and enhancing the overall reliability, power quality, and security of power systems.

2. Overview of distributed energy storage technologies

A number of energy storage technologies have been developed or are under development for power system applications. These systems use different energy storage technologies, including conventional energy storage that have been extensively proven over many years, and recently developed technologies with high potential for applications in modern power systems, especially in electrical microgrids.

Four energy storage methodologies gather these technologies, i.e. chemical, electric, mechanic, and thermal energy storage (Molina & Mercado, 2001, 2003). Chemical storage methods use a reversible chemical reaction that takes place in the presence of an electrolyte for storing/producing DC electricity. This approach includes both, battery systems and fuel cells. Batteries contain the classic and well-known lead-acid type as well as the modern redox (reduction-oxidation) flow batteries and the advanced battery energy storage systems (ABESSs). ABESSs comprise new alkaline batteries, nickel chemistry (nickel-metal hydride–NiMH, and nickel-cadmium–NiCd), lithium chemistry (lithium–Li, and lithium-ion–Li-Ion), and sodium chemistry (sodium-sulfur–NaS, and sodium-salt–NaNiCl). Fuel cells (FC–hydrogen cycle and reversible/regenerative FCs) include five major types, that is alkaline fuel cells (AFC), proton exchange membrane fuel cells (PEMFC), phosphoric acid fuel cells (PAFC), molten carbonate fuel cells (MCFC), direct methanol fuel cells (DMFC), and solid oxide fuel cells (SOFC). Electric storage methods store energy directly as DC electricity in an electric or magnetic field, with no other intermediate energy transformation. This approach includes recent developments in superconducting magnetic energy storage (SMES) and the so-called super (or ultra) capacitor energy storage (SCES or UCES, respectively). Modern mechanical storage methods exchange their energy with the power system directly as AC electricity using a synchronous or asynchronous motor/generator. This methodology comprises updating of popular and well-proven pumped hydro, modern flywheels, and compressed air energy storage (CAES) systems. Thermal storage systems store energy as super-heated oil or molten salts. The heat of the salt or oil is used for steam generation and then to run a turbine coupled to an electric motor/generator.
Most of these technologies have been classified in terms of power and energy applications, grouped in short-term and long-term energy storage capabilities, as shown in Fig. 1 (Energy Storage Association, 2003). In general terms, power applications refer to energy storage systems rated for one hour or less, whereas energy applications would be for longer periods.

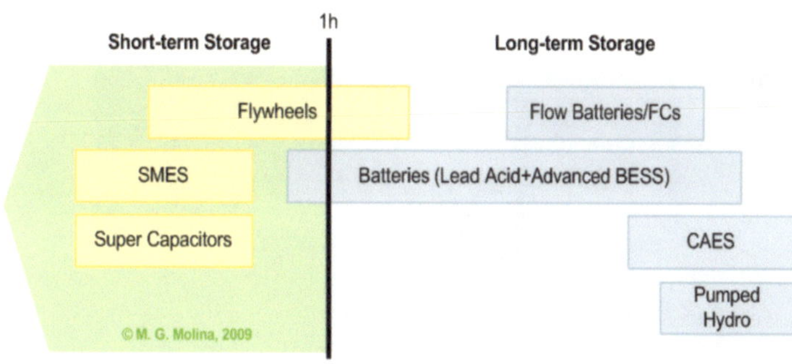

Fig. 1. Classification of energy storage technologies based on the storage capability

Energy storage in interconnected power systems has been studied for many years and the benefits are well-known and in general understood (Nourai, 2002; Energy Storage Association, 2003). In contrast, much less has been done particularly on distributed energy storage, but most of the same benefits apply. In both cases, storage costs, limited sitting opportunities, and technology limitations have restricted the use of energy storage during last decades. This chapter will address DES technologies for power applications in microgrids, i.e. considering only short-term energy storage capability requirements, since they are essential for allowing the microgrid operation in autonomous fashion and even more with high penetrations of intermittent renewable energy sources. They play the major role in control and operation of a microgrid by providing an instantaneous bridge in meeting the power and energy requirements of the microgrid when DG sources primary reserve is not sufficient to meet the demand, particularly in response time. The analysis presented is focused on the three foremost advanced short-term energy storage systems, such as super capacitors, SMESs and flywheels.

2.1 Superconducting Magnetic Energy Storage – SMES

SMES is a type of energy storage system where energy is permanently stored in a magnetic field generated by the flow of DC current in a superconducting coil (SC). This coil is cryogenically cooled to a temperature below its critical temperature to exhibit its superconductivity property. The basic principle of a SMES is that once the superconducting coil is charged, the current will not decay and the magnetic energy can be stored indefinitely. This stored energy can be released back into the electric network by simply discharging the coil (Buckles & Hassenzahl, 2000). An attractive and a potentially cost-effective option for modern SMES systems is to use a high-temperature superconductor (HTS: Ceramic oxide compound) SMES cooled by liquid nitrogen instead of the usual low-temperature superconductor (LTS: Niobium-titanium alloy) SMES cooled by liquid helium to provide a short-term buffer during a disturbance in the power system.
The basic structure of a SMES device is shown in Fig. 2. The base of the SMES unit is a large superconducting coil, whose basic structure is composed of the cold components itself (the SC with its support and connection components, and the cryostat) and the cryogenic refrigerating system (Arsoy et al., 2003). On the other hand, the power conditioning system provides a power electronic interface between the AC power system and the SC, aiming at achieving two goals: one is to convert electric power from DC to AC, and the other is to charge/discharge efficiently the superconducting coil.

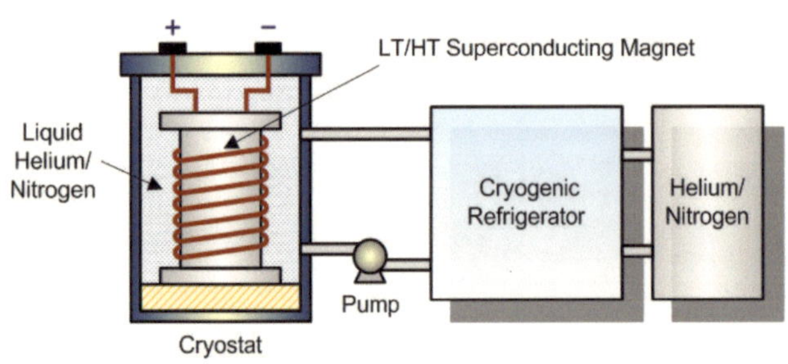

Fig. 2. Basic structure of a SMES device

SMES systems have many advantages over typical storage systems. The dynamic performance of a SMES system is far superior to other technologies. The superconducting feature of the SMES coil implies the "permanent" storage of energy because it has no internal resistance, which makes the stored energy not to be dissipated as heat. Moreover, this allows the coil to release all its stored energy almost instantaneously, a reason why they are very quick and have very short response times, limited by the switching time of the solid state components responsible of the energy conversion. On the other hand, the operation of the system and the lifetime are not influenced by the number of service cycles or the depth of discharge as in the case of traditional batteries. Additionally, a SMES system is highly efficient with more than 95% efficiency from input back to output, as well as highly reliable because of no using moving parts to carry out the energy storing.

Among the disadvantages of the SMES device is the high cost of superconducting wires and the large energy requirements for the refrigeration of the SMES system at cryogenic temperatures, particularly in conventional units (LTS); although this demand is considerably reduced by using modern HTS materials. In addition to these drawbacks is the use of huge magnetic fields, which can overcome 9 T.

2.2 Super Capacitor Energy Storage – SCES

Capacitors store electric energy through the electric field formed between two conducting plates (electrodes), when a DC voltage is applied across them. The so-called super capacitor energy storage (SCES), aka ultra capacitor energy storage (UCES), are a relative recent technology in the field of short-term energy storage systems and consist of a porous structure of activated carbon for one or both electrodes, which are immersed into an electrolytic solution (typically potassium hydroxide or sulphuric acid) and a separator that prevents physical contact of the electrodes but allows ion transfer between them (Barker, 2002). This structure effectively creates two equivalent capacitors (between each electrode and the electrolyte) connected in series, as shown in the schematic view of its internal components of Fig. 3. Energy is stored as a charge separation in the double layer formed at the interface between the solid electrode material surface and the liquid electrolyte in the micropores of the electrodes. Due to this feature, these capacitors are also known as electric double layer capacitors (EDLC) or simply advanced electrochemical capacitors.

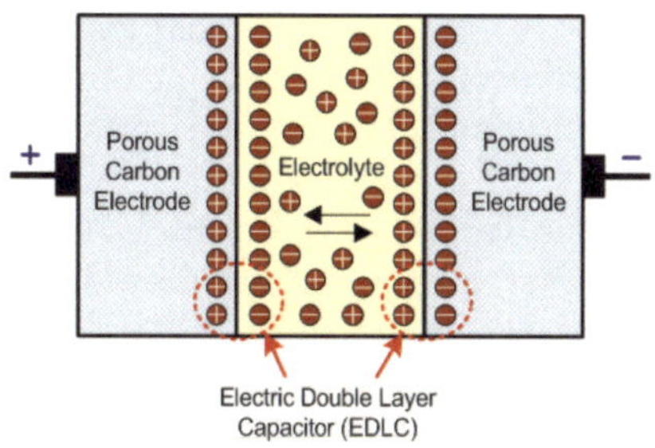

Fig. 3. Schematic view of a super capacitor

A super capacitor largely is subject to the same physics as a standard capacitor. That is, the capacitance is determined by the effective area of the electrodes, the separation distance of them and the dielectric constant of the separating medium. However, the key difference of the super capacitor is that with its structure of liquid electrolyte and porous electrodes (activated carbon material), an extremely high specific surface area is obtained (hundreds of m^2/g) compared to the conventional electrode structure (Conway, 1999). Furthermore, it ensures an extremely short distance at the interface between electrode and electrolyte (less than 1 μm). These two factors lead to a very high capacitance per unit of volume, which can be from hundreds to thousands times larger than electrolytic capacitors, up to a few thousand Farads (typically 5000 F) (Schindall, 2007). Unfortunately, the maximum voltage is limited to a few volts (normally up to 3 V) by the decomposition voltage of the electrolyte, mainly because of the presence of impurities.

Super capacitors have big advantages which make them almost non comparable in many applications. Because they have no moving parts, and require neither cooling nor heating, and because they undergo no internal chemical changes as part of their function, they are robust and very efficient, reaching a cycle efficiency of 95% or more. Also, they require practically no maintenance and the lifetime is exceptionally high, with no lifetime degradation due to frequent and deep cycling. Presently, the life cycle of a typical super capacitor reaches over hundred thousands of duty cycles or more than 10 year life. Since super capacitors are capable of very fast charges and discharges, they make a perfect fit for voltage regulation in the power world.

Unfortunately, the most important disadvantage of super capacitors is that they are in the earliest stages of development as an ESS for power system applications and consequently costs are still extremely high. Presently, very small super capacitors in the range of seven to ten watts are widely available commercially for consumer power quality applications and are commonly found in household electrical devices. Development of larger-scale capacitors has been focused on electric vehicles. Presently, small-scale power quality (up to 250 kW) is considered to be the most promising utility use for advanced capacitors.

2.3 Flywheel Energy Storage – FES

A flywheel device stores electric energy as kinetic (or inertial) energy of the rotor mass spinning at very high speeds. Fig. 4 shows the structure of a conventional flywheel unit. The charging/discharging of the device is carried out through an integrated electrical machine operating either as a motor to accelerate the rotor up to the required high speeds by absorbing power from the electric grid (charge mode) or as a generator to produce electrical power on demand using the energy stored in the flywheel mass by decelerating the rotor (discharge mode). The system has very low rotational losses due to the use of magnetic bearings which prevent the contact between the stationary and rotating parts, thus decreasing the friction. In addition, because the system operates in vacuum, the aerodynamic resistance of the rotor is outstandingly reduced. These features permit the system to reach efficiencies higher than 80% (Nourai et al., 2005).

Flywheels have the ability to charge and discharge rapidly, and are almost immune to temperature fluctuations. They take up relatively little space, have lower maintenance requirements than batteries, and have a long life span. Flywheel devices are relatively tolerant of abuse, i.e. the lifetime of a flywheel system will not be shortened by a deep discharge unlike a battery. The stored energy is directly proportional to the flywheel rotor momentum and the square of the angular momentum, a reason why increments in the rotation speed yield large benefits on the storage energy density. Keeping this in mind, the classification in two types of flywheels arises: high speed flywheels (HS: approximately 40 000 rpm) and low speed flywheels (LS: approximately 7 000 rpm). High-speed flywheels allow obtaining very compact units with high energy densities (Liu & Jiang, 2007).

Conventional magnetic bearings have low specific power consumption (W/g), which is dissipated as heat in the copper of the bearing electromagnets. This power depends on the structure of the bearing and the utilized control system. Modern superconducting magnetic bearings, on the other hand, have demonstrated very low losses (10^{-2}–10^{-3}W/kg) in rotors at low speeds. This leads to a very high overall efficiency of the system, exceeding 90%.

Although most of the flywheel technology was developed in the automobile and aerospace industry, it is expected that flywheels have most commercial success targeted for power delivery capabilities of up to 1 MW. They are particularly suitable for the PQ and reliability market, but no large-scale applications of the technology have been installed to date. A big disadvantage of modern high-temperature superconducting flywheel devices is that they constitute a new technology, which is currently under development. Such systems would offer inherent stability, minimal power loss, and simplicity of operation as well as increased energy storage capacity, which may show a promising future for use in the power sector.

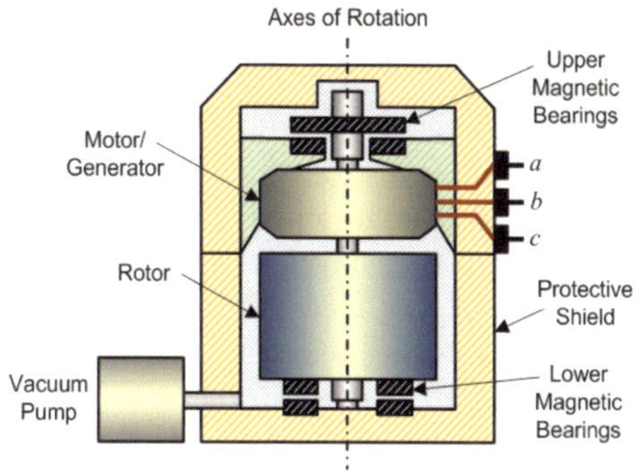

Fig. 4. Structure of a conventional flywheel

3. Application of advanced distributed energy storage in microgrids

For microgrids to work properly, an upstream interconnection switch must open typically during an unacceptable power quality (PQ) condition, and the DER must be able to provide electrical power to the islanded loads. This includes maintaining appropriate voltage and frequency levels for the islanded subsystem. In this way, the DER must be able to supply the active and reactive power requirements during islanded operation, so that fast-acting generation reserve is required. As a result, for stable operation to balance any instantaneous mismatch in active power, efficient distributed energy storage, such as super capacitors, SMESs and flywheels, must be used (Katiraei et al., 2008).

In a distributed energy storage system, the power conditioning system (PCS) is the interface that allows the effective connection to the electric power system. The PCS provides a power electronic interface between the AC electric system and the DES, aiming at achieving two major goals: one is to convert electric power from DC (or in some cases uncontrolled AC) to AC (established by the utility grid), and the other is to charge/discharge efficiently the DES device. The dynamics of the PCS directly influences the validity of the DES unit in the dynamic control of the microgrid. With the appropriate topology of the PCS and its control system design, the DES unit is capable of simultaneously performing both instantaneous active and reactive power flow control, as required in modern microgrid applications.

The progress in new technologies of power electronics devices (Bose, 2002; Carrasco et al., 2006), named flexible AC transmission systems (FACTS), is presently leading the use of advanced energy storage solutions in order to enhance the electrical grid performance, providing the enough flexibility to adapt to the specific conditions of the microgrid and operating in an autonomous fashion. Just as flexible FACTS controllers permit to improve the reliability and quality of transmission systems, these devices can be used in the distribution level with comparable benefits for bringing solutions to a wide range of problems. In this sense, FACTS-based power electronic controllers for distribution systems, namely custom power (CP) devices (or simply distribution FACTS), are able to enhance the reliability and the quality of power delivered to customers (Molina & Mercado, 2006). A distribution static synchronous compensator (DSTATCOM) is a fast response, solid-state power controller that belongs to advanced shunt-connected CP devices and provides flexible voltage control at the point of common coupling (PCC) to the utility distribution

feeder for power quality and stability improvements. It can exchange both active and reactive powers with the distribution system by varying the amplitude and phase angle of the PCS voltage with respect to the PCC voltage, if an energy storage system is included into the inner DC bus. The effect is a controlled current flow through the tie reactance between the DSTATCOM and the distribution network, this enabling the DSTATCOM to mitigate voltage fluctuations such as sags, swells and transients. Furthermore, it can be utilized for providing voltage regulation, power factor correction, harmonics compensation and stability augmentation. The addition of energy storage to the power custom device, through an appropriate interface, leads to a more flexible integrated controller. The ability of the DSTATCOM-DES (also known simply as DES system) to supply effectively active power allows expanding its compensation actions, reducing transmission losses and enhancing the operation of the electric microgrid (Molina et al., 2007).
Fig. 5 depicts a functional model of various advanced energy storage devices integrated with the appropriate power conditioning system for microgrid applications. This model consists mainly of a DSTATCOM, the energy storage system and the interface between the DSTATCOM and the DES, represented by the bidirectional converter.

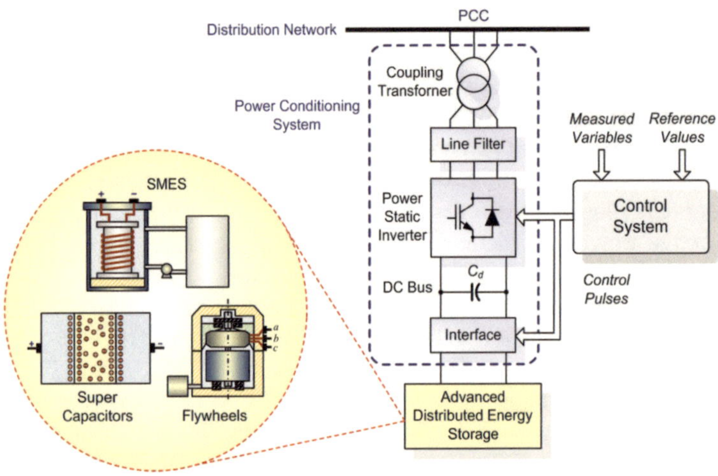

Fig. 5. Basic circuit of a custom power device integrated with advanced energy storage

The DSTATCOM consists mainly of a three-phase power inverter shunt-connected to the distribution network by means of a coupling transformer with line filter and the corresponding control scheme. The integration of the DES into the DC bus of the DSTATCOM device requires a rapid and robust bidirectional interface to adapt the wide range of variation in voltage and current levels between both devices, according to the specific DES employed. Controlling the DES rate of charge/discharge requires varying the voltage magnitude (and polarity in some cases) according to the state-of-operation, while keeping essentially constant the DC bus voltage of the DSTATCOM inverter. To this aim, a two-quadrant converter topology according to the DES unit employed is proposed in order to obtain a suitable control performance of the overall system.

4. Dynamic modelling and control design of the SMES system

A SMES system consists of several sub-systems, which must be carefully designed in order to obtain a high performance compensation device for microgrid applications. The base of the SMES unit is a large superconducting coil (SC). On the other hand, the power conditioning system provides a power electronic interface between the AC electric system and the SC, allowing the grid-connected operation of the DES. Fig. 6 shows the proposed detailed model of the entire SMES system for applications in the distribution level. This model consists of the SMES coil with its filtering and protection system and the PCS for coupling to the electric grid.

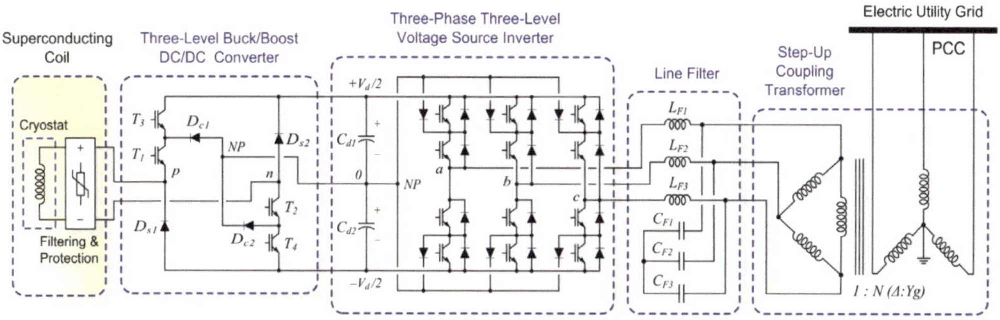

Fig. 6. Full detailed model of the proposed SMES system

4.1 Power conditioning system of the SMES

4.1.1 Three-phase three-level DSTATCOM

The key part of the PCS is the DSTATCOM device, and is shared by the three advanced selected DES systems, as will be described later. The proposed DSTATCOM essentially consists of a three-phase voltage source inverter (VSI) built with semiconductors devices having turn-off capabilities. This device is shunt-connected to the distribution network by means of a coupling transformer and the corresponding line sinusoidal filter. Its topology allows the device to generate at the point of common coupling to the AC network (PCC) a set of three almost sinusoidal voltage waveforms at the fundamental frequency phase-shifted 120° between each other, with controllable amplitude and phase angle. Since the SMES coil is basically a stiff current source, the use of a current source inverter (CSI) would emerge as the natural selection. However, the wide range of variation of the coil current and voltage would cause the device to exceed its rating, which makes impractical the use of conventional CSIs. On this basis, an analyses were performed to evaluate hybrid current source inverters (HCSI) and voltage source inverters (VSI); concluding that the later ones are a more cost-effective solution for the present application (Molina et al., 2007).

The three-phase VSI corresponds to a DC/AC switching power inverter using high-power insulated gate bipolar transistors (IGBTs). This semiconductor device is employed due to its lower switching losses and reduced size when compared to other devices. In addition, as the power rating of the inverter goes up to medium levels for typical DER applications (less than few MWs), the output voltage control of the VSI can be efficiently achieved through sinusoidal pulse width modulation (SPWM) techniques. The connection to the utility grid is made by means of a step-up Δ-Y coupling transformer, and second-order low pass sine wave filters are included in order to reduce the perturbation on the distribution system from high-frequency switching harmonics generated by the PWM control of the VSI. Since two ways for linking the filter can be employed, i.e. placing it before and after the coupling transformer, here it is preferred the first option because reduce notably the harmonics contents into the transformer windings, thus reducing losses and avoiding its overrating.

The VSI structure proposed is designed to make use of a three-level twelve pulse pole structure, also called neutral point clamped (NPC), instead of a standard two-level six pulse inverter structure (Rodriguez et al., 2002, Soto & Green, 2002). This three-level VSI topology generates a more smoothly sinusoidal output voltage waveform than conventional two-level structures without increasing the switching frequency and effectively doubles the power rating of the VSI for a given semiconductor device. Moreover, the three level pole attempts to address some limitations of the standard two-level by offering an additional flexibility of a level in the output voltage, which can be controlled in duration, either to vary the fundamental output voltage or to assist in the output waveform construction. This extra feature is used here to assist in the output waveform structure. In this way, the harmonic performance of the inverter is improved, also obtaining better efficiency and reliability. The output line voltage waveforms of a three-level VSI connected to a 380 V utility system are shown in Fig. 7. It is to be noted that in steady-state the VSI generates at its output terminals a switched line voltage waveform with high harmonics content, reaching the voltage total harmonic distortion (VTHD) almost 45% when unloaded. At the output terminals of the low pass sine wave filters proposed, the VTHD is reduced to as low as 1%, decreasing this quantity to even a half at the coupling transformer secondary output terminals (PCC). In this way, the quality of the voltage waveforms introduced by the PWM control to the power utility is improved and the requirements of IEEE Standard 519-1992 relative to power quality (VTHD limit in 5 %) are entirely fulfilled (Bollen, 2000).

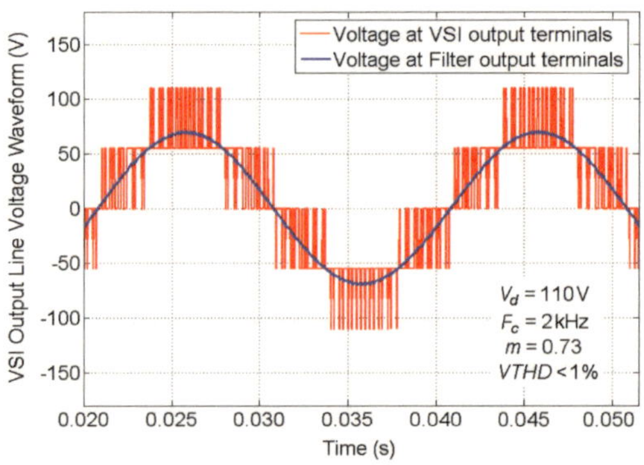

Fig. 7. Three-level NPC voltage source inverter output line voltage waveforms

The mathematical equations describing and representing the operation of the DSTATCOM can be derived from the detailed model shown in Fig. 6 by taking into account some assumptions respect to the operating conditions of the inverter. For this purpose, a simplified equivalent VSI connected to the electric system is considered, also referred to as an averaged model, which assumes the inverter operation under balanced conditions as ideal, i.e. the voltage source inverter is seen as an ideal sinusoidal voltage source operating at fundamental frequency, as depicted in Fig. 8. This consideration is valid since, as shown in Fig. 7, the high-frequency harmonics produced by the inverter as result of the sinusoidal PWM control techniques are mostly filtered by the low pass sine wave filters and the net instantaneous output voltages at the point of common coupling resembles three sinusoidal waveforms phase-shifted 120º between each other.

This ideal inverter is shunt-connected to the network at the PCC through an equivalent inductance L_s, accounting for the leakage of the step-up coupling transformer and an

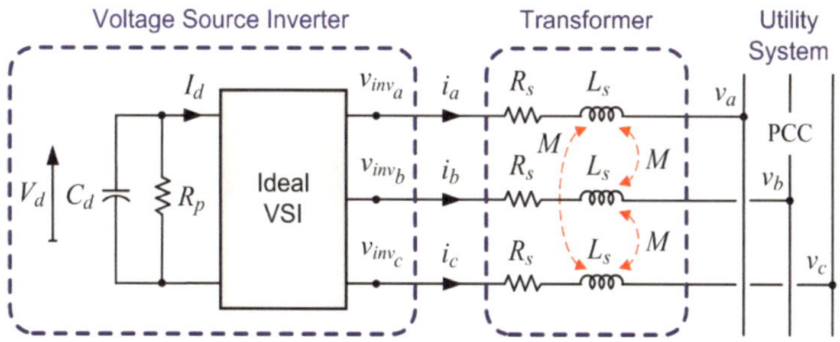

Fig. 8. Equivalent circuit diagram of the proposed inverter connected to the AC system

equivalent series resistance R_s, representing the transformers winding resistance and VSI semiconductors conduction losses. The magnetizing inductance of the step-up transformer can also be taken into consideration through a mutual equivalent inductance M. In the DC side, the equivalent capacitance of the two DC bus capacitors, C_{d1} and C_{d2} (C_{d1}=C_{d2}), is described through C_d=$C_{d1}/2$=$C_{d2}/2$ whereas the switching losses of the VSI and power losses in the DC capacitors are considered by a parallel resistance R_p. As a result, the dynamics equations governing the instantaneous values of the three-phase output voltages in the AC side of the VSI and the current exchanged with the utility grid can be directly derived from Fig. 8 by applying Kirchhoff's voltage law (KVL) as follows:

$$\begin{bmatrix} v_{inv_a} \\ v_{inv_b} \\ v_{inv_c} \end{bmatrix} - \begin{bmatrix} v_a \\ v_b \\ v_c \end{bmatrix} = \left(\mathrm{R_S} + s\mathrm{L_S}\right) \begin{bmatrix} i_a \\ i_b \\ i_c \end{bmatrix}, \tag{1}$$

where:
s: Laplace variable, being $s = d/dt$ for t > 0 (Heaviside operator p also used)

$$\mathrm{R_S} = \begin{bmatrix} R_s & 0 & 0 \\ 0 & R_s & 0 \\ 0 & 0 & R_s \end{bmatrix}, \; \mathrm{L_S} = \begin{bmatrix} L_s & M & M \\ M & L_s & M \\ M & M & L_s \end{bmatrix} \tag{2}$$

Under the assumption that the system has no zero sequence components (operation under balanced conditions), all currents and voltages can be uniquely transformed into the synchronous-rotating orthogonal two-axes reference frame, in which each vector is described by means of its d and q components, instead of its three a, b, c components. Thus, the new coordinate system is defined with the d-axis always coincident with the instantaneous voltage vector, as described in Fig. 9. By defining the d-axis to be always coincident with the instantaneous voltage vector v, yields v_d equals $|v|$, while v_q is null. Consequently, the d-axis current component contributes to the instantaneous active power and the q-axis current component represents the instantaneous reactive power. This operation permits to develop a simpler and more accurate dynamic model of the DSTATCOM.

By applying Park's transformation (Krause, 1992) stated by equation (3), equations (1) and (2) can be transformed into the synchronous rotating d-q reference frame as follows (equations (4) through (7)):

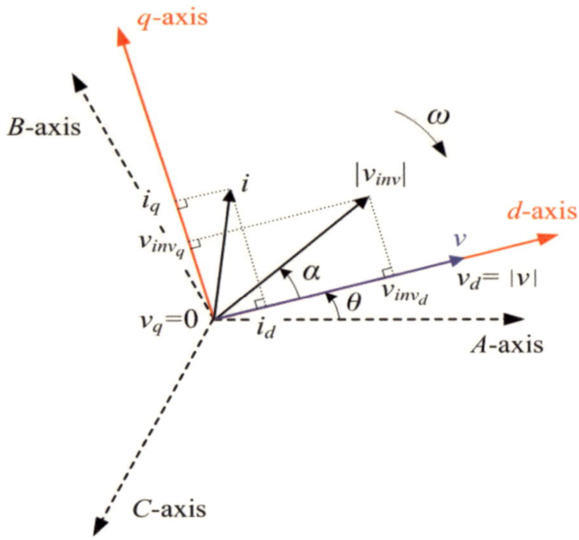

Fig. 9. DSTATCOM vectors in the synchronous rotating *d-q* reference frame

$$\mathrm{K_s} = \frac{2}{3}\begin{bmatrix} \cos\theta & \cos\left(\theta - \frac{2\pi}{3}\right) & \cos\left(\theta + \frac{2\pi}{3}\right) \\ -\sin\theta & -\sin\left(\theta - \frac{2\pi}{3}\right) & -\sin\left(\theta + \frac{2\pi}{3}\right) \\ \frac{1}{2} & \frac{1}{2} & \frac{1}{2} \end{bmatrix}, \tag{3}$$

with:

$\theta = \int_0^t \omega(\xi)d\xi + \theta(0)$: angle between the *d*-axis and the reference phase axis,

and ξ: integration variable

ω: synchronous angular speed of the network voltage at the fundamental system frequency f (50 Hz throughout this chapter).

Thus,

$$\begin{bmatrix} v_{inv_d} - v_d \\ v_{inv_q} - v_q \\ v_{inv_0} - v_0 \end{bmatrix} = \mathrm{K_s}\begin{bmatrix} v_{inv_a} - v_a \\ v_{inv_b} - v_b \\ v_{inv_c} - v_c \end{bmatrix}, \quad \begin{bmatrix} i_d \\ i_q \\ i_0 \end{bmatrix} = \mathrm{K_s}\begin{bmatrix} i_a \\ i_b \\ i_c \end{bmatrix} \tag{4}$$

Then, by neglecting the zero sequence components, equations (5) and (6) are derived.

$$\begin{bmatrix} v_{inv_d} \\ v_{inv_q} \end{bmatrix} - \begin{bmatrix} v_d \\ v_q \end{bmatrix} = \left(\mathrm{R_s} + s\mathrm{L}'_{\mathrm{s}}\right)\begin{bmatrix} i_d \\ i_q \end{bmatrix} + \begin{bmatrix} -\omega & 0 \\ 0 & \omega \end{bmatrix}\mathrm{L}'_{\mathrm{s}}\begin{bmatrix} i_q \\ i_d \end{bmatrix}, \tag{5}$$

where:

$$\mathrm{R_s} = \begin{bmatrix} R_s & 0 \\ 0 & R_s \end{bmatrix},\ \mathrm{L'_s} = \begin{bmatrix} L'_s & 0 \\ 0 & L'_s \end{bmatrix} = \begin{bmatrix} L_s - M & 0 \\ 0 & L_s - M \end{bmatrix} \tag{6}$$

It is to be noted that the coupling of phases *abc* through the term M in matrix $\mathrm{L_s}$ (equation (2)), was fully eliminated in the d-q reference frame when the DSTATCOM transformers are magnetically symmetric, as is usually the case. This decoupling of phases in the synchronous-rotating system allows simplifying the control system design.
By rewriting equation (5), the following state equation can be obtained:

$$s\begin{bmatrix} i_d \\ i_q \end{bmatrix} = \begin{bmatrix} \dfrac{-R_s}{L'_s} & \omega \\ -\omega & \dfrac{-R_s}{L'_s} \end{bmatrix} \begin{bmatrix} i_d \\ i_q \end{bmatrix} + \frac{1}{L'_s} \begin{bmatrix} v_{inv_d} - |v| \\ v_{inv_q} \end{bmatrix} \tag{7}$$

A further major issue of the d-q transformation is its frequency dependence (ω). In this way, with appropriate synchronization to the network (through angle θ), the control variables in steady state are transformed into DC quantities. This feature is quite useful to develop an efficient decoupled control system of the two current components. Although the model is fundamental frequency-dependent, the instantaneous variables in the d-q reference frame contain all the information concerning the three-phase variables, including steady-state unbalance, harmonic waveform distortions and transient components.
The relation between the DC-side voltage V_d and the generated AC voltage v_{inv} can be described through the average switching function matrix in the dq reference frame $\mathbf{S}_{\mathbf{av},dq}$ of the proposed inverter, as given by equation (8). This relation assumes that the DC capacitors voltages are balanced and equal to $V_d/2$.

$$\begin{bmatrix} v_{inv_d} \\ v_{inv_q} \end{bmatrix} = \mathbf{S}_{\mathbf{av},\,\boldsymbol{dq}}\, V_d\,, \tag{8}$$

and the average switching function matrix in dq coordinates is computed as:

$$\mathbf{S}_{\mathbf{av},\,\boldsymbol{dq}} = \begin{bmatrix} S_{av,d} \\ S_{av,q} \end{bmatrix} = \frac{1}{2} m_i\, a \begin{bmatrix} \cos\alpha \\ \sin\alpha \end{bmatrix}, \tag{9}$$

being,
m_i: modulation index of the voltage source inverter, $m_i \in [0, 1]$.
$a = \dfrac{\sqrt{3}}{\sqrt{2}} \dfrac{n_2}{n_1}$: turns ratio of the step-up Δ-Y coupling transformer,
α: phase-shift of the DSTATCOM output voltage from the reference position,
The AC power exchanged by the DSTATCOM is related with the DC bus power on an instantaneous basis in such a way that a power balance must exist between the input and the output of the inverter. In this way, the AC power should be equal to the sum of the DC resistance (R_p) power, representing losses (IGBTs switching and DC capacitors) and to the charging rate of the DC equivalent capacitor (C_d) (neglecting the SMES action):

$$P_{AC} = P_{DC} \tag{10}$$

$$\frac{3}{2}\left(v_{inv_d} i_d + v_{inv_q} i_q\right) = -\frac{C_d}{2} V_d s V_d - \frac{V_d^2}{R_p} \tag{11}$$

Essentially, equations (1) through (11) can be summarized in the state-space as described by equation (12). This continuous state-space averaged mathematical model describes the steady-state dynamics of the ideal DSTATCOM in the *dq* reference frame, and will be subsequently used as a basis for designing the middle level control scheme to be proposed.
As reported by Acha et al. (2002), modelling of static inverters by using a synchronous-rotating orthogonal *d-q* reference frame offer higher accuracy than employing stationary coordinates. Moreover, this operation allows designing a simpler control system than using *abc* or $\alpha\beta$.

$$s\begin{bmatrix} i_d \\ i_q \\ V_d \end{bmatrix} = \begin{bmatrix} \frac{-R_s}{L'_s} & \omega & \frac{S_{av,d}}{2L'_s} \\ -\omega & \frac{-R_s}{L'_s} & \frac{S_{av,q}}{2L'_s} \\ -\frac{3}{2C_d}S_{av,d} & -\frac{3}{2C_d}S_{av,q} & -\frac{2}{R_p C_d} \end{bmatrix} \begin{bmatrix} i_d \\ i_q \\ V_d \end{bmatrix} - \begin{bmatrix} \frac{|v|}{L'_s} \\ 0 \\ 0 \end{bmatrix} \tag{12}$$

4.1.2 Two-quadrant three-level DC/DC converter

The inclusion of a SMES coil into the DC bus of the DSTATCOM VSI demands the use of a rapid and robust bidirectional interface to adapt the wide range of variation in voltage and current levels between both devices. Controlling the SMES coil rate of charge/discharge requires varying as much the coil voltage magnitude as the polarity according to the coil state-of-charge, while keeping essentially constant and balanced the voltage of the VSI DC link capacitors. To this aim, a two-quadrant three-level IGBT DC/DC converter or chopper is proposed to be employed, as shown in Fig. 6 (upper left side). This converter allows decreasing the ratings of the overall PCS (specifically VSI and transformers) by regulating the current flowing from the SMES coil to the inverter of the VSI and vice versa.
The three-level VSI topology previously described can be applied to reactive power generation almost without voltage imbalance problems. But when active power exchange is included, the inverter could not have balanced voltages without sacrificing output voltage performance and auxiliary converters would be needed in order to provide a compensating power flow between the capacitors of the DC link. For this reason, the use of a two-quadrant three-level DC/DC converter as interface between the DSTATCOM and the SMES is proposed instead of the commonly used standard two-level one (Molina & Mercado, 2007). This converter makes use of the extra level to solve the above-mentioned possible voltage imbalance problems, as will be described below. Major advantages of three-level DC/DC chopper topologies compared to traditional two-level ones include reduction of voltage stress of each IGBT by half, permitting to increase the chopper power ratings while maintaining high dynamic performance and decreasing the harmonics distortion produced. Furthermore, it includes the availability of redundant switching states, which allow generating the same output voltage vector through various states. This last feature is very significant to reduce switching losses and the VSI DC current ripple, but mainly to maintain the charge balance of the DC capacitors, thus avoiding generating additional distortion.

Table 1 lists all possible combinations of the chopper output voltage vectors, V_{pn} (defining the SMES side of the circuit as the output side) and their corresponding IGBT switching states. As derived, the chopper can be thought of as a switching matrix device that combines various states for applying either a positive, negative or null voltage to the SC coil. The addition of an extra level to the DC/DC chopper allows enlarging its degrees of freedom. As a result, the charge balance of the DC bus capacitors can be controlled by using the extra switching states, at the same time acting as an enhanced conventional DC/DC converter. The output voltage vectors can be selected based on the required SMES coil voltage and DC bus neutral point (*NP*) voltage. In this way, multiple subtopologies can be used in order to obtain output voltage vectors of magnitude *0* and $V_d/2$, in such a way that different vectors of magnitude $V_d/2$ produce opposite currents flowing from/to the neutral point. This condition causes a fluctuation in the *NP* potential which permits to maintain the charge balance of the dc link capacitors. By properly selecting the duration of the different output voltage vectors, an efficient DC/DC controller with *NP* voltage control capabilities is obtained.

States	T_1	T_2	T_3	T_4	V_{pn}
1	1	1	1	1	$+V_d$
2	0	0	0	0	$-V_d$
3	0	1	0	1	0
4	1	0	1	0	0
5	1	1	0	0	0
6	1	1	0	1	$+V_d/2$
7	1	1	1	0	$+V_d/2$
8	1	0	0	0	$-V_d/2$
9	0	1	0	0	$-V_d/2$

Table 1. Three-level chopper output voltage vectors and their resultant switching states

The DC/DC chopper has basically three modes of operation, namely the buck or charge mode, the stand-by or free-wheeling mode and the boost or discharge mode. These modes are obtained here by using a buck/boost topology control mode contrary to a bang-bang control mode (Aware & Sutanto, 2004), which is much simpler yet produces higher AC losses in the superconducting coil. The behaviour of the chopper for each mode of operation can be explained in terms of operating a combination of three of the switching states shown in Table 1 during a switching cycle T_s. The purpose of the chopper is to apply a positive, null, or negative average voltage to the SMES coil, according to the mode of operation.
In the first mode of operation, that is the charge mode, the chopper works as a step-down (buck) converter. Since power is supplied to the SC from the electric power system, this mode can also be called powering mode, and makes use of a combination of positive and null vectors. This is achieved through the switching states *1*, *5* and *6* or *7* in order to produce output voltage vectors $+V_d$, *0* and $+V_d/2$, respectively, with separate contribution of charge at the *NP* from capacitors C_{d1} and C_{d2}. In this mode, transistors T_1 and T_2 are always kept on, while transistors T_3 and T_4 are modulated to obtain the appropriate output voltage, V_{pn}, across the SMES coil. In this way, only subtopologies closest to the state *1* are used. In consequence, only one semiconductor device is switched per switching cycle; this reducing the switching losses compared to the standard two-level converter and thus also reducing the input/output current ripple.

Fig. 10(a) shows the switching function S_{ch} of the three-level chopper operating in buck mode. This function, which is stated in equation (13), is valid for the charge mode independently of the switching states utilized for maintaining the charge balance of the DC bus capacitors (states *6* or *7*).

$$S_{ch} = D_1 + D_2 + \sum_{h=1}^{\infty}\left[2\frac{\sin(h\pi D_2)}{h\pi}\cos\left[h\omega(t-\gamma_2-2\gamma_1)\right]\right] + \sum_{h=1}^{\infty}\left[\frac{\sin(2h\pi D_1)}{h\pi}\cos\left[h\omega(t-\gamma_1)\right]\right], \quad (13)$$

where, h=1, 2, 3 ...

$D_1 = t_{on1}/2T_s$: duty cycle for switching states *6* or *7*

$D_2 = t_{on2}/T_s$: duty cycle for switching state 1

$\gamma_1 = D_1/f$: harmonic phase angle due to D_1

$\gamma_2 = D_2/2f$: harmonic phase angle due to D_2,

with f, being the fundamental electric grid frequency.

Once completed the charging of the SMES coil, the operating mode of the converter is changed to the stand-by mode, for which only the state *5* is used. In this second mode of operation transistors T_3 and T_4 are switched off, while transistors T_1 and T_2 are kept on all the time. In this way, the SMES coil current circulates in a closed loop, so that this mode is also known as free-wheeling mode. As in this mode no significant power losses are developed through semiconductors, the current remains fairly constant.

In the third mode of operation, that is the discharge mode, the chopper works as a step-up (boost) converter. Since power is returned back from the SC to the electric grid, this mode can also be called regenerative mode, and makes use of a combination of negative and null vectors. This is achieved through the switching states *2*, *5* and *8* or *9* in order to produce output voltage vectors $-V_d$, *0* and $-V_d/2$ with independent contribution of charge at the *NP* from capacitors C_{d1} and C_{d2}. As can be observed from Fig. 10(b), in this mode transistors T_3 and T_4 are constantly kept off while transistors T_1 and T_2 are controlled to obtain the suitable voltage V_{pn}, across the SMES coil. In this way, only subtopologies closest to the state *2* are used. In consequence, as in the case of the charge mode, only one semiconductor device is switched per switching cycle.

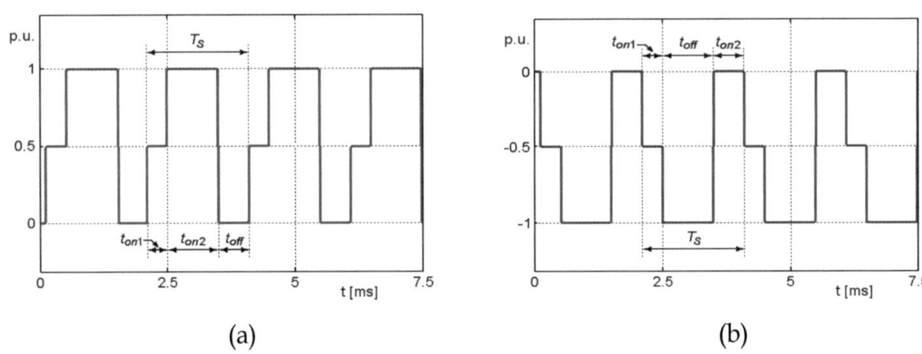

Fig. 10. Chopper switching functions. (a) Buck mode, S_{ch}. (b) Boost mode, S_{dch}

Fig. 10(b) shows the switching function S_{dch} of the three-level chopper operating in boost mode. This function, which is stated in equation (14), is valid for the discharge mode independently of the switching states utilized for maintaining the charge balance of the DC capacitors (states *8* or *9*).

$$-S_{dch} = 1 - D_1 - D_2 + \sum_{h=1}^{\infty}\left[2\frac{\sin\left(h\,\pi\left(1-D_2\right)\right)}{h\pi}\cos\left[h\omega\left(t-\zeta_2-2\zeta_1\right)\right]\right] + \sum_{h=1}^{\infty}\left[\frac{\sin\left(2h\,\pi\left(1-D_1\right)\right)}{h\pi}\cos\left[h\omega\left(t-\zeta_1\right)\right]\right], \quad (14)$$

where, h=1, 2, 3 …

$\zeta_1 = \left(1-D_1\right)/f$: harmonic phase angle due to D_1

$\zeta_2 = \left(1-D_2\right)/2f$:harmonic phase angle due to D_2

By averaging the switching functions S_{ch} and S_{dch}, which results analogous to neglecting harmonics, a general expression relating the chopper average output voltage V_{ab} to the VSI average DC bus voltage V_d, can be derived through equation (15):

$$V_{ab} = m\,V_d, \quad (15)$$

being m, the modulation index expressed as:

$m = (D_1 + D_2)$: chopper in buck mode (charge)

$m = -(1 - D_1 - D_2)$: chopper in boost mode (discharge)

4.2 SMES coil

The equivalent circuit of the SMES coil makes use of a lumped parameter network implemented by a six-segment model based on Steurer & Hribernik (2005) and Chen et al. (2006), as described in Fig. 11. This representation allows characterizing the voltage distribution and frequency response of the SC coil with reasonable accuracy over a frequency range from DC to several thousand Hertz. The model comprises self inductances (L_i), mutual couplings between segments (i and j, M_{ij}), AC loss resistances (R_{Si}), skin effect-related resistances (R_{Shi}), turn-ground (shunt-C_{Shi}) and turn-turn capacitances (series-C_{Si}). A metal oxide semiconductor (MOV) protection for transient voltage surge suppression is included between the SMES model and the DC/DC converter.

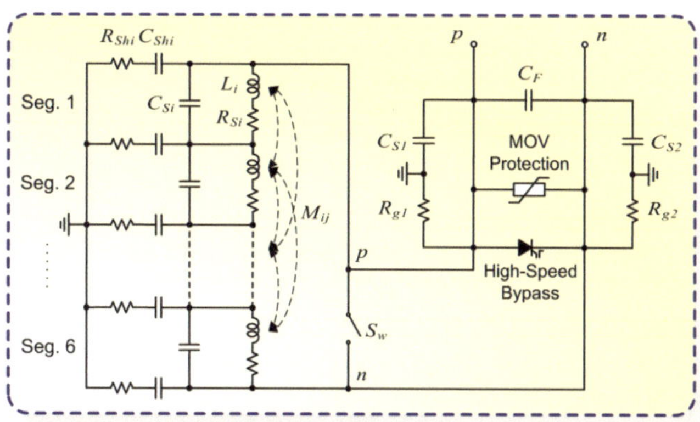

Fig. 11. Multi-segment model of the SMES coil

Fig. 12 shows the frequency domain analysis of the six-segment SMES model, measuring the impedance of the SC across its terminals (Z_{pn}) for the case of the coil including (solid-lines) and not including (dashed-lines) surge capacitors (C_{s1} and C_{s2}) in parallel with grounding-balance resistors (R_{g1} and R_{g2}) as well as a filter capacitor C_F for reducing the effect of resonance phenomena. As can be seen from the magnitude of the terminal impedance, the coil has parallel resonance (higher magnitudes of Z_{pn}) frequencies at around 70 Hz, 120 Hz, 200 Hz and series resonance (lower magnitudes of Z_{pn}) frequencies at about 110 Hz and 190 Hz. The chopper output voltage V_{pn} contains both even and odd harmonics of the switching frequency, which may excite coil resonances and cause significant voltage amplification of transients with the consequent addition of insulation stress within the SMES coil. Since the coil has a rather high inductance, these resonance frequencies become lower, turning this phenomena an issue for selecting the chopper operating frequency. In addition, high power DC/DC converters (several MWs) utilize low operating frequencies in order to minimize losses, being significant in consequence to take into consideration the coil resonance phenomena for choosing a safety frequency band of operation for the chopper. Fortunately, the negative effects of the harmonics decrease faster than the inverse of the harmonic order due to the skin effect occurring in the superconductor. In this way, for the case presented here, the chopper operating frequency can be set as low as 500 Hz without producing severe voltage amplification inside the SMES coil.

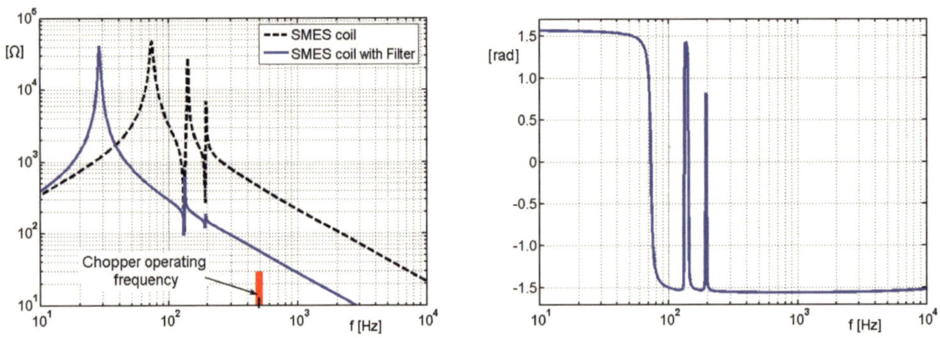

(a) (b)

Fig. 12. SMES coil terminal impedance Z_{pn} versus frequency: (a) Magnitude of SMES coil impedance (b) Phase angle of SMES coil impedance

The current and voltage of the superconducting inductor are related as:

$$i_{SC} = \frac{1}{L_{SC}} \int_{t_0}^{t} V_{SC}\, d\tau + I_{SC0} \tag{16}$$

where,

L_{SC}: equivalent full inductance of the SMES coil, accounting for all series self inductances L_i

I_{SC0}: initial current of the inductor

The amount of energy drawn from the SC coil is directly proportional to the equivalent inductance and to the change in the coil current (i_{SCi}–initial and i_{SCf}–final currents) as:

$$E_{SMES} = \frac{1}{2} L_{SC} \left(i_{SCi}{}^2 - i_{SCf}{}^2 \right) \tag{17}$$

4.3 Proposed control scheme of the SMES system

The proposed hierarchical three-level control scheme of the SMES unit consists of an external, middle and internal level. Its design is based on concepts of instantaneous power on the synchronous-rotating *d-q* reference frame, as depicted in Fig. 13. This structure has the goal of rapidly and simultaneously controlling the active and reactive powers provided by the SMES (Molina & Mercado, 2009). To this aim, the controller must ensure the instantaneous energy balance among all the SMES components. In this way, the stored energy is regulated through the PCS in a controlled manner for achieving the charging and discharging of the SC coil.

4.3.1 External level control design

The external level control, which is outlined in Fig. 13 (left side) in a simplified form, is responsible for determining the active and reactive power exchange between the DSTATCOM-SMES device and the utility system. This control strategy is designed for performing two major control objectives: the voltage control mode (VCM) with only reactive power compensation capabilities and the active power control mode (APCM) for dynamic active power exchange between the SMES and the electric grid. To this aim, the instantaneous voltage at the PCC is computed by employing a synchronous-rotating reference frame. In consequence, by applying Park's transformation, the instantaneous values of the three-phase AC bus voltages are transformed into *d-q* components, v_d and v_q respectively, and then filtered to extract the fundamental components, v_{d1} and v_{q1}. As formerly described, the *d-axis* was defined always coincident with the instantaneous voltage vector v, then v_{d1} results in steady-state equal to $|v|$ while v_{q1} is null. Consequently, the *d*-axis current component of the VSI contributes to the instantaneous active power p while the q-axis current component represents the instantaneous reactive power q, as stated in equations (18) and (19). Thus, to achieve a decoupled active and reactive power control, it is required to provide a decoupled control strategy for i_{d1} and i_{q1}.

$$p = \frac{3}{2}(v_{d1}i_{d1} + v_{q1}i_{q1}) = \frac{3}{2}|v|\,i_{d1}\,, \tag{18}$$

$$q = \frac{3}{2}(v_{d1}i_{q1} - v_{q1}i_{d1}) = \frac{3}{2}|v|\,i_{q1}\,, \tag{19}$$

In this way, only v_d is used for computing the resultant current reference signals required for the desired SMES output active and reactive powers. Independent limiters are use for restrict both the power and current signals before setting the references i_{dr1} and i_{qr1}. Additionally, the instantaneous actual output currents of the SMES, i_{d1} and i_{q1}, are computed for use in the middle level control. In all cases, the signals are filtered by using second-order low-pass filters to obtain the fundamental components employed by the control system. A phase locked loop (PLL) is used for synchronizing, through the phase θ_s, the coordinate transformations from *abc* to *dq* components in the voltage and current measurement system. The phase signal is derived from the positive sequence components of the AC voltage vector measured at the PCC of the DSTATCOM-SMES.

The standard control loop of the external level is the VCM and consists in controlling (supporting and regulating) the voltage at the PCC through the modulation of the reactive component of the DSTATCOM output current, i_{q1}. This control mode has proved a very

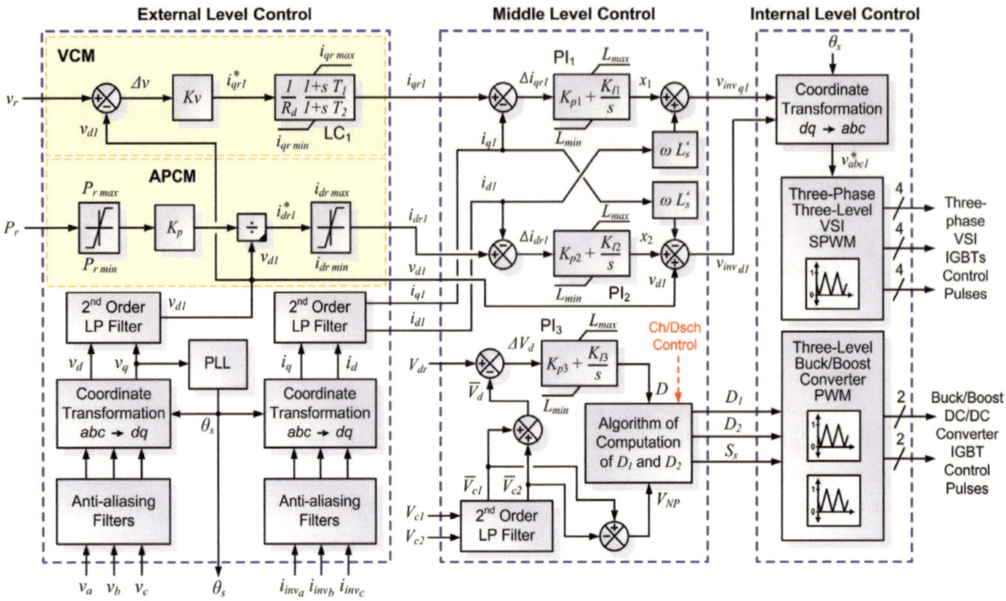

Fig. 13. Multi-level control scheme of the SMES system

good performance in conventional DSTATCOM controllers (with no energy storage). The design of this control loop in the rotating frame is simpler than using stationary frame techniques, and employs a standard proportional-integral (PI) compensator including an anti-windup system to enhance the dynamic performance of the VCM system. This control mode compares the reference voltage set by the operator with the actual measured value in order to eliminate the steady-state voltage offset via the PI compensator. A voltage regulation droop (typically 5%) R_d is included in order to allow the terminal voltage of the DSTATCOM-SMES to vary in proportion with the compensating reactive current. Thus, the PI controller with droop characteristics becomes a simple phase-lag compensator (LC_1), resulting in a stable fast response compensator. This feature is particularly significant in cases that more high-speed voltage compensators are operating in the area. This characteristic is comparable to the one included in generators´ voltage regulators.

The APCM allows controlling the active power exchanged with the electric system. The control strategy to be applied can be designed for performing various control objectives with dissimilar priorities, as widely presented in the literature (Molina & Mercado, 2006, 2007, 2009). In this chapter, a general active power command to achieve the desired system response is provided. To this aim, the in-phase output current component reference signal of the DSTATCOM, i_{dr1} is straightforwardly derived from the reference active power. In this way, the active power flow between the DSTATCOM-SMES and the power system can be controlled so as to force the SC to absorb active power when P_r is negative, i.e. operating in the charge mode, or to inject active power when P_r is positive, that is operating in the discharge mode.

4.3.2 Middle level control design

The middle level control makes the expected output, i.e. positive sequence components of i_d and i_q, to dynamically track the reference values set by the external level. The middle level control design, which is depicted in Fig. 13 (middle side), is based on a linearization of the state-space averaged model of the SMES VSI in d-q coordinates, described in equation (12). Inspection of this equation shows a cross-coupling of both components of the SMES output current through ω. Therefore, in order to fully decouple the control of i_d and i_q, appropriate control signals have to be generated. To this aim, it is proposed the use of two control signals x_1 and x_2, which are derived from assumption of zero derivatives of currents ($s\,i_d$ and $s\,i_q$) in the upper part (AC side) of equation (12). This condition is assured by employing conventional PI controllers with proper feedback of the SMES actual output current components, as shown in Fig. 13. Thus, i_d and i_q respond in steady-state to x_1 and x_2 respectively with no crosscoupling, as derived from equation (20). As can be noticed, with the introduction of these new variables this control approach allows to obtain a quite effective decoupled control with the VSI model (AC side) reduced to first-order functions.

$$s\begin{bmatrix} i_d \\ i_q \end{bmatrix} = \begin{bmatrix} \frac{-R_s}{L'_s} & 0 \\ 0 & \frac{-R_s}{L'_s} \end{bmatrix} \begin{bmatrix} i_d \\ i_q \end{bmatrix} - \begin{bmatrix} x_1 \\ x_2 \end{bmatrix} \tag{20}$$

From equation (12), it can be seen the additional coupling resulting from the DC capacitors voltage V_d, as much in the DC side (lower part) as in the AC side (upper part). This difficulty demands to maintain the DC bus voltage as constant as possible, in order to decrease the influence of the dynamics of V_d. The solution to this problem is obtained by using another PI compensator which allows eliminating the steady-state voltage variations at the DC bus, by forcing the instantaneous balance of power between the DC and the AC sides of the DSTATCOM through the modulation of the duty cycle (D) of the DC/DC chopper. Finally, duty cycles D_1 and D_2 are computed through the novel controller in order to prevent dc bus capacitors voltage drift/imbalance, as formerly explained. This novel extra DC voltage control block provides the availability of managing the redundant switching states of the chopper according to the capacitors charge unbalance measured through the neutral point voltage, $V_{PN} = \overline{V_{c1}} - \overline{V_{c2}}$. This specific loop modifying the modulating waveforms of the internal level control is also proposed for reducing instability problems caused by harmonics as much in the SMES device as in the electric system. The application of a static determination of D_1 and D_2, such as the case of D_1=D_2=$D/2$, has proved to be good enough for reaching an efficient equalization of the DC bus capacitors over the full range of VSI output voltages and active/reactive power requirements.

4.3.3 Internal level control design

The internal level provides dynamic control of input signals for the DC/DC and DC/AC converters. This level is responsible for generating the switching control signals for the twelve valves of the three-level VSI, according to the control mode (SPWM) and types of valves (IGBTs) used and for the four IGBTs of the buck/boost three-level DC/DC converter. Fig. 13 (right side) shows a basic scheme of the internal level control of the SMES unit. This level is mainly composed of a line synchronization module and a firing pulses generator for both the VSI and the chopper. The coordinate transformation from Cartesian to Polar yields the required magnitude of the output voltage vector V_{inv} produced by the VSI, and its absolute phase-shift rating α. The line synchronization module simply synchronizes the

SMES device switching pulses with the positive sequence components of the AC voltage vector at the PCC through the PLL phase signal, θ_s.
In the case of the sinusoidal PWM pulses generator block, the controller of the VSI generates pulses for the carrier-based three-phase PWM inverter using three-level topology. Thus, the expected sinusoidal-based output voltage waveform V_{abc^*} of the DSTACOM-SMES, which is set by the middle level control, is compared to triangular signals generated by the carriers generator for producing three-state PWM vectors (1, 0, -1). These states are decoded by the states-to-pulses decoder via a look-up-table that relates each state with the corresponding firing pulse for each IGBT of the four ones in each leg of the three-phase three-level VSI.
In the case of the DC/DC converter firing pulses generator block, the three-level PWM modulator is built using a compound signal obtained as the difference of two standard two-level PWM signals. According to the mode of operation of the chopper (charge/discharge), switching functions S_{ch} and S_{dch} are synthesized using equations (13) and (14).

5. Dynamic modelling and control design of the SCES system

Super capacitor energy storage (SCES) systems consist of several sub-systems, but share most of them with SMES systems since both operate at DC voltage levels. The base of the SCES system is the super capacitors bank. On the other hand, the power conditioning system provides an electronic interface between the AC electric system and the super capacitors, allowing the grid-connected operation of the DES. Fig. 14 shows the proposed detailed model of the entire SCES system for applications in the distribution level. This model consists of the super capacitors bank and the PCS for coupling to the electric grid (Molina & Mercado, 2008).

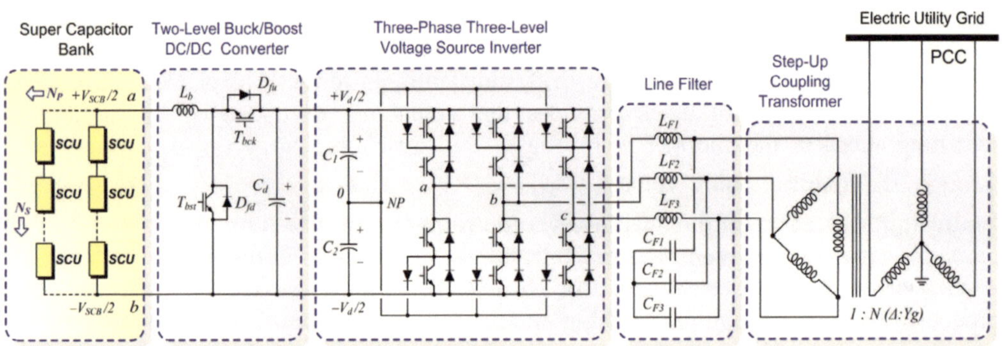

Fig. 14. Detailed model of the proposed SCES

5.1 Power conditioning system of the SCES

5.1.1 Three-phase three-level DSTATCOM

As in the prior case of the SMES system, the key part of the PCS is the DSTATCOM device, and utilizes the same topology that SMESs. The proposed DSTATCOM essentially consists of a three-phase three-level VSI built with semiconductors devices having turn-off capabilities, such as IGBTs, as shown in Fig. 14 (right side). This device is shunt-connected to the distribution network by means of a coupling transformer and the corresponding line sinusoidal filter. Equations governing the steady-state dynamics of the ideal DSTATCOM in the dq reference frame were previously derived and summarized in equation (12).

5.1.2 Two-quadrant two-level DC/DC converter

The integration of the SCES system into the DC bus of the DSTATCOM device requires a rapid and robust bidirectional interface to adapt the wide range of variation in voltage and current levels between both devices, especially because of the super capacitors dynamic behaviour, during both charge and discharge modes. Controlling the SCES system rate of charge/discharge requires varying the voltage magnitude according to the SCU state-of-operation, while keeping essentially constant the DC bus voltage of the DSTATCOM VSI (in contrast to SMES systems, in SCESs polarity does not change). To this aim, a combined two-quadrant two-level buck/boost DC/DC converter topology by using high-power fast-switched IGBTs is proposed in order to obtain a suitable control performance of the overall system. This step-down and step-up converter allows decreasing the ratings of the overall power devices by regulating the current flowing from the SCES to the inverter of the DSTATCOM and vice versa. Since there are no requirement for electrical isolation between input and output, no isolation circuit is considered in this work.

The basic structure of the DC/DC boost converter proposed is shown in Fig. 14. This switching-mode power device contains basically two couples of semiconductor switches (two power IGBT transistors connected in anti-parallel to respective free-wheeling diodes, T_{bck}–D_{fu} and T_{bst}–D_{fd}) and two energy storage devices (an inductor L_b and a capacitor C_d) for producing a single polarity DC voltage output with greater or lower level than its input DC voltage, according to the operation mode of the SCES. This bidirectional DC/DC converter has basically the three standard modes of operation, namely the charge mode, the discharge mode and the stand-by mode. In the charge mode, the chopper works as a step-down (buck) converter employing T_{bck}, D_{fd} and L_b. This topology makes use of modulation of transistor T_{bck} (upper IGBT in the leg), while keeping T_{bst} off at all times, in order to produce a power flow from the DC bus of the DSTATCOM to the UCES system. Once completed the charging of the UCES, the operating mode of the DC/DC converter is changed to the stand-by mode, for which both IGBTs are maintained continually switched off. In the discharge mode, the chopper operates as a step-up (boost) converter using T_{bst}, D_{fu}, L_b and C_d. This topology employs the modulation of the lower IGBT of the leg, i.e. T_{bst}, while preserves T_{bck} off all the time in order to produce a power flow from the UCES to the DSTATCOM DC bus.

The operation of the DC/DC converter in the continuous (current) conduction mode (CCM), i.e. the current flows continuously in the inductor L_b during the entire switching cycle, facilitates the development of the state-space model because only two switch states are possible during a switching cycle for each operation mode, namely, (i) the power switch T_{bck} is on and the diode D_{fd} is off; or (ii) T_{bck} is off and D_{fd} is on, for the charge mode, and (i) the power switch T_{bst} is on and the diode D_{fu} is off; or (ii) T_{bst} is off and D_{fu} is on, for the discharge mode. In steady-state CCM operation, the state-space equation that describes the dynamics of the DC/DC converter is given by equation (21).

$$s\begin{bmatrix} I_{SCB} \\ V_d \end{bmatrix} = \begin{bmatrix} 0 & -\dfrac{S_{dc}}{L_b} \\ -\dfrac{S_{dc}}{C_d} & 0 \end{bmatrix}\begin{bmatrix} I_{SCB} \\ V_d \end{bmatrix} + \begin{bmatrix} \dfrac{1}{L} & 0 \\ 0 & -\dfrac{1}{C} \end{bmatrix}\begin{bmatrix} V_{SCB} \\ I_d \end{bmatrix}, \tag{21}$$

where:

I_{SCB}: Chopper input current, matching the SCES output current.

V_{SCB}: Chopper input voltage, the same as the SCES output voltage.
V_d: Chopper output voltage, coinciding with the VSI DC bus voltage.
i_d: Chopper output current.
S_{dc}: Switching function of the buck/boost DC/DC converter.
The switching function S_{dc} is a two-levelled waveform characterizing the signal that drives the power switch of the DC/DC buck/boost converter, according to the operation mode.
If the switching frequency of the power switches is significantly higher than the natural frequencies of the DC/DC converter, this discontinuous model can be approximated by a continuous state-space averaged (SSA) model, where a new variable m_c is introduced. In the [0, 1] interval, m_c is a continuous function and represents the modulation index of the DC/DC converter. This variable is used for replacing the switching function in equation (21), yielding the following SSA expression:

$$s\begin{bmatrix} I_{UCB} \\ V_d \end{bmatrix} = \begin{bmatrix} 0 & -\dfrac{m_c}{L_b} \\ -\dfrac{m_c}{C_d} & 0 \end{bmatrix}\begin{bmatrix} I_{UCB} \\ V_d \end{bmatrix} + \begin{bmatrix} \dfrac{1}{L} & 0 \\ 0 & -\dfrac{1}{C} \end{bmatrix}\begin{bmatrix} V_{UCB} \\ I_d \end{bmatrix}, \tag{22}$$

Since, in steady-state conditions the inductor current variation during both, on and off times of T_b are essentially equal, so there is not net change of the inductor current from cycle to cycle, and assuming a constant DC output voltage of the bidirectional converter, the steady-state input-to-output voltage conversion relationship of the buck/boost converter is easily derived from equation (22), by setting the inductor current derivative at zero, yielding equation (23).

$$V_{SCB} = m_c V_d \tag{23}$$

In the same way, the relationship between the average input current I_{SCB} and the DC/DC converter output current I_d in the CCM can be derived as follows:

$$I_d = m_c I_{SCB} \tag{24}$$

As can be observed, both the steady-state input-to-output current and voltage conversion relationships coincide with the modulation index m_c, which is defined as:
$m_c = D$: for the bidirectional chopper in buck mode (charge),
$m_c = (1- D)$: for the bidirectional chopper in boost mode (discharge),
where $D \in [0, 1]$ is the duty cycle for switching T_{bck} or T_{bst} according to the operation mode, defined as the ratio of time during which the particular power switch is turned-on to the period of one complete switching cycle, T_s.

5.2 Super capacitors bank

The super capacitor unit (SCU) performance is based mainly on an electrostatic effect, which is purely physical reversible, rather than employing faradic reactions as is the case for batteries, although includes an additional pseudocapacitive layer contributing to the overall capacitance. Because of the complex physical phenomena in the double layer interface, traditional simple models such as the classical lumped-parameter electrical model (Spyker & Nelms, 2000) represented by a simple RC circuit composed only of a capacitance with an equivalent series resistance (ESR), and an equivalent parallel resistance (EPR) are inadequate for modelling EDLCs. These models yield a large inaccuracy when compared with experimental results. Therefore, this work proposes the use of an enhanced electric model of a super capacitor, based on the ones previously proposed by Rafika et al. (2007) and Zubieta & Bonert (2000), which reflects with high precision the effects of frequency, voltage and temperature in the dynamic behaviour. This solution is easy to implement in any software environment (such as MATLAB, PSCAD, EMTP, etc) and allows an adequate simulation time when the SCES is used in applications containing many states and non-linear blocks such as the case of incorporating power electronic devices into electric power systems. The model proposed describes the terminal behaviour of the EDLC unit over the frequency range from DC to several thousand Hertz with sufficient accuracy.

The equivalent electric circuit model of the super capacitor unit is depicted in Fig. 15. In order to define the structure of this equivalent circuit, three major aspects of the physics of the double-layer capacitor should be taken into account. Firstly, based on the electrochemistry of the interface between two materials in different phases, the double layer capacitance is modelled by two ladder circuits consisting in resistive-capacitive branches with different time constants (R_E, R_I–C_A, R_V–C_V). Secondly, based on the theory of the interfacial tension in the double layer, the capacitance of the device turns out to be in a dependence on the potential difference, so that in order to reflect the voltage dependence of the capacitance, C_V is assumed to vary linearly with the voltage at its terminals (V_{SCB}) by the relation $C_V = 2K_V\ V_{UC}$, while C_A represents the constant capacitance and is empirically determined in the order of 2/3 of the nominal capacitance value provided by the manufacturer. Thirdly, the double-layer capacitor has a certain self-discharge as a consequence of the diffusion of the excess ionic charges at the interface between the electrode and the electrolyte, and due to the impurities in the SCU materials. This low current-leakage pathway between the SCU terminals determines the duration time of stored energy in open circuit, and is dependent of voltage and temperature. Hence, the super capacitor self-discharge cannot be represented by a simple single resistance. It is necessary to use two different time constant circuits, formed by R_{P1}–C_{P1} and R_{P2}–C_{P2}, which depend on the voltage V_{SCU} and on the SCU operating temperature T_{SC}. A parallel R_L resistance giving the long time leakage current contribution is also included. Circuit made up of R_I-C_I is introduced into the model to take into account the electrolyte ionic resistance temperature dependence in the low frequency range, with $R_I(T)$, while cancelling its effect in the high

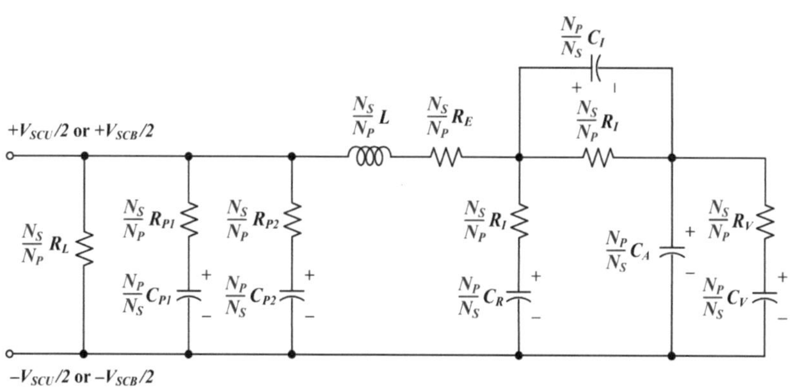

Fig. 15. Advanced equivalent electric circuit model of the super capacitor unit/bank

frequency range, through C_I. Circuit formed by R_I–C_R gives more precision to the model by increasing the value of the differential capacitance for the average frequencies. Eventually, a small equivalent series inductance (nano Henrys) is added to the model for pulsed applications.

Since the frequency characteristics of the complex impedance of electrochemical cells are useful for characterizing a UCES unit, electrochemical impedance spectroscopy (EIS) has been also performed on a BCAP0010 super capacitor (Maxwell Technologies, 2008) for extending the analysis from the time domain to the frequency domain. Thus, the EDLC is swept in frequency for various voltage levels and with different temperatures. Fig. 16 plots the real and imaginary components of super capacitor impedance as a function of frequency for a bias voltage of 2.5 V and a temperature of 20 °C. As can be observed from the real part, the dependence of impedance on frequency can be divided into four distinct frequency zones. Zone I, in the range 1 mHz–10 mHz with characteristic time constant from 100 to 1000 s, is determined by series (R_I, R_E) and parallel resistances. However, at very low frequencies, leakage current represented by parallel resistance R_L dominates the contribution. Zone II, between 10 mHz and 10 Hz gives the information on the series resistances R_I and R_E. In this zone, the effect of parallel resistance is negligible and both, R_I and R_E contribute at 10 mHz to form the so-called DC series resistance ESR–DC given by manufacturers. Zone III, in the range 10 Hz–1 kHz shows mainly the resistance R_E due to all the connections, particularly the contact resistance between the activated carbon and the current collector as well as the minimal resistance of the electrolyte. In this range, manufacturers specify this series resistance as an AC series resistance, also called ESR–1 kHz. Zone IV, between 1 and 10 kHz is due to the super capacitor inductance and the parasitic inductance of the all connecting cables. As can be derived from the imaginary part of frequency characteristics of the SCES complex impedance, there exists a resonance frequency around 25 Hz below which the SCU behaviour is entirely capacitive. During more than ±1/2 decade of this resonance frequency, the imaginary component of the impedance magnitude is relatively flat and approximately zero, this demonstrating a purely resistive EDLC behaviour in this mid-frequency range. Above this frequency, the magnitude begins increasing indicating a completely inductive effect.

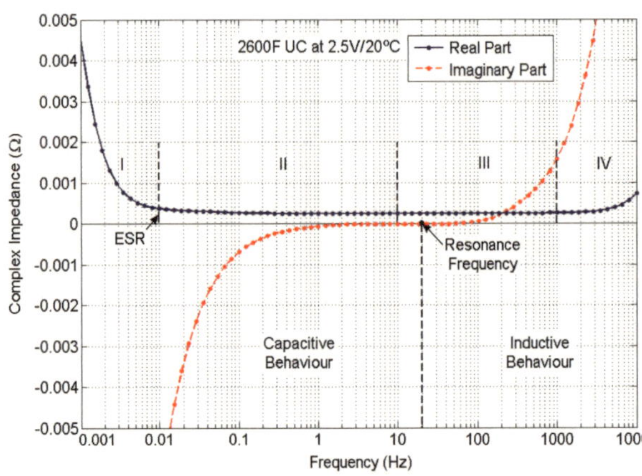

Fig. 16. Impedance real and imaginary part of 2600F super capacitor (BCAP0010) as a function of frequency with a bias voltage of 2.5V and a temperature of 20°C

The amount of energy drawn from the super capacitor unit is directly proportional to the differential capacitance and to the change in the terminal voltage (V_{SCUi}–initial and V_{SCUf}–final voltages), as given by equation (28).

$$E_{SCU} = \frac{1}{2} C_{SCU} \left(V_{SCUi}^{\ 2} - V_{SCUf}^{\ 2} \right) \tag{25}$$

For practical applications in power systems, the required amount of terminal voltage and energy of UCES exceed largely the quantities provided by an SCU. In this way, an SCES system can be built by using multiple SCUs connected in series to form a SCES string and in parallel to build a bank of SCUs (SCB), as depicted in Fig 14. For this topology, the terminal voltage determines the number of capacitors N_s which must be connected in series to form a string, and the total capacitance determines the number of super capacitors strings N_p which must be connected in parallel in the bank. The equivalent electric circuit model of the super capacitor unit can be extended to the SCB by directly computing the total resistances, capacitances and inductances according to the series and parallel contribution of each parameter, as depicted in Fig. 15 (blue text). This proposed advanced dynamic model of SCB shows a very good agreement with measured data at all the operating frequency range.

5.3 Proposed control scheme of the SCES system

The proposed hierarchical three-level control scheme of the SCES system consists of an external, middle and internal level, of which each level has its own control objectives. Its design, as in the case of the SMES device, is also based on the synchronous-rotating *d-q* reference frame, as depicted in Fig. 17 (Molina & Mercado, 2008).

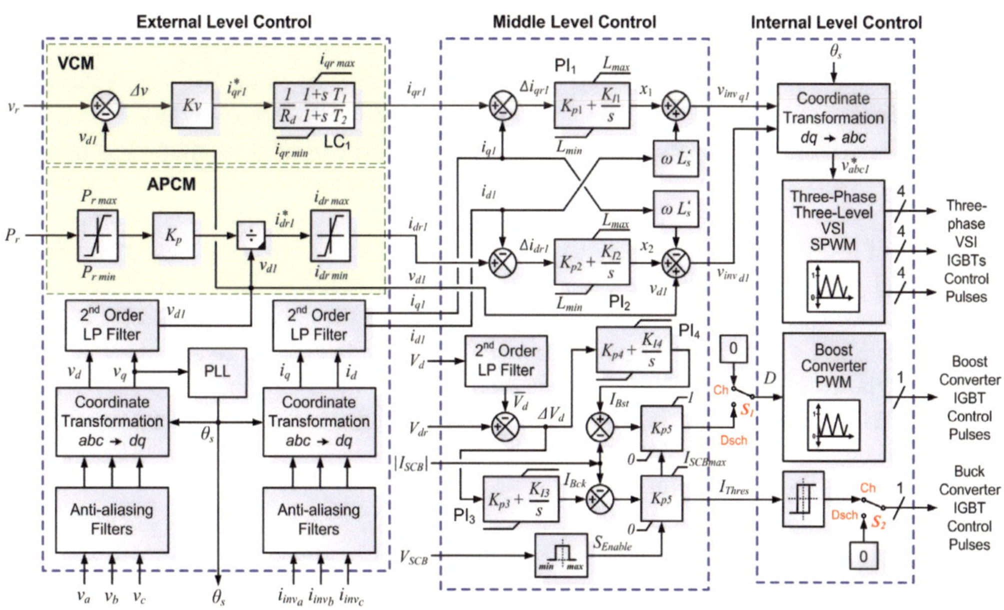

Fig. 17. Multi-level control scheme of the SCES system

5.3.1 External level control design

As in the former case of the SMES system, the external level control, which is outlined in Fig. 17 (left side), is responsible for determining the active and reactive power exchange between the DSTATCOM-SCES device and the electric grid. This control strategy is designed for performing the same major control objectives as SMES, i.e. VCM with only reactive power compensation capabilities produced locally by the DSTATCOM and independently of the storage device and the active power control mode (APCM) for dynamic active power exchange between the SCES and the electric grid.

5.3.2 Middle level control design

The middle level control shares part of the algorithms corresponding to the SMES one, since both devices utilize the same DSTATCOM topology and then the control of this last device is identical. The difference with the SMES system is in the control of the DC/DC converter, which is now specific for the SCB.

In the charge operation mode of the SCES, switches S_1 and S_2 are set at position Ch (charge), so that the DC/DC converter acts as a buck or step-down chopper. In this way, only the upper IGBT is switched while the lower one is kept off all the time. Since the super capacitor current is highly responsive to the voltage applied, being this relation especially increased by the SCES properties, i.e. the exceptionally low ESR and large capacitance, a hysteresis current control (HCC) method is proposed here for this operation mode. The HCC technique with fixed-band gives good performance, ensuring fast response and simplicity of implementation but with the main drawback of varying the IGBT switching frequency and then generating a variable-frequency harmonic content. To overcome this problem, an adaptive hysteresis (nearly constant-frequency) current control technique (AHCC) for the DC/DC converter operating in continuous conduction mode of I_{SCB} is proposed (Ninkovic, 2002). The basic concept in this hysteresis control is to switch the buck DC/DC converter IGBT to the opposite state (on-off) whenever the measured super capacitor current reaches above or below a given boundary determined by the hysteresis band. The AHCC is based on cycle-by-cycle hysteresis calculator, which generates the hysteresis window that will keep the switching frequency in a very narrow band centred on a programmed average value. The accuracy remains outstanding, and the ripple content allows the use of a smaller filter than typical HCC. This technique gives good performance, ensuring fast response and simplicity of implementation. In this way, the charging of the UCES is rapidly accomplished at a current I_{Thres} computed by the external level control, provided that the voltage V_{SCB} is below the limit V_{SCBmax}. During this process, the VSI DC bus voltage is controlled at a nearly constant level via a PI control of the error signal between the reference and the measured voltage at the DC bus, in such a way that a balance of powers are obtained between the DSTATCOM inverter and the SCB. When the super capacitor maximum voltage is reached, the DC/DC buck converter IGBT is switched-off and the charge operation mode of the UCES is changed to the stand-by mode.

In the discharge operation mode of the SCES, switches S_1 and S_2 are set at position Dsch (discharge), so that the DC/DC converter acts as a boost or step-up chopper. In this way, only the lower IGBT T_{bst} is switched while the upper one is kept off at all times. Since the ultracapacitor discharge current is to be controlled by the DC/DC converter input impedance, a pulse-width modulation (PWM) control technique with double-loop control strategy is proposed to be employed. This control mode has low harmonic content at a constant-frequency and reduced switching losses. In this way, the discharging of the SCES is rapidly accomplished at a level determined by the external level control, provided that the voltage V_{SCB} is above the limit V_{SCBmin}. During this process, the VSI DC bus voltage is regulated at a constant level via a PI control of the error signal between the reference and the measured voltage at the DC bus. Thus, by adjusting the duty cycle D of the boost chopper, the energy released from the ultracapacitor unit towards the VSI is regulated. An inner current loop is introduced into the voltage loop to achieve an enhanced dynamic response of the ultracapacitor current I_{SCB}, so that rapid response can be derived from the DC/DC boost converter.

5.3.3 Internal level control design

The internal level (right side of Fig. 17) is responsible for generating the switching signals for the twelve valves of the DSTATCOM three-level VSI, in the same way as the SMES internal control, and for both IGBTs of the buck/boost DC/DC converter. This level is mainly composed of a line synchronization module, the three-phase three-level SPWM firing pulses generator, an adaptive hysteresis current control generator for the IGBT of the buck chopper and a PWM generator for the IGBT of the boost DC/DC converter.

6. Dynamic modelling and control design of the FES system

Flywheel energy storage (FES) systems are mainly composed of several sub-systems, such as the rotor, the bearing system, the driving motor/generator and housing, and the PCS for coupling to the electric grid. Unlike SMESs and SCESs that operate at DC voltage levels, FES systems use an electric machine, such as a permanent magnet synchronous machine (PMSM) in the proposed topology, in order to generate a set of three sinusoidal voltage waveforms phase-shifted 120° between each other, with variable amplitude and frequency. On the other hand, the power conditioning system provides an electronic interface between the two AC electric systems, i.e. the electric utility grid and the flywheel machine, allowing the grid-connected operation of the DES. The proposed detailed model and the global control scheme of an economical and reliable FES system for applications in the distribution level is depicted in Fig. 18.

6.1 Power conditioning system of the FES

The power conditioning system (PCS) used for connecting RESs to the distribution grid requires the flexible, efficient and reliable generation of high quality electric power. The PCS proposed in this work is composed of a back-to-back AC/DC/AC converter that fulfills all the requirements stated above. Since the variable speed rotor of the flywheel is directly coupled to the synchronous motor/generator, this later produces an output voltage with variable amplitude and frequency. This condition demands the use of an extra conditioner to meet the amplitude and frequency requirements of the utility grid, resulting in a back-to-back converter topology (Suvire & Mercado, 2008). Two voltage source inverters compose the core of the back-to-back converter, i.e. a machine-side inverter and a grid-side one. As can be clearly seen for Fig. 18, the grid-side VSI is part of the well-known DSTATCOM device employed in both SMESs and SCESs systems.

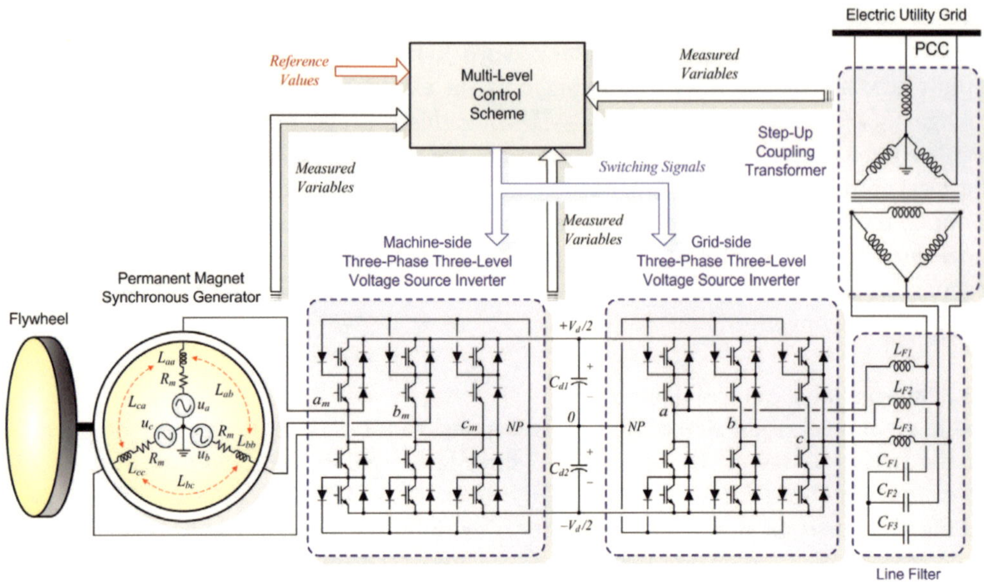

Fig. 18. Full detailed model of the proposed flywheel system

6.1.1 Three-phase three-level DSTATCOM

As in both prior cases of the SMES and SCES system, the key part of the PCS is the DSTATCOM device, and utilizes the same topology previously described. The proposed DSTATCOM essentially consists of a three-phase three-level VSI made with IGBTs, as shown in Fig. 18 (right side). This device is shunt-connected to the distribution network by means of a coupling transformer and the corresponding line sinusoidal filter. Equations governing the steady-state dynamics of the ideal DSTATCOM in the *dq* reference frame were previously derived and summarized in equation (12).

6.1.2 Two-quadrant three-level AC/DC converter

The machine-side three-phase three-level VSI corresponds to an AC/DC switching power inverter using high-power insulated gate bipolar transistors (IGBTs). This device is analogous to the grid-side VSI (DSTATCOM part) and converts the variable amplitude and frequency output voltage of the PMSM into a roughly constant DC voltage level of the DSTATCOM inner bus. The VSI structure proposed is equal to the DSTATCOM VSI, i.e. a three-level twelve pulse NPC structure, instead of a standard two-level six pulse inverter structure. This three-level VSI topology generates a more smoothly sinusoidal output voltage waveform than conventional two-level structures without increasing the switching frequency and effectively doubles the power rating of the VSI for a given semiconductor device while maintaining high dynamic performance. This feature is essential in order to reduce power loses in the electric machine and then for improving the efficiency of the entire FES system, but also mainly to maintain the charge balance of the intermediate DC bus capacitors, thus avoiding contributing to both AC systems (PMSG and electric grid) with additional distortion. Equations governing the steady-state dynamics of the ideal machine-side VSI in the *dq* reference frame are basically derived from the DSTATCOM VSI mathematical model described by equation (12), but modifying the electrical parameters of the grid by the PMSM as will be later explained.

6.2 Flywheels

The flywheel energy storage system is based on the principle that a rotating mass at high speed can be used to store and retrieve energy. Thus, the flywheel itself is just a mass with high inertia, which is coupled to an electric machine to form the DES. The use of a PMSM is proposed for this application since results very attractive due to advantages such as the inclusion of self-excitation, high power factor, and especially high efficiency and fast dynamic response (Zhou & Qi, 2009). This means that modelling the electrical behaviour of the system can be determined by modelling a PMSM with high inertia.

The permanent magnet synchronous machine can be electrically described using a simple equivalent circuit with an armature equation including back electromotive forces (emfs). This model assumes that saturation is neglected, the induced emfs are sinusoidal, the eddy currents and hysteresis losses are negligible, and that there are no field current dynamics (Samineni et al., 2003). In this way, voltage equations for the PMSM are given by:

$$\begin{bmatrix} u_{am} \\ u_{bm} \\ u_{cm} \end{bmatrix} - \begin{bmatrix} u_a \\ u_b \\ u_c \end{bmatrix} = \left(\mathrm{R_m} + s\mathrm{L}\right) \begin{bmatrix} i_{am} \\ i_{bm} \\ i_{cm} \end{bmatrix}, \tag{26}$$

where:

$$\mathrm{R_m} = \begin{bmatrix} R_m & 0 & 0 \\ 0 & R_m & 0 \\ 0 & 0 & R_m \end{bmatrix}, \ \mathrm{L} = \begin{bmatrix} L_{aa} & L_{ab} & L_{ac} \\ L_{ab} & L_{bb} & L_{bc} \\ L_{ac} & L_{bc} & L_{cc} \end{bmatrix}, \tag{27}$$

being:

u_{im} (i=a, b, c): stator phase voltages in *abc* coordinates

u_i: back emfs in *abc* coordinates

i_{im}: stator currents in *abc* coordinates

L_{ij}: stator winding inductances, including self and mutual ones (combinations of i and j=a, b, c). It is considered symmetry for mutual inductances, so that L_{ij}=L_{ji}

The terminal voltages applied from the machine-side VSI to the stator, u_{im} and the back emfs, u_i are balanced three-phase voltages, being the later defined as follows:

$$u_i = \omega_s \Psi_{mi}, \tag{28}$$

with:

Ψ_{mi}: permanent-magnet flux linkage in *abc* coordinates

ω_s: synchronous angular speed of the electric machine, aka rotor electrical speed.

Since there is no functional equation for instantaneous reactive power in the *abc* reference frame, it is useful to apply a transformation to the synchronous-rotating orthogonal *d-q* set aligned with the rotor flux to equations (26) and (27) in order to analyze the electric machine. This is performed by applying Park's transformation defined in equation (3), replacing ω with the rotor electrical speed, ω_s and defining the q-axis to be always coincident with the instantaneous stator mmfs, which rotate at the same speed as that of the rotor (yielding u_q equals $|u|$, while u_d is null). This is beneficial because any AC signals that spins at w_s become DC quantities in the rotor *dq* frame. Then, by neglecting the zero sequence components, equations (29) and (30) are derived.

$$\begin{bmatrix} u_{dm} \\ u_{qm} \end{bmatrix} - \begin{bmatrix} u_d \\ u_q \end{bmatrix} = (\mathrm{R_m} + s\mathrm{L}'_s) \begin{bmatrix} i_{dm} \\ i_{qm} \end{bmatrix} + \begin{bmatrix} -\omega_s & 0 \\ 0 & \omega_s \end{bmatrix} \mathrm{L}'_s \begin{bmatrix} i_{qm} \\ i_{dm} \end{bmatrix}, \quad (29)$$

where:

$$\mathrm{R_m} = \begin{bmatrix} R_m & 0 \\ 0 & R_m \end{bmatrix}, \ \mathrm{L}'_s = \begin{bmatrix} L_d & 0 \\ 0 & L_q \end{bmatrix}, \ u_d = \omega_s \Psi_{qm}, \ u_q = \omega_s \Psi_{dm} \quad (30)$$

Flux Linkages in the *dq* frame can be expressed in terms of the stator currents, inductances, and the flux linkage due to the permanent magnets of the rotor linking the stator, Ψ_m as:

$$\Psi_{dm} = L_d i_{dm} + \Psi_m \quad (31)$$

$$\Psi_{qm} = L_q i_{qm} \quad (32)$$

By rewriting equation (29), the following state equation can be obtained:

$$s\begin{bmatrix} i_{dm} \\ i_{qm} \end{bmatrix} = \begin{bmatrix} \dfrac{-R_m}{L_d} & \omega_s \\ -\omega_s & \dfrac{-R_m}{L_q} \end{bmatrix} \begin{bmatrix} i_{dm} \\ i_{qm} \end{bmatrix} + \begin{bmatrix} \dfrac{u_{dm}}{L_d} \\ \dfrac{u_{qm} - |u|}{L_q} \end{bmatrix}, \quad (33)$$

being $|u| = \omega_s \Psi_m$

In the rotor *dq* frame, the active and reactive powers are calculated as follows:

$$p = \frac{3}{2}(v_{dm} i_{dm} + v_{qm} i_{qm}) \quad (34)$$

$$q = \frac{3}{2}(v_{dm} i_{qm} - v_{qm} i_{dm}) \quad (35)$$

The developed electromagnetic torque of the electric machine takes the following convenient form:

$$T_e = \frac{3}{2} p_p \left[\psi_m i_{qm} + (L_d - L_q)\, i_{dm} i_{qm} \right], \quad (36)$$

where p_p is the number of pole-pairs of the PMSM.

For a non-salient-pole machine, as the employed here, the stator winding direct and quadrature inductances L_d and L_q, are approximately equal. Indeed this application uses a surface mount permanent magnet synchronous machine (SPMSM) which has zero saliency. This means that the direct-axis current i_{dm} does not contribute to the electrical torque T_e, as described by equation (37). The key concept is to keep null the direct current, i_{dm} by an appropriate transformation synchronization in order to obtain maximal torque with minimum current, i_{qm}.

$$T_e = \frac{3}{2} p_p \, \psi_m i_{qm} = K_{Te}\, i_{qm} \quad (37)$$

Using the convenient forms of active and reactive powers in the *d-q* reference frame, it can be derived a simple controller for the proposed machine.
The FES system rotor dynamics can be mechanically modelled using a single-mass model given by equation (38). In other word, as previously discussed, the flywheel is modelled as an additional inertia to the rotor of the PMSM.

$$T_e = T_l + B\omega_m + J_c \frac{d\omega_m}{dt}, \qquad (38)$$

where:
T_l: load torque
B: viscous friction coefficient
J_c: combined inertia moment of the FES system (PMSM inertia, J_m plus flywheel rotor inertia, J_f)
ω_m: rotor mechanical speed (whereas ω_s is the rotor electrical speed)
Solving equation (38) for the rotor mechanical speed, it is obtained:

$$\omega_m = \int \left(\frac{T_e - T_l - B\omega_m}{J_c} \right) dt, \qquad (39)$$

and

$$\omega_m = \frac{\omega_r}{p_p} \qquad (40)$$

As can be noted, the flywheel rotor mechanical speed depends on the torque, the friction coefficient and on the inertia of the coupling flywheel-electric machine.
The machine torque can be then easily defined by the *emf* power, P_e:

$$T_e = \frac{P_e}{\omega_m} \qquad (41)$$

The amount of energy drawn from the flywheel unit is directly proportional to the combined inertia of the flywheel-machine and to the change in rotation speed (ω_{mi}–initial and ω_{mf}–final speeds), as given by equation (42).

$$E_{FES} = \frac{1}{2} J_c \left(\omega_{mi}^{\ 2} - \omega_{mf}^{\ 2} \right) \qquad (42)$$

6.3 Proposed Control Scheme of the FES System

As in both prior cases of the SMES and SCES system, the proposed three-level control scheme of the FES system consists of an external, middle and internal level. Since each control level has its own control objectives, independently of the other levels, some structures are identical to previous DES systems controllers. Its design is also performed in the synchronous-rotating *d-q* reference frame, as depicted in Fig. 19. This arrangement has the goal of rapidly and simultaneously controlling the reactive power generated by the DSTATCOM and the active power provided by the FES system during the charging/discharging process.

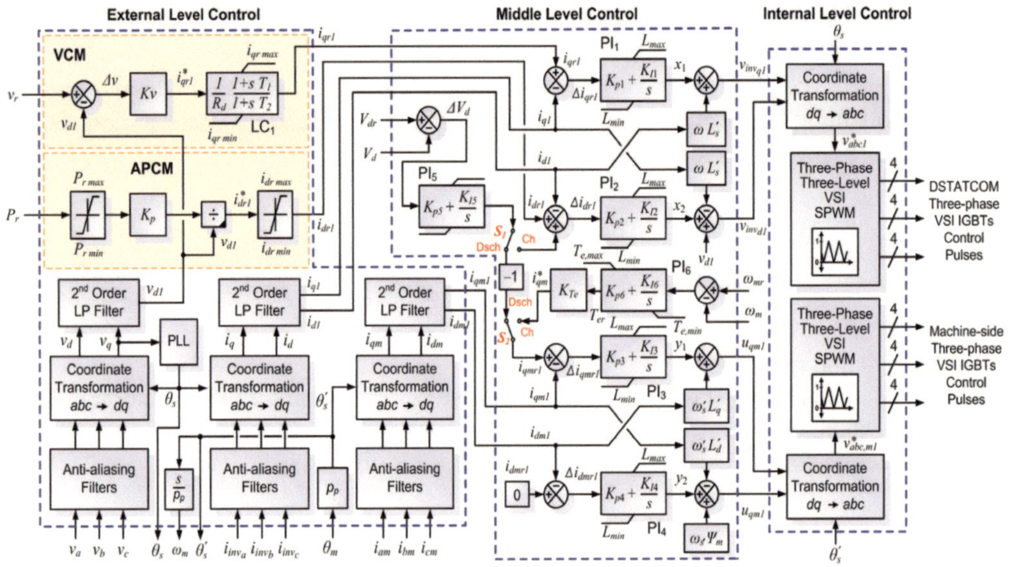

Fig. 19. Multi-level control scheme of the FES system

6.3.1 External level control design

As in the earlier both DES cases described, the external level control, which is outlined in Fig. 19 (left side), is responsible for determining the active and reactive power exchange between the DSTATCOM-FES device and the electric grid. This control strategy is designed for performing the same major control objectives, i.e. VCM with only reactive power compensation capabilities produced locally by the DSTATCOM and APCM for dynamic active power exchange between the FES and the microgrid. The only blocks added in the case of the FES control is the measurement system related to the PMSG. This block includes the stator instantaneous currents sensing and the *dq* transformation and filtering block in order to extract the fundamental components, i_{dm1} and $i_{dq1.}$ This method computes the rotor flux angle indirectly based on the measured rotor position, θ_m of the electric machine. As formerly described, the *q-axis* was defined always coincident with the instantaneous stator mmfs, such that only the quadrature-axis current i_{qm} contribute to the electrical torque T_e, this notably optimizing the machine torque and simplifying the middle level control design.

6.3.2 Middle level control design

The middle level control makes the expected output, i.e. positive sequence components of i_{dm} and i_{qm}, to dynamically track the reference values set by the external level. This level control design, which is depicted in Fig. 19 (middle side), is based on a linearization of the state-space averaged model of the FES system PCS. The dynamic performance of the proposed PCS, consisting of a back-to-back converter topology with two VSIs (a machine-side AC/DC converter and a grid-side DC/AC one), is described using equations (12) and (33), respectively. As can be noted, since all the presented DES devices utilize the same DSTATCOM topology as part of their respective PCSs, some algorithms corresponding to the middle level control are shared. The major difference is in the control of the AC/DC converter, which is now particular for the used electric machine drive (Toliyat et al., 2005).

Inspection of equation (33) shows a cross-coupling of both components of the PMSM output current through ω. Therefore, in order to fully decouple the control of i_{dm} and i_{qm}, appropriate control signals have to be generated. To this aim, two conventional PI controllers with proper feedback of the PMSM actual output current components are used, consequently responding in steady-state with no crosscoupling, as in the case of the DSTACOM VSI control.

Control of the FES system is in essence controlling the motor/generator that is coupled to the flywheel. The FES PCS has basically three modes of operation, namely the charge mode, the stand-by or free-wheeling mode and the discharge mode.

A typical setup when energy is stored into the device is allowing electrical power to flow into the electric machine (PMSM working as a motor), creating a torque which accelerates the speed of the rotating mass (flywheel). In the charge operation mode of the FES, switches S_1 and S_2 are set at position Ch (charge), so that the DC bus voltage is regulated by the DSTATCOM inverter (grid-side VSI), while the machine-side inverter is used for controlling the rotor mechanical speed. In this startup stage, since a high torque is required, a current control is essential. Thus, a reference torque command is employed from a speed PI controller acting on the speed error (ω_{mr}–ω_m). When the FES system maximum speed is reached, the PCS achieves the stand-by mode, which maintains stable the rotor speed.

When power is drawn from the FES device, the rotating mass is allowed to decelerate (PMSM working as a generator) and apply a torque to the electric machine, which discharges power at the machine terminals to the electric grid. In the discharge operation mode of the FES, switches S_1 and S_2 are set at position Dsch (discharge), so that the FES system itself regulates the DC bus voltage by decelerating the flywheel, when T_e is obtained from PI voltage controller acting on the voltage error (V_{dr}–V_d). Additionally, a negative gain is needed in the PI voltage controller because when the FES system releases energy, the current flows from the machine-side converter to the grid-side converter (opposite to the charge mode).

6.3.3 Internal level control design

The internal level (right side of Fig. 19) is responsible for generating the switching signals for the twelve IGBTs of the DSTATCOM three-level VSI (grid-side), and for the twelve IGBTs of the machine-side three-level VSI. This level is mainly composed of line and flux synchronization module, and the three-phase three-level SPWM firing pulses generator for both inverters of the back-to-back converter.

7. Digital simulation results

The distribution power system used to validate the proposed full detailed modelling and control approaches of the selected DSTATCOM-DES devices is depicted in Fig. 20 as a single-line diagram. This power system implements a substation feeding an electrical microgrid, which includes the selected advanced DES units. The small microgrid does not include any distributed generation for simplifying the study. The utility system is represented by a classical single machine-infinite bus type (SMIB) system. This basic 7-bus distribution network operates at 25 kV/50 Hz, and implements a 50 MW short circuit power level infinite bus through a Thevenin equivalent. A set of linear loads are grouped at bus 4 in the microgrid, and are modelled by constant impedances. A microgrid central breaker

(MGCB) with automatic reclosing capabilities is employed for the interconnection of the point of common coupling (PCC) of the MG (bus 4) to the substation of the utility distribution system through a 15 km tie-line. The proposed DSTATCOM-DES devices to be studied are placed at bus 4 and includes a 25 kV/1.2 kV step-up transformer with a ±1.5 MVA/2.5 kV DC bus DSTATCOM and an advanced 0.75 MW/4 MJ DES. DES devices included all previously modelled advanced ESSs, i.e. SMES, SCES and FES.

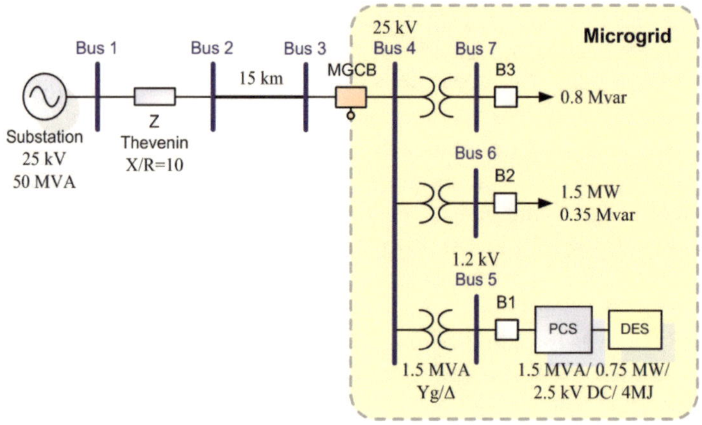

Fig. 20. Single-line diagram of the test power system with the microgrid containing DES

The dynamic performance of the proposed dynamic modelling and control schemes of the selected DES systems is assessed through digital simulations carried out in the MATLAB/Simulink environment (The MathWorks Inc., 2009), by using SimPowerSystems.

For full dynamic performance studies, independent control of active and reactive powers exchanged between the DES and the electric grid is carried out. To this aim, all DES systems are firstly charged to be initialized at the same energy level of 2 MJ (half capacity). Thus, the two control modes of the DSTATCOM-DES systems are analyzed using two case studies.

The first case study (Scenario 1) corresponds to the DSTATCOM-DES device operating in VCM. In this case, the topology presented in the test system without the activation of the DSTATCOM-DES, the so-called base case, is used as a benchmark for the reactive power studies. Under this situation, the distribution utility feeds the load of 1.5 MW/0.35 Mvar, i.e. only the breaker B2 is closed. The supply voltages and currents are balanced and in steady-state. The voltage obtained at bus 3 in this steady-state is 0.94 p.u. (base voltage at 25 kV). At t=0.4 s, a reactive load of 0.8 Mvar is suddenly connected at bus 3 by closing B3 and later disconnected at t=0.6 s. Fig. 21 presents the system response before, during and after the contingency described. As can be seen, the increase of the inductive reactive load produces a voltage sag (aka dip) at bus 3 of near 21 % respect to the value in steady-state during 200 ms, until the reactive load is disconnected. Although the DSTATCOM-DES is not operating, i.e. not exchanging power with the grid as can be seen from response of *d* and *q* current components, the DSTATCOM-DES is connected (B1 is closed) and still forced to generate an output voltage waveform accurately synchronized in amplitude and in phase with the grid positive sequence voltage at the PCC for being ready to be quickly activated when necessary. The DSTATCOM-DES signals of Fig. 21 were introduced for comparison purposes with the subsequent cases studied.

The second case study (Scenario 2) corresponds to the DSTATCOM-DES device operating in APCM. This case study is particular for each energy storage technology considered, since each DES device modifies in a different way the dynamics of the DSTATCOM device.
The SMES system studied is composed of a stack of 4 Bi-2212 HTS coils with a total equivalent nominal inductance of 8.3 H operated at 30 K, and a critical current of 1.2 kA. The SMES arrangement was initialized at about 2 MJ, so that the consequent initial coil current is set at about 722 A. The SCES system is made up of a string of 468 Maxwell Boostcap BCAP0010 (2600 F/2.5 V/20°C) super capacitors with a total equivalent nominal capacitance of about 5.6 F and a maximum voltage of 1170 V at 20°C. The super capacitors bank was also initialized at about 2 MJ, so that the corresponding initial voltage is fixed at near 850 V. In the case of the proposed FES system, it consists of a high speed flywheel with operating speed range of 14 000 rpm–28 000 rpm and total system inertia of 14e-3 kg-m^2. The PMSM is a three phase, two pair poles one and operates in the frequency range of 467 Hz–933 Hz. Since, the FES system is also initialized at 2 MJ, the initial rotor speed is fixed at about 22 000 rpm. The base case used for this study is the same previously described, but considering only the steady-state scenario prior to the voltage sag, i.e. until 0.4 s with the utility grid feeding only the load of 1.5 MW/0.35 Mvar (breaker B2 closed). In this case, the topology presented in the test system without the activation of the DSTATCOM-DES (base case) is also used as a benchmark for the APCM case study.

7.1 Scenario 1: Connection of the DSTATCOM-DES in voltage control mode

The dynamic response in controlling the reactive power locally generated by the DSTATCOM-DES independently of the active power exchange is now studied through the simulation results of Fig. 22. The good performance of the voltage regulator of the DSTATCOM device is evidently depicted by the rapid compensation of reactive power and the consequent improvement of the voltage profile, after activation at t= 0.2 s, and even more during the voltage sag between 0.4 s and 0.6 s. As can be noted from actual and reference values of i_q, the only reactive power exchange with the utility system, independent of the active power, allows efficiently regulating the voltage at bus 3, from 0.94 p.u. in the base case up to the reference value of near 1 p.u., and particularly during the sag, when the voltage goes down to 0.75 p.u. in the base case and the VCM allows restoring quickly the voltage back to about 1 p.u. and thus mitigating completely the voltage perturbation. The DSTATCOM-DES provides near 0.83 Mvar of capacitive reactive power for improving the voltage profile during the sag and about 0.22 Mvar during the previous steady-state. As a consequence of the global improvement of the voltage profile at bus 3 (PCC), the active power demanded by loads is slightly enlarged. The decoupling characteristics between the active and reactive powers are excellent because of the full decoupled current control strategy implemented in the *d-q* frame. It is significant to note that, since only reactive power is exchanged with the grid in this control mode, there is no need for energy storage or any other external energy source. In fact, this reactive power is locally and electronically generated just by the DSTATCOM, so that the results of Fig. 21 and 22 are valid for any DES coupled to the DSTATCOM. This DES is maintained idle (or in stand-by mode) during the entire VCM operation by using the electronic interface which couples it to the DSTATCOM. Since in this control mode only reactive power is injected/absorbed at the PCC, the maximum apparent power of the DSTATCOM VSI, i.e. 1.5 MVA, can be used for compensating deeper sags. When active power is included in the control goals, some criterion of dynamic distribution of limits should be considered according to priorities set by the DSTATCOM-DES operator.

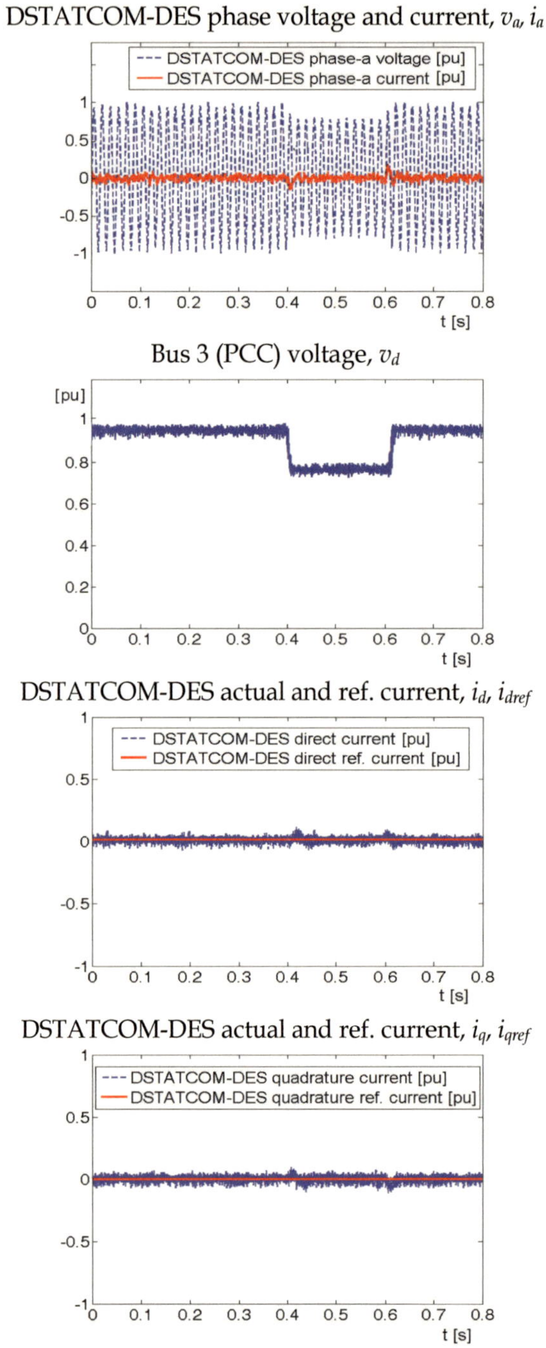

Fig. 21. Simulation results for the base case (with no activation of DSTATCOM-DES)

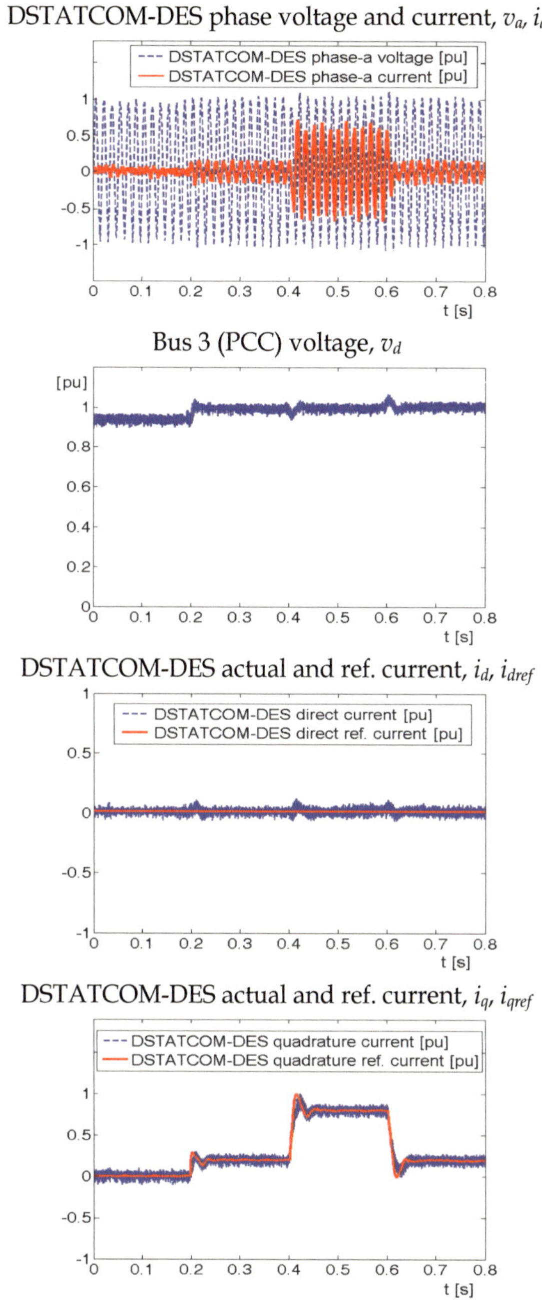

Fig. 22. Simulation results for the case with the DSTATCOM-DES in VCM

7.2 Scenario 2: Connection of the DSTATCOM-DES in active power control mode

The full dynamic response in controlling the active power flow injected/absorbed by the DES unit independently of the reactive power generated is now analyzed through the simulation results of Fig. 23. This case study is particular for each energy storage technology, but the three DESs selected for power applications in microgrids shown some almost coincident responses, so that the study is focused on the SMES device dynamic behaviour analysis and the difference with the other devices will be remarked when is required. In this case study, an active power command P_r is set to make step changes of 0.5 MW during 200 ms as much in the discharge as in the charge modes of operation with the VCM control scheme deactivated. Thus, reactive power is not generated and the device is fully used to exchange active power with the microgrid. Under these circumstances, an active power of around 30 % of the active power demanded by the load is injected during the discharge mode and absorbed during the charge mode of the SMES coil. As can be noted from actual and reference values of i_d and i_q shown in Fig. 23 only active power is rapidly exchanged with the utility system, in both discharge/charge modes of operation, independently of the reactive power. As can be seen, there exists a very low transient

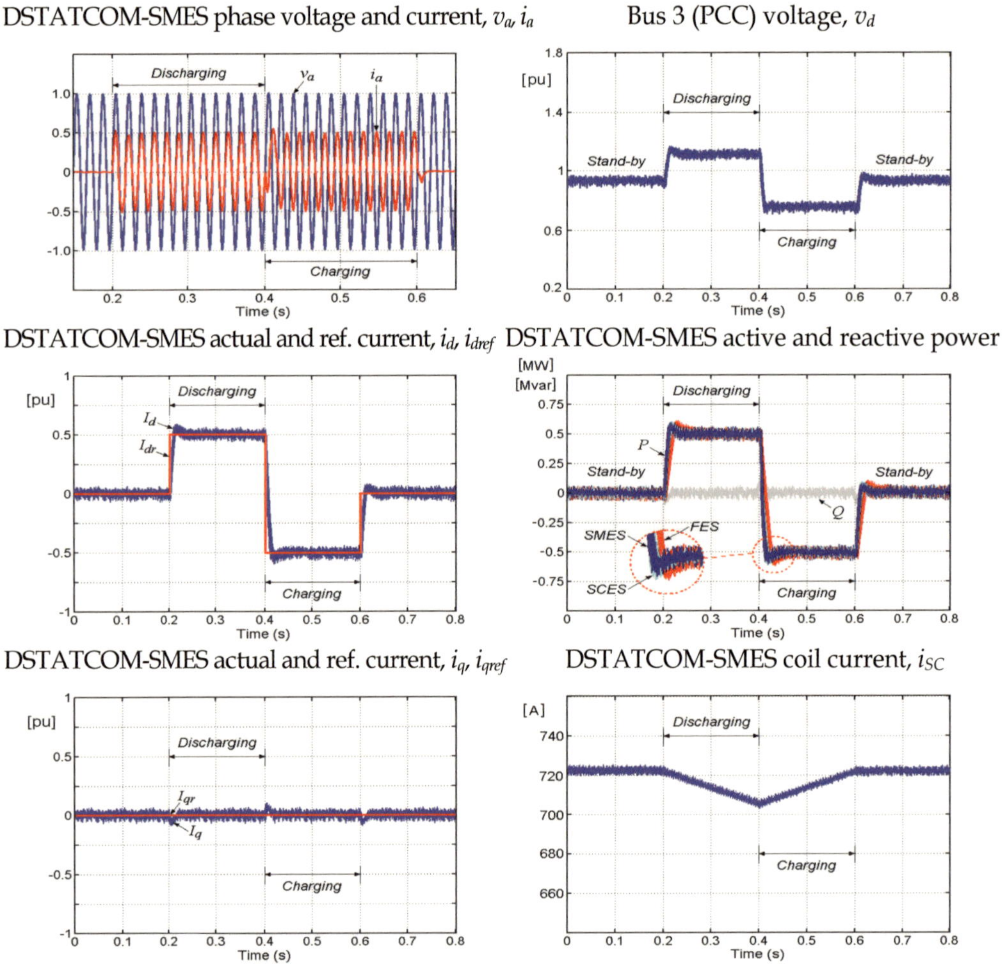

Fig. 23. Simulation results for the case with the DSTATCOM-DES in active power control mode

coupling between the active and reactive powers exchanged by the SMES due to the full decoupled current control strategy in the synchronous-rotating *d-q* reference frame. As expected, the phase ´a´ voltage at the PCC (bus 3) is in-phase with the SMES DSTATCOM output current during the active power injection (discharge mode) and in opposite-phase during the active power absorption (charge mode). This active power exchange produces substantial changes in the terminal voltage v_{d1}, because the test power grid studied is pretty weak. A significant issue to be noted is that the dynamic active power response of the SMES in APCM is very fast and better than the reactive power one in VCM. This is a consequence of the PI compensator included for voltage regulation at the PCC, which inevitably adds a lag in the response. As can be also seen from the comparison of transient responses of the three selected DES devices, SMESs and SCESs are the faster DES devices and response almost identically in one and a half cycle, with a settling time of approximately 30 ms. In the same way, the FES device is hardly slower than both later and its response exceed the two cycles with a settling time of almost 45 ms. The discharging and charging processes performed produce a variation of about 0.1 MJ of the energy stored in the DES devices. In the case of the SMES system, this variation is carried out by reducing the coil current from 722 A down to about 705 A and then returning to the initial value (without considering loses). The SCES bank obtains this energy variation by changing the terminal voltage from 850 V in the initial state to 828 V and then going back to the original state of charge. In the case of the FES device, the energy change is performed by decelerating the flywheel rotor speed from 22 000 rpm to 21 673 rpm and then accelerating back to the previous condition.

8. Conclusion

This chapter has thoroughly discussed the power application of advanced distributed energy storage systems in modern electrical microgrids. More specifically, of the various advanced storage systems nowadays existing, the three foremost ones for power applications have been considered, i.e. ultra capacitors, SMESs and flywheels. To this aim, major operating characteristics of these modern devices have been analyzed and a real detailed full dynamic model of all DES units has been studied. Moreover, a novel power conditioning system of the selected DES units to simultaneously and independently control active and reactive power flow in the distribution network level and a new three-level control scheme have been proposed, comprising a full decoupled current control strategy in the synchronous-rotating *d-q* reference frame. The dynamic performance of the proposed systems has been fully validated by digital simulations carried out by using SimPowerSystems of MATLAB/Simulink. The dynamic modelling approaches proposed describe the dynamic behaviour of the DES units over the frequency range from DC to several thousand Hertz with sufficient accuracy. The results show that the novel multi-level control schemes ensure fast controllability and minimum oscillatory behaviour of the DES systems operating in the four-quadrant modes, which enables to effectively increase the transient and dynamic stability of the power system. The improved capabilities of the integrated DSTATCOM-DES controllers to rapidly control the active power exchange between the DES and the utility system, simultaneously and independently of the reactive power exchange, permit to greatly enhance the operation and control of the electric system. The fast response DES devices show to be very effective in enhancing the distribution power quality, successfully mitigating disturbances such as voltage sags and voltage/current harmonic distortion, among others.

9. Acknowledgments

The author wishes to thank CONICET (Argentinean National Research Council for Science and Technology), IEE/UNSJ (Institute of Electrical Energy at the National University of San Juan) and ANPCyT (National Agency for Scientific and Technological Promotion) under grant FONCYT PICT 2005 - Cod. No. 33407, for the financial support of this work.

10. References

Acha, E. & Agelidis, V.; Anaya-Lara, O. & Miller, T. (2002). *Power Electronic Control in Electrical Systems*. Newness, 1st ed., UK.

Arsoy, A. B.; Liu, Y.; Ribeiro, P. F. & Wang, F. (2003). STATCOM-SMES. *IEEE Industry Applications Magazine*, Vol. 2, pp. 21-28.

Aware, M.V. & Sutanto, D. (2004). SMES for Protection of Distributed Critical Loads. *IEEE Transactions on Power Delivery*, Vol. 19, No 3, pp. 1267–1275.

Barker P. P. (2002). Ultracapacitors for Use in Power Quality and Distributed Resource Applications, *Proceedings of IEEE Power Engineering Society 2002 Summer Meeting*, Chicago, Illinois, USA, July, 2002.

Battaglini, A.; Lilliestam, J.; Haas, A. & Patt, A. (2009). Development of SuperSmart Grids for a More Efficient Utilisation of Electricity from Renewable Sources, *Journal of Cleaner Production*, Vol. 17, No. 10, pp. 911-918.

Bollen, M. H. J. (2000). *Understanding Power Quality Problems*. IEEE Press, Piscataway, New Jersey, USA.

Bose, B. K. (2002). *Modern Power Electronics and AC Drives*, Prentice Hall, 2nd edition, New Jersey, USA.

Buckles W. & Hassenzahl W. V. (2000). Superconducting Magnetic Energy Storage, *IEEE Power Engineering Review*, 2000, pp. 16-23.

Carrasco J. M.; Garcia-Franquelo, L.; Bialasiewicz, J. T.; Galván, E; Portillo-Guisado, R. C.; Martín-Prats, M. A.; León, J. I. & Moreno-Alfonso, N. (2006). Power Electronic Systems for the Grid Integration of Renewable Energy Sources: A Survey. *IEEE Trans. on Industrial Electronics*, Vol. 53, No. 4, pp. 1002-1016.

Chen, L.; Liu, Y.; Arsoy, A. B.; Ribeiro, P. F.; Steurer, M. & Iravani, M.R. (2006). Detailed Modeling of Superconducting Magnetic Energy Storage (SMES) System. *IEEE Transactions on Power Delivery*, Vol. 21, No. 2, pp. 699-710.

Conway, B. E. (1999). *Electrochemical Supercapacitors: Scientific Fundamentals and Technological Applications*, Kluwer Academic Press/Plenum Publishers, 1st ed., New York, USA.

Dail, Y.; Zhao, T.; Tian, Y. & Gao, L. (2007). Research on the Influence of Primary Frequency Control Distribution on Power System Security and Stability, *Proceedings of 2nd IEEE Conference on Industrial Electronics and Applications*, IEEE, USA, pp. 222-226.

El-Khattam, W. & Salama, M.M.A. (2004). Distributed Generation Technologies, Definitions and Benefits, *Electric Power Systems Research*, Vol. 71, No. 2, pp. 119-128.

Energy Storage Association. (2003). *Applications of Electricity Storage*. Available from http://electricitystorage.org/technologies_applications.htm, [Aug., 2009].

Hingorani, N. G. & Gyugyi, L. (2000). *Understanding FACTS*, IEEE Press, 1st ed., New York, USA.

Katiraei, F. ; Iravani, R. ; Hatziargyriou, N. & Dimeas, A. (2008). Microgrids Management: Controls and Operation Aspects of Microgrids, *IEEE Power & Energy Magazine*, Vol. 6, No. 3, pp. 54-65.

Krause, P.C. (1992). *Analysis of Electric Machinery*, Mc Graw-Hill, New York, USA.

Kroposki, B.; Lasseter, R.; Ise,T. ; Morozumi, S. ; Papatlianassiou, S. & Hatziargyriou, N. (2008). Making Microgrids Work, *IEEE Power & Energy Mag.*, Vol. 6, No. 3, pp.40-53.

Liu, H. & Jiang, J. (2007), Flywheel Energy Storage - An Upswing Technology for Energy Sustainability, *Energy and Buildings*, Vol. 39, No.5, pp. 599-604.

Maxwell Technologies. *Electric double layer capacitor: boostcap BCAP0010 Ultracapacitor.* Available from http://www.b-l-l.com/maxwell/contents/ultracapacitors/data sheets/BCAP_Series.pdf [April, 2008].

Molina M. G. & Mercado P. E. (2001). Evaluation of Energy Storage Systems for Application in the Frequency Control", *Proceedings of the 6th COBEP*, ISOBRAEP, Florianopolis, SC-Brazil, pp. 479-484, Nov. 2001.

Molina M. G. & Mercado P. E. (2003). New Energy Storage Devices for Applications on Frequency Control of the Power System using FACTS Controllers, *Proceedings of X ERLAC,* CIGRÉ, Iguazú, Argentina, pp. 222-226, May 2006.

Molina M. G. & Mercado P. E. (2006). Control Design and Simulation of DSTATCOM with Energy Storage for Power Quality Improvements, *Proceedings of IEEE/PES Transm. and Distribution Conference Latin America*, Caracas, Venezuela, Aug. 2006.

Molina M. G., Mercado P. E. & Watanabe E. H. (2007). Static Synchronous Compensator with Superconducting Magnetic Energy Storage for High Power Utility Applications, *Energy Conversion and Management*, Vol. 48, No. 8, pp. 2316-2331.

Molina M. G. & Mercado P. E. (2008). Dynamic Modeling and Control Design of DSTATCOM with Ultra-Capacitor Energy Storage for Power Quality Improvements. *Proceedings of IEEE/PES Transm. and Distrib. Conf. Latin America*, Bogotá, Colombia, Aug. 2008.

Molina M. G. & Mercado P. E. (2009). Control of Tie-Line Power Flow of Microgrid Including Wind Generation by DSTATCOM-SMES Controller. *Proceedings of IEEE Energy Conversion Congress and Expo.*, San José-CA, USA, Sept. 2009, pp. 2014-2021.

Nourai, A. (2002). Large-Scale Electricity Storage Technologies for Energy Managment, *Proceedings of IEEE PES 2002 Summer Meeting*, IEEE, Chicago, USA, July 2002.

Nourai, A.; Martin, B. P. & Fitchett, D. R. (2005). Testing the limits [electricity storage technologies], *IEEE Power and Energy Magazine*, Vol. 3, No. 2, pp. 40-46.

Ninkovic, P. S. (2002). A Novel Constant-Frequency Hysteresis Current Control of PFC Converters. *Proceedings of IEEE International Symposium on Industrial Electronics (ISIE)*, L´Aquila, Italy, 2002.

Pourbeik, P.; Kundur, P. S. & Taylor, C. W. (2006). The Anatomy of A Power Grid Blackout - Root Causes and Dynamics of Recent Major Blackouts, *IEEE Power and Energy Magazine*, Vol. 4, No. 5. pp. 22-29.

Pourbeik, P.; Bahrman, M.; John,E. & Wong, W. (2006a) Modern Countermeasures to Blackouts, *IEEE Power and Energy Magazine*, Vol. 4, No. 5, pp. 36-45.

Rafika, F.; Gualous, H.; Gallay, R.; Crausaz, A. & Berthon, A. (2007). Frequency, Thermal and Voltage Supercapacitor Characterization and Modeling. *Journal of Power Sources*, Vol. 165, No. 2, pp. 928-34.

Rahman, S. (2003). Going Green: The Growth of Renewable Energy, *IEEE Power & Energy Magazine*, Vol. 1, No. 6, pp. 16-18.

Rodríguez, J.; Lai, J. S. & Peng, F.Z. (2002). Multilevel Inverters: A Survey of Topologies, Controls, and Applications. *IEEE Transactions on Industrial Electronics*, Vol. 49, No. 4, pp. 724-738.

Samineni, S.; Johnson, B. K. Hess, H. L. & Law, J. D. (2003). Modeling and Analysis of A Flywheel Energy Storage System for Voltage Sag Correction, *Proceedings of IEEE International Electric Machines and Drives Conference*, pp. 1813 - 1818, June 2003.

Schindall, J. (2007). The Charge of the Ultra-capacitors. *IEEE Spectrum Magazine*, Vol. 44, No. 11, pp. 42–46.

Slootweg J. G. & Kling, W. L. (2003). The Impact of Large Scale Wind Power Generation on Power System Oscillations, *Electric Power Systems Research*, Vol. 67, No. 1, pp. 9-20.

Song Y. H. & Johns, A. T. (1999). *Flexible AC Transmission Systems (FACTS)*. IEE Press, 1st ed., London, UK.

Soto, D. & Green, T. C. (2002). A Comparison of High-Power Converter Topologies for the Implementation of FACTS Controllers. *IEEE Trans. on Industrial Electronics*, Vol. 49, No. 5, pp. 1072-1080.

Spyker, R. L. & Nelms, R. M. (2000). Classical Equivalent Circuit Parameters for a Double-Layer Capacitor. *IEEE Trans. on Aerospace and Elec. System*, Vol.36, No.3, pp.829–836.

Steurer, M. & Hribernik, W. (2005). Frequency Response Characteristics of A 100 MJ SMES Coil - Measurements and Model Refinement. *IEEE Transactions on Applied Superconductivity*, Vol. 15, 1887-1890.

Suvire, G. O. & Mercado, P. E. (2008). Wind Farm: Dynamic Model and Impact on a Weak Power System, *Proceedings of IEEE/PES Transm. and Distribution Conference Latin America*, Bogotá, Colombia, Aug. 2008.

The MathWorks Inc. (2009). *SimPowerSystems for use with Simulink: User's Guide*, R2009a, Available from http://www.mathworks.com [July, 2009].

Toliyat, H.; Talebi, S.; McMullen, P.; Huynh, C. & Filatov, A. (2005). Advanced High-Speed Flywheel Energy Storage Systems for Pulsed Power Applications, *IEEE Electric Ship Technologies Symposium*, 2005.

Zhou, L. & Qi, Z. (2009). Modeling and Simulation of Flywheel Energy Storage System with IPMSM for Voltage Sags in Distributed Power Network, *Proceedings of the 2009 IEEE Int. Conference on Mechatronics and Automation*, Changchun, China, August 2009.

Zubieta, L. & Bonert, R. (2000). Characterization of Double-Layer Capacitorsf Power Electronics Applications, *IEEE Trans. on Ind. Applications*, Vol. 36, No. 1, pp.199-205.

5

Improving the Kill Chain for Prosecution of Time Sensitive Targets

Edward H. S. Lo and T. Andrew Au
Defence Science and Technology Organisation
Australia

1. Introduction

Command and control (C2) is an essential part of all military operations and activities. It is the means by which a commander recognises what to achieve and the means to ensure that appropriate actions are taken. C2 helps the commander achieve organised engagements with the enemy through the coordinated use of soldiers, platforms and information. However, war is a poorly understood phenomenon characterised by one complex system interacting with another in a fiercely competitive way. In order to effectively control such a dynamic and complex environment, the commander needs at their disposal a C2 system that can capture the battlespace dynamics and be capable of reacting and undertaking actions that produce desired effects. Through planning (whether immediate or deliberate), the commander determines the aims and objectives of the operation, develops concepts of operation, then allocates resources and provides for necessary coordination accordingly.

The term "fog of war" succinctly describes the level of ambiguity in situational awareness in military operations. Good C2 aims to deal with uncertainty so that the commander can decide on an appropriate course of action to positively shape the campaign. One may break through the fog of war by acquiring more knowledge of the situation, but it takes time to gain and process information. Unfortunately, any C2 system also needs to be fast, at least faster than the adversary's OODA (Observe, Orient, Decide and Act) loop (Brehmer, 2005). The resulting tension between coping with uncertainty and time constraints presents a fundamental challenge of C2 (Department of the Navy, 1996).

An essential element of a C2 system is its organisation of people (Wilcox, 2005) working to achieve the commander's intent through formal processes, networks, and the application of sensors and weapons systems. C2 staff gather information, make decisions, take action, communicate and cooperate with one another in the accomplishment of a common goal. Not surprisingly, a C2 system sometimes fails to respond to clear opportunities because the people lack the coordinating abilities required to manage resources effectively and efficiently. The cognitive and cooperative skills of such a C2 organisation prosecuting the mission could ultimately determine the success or failure of military operations (Bakken *et al.*, 2004).

1.1 Air power and targeting

Application of air power is a primary element of modern military campaigns. Central to successful application of air power is the selection and prosecution of targets that represent critical vulnerabilities of an adversary. Responsibility for planning, tasking and controlling assigned air and space assets is typically assigned to an Air and Space Operations Centre (AOC). Targeting is a central function of an AOC, selecting and prioritising targets and matching appropriate actions to those targets to produce desired effects (Royal Australian Air Force, 2008).

An AOC is a high tempo multitask environment staffed by a dedicated team of specialists who exercise multiple responsibilities to ensure that air assets are coordinated to achieve maximum effect. Two forms of targeting are used in an AOC. Execution of present-day air campaigns is based on a systematic process, called the air tasking cycle, to conduct deliberate targeting. The air tasking cycle consists of six phases, as shown in Fig. 1, in which the first four involve planning and tasking, followed by force execution and completed by operational assessment (US Air Force, 2006). The product of planning is an Air Battle Plan (ABP) containing an Air Tasking Order (ATO) for scheduling sorties.

Fig. 1. Phases of the air tasking cycle.

The air tasking cycle is the central mechanism employed by an AOC that translates the commander's intent into actions against targets. The intent informs strategy development that is used to decide on the desired effects together with the military orders (actions) consisting of the best available means to achieve the stated objectives. Through this cyclical process, an AOC plans, tasks and controls joint air missions to coordinate and synchronise joint fires (Air Force actions in conjunction with other force element strike capability) executed by individual components under the control of the Joint Force Commander.

The air tasking cycle spans multiple days and is useful against fixed targets like buildings and infrastructure. Typically, the air tasking cycle is a three-day process from strategy development up to the end of the force execution phase. Of these, two days are devoted to planning and tasking while one day is allocated to execution (Department of Defence, 2006). Multiple overlapping air tasking cycles can be scheduled one day apart to allow for daily force execution.

While the air tasking cycle is appropriate for static targets, it lacks the responsiveness needed to engage dynamic and emergent targets (Hinen, 2002; Hazlegrove, 2000), as witnessed in recent conflicts where coalition forces encountered both mobile targets and an adversary strategy of concealment, dispersal and deception. An important function of an AOC is prosecution of targets requiring immediate response, known as time-sensitive targets (TSTs); these include mobile SCUD launchers, surface-to-air missiles and high-payoff targets. Prosecution of such targets is facilitated through the use of a dynamic targeting process, a procedure whose successful implementation depends on timely and accurate decision making by key players. The dynamic targeting process has six distinct phases: Find, Fix, Track, Target, Engage and Assess (F2T2EA), also known as the kill chain or the F2T2EA process.

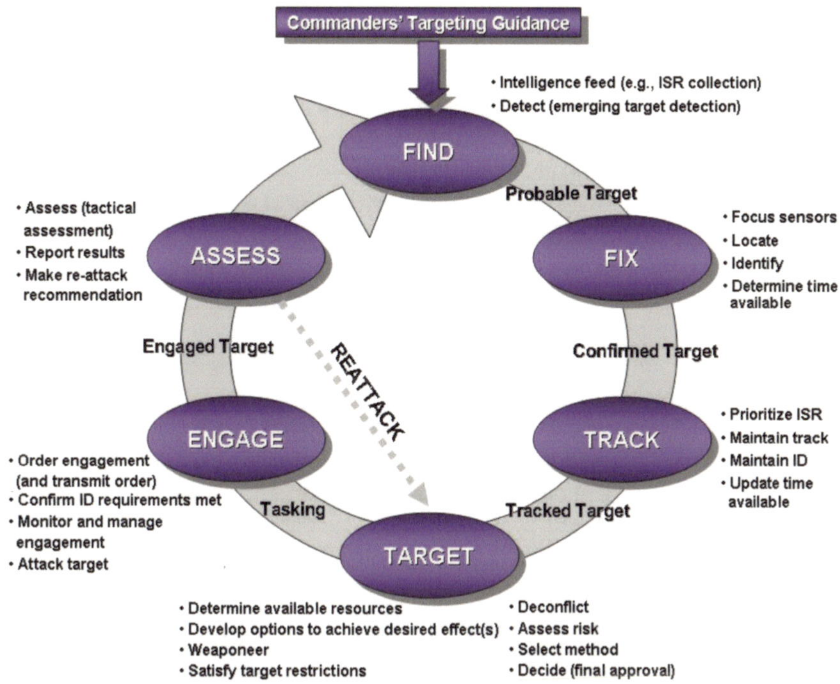

Fig. 2. Phases of the dynamic targeting process (US Air Force, 2006).

1.2 A dynamic modelling approach

Due to the inability to experiment with the kill chain during live exercises and the difficulty of human-in-the-loop simulations, we have constructed an executable dynamic model of human interaction and tasks engaged in the F2T2EA process. We used the simulation and analysis tool C3TRACE (Command, Control and Communications: Techniques for the Reliable Assessment of Concept Execution) developed by the US Army Research Laboratory to represent the operators, the tasks and functions they perform, and their communications patterns. The process model developed is able to quantify task performance and human workload for various organisational configurations.

In modelling the kill chain, it is necessary to capture the activities and measure the duration of tasks performed by operators while engaging in the dynamic targeting process. While technology plays an important role, the kill chain is essentially a human-centric activity involving complex (work-related) social interactions over a limited period of time. For this reason, we capture and study this process through a social network analysis (SNA) approach. Traditional SNA techniques seek to describe the underlying network structure between individuals through communication links. The resulting network can then be subjected to mathematical analysis using graph theory. Nevertheless, when analysing dynamic targeting we regard exclusion of timing and other contextual information as a shortcoming of the basic SNA approach.

To quantify the variety of social interactions over time, we enriched the traditional methodology of social network analysis by capturing and time-stamping dynamic information. Specifically, this included speech utterances, chat messages, operator actions and changing levels of situational awareness. This extension allowed us to capture in detail the dynamic targeting process as used in an AOC. A software tool we developed that can replay the team's dynamic interactions helps not only in the construction of the dynamic model but also in further analysis of activities within the kill chain.

The goal of our endeavour is to use this multi-faceted dynamic modelling approach to facilitate improvements in the kill chain. The network of tasks performed by the team can be analysed by executing the process model to generate typical outcomes, operator utilisation and durations as well as rates of output in the kill chain. Subjecting the F2T2EA process to stress tests helped us identify possible information-processing bottlenecks and overloads. Subsequent to the simulation, we could usually suggest modified work arrangements to address any identified shortcomings. These proposals, including techniques adapted from those typically used to address resource constrained workflows, led to positive outcomes when tested in a recent exercise.

This paper is divided into six sections. Section 2 following introduces the concept of dynamic targeting used in an AOC and describes how it fits into the deliberate targeting process. Section 3 covers process modelling and simulation and its application to analysis of C2 systems. Section 4 examines our approach for capturing the dynamic targeting sequence and briefly describes C3TRACE, the tool employed herein for modelling and analysis. Section 5 illustrates steps in building a dynamic targeting model in C3TRACE using publicly available data, together with the approach used for analysing the process using the simulation results. Section 6 summarises our work here and discusses how human-in-the-loop experiments could be used to assess alternatives for improving the dynamic targeting process.

2. Dynamic targeting in an air and space operations centre

Spanning multiple days makes the air tasking cycle suitable for prosecuting fixed targets but unsuitable for those targets requiring immediate response. Time-sensitive targets (TSTs) requiring immediate response are prosecuted using a separate dynamic targeting process. An AOC coordinates this process while the air tasking cycle is in its execution and assessment phases. The dynamic targeting process provides the command authority with a decision to engage a TST using a compressed timeframe.

2.1 Command and control structure for dynamic targeting

An AOC has an offensive operations team and a defensive operations team, organised, in part, around the dynamic targeting process, with most of the activities related to offensive operations. The goal of the dynamic targeting process is to provide the command authority with a correct decision, even if the decision is not to engage the target. It is very dependent on the situation, available resources, the theatre, and the commander's specific intent. One aspect of the process that demands high workload and time is the need to coordinate activities with the rest of the campaign (execution of the air tasking cycle).

We modelled the dynamic targeting process by considering a command and control structure comprising the following roles (Department of Air Force, 2005; US Air Force, 2006; Case *et al.*, 2006; Air Land Sea Application Center, 2001):

- CCO: Chief of Combat Operations
- DTO: Dynamic Targeting Officer
- SIDO: Senior Intelligence Duty Officer
- SODO: Senior Offensive Duty Officer
- SADO/C2DO: Senior Air Defence Officer / Command & Control Duty Officer (a dual-hatted role)
- Liaison Officers:
  - BCD: Battlefield Coordination Detachment (from Army)
  - SOLE: Special Operations Liaison Element (from Special Operations Command)
  - NALE: Naval and Amphibious Liaison Element (from Navy)
  - MARLO: Marine Liaison Officer (from Marine Corps Forces)

The CCO has prime responsibility for monitoring and directing the current air situation with assistance from the offensive operations team. Within the offensive operations team, the DTO has the key role in the AOC for coordinating the dynamic targeting process.

2.2 The dynamic targeting process

The dynamic targeting process has six distinct phases of Find, Fix, Track, Target, Engage and Assess (F2T2EA) (see Fig. 2). The find phase involves detection of an emerging target that fits the description of an expected TST. This detection results in an alert received by the DTO to proceed in coordinating the decision making process to determine whether or not to prosecute the target. The Fix phase commences when positive identification of the target is requested by the DTO and accomplished by the intelligence cell through the SIDO (Case *et al.*, 2006). During the Track phase, a track is maintained on the target while the desired effect is confirmed against it (US Air Force, 2006). The formulation of the desired effect and the targeting solution against the target takes place during the target phase of the dynamic targeting process. During this phase, the current Air Tasking Order (ATO)[1] is searched for suitable weapons platforms that can engage the TST and a collateral damage estimate performed (to prevent fratricide) (Department of Air Force, 2005). The mission package is reviewed against the rules of engagement (ROE) and then submitted to the CCO or higher level commander for engagement approval (Case *et al.*, 2006). The target phase is often the lengthiest process due to the large number of requirements that must be satisfied (US Air Force, 2006).

The engage phase commences once the engagement is ordered by the commander. A fifteen-line brief drafted by the DTO and the C2DO is transmitted to the pilot of the designated weapons platform who acknowledges both the receipt of the message and comprehension of its contents. This phase concludes once the pilot engages the target. A successful battle damage assessment report completes the dynamic targeting (F2T2EA) process (Case *et al.*, 2006).

---

[1] The ATO defines the actions during the execution phase of a specific air tasking cycle and is the basis for the monitoring of execution and the assessment of results from sortie action.

Success in dynamic targeting requires timely and accurate decisions. Any delay in the process will ultimately affect the outcome of any dynamic targeting endeavour. There is often very little time allowed between detection of a TST and its possible engagement and execution. The timeliness of this process varies widely. Newman *et al.* (2005) reports an average duration of 20 minutes for dynamic targeting whereas it took approximately one hour by Molan's (2008) account.

An inherent delay in engaging TSTs is the human element of the decision-making process. In making decisions, the AOC has to consider several important factors to make sure that the best possible plan is carried out. Under such time constraints, the command team might make errors due simply to the complexity of the environment or the stress that such a situation generates.

3. Prior work of C2 modelling

Model building is useful in gaining an understanding of C2 systems because it involves abstracting the salient aspects of the underlying process (Aslaksen & Belcher, 1992). Our focus is on modelling the functional aspects of the process in terms of the sequence of tasks performed. Simulation is the act of executing the model to produce typical results expected from undertaking real world activity; it can be quite useful in predicting how a system might behave outside of its usual operating environment (Hannon & Ruth, 1994). The modelling and simulation paradigm through process modelling is thus used herein to study the dynamic targeting process.

3.1 Process modelling and simulation

A dynamic model expresses the behaviour of a system over time. While mathematical models have been used to model dynamic systems, these approaches have generally been applicable to problems where an analytical solution exists (Law & Kelton, 1991). More complex systems require alternative approaches such as process modelling (Hlupic & Robinson, 1998), which is the focus of this chapter.

The underlying technology behind process modelling is discrete-event simulation. A discrete-event simulation models the evolution of a system over time by a representation in which the state variables change only at specific moments in time (Law & Kelton, 1991). These points in time are when events occur and cause an instantaneous change to the system's state. While the model is being executed, the discrete-event simulation keeps track of simulated time and advances the clock as required. Simulation time is typically managed through the next-event approach to time advance. On commencement, the scheduler initialises simulation time to zero then determines the trigger times of subsequent events. Model execution occurs by advancing the simulation clock to when each event occurs in time order and modifying the state variables as required.

In process modelling, the functions of an organisation are encoded as a network of tasks. Simulation involves triggering activities in the workflow with entities that flow through the system. The invocation and completion of tasks gives rise to events that are executed by the discrete-event simulation. There may be times when tasks lack sufficient resources to immediately service requests, resulting in queuing of entities. Process modelling has direct underpinnings from queuing theory (Law & Kelton, 1991) and thus is useful for analysing how well an organisation services its work requirements.

3.2 Process modelling of C2 systems

Kalloniatis and colleagues (Kalloniatis *et al.*, 2009; Kalloniatis & Wong, 2007) have used Websphere Business Modeler Advanced to construct executable models of operational level Joint military headquarters for assessing appropriate staff numbers and structures. Their estimation of relative risk in terms of backlogs in the simulation of processes and cyclic activities indicated areas with the greatest need of augmentation when dealing with a surge in workload.

Newman *et al.* (2005) used the Extend process modelling tool (Krahl, 2003) to model the dynamic targeting process. The model was built from information gained through interviews, observations and system logs. They evaluated the effects of process modifications by comparing the simulation results against a baseline model. At the macro level, they assessed process timeliness and throughput while at the individual level they examined queue rates, actual process time and utilisation rates. Their quantitative analysis enabled their team to suggest recommendations for improving the dynamic targeting process. Extend has also been used in modelling the Standing Joint Force Headquarters (SJFHQ) concept (Hutchins *et al.*, 2005). Findings from the simulation results were used to support decisions on structuring the emerging command centre.

4. Capturing and modelling the dynamic targeting process

The US Army Research Laboratory developed a tool called Command, Control and Communications: Techniques for the Reliable Assessment of Concept Execution (C3TRACE) that combines dynamic modelling with human workload modelling (Kilduff *et al.*, 2005). They successfully used C3TRACE to understand how technology affects decision quality in an infantry company (Kilduff *et al.*, 2006). Their analysis revealed that these troops suffered from information overload and occasionally made decisions based on poor information quality.

C3TRACE provides the capability to represent different organisational levels, the staff assigned to them, the tasks and functions they perform, and the communications patterns within and outside the organisation, all as a function of the frequency, criticality, and quality of incoming information. In our study, we used C3TRACE to model human interaction and tasks within the dynamic targeting sequence. The executable model helps us identify communication bottlenecks, workload peaks, and decision-making vulnerabilities so that the overall effectiveness of a proposed configuration change can be assessed.

Three main input categories are required to build a C3TRACE model: the organisational structure (i.e., personnel), the functions and tasks that are executed by the personnel (i.e., sequencing, decisions and queues), and the communication events (messages in the form of face-to-face, digital, voice, etc.). The output of the model includes operator utilisation and performance, decision quality and workload. The advantage of C3TRACE over other process modelling tools (Kalloniatis *et al.*, 2009; Krahl, 2003) is its support for integrating human operators and its ability to account for the human aspect in a work process (Keller, 2002). The analysis of workload allows one to determine the utilisation of operators based on multiple resource theory (Bierbaum *et al.*, 1987). It assumes that workload is the result of several processing resources described by four components: visual, auditory, cognitive, and psychomotor (VACP). The visual and auditory components refer to external stimuli. The cognitive component relates to the level of information processing required and the psychomotor component refers to physical actions. Tasks performed by an operator are therefore broken down into these four components. Workload according to each component is measured on a scale from 0.0 (no activity) to 7.0 (maximum activity). This allows us to capture operator activities including: reading, listening to speech, evaluating between options, speaking, writing and typing on the keyboard (Bierbaum *et al.*, 1987).

The ability for the model to provide meaningful insights into the dynamic targeting process is dependent on how accurately salient aspects of the underlying process are captured. Our close engagement with an AOC has provided an opportunity to observe details of the dynamic targeting process during major joint military exercises. The model we created was constructed from doctrine and procedure manuals, as well as analyses of the data from:

- Capturing the interactions and work practices in the AOC,
- Interviews and workshops with operators,
- Conducting surveys,
- Documents produced during the dynamic targeting process, and
- Logs from computer applications and the Chat application.

Once built, the model was checked by AOC specialists to ensure the process was correctly modelled and that valid simulation results were being produced. The following section describes in further detail the approach used to capture the dynamic targeting process.

4.1 Capturing social interactions during dynamic targeting

Our approach to data collection sought to capture fine-grain events in the AOC down to interactions between operators (Stanton *et al.*, 2008). Our observations included recording operators' speech utterances, passing of information and comments on observed events and activities. Additional timing data (hh:mm) was appended to each entry to allow post processing and evaluation of work efficiency. Collecting data this way documented the sequence of events and the decision making process, and identified the activities undertaken by operators during dynamic targeting. Over 50 hours of observations were recorded this way, some captured from multiple vantage points by different observers (Lo *et al.*, 2009).

Information contained in the Chat logs was extracted to supplement the observer notes. The Chat logs provided time-stamped messages exchanged between operators in the AOC during the exercise activities (Joint Warfighting Center, 2002). Chat helped facilitate the communication between different functional entities in the AOC and often triggered respective coordinating activities. Manual observations were synchronised to the system time observed in Chat to facilitate merging of Chat messages with other records. Logs from a specialised AOC status tool provided timed information about the state of progress by operators on each TST.

4.2 Merging the disparate sources of data

Disparate sources of data were merged into a single consolidated view for each time step. This was facilitated through a spreadsheet, as illustrated using a fictitious scenario and data in Fig. 3. For our purpose, observations were categorised into different activities and annotated with the following keywords in the columns of the spreadsheet:

- 'Speaks' in *Activity* column denotes a speech event between operator(s) in *Speakers* column and those in *Listeners* column. To simplify entry of broadcasts, the ALL keyword in *Listeners* column was used to represent all operators on the floor. Actual speech utterances were stored under *Comment* column,
- ROIP (radio over IP) indicates a speech event through the radio communications system. Due to difficulty in ascertaining the identity of the operator on the other end of the line, that operator was simply denoted as 'Radio',

- Chat describes a message transfer using the Chat application,
- *Comment* column contains observer comments,
- Progress specifies an event relating to the progress observed in prosecuting a TST in terms of the traffic light colour scheme. Column F identifies the TST (1 - 4), while the fields under columns G - O annotates the current state, either R, Y or G (Red, Yellow or Green), and
- <software application> indicates an observed use of a software application. The software application name was recorded in *Activity* column while user name was recorded in *Speakers* column.

Merging data from disparate sources can involve a degree of data deconfliction. In the case of merging records from two or more observers, there may be a need to remove duplicate observations of the same event. Similarly, events recorded in Chat or other software application logs may also have been recorded by observers (glanced from computer terminals or projected onto shared displays). The codes field in the spreadsheet of Fig. 3, allows the analyst to tag each line with user defined codes that annotate the data. A possible use is to assign a letter identifying the observer who produced the entry. Such an approach aided data deconfliction.

Our approach extends that used by Dietz (2006) in capturing the individual interactions between operators during the decision making process, in addition to capturing the traffic patterns between command posts. Through use of multiple data sources and observers the risk of missing key event data was minimised.

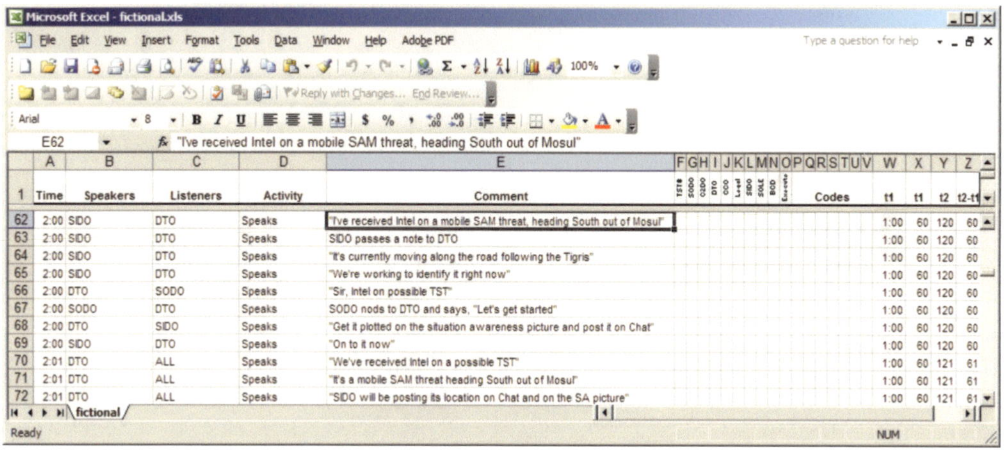

	Time	Speakers	Listeners	Activity	Comment	Codes	t1	t1	t2	t2-t1
62	2:00	SIDO	DTO	Speaks	"I've received Intel on a mobile SAM threat, heading South out of Mosul"		1:00	60	120	60
63	2:00	SIDO	DTO	Speaks	SIDO passes a note to DTO		1:00	60	120	60
64	2:00	SIDO	DTO	Speaks	"It's currently moving along the road following the Tigris"		1:00	60	120	60
65	2:00	SIDO	DTO	Speaks	"We're working to identify it right now"		1:00	60	120	60
66	2:00	DTO	SODO	Speaks	"Sir, Intel on possible TST"		1:00	60	120	60
67	2:00	SODO	DTO	Speaks	SODO nods to DTO and says, "Let's get started"		1:00	60	120	60
68	2:00	DTO	SIDO	Speaks	"Get it plotted on the situation awareness picture and post it on Chat"		1:00	60	120	60
69	2:00	SIDO	DTO	Speaks	"On to it now"		1:00	60	120	60
70	2:01	DTO	ALL	Speaks	"We've received Intel on a possible TST"		1:00	60	121	61
71	2:01	DTO	ALL	Speaks	"It's a mobile SAM threat heading South out of Mosul"		1:00	60	121	61
72	2:01	DTO	ALL	Speaks	"SIDO will be posting its location on Chat and on the SA picture"		1:00	60	121	61

Fig. 3. Different sources of data merged into a single spreadsheet (based on fictitious data).

4.3 Analysing the social interactions in dynamic targeting

To replay events captured for dynamic targeting a software tool, simply called SNA Viewer, was developed (Lo *et al.*, 2009). Written in Java, SNA Viewer displays social network diagrams produced by the Pajek network analysis package (Batagelj & Mrvar, 2003), together with relevant contextual information from the spreadsheet and an indicator of the progress of activity for the TST being prosecuted (see Fig. 4). This combination of views enables after-action study of the dynamic targeting process by playing out, in time sequence, the captured events in detail.

The slider at the bottom of the user interface (see Fig. 4) enabled us to quickly navigate through the events by time sequence. Positioning the slider updates each of the three views with information relating to the selected time. Activities are assessed by browsing through events of interest in the recorded comments and reviewing key information, such as actors and duration. The additional comments provide an account of the information flows and the decision making process that took place during prosecution of a TST. Together, the timing data and comments enable decision effectiveness to be assessed.

Progress of the dynamic targeting process is represented with traffic light colours (Newman *et al.*, 2005) in Fig. 4 where red, yellow and green denotes halted, in-progress and approved, respectively. The state of each operator is triggered by the value in columns F - O in Fig. 3 (R, Y or G) while the identifier in column F identifies the TST being prosecuted (1 - 4 for identifying multiple targets). This feature can be used to measure the level of shared situational awareness because individual operators might not update their responsible traffic lights immediately to reflect their work progress in the dynamic targeting process. Recording the changing traffic lights in this way facilitates the assessment of teamwork for dynamic targeting at the indicated time.

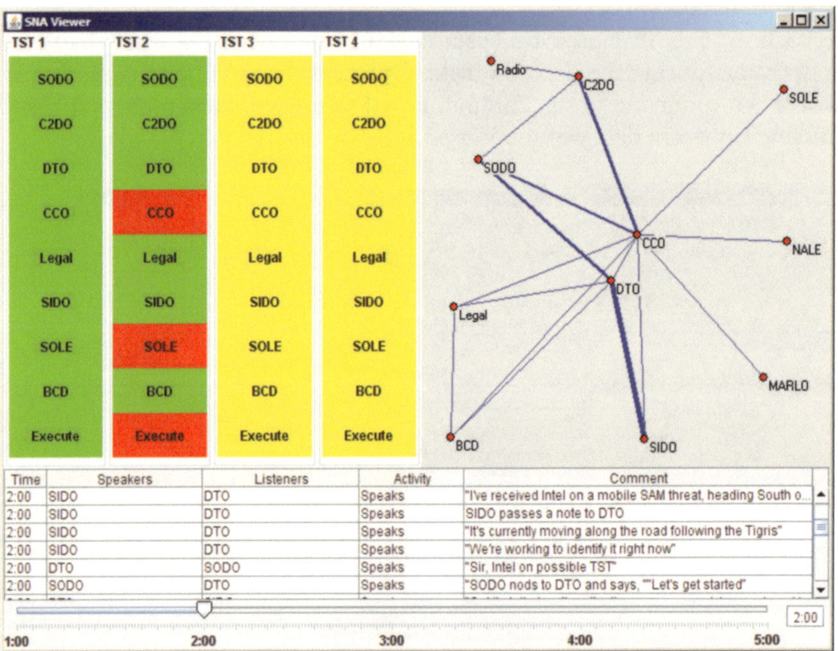

Fig. 4. Screen capture of the Temporal SNA model (based on fictitious data).

The purpose of the social network diagram is to provide a pictorial representation of the evolving interactions between operators when prosecuting a TST. In isolation, SNA allows an analyst to determine the frequency of communication between operators (through verbal communication, ROIP and Chat). Operators in Fig. 4 have been laid out according to the Kamada-Kawai model (Kamada & Kawai, 1989), which positions highly connected operators (over the entire session) in the centre of the diagram. Recorded events (comments, speech utterances and messages from Chat) in the table below, together with the view of TST progress complement the social network diagram with important contextual information.

The current version of SNA Viewer uses the Pajek package to produce the social network diagrams (Batagelj & Mrvar, 2003). Contents of each session were exported in text format and parsed with a program we developed to produce valid Pajek code. Specifically, the code took the form of a time-event network that enumerated and labelled each node and defined when edges were added and removed from the network. Nodes connected with multiple edges are displayed in Pajek using a thicker line. The network diagram for each time sequence was individually exported to an image file for display in SNA Viewer.

The ability to program a time-event network in Pajek enabled the exploration of different ways of representing the social network diagrams. For example, the following options were considered for the network diagram:

- Displaying the communications events at each instance in time,
- Showing the communications events accumulated since start time, and
- Representing the network diagram as a heatmap by allowing edges to remain on the network diagram for a fixed period.

These effects weren't a feature of Pajek but instead were produced in our program that automatically parses captured data to produce valid Pajek code. Of those options, the heatmap approach was assessed as producing the most meaningful social network diagrams for our purpose. In the network diagram in Fig. 4, each edge was set to remain on display for 10 minutes after its inclusion in the graph. The frequency of interaction between operators is indicated by the relative edge thickness.

Capturing the detailed aspects of the dynamic targeting process enabled the workflow to be decomposed, facilitating understanding of its sub-processes. In particular, we were able to deduce task durations for the process from captured recordings and construct the workflow with data in the operator manuals. Furthermore, the collection of multiple observations from several vignettes has helped us to compute the state transition probabilities for branched workflows. This understanding underpinned the construction of an executable dynamic targeting model using C3TRACE (Lo & Au, 2007).

4.4 Conducting surveys and interviews with operators

Exercise participants were asked to complete surveys at the end of each shift to assess their own levels of workload and to identify issues faced. Furthermore, interviews with operators conducted during lull periods were useful in eliciting deeper understanding of operator activities and issues related to dynamic targeting. The information received allowed the dynamic targeting process to be decomposed into its component tasks, provided average durations, identified actors in each task and estimated the probability values for each conditional branch in the network of tasks. The operators were also asked to rate their workload according to the VACP scale. The knowledge gained through this approach is invaluable and helps to supplement the observed notes because of our inability to remain cognisant of all activities concurrently being undertaken by operators in the dynamic targeting process, particularly when represented by a single observer.

5. Illustrating model development

The dynamic targeting process is modelled herein with publicly available information using the operator configuration described in Section 2.2 with each role filled by a single operator. The process model was generated by capturing the work performed by the operators according to the F2T2EA process (Department of Air Force, 2005; Case *et al.*, 2006).

Simulation of the actual dynamic targeting sequence allows identification of possible bottlenecks in the process. To illustrate the modelling process, the model was populated with fictitious timing and probability to generate simulation results in this chapter that illustrate the concept.
An important part of constructing a process model involves encoding the functions of the workflow as a network of multiple tasks performed by different processing entities (people or machines). During simulation, execution of the process model is controlled by a flow of tokens. A fragment of the process model is illustrated in Fig. 5 and the corresponding sequence of events is as follows (Case et al., 2006):

1. ... CCO or SODO approves tasking order
2. Tasking order (15-line text message) is drafted by C2DO and transmitted by ground track coordinator (GTC) via Link-16 or voice to airborne weapons controller, e.g., Airborne Warning and Control System (AWACS)
3. AWACS acknowledges receipt and passes information to weapon platform which either accepts or rejects tasking
4. Acknowledgement is provided to the C2DO with the estimated time-over-target (TOT) from the weapon platform
5. Target is prosecuted

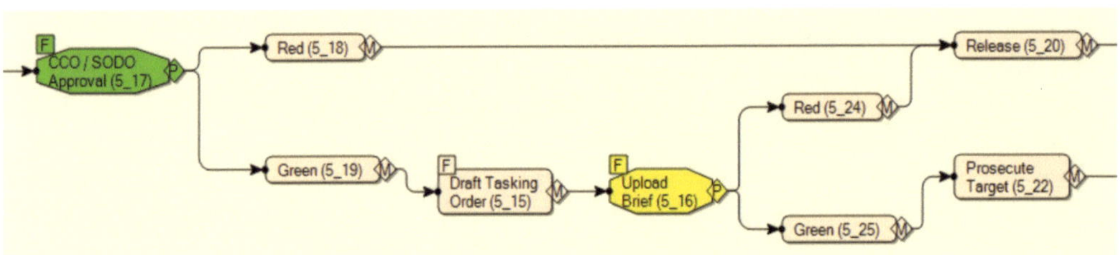

Fig. 5. A fragment of the dynamic targeting process model in C3TRACE.

C3TRACE allows modelling of operators and assignment of operators to tasks. If the required operators become unavailable, tokens queue for service and the corresponding tasks will be delayed. Hence, tasks 5_17, 5_15 and 5_16 in Fig. 5 are each configured with a simple First In, First Out (FIFO) queue (as denoted by the symbol F). The transition to multiple decision outcomes (such as Green denoting success and Red representing failure) are modelled using probabilistic branching (as indicated by the symbol P) and handled appropriately. Task 5_22 captures the inherent delay in the target engagement by the chosen weapons system.

5.1 Analysis of the dynamic targeting model

To study process throughput, the dynamic targeting model was subjected to various rates of emerging TSTs so that the process was stressed beyond its normal operating conditions. Each simulation run involved initiating the F2T2EA process using 25 tokens over a range of different rates of occurrence, from a low rate of emerging TSTs sensed 90 minutes apart to a high rate of targets sensed 5 minutes apart. Results were obtained by averaging ten independent runs with each rate and the resultant task timeline was analysed according to the output rate of the process.
Fig. 6 shows the throughput performance in terms of the ratio of output to input rates against a range of initiation rates. An output rate that equals the input rate indicates the

process is working within its limitations. A lower output rate than the input rate shows that the dynamic targeting process is stressed and building up backlogs. For the data employed for this study, the results indicate that the dynamic targeting process works efficiently when the rate of initiation is slower than one TST every 30 minutes. Pushing the process any faster simply results in a backlog of outstanding tasks that cause the delayed prosecution of TSTs. This defeats the purpose of dynamic targeting because the process is designed to enable an immediate targeting response.

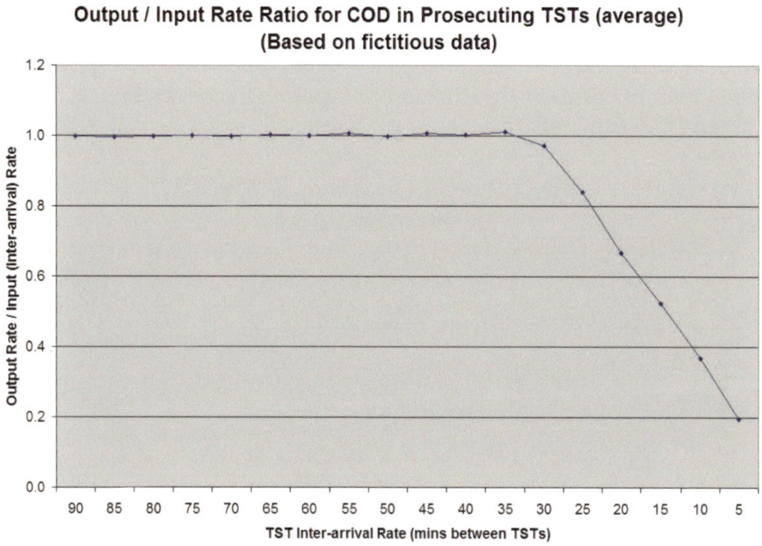

Fig. 6. Performance of the dynamic targeting process over a range of input rates.

Fig. 7 plots the utilisation of operators in prosecuting TST requests arriving 30 minutes apart. This is the maximum capacity at which the process can manage to respond to

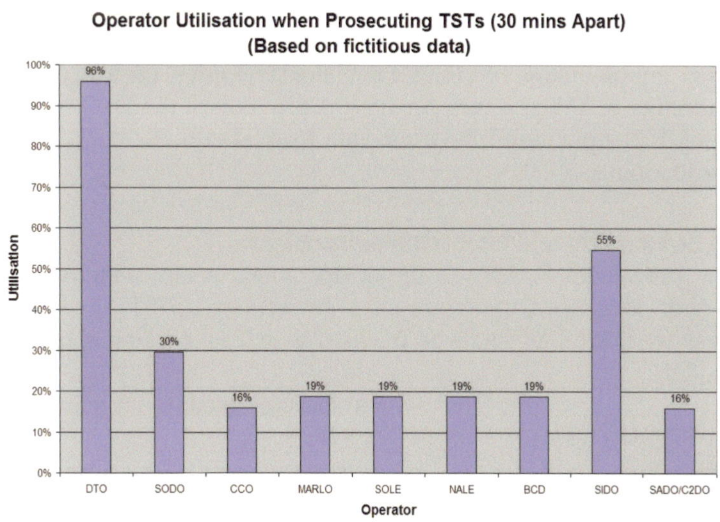

Fig. 7. Operator utilisation when prosecuting TSTs spaced 30 minutes apart.

incoming requests immediately. Note that the graph only plots the utilisation of operators undertaking the dynamic targeting process and does not account for their routine work during the execution phase of the air tasking cycle. Clearly the DTO is highly utilised in the dynamic targeting process at the indicated input rate. The SIDO is another operator who is substantially utilised in the prosecution of TSTs.

To investigate potential process bottlenecks, we present in Fig. 8 utilisation of the DTO over a range of input rates in prosecuting TSTs. This reveals that utilisation of the DTO is highly correlated with the input rate of TST requests. The maximum DTO utilisation is reached when the input rate reaches one TST every 30 minutes and 100% utilisation is maintained at higher input rates at the expense of prolonged process time. This knee point corresponds to the input rate that maximises the throughput performance in Fig. 6. This correlation indicates that the DTO is the likely cause of the bottleneck in process performance.

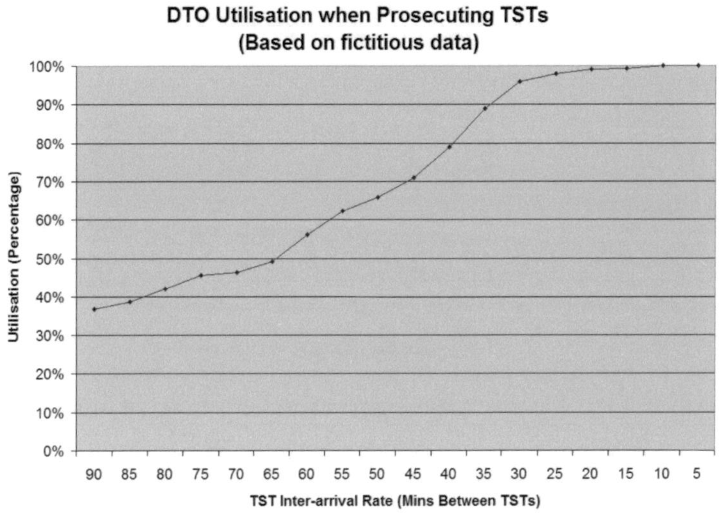

Fig. 8. Utilisation of the DTO over a range of input rates for the prosecution of TSTs.

Fig. 9 is another representation of utilisation of the DTO using the TST inter-arrival rate in terms of the number of TST requests per hour. Utilisation of the DTO is highly correlated with the rate of TST inputs until the input rate reaches two TSTs per hour, i.e., one TST arriving every 30 minutes.

5.2 Relieving bottlenecks and improving performance

The increasing prevalence of TSTs in recent operations necessitates improvement in the performance of the dynamic targeting process. Prosecution of TSTs involves a race against the clock. Some avenues that might be pursued to relieve existing shortfalls of dynamic targeting include:

- Additional human resources (augmentees) to assist dynamic targeting when the rate of emerging TSTs increases
- Specialised training to ensure that operators are able to meet performance targets
- Appropriate training to produce multi-skilled operators who are capable of taking on different roles to help balance workloads in overstressed situations

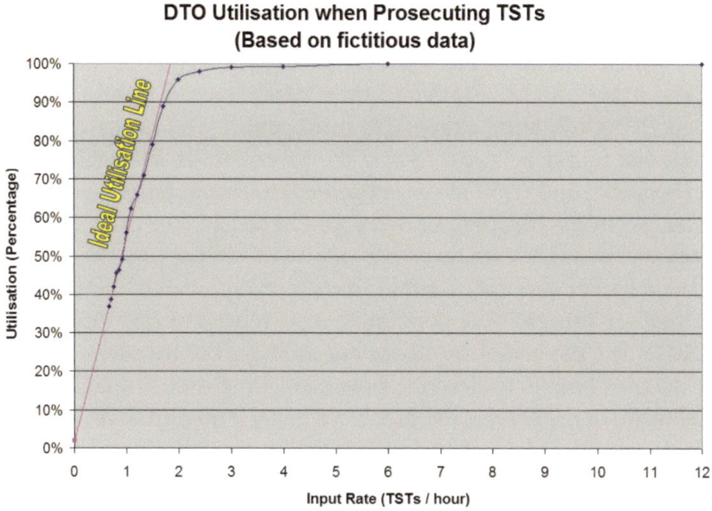

Fig. 9. Ideal utilisation range of the DTO when prosecuting TSTs.

- Use of technology to facilitate human operations
- Simplifying the dynamic targeting process to enable faster decision making

As the DTO is highly utilised in the dynamic targeting process, forming a dynamic targeting cell (DTC) with a team of multiple operators performing the functions of the overworked DTO can relieve any bottlenecks here (Department of Air Force, 2005). The decision of when to use augmentees is mainly based on anecdotal evidence resulting from observations and feedback during exercises.

6. Conclusion and future work

Although C2 is a critical component of military forces, C2 systems are complex and may exhibit unpredictable behaviour. Even with clearly established goals and defined limitations, it is not straightforward to provide coordinated engagement reliably in an efficient manner. Dynamic targeting is an important C2 process in the AOC because it is used to rapidly engage high value time-sensitive targets. This process is subject to a highly dynamic environment due to differences and variations in such variables as:

- The target to prosecute
- Battlespace conditions
- Red force capability
- Operator workloads in an AOC
- Outcomes of decision making
- Order and timing for tasks undertaken

Prosecuting time-sensitive targets is inherently difficult and complex because the process involves choosing among geographically distributed assets and personnel. The need to coordinate actions throughout a theatre of combat is constantly in tension with the need to prosecute quickly and efficiently.

In this chapter we report studies of dynamic targeting in an AOC by capturing the social interactions involved in the process and using C3TRACE as a simulation and analysis tool.

An advantage of C3TRACE is that it allows for limitations of human operators in developing executable process models. Our model has incorporated the human aspect in the work process because humans are central to C2 in terms of decision making and collaboration. The initial model was based on a baseline configuration in which only one DTO is involved in coordinating every TST prosecution. The limits of dynamic targeting with this model were found by stress testing the process over a range of rates of initiation. Stressing the process beyond its inherent capacity results in a failure to prosecute targets in a timely manner. A study of operator workload revealed the cause of the performance bottlenecks correlates strongly with an overworked DTO in the process.

The model in this chapter was constructed from publicly available information describing the dynamic targeting process and populated with representative but fictitious data and probabilities. Therefore, the actual results of our analysis are for illustrative purposes only. In this respect the aim here is to describe how modelling and simulation using C3TRACE can reveal insights about organisational processes using a quantitative approach. The results generated provide confidence in applying C3TRACE modelling and simulation to assess potential AOC refinements before committing to actual process evaluations on the operations floor.

Related, but necessarily classified work, has extended to the analysis of data captured from observing real processes in an AOC. We plan human-in-the-loop experimentation to evaluate the effectiveness of different options for overcoming issues identified through such analysis. The environment described by Case *et al.* (2006) provides a reference for establishing our own instrumented facility. In particular, we are keen to employ this environment to assess how augmentees can be tasked to overcome the throughput limitations of the process and to determine whether changes to the workflow can improve timeliness. We expect that video and audio capture will supplement manually observed data and help to further reduce the risk of missing important events.

7. References

Air Land Sea Application Center (2001). *Multiservice Procedures for Joint Air Operations Center (JAOC) and Army Air and Missile Defense Command (AAMDC) Coordination*, FM 3-01.20, Air Land Sea Application Center, Department of Defense, Washington, USA.

Aslaksen, E. & Belcher, R. (1992). *Systems Engineering*, Prentice Hall, Sydney.

Bakken, B. T.; Gilljam, M. & Haerem, T. (2004). Perception and Handling of Complex Problems in Dynamic Settings - Three Cases of Relevance to Military Command and Crisis Management, *Proceedings of the International System Dynamics Conference*, Oxford, England, July 2004, System Dynamics Society.

Batagelj, V. & Mrvar, A. (2003). Pajek - Analysis and Visualization of Large Networks, In *Graph Drawing Software*, Jünger, M. & Mutzel, P. (Ed.), Springer, Berlin.

Bierbaum, C. R.; Szabo, S. M. & Aldrich, T. B. (1987). *A Comprehensive Task Analysis of the UH-60 Mission with Crew Workload Estimates and Preliminary Decision Rules for Developing a UH-60 Workload Prediction Model*, Anacapa Sciences, Fort Rucker, USA, Technical report: ASI690-302-87.

Brehmer, B. (2005). The Dynamic OODA Loop: Amalgamating Boyd's OODA Loop and the Cybernetic Approach to Command and Control, *Proceedings of the International Command and Control Research and Technology Symposium*, McLean, USA, June 2005, CCRP.

Case, F. T.; Koterba, N.; Conrad, G. & Ockerman, J. (2006). An Instrumentation Capability for Dynamic Targeting, *Proceedings of the Command and Control Research and Technology Symposium*, San Diego, USA, June 2006, CCRP.

Deitz, P. H. (2006). Social Networks and Network Structures, *Presented in the Army Science Conference*, Orlando, USA, November 2006, ASC.

Department of Air Force (2005). *Operational Procedures - Air and Space Operations Center*, Department of Air Force, Department of Defense, Washington, USA.

Department of Defence (2006). *Exercise Pitch Black 06*, Department of Defence, viewed September 2009, <http://www.defence.gov.au/pitchblack06/background.htm>.

Department of the Navy (1996). *Command and Control, MCDP 6*, Headquarters United States Marine Corps, Washington, USA.

Hannon, B. & Ruth, M. (1994). *Dynamic Modeling*, Springer-Verlag, New York.

Hazlegrove, A. P. (2000). Desert Storm Time-Sensitive Surface Targeting: A Successful Failure or a Failed Success? *Defense and Security Analysis*, Vol. 16(2), pp. 113–149.

Hinen, A. L. (2002). Kosovo: "The Limits of Air Power II. *Air & Space Power Journal*.

Hlupic, V. & Robinson, S. (1998). Business Process Modelling and Analysis using Discrete-Event Simulation, *Proceedings of the Winter Simulation Conference*, Washington DC, USA, pp. 1363–1369, December 1998, ACM.

Hutchins, S. G.; Schacher, G. E.; Dailey, J.; Looney, J. P.; Saylor, S. E.; Jensen, J. J. & Osmundson, J. S. (2005). Modeling and Simulation Support for the Standing Joint Force Headquarters Concept, *Proceedings of the International Command and Control Research and Technology Symposium*, McLean, USA, June 2005, CCRP.

Joint Warfighting Center (2002). *Commander's Handbook for Joint Time-Sensitive Targeting*, Joint Warfighting Center, US Joint Forces Command, Suffolk, USA.

Kalloniatis, A. C.; Macleod, I. D. G. & La, P. (2009). Process versus Battle-Rhythm: Modelling Operational Command and Control, *Proceedings of the World IMACS / MODSIM09 International Congress*, Cairns, Australia, pp. 1622–1628, July 2009, MSSANZ & IAMCS.

Kalloniatis, A. C. & Wong, P. (2007). Application of Business Process Modelling to Military Organisations, *Proceedings of the SimTect Conference*, Brisbane, Australia, June 2007, SIAA.

Kamada, T. & Kawai, S. (1989). An Algorithm for Drawing General Undirected Graphs. *Information Processing Letters*, Vol. 31(1), pp. 7–15.

Keller, J. (2002). Human Performance Modeling for Discrete-Event Simulation: Workload, *Proceedings of the Winter Simulation Conference*, San Diego, USA, pp. 157–162, December 2002, ACM.

Kilduff, P. W.; Swoboda, J. C. & Barnette, D. B. (2005). *Command, Control, and Communications: Techniques for the Reliable Assessment of Concept Execution (C3TRACE) Modeling Environment: The Tool*, Army Research Laboratory, Aberdeen Proving Ground, USA, Technical report: ARL-MR-0617.

Kilduff, P. W.; Swoboda, J. C. & Katz, J. (2006). *A Platoon-Level Model of Communication Flow and the Effects on Operator Performance*, Army Research Laboratory, Aberdeen Proving Ground, USA, Technical report: ARL-MR-0656.

Krahl, D. (2003). Extend: An Interactive Simulation Tool, *Proceedings of the Winter Simulation Conference*, New Orleans, USA, pp. 188–196, December 2003, ACM.

Law, A. M. & Kelton, W. D. (1991). *Simulation Modeling and Analysis*, second edition McGraw-Hill, New York.

Lo, E. H. S. & Au, T. A. (2007). Modelling of Dynamic Targeting in the Air Operations Centre, *Proceedings of the Conference on Microelectronics, MEMS and Nanotechnology*, Canberra, Australia, December 2007, SPIE.

Lo, E. H. S.; Au, T. A.; Hoek, P. J. & La, P. D. (2009). Analysis of Team Interactions in Dynamic Targeting, *Proceedings of the SimTect Conference*, Adelaide, Australia, June 2009, SIAA.

Molan, J. (2008). *Running the War in Iraq*, Harper Collins, Sydney.

Newman, A.; Sokoly, S.; Kennedy, K.; Knight, B.; Sadorra, O.; Baker, M.; Brown, I.; Bemmerzouk, S.; Ernest, K.; Leonard, R. & Sullivan, W. J. (2005). Time Sensitive / Dynamic Targeting Analysis: Techniques and Results, *Proceedings of the International Command and Control Research and Technology Symposium*, McLean, USA, April 2005, CCRP.

Royal Australian Air Force (2008). *The Air Power Manual*, Air Power Development Centre, Canberra, Australia.

Stanton, N. A.; Baber, C. & Harris, D. (2008). *Modelling Command and Control: Event Analysis of Systemic Teamwork*, Ashgate, Hampshire, England.

US Air Force (2006). *Targeting - Air Force Doctrine Document 2-1.9*, Air Force Doctrine Center, Maxwell Air Force Base, USA.

Wilcox, R. (2005). A Systems Engineering Approach to Metrics Identification for Command and Control, *Proceedings of the International Command and Control Research and Technology Symposium*, McLean, USA, June 2005, CCRP.

6

Investment in Container Ships for the Yangtze River: A System Dynamics Model

Yan Jin
School of transportation, Wuhan University of Technology, Wuhan, Hubei, 430063, China

1. Introduction

The Yangtze River, especially the Three-Gorge Reservoir, is becoming an important container transport route in the region of western China and some new container terminals have been built or are being planned or under construction (Fig.1). As the volume of the container goods grows, the trading of container ships in the area is likely to increase considerably.

But the special hydrographical condition raises a number of questions concerning the quality and operational suitability of existing container ships at present. Seasonal varying depth and water speed at different voyage passages in the Yangtze River and Three-Gorge Reservoir disturb the container ship sailing. As a consequence, traditional types of container ships serve without economic benefit. But the booming transport demand of containerized goods on the Yangtze River, especially in upstream and middle part, needs suitable and profitable container ships urgently. So the most important task is to invest in capacity of container ships to cope with the growing demand.

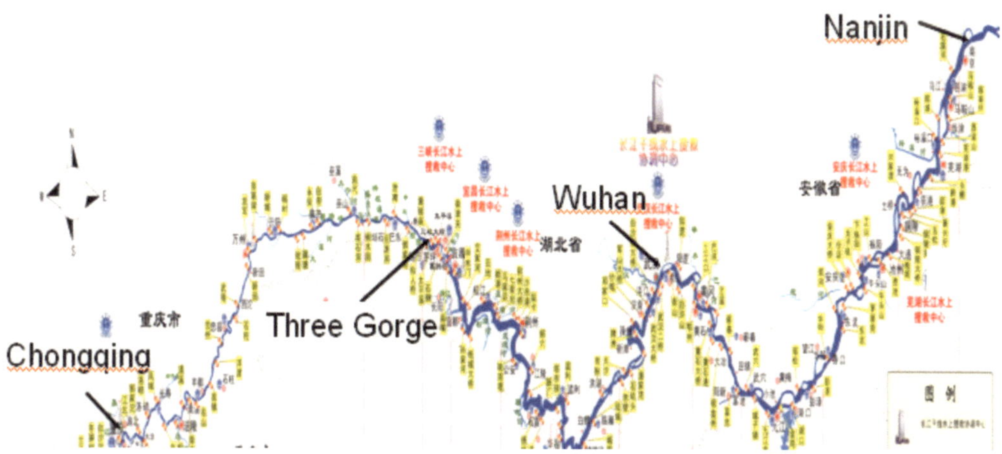

Fig. 1. Location of the main terminals in the Yangtze River
(Source: Jiangsu Marine Safety Administration)

Shipping is a capital-intensive industry with a history of sudden freight market booms and collapses. Estimating future transport demand and the ensuing adjustment of container ship supply has proved to be extremely difficult (Tvedt, 2003). Depending on the available shipyard capacity, shipbuilding is a long process, taking usually two to three years. So investment decisions are made while freight rates and market demand are sprouting, but new capacity enters the market with a substantial time lag, possibly when both demand and prices are weak (Stopford, 2002). The fact that container ships tend to be expensive and nobody can make investment decisions easily, especially for ship owners who are willing to take their share of the growing container market in Yangtze River. A system dynamics method will be introduced in this paper to simulate the pattern of the container ships growing after making investment decision.

This paper is structured as follows. In the following two sections, system dynamics approach in shipping market is introduced through literature review and general introduction of the system dynamics theory. Then the complicated condition of the Yangtze River and the Three-Gorge Reservoir is presented in detail. In the system-dynamics simulation section, existing date on the container terminal capacity, number of vessel fleet and delay in new building of container ships are used to analyze the development of new types of container ships. In the last part the simulation results are analyzed which suggest that the change of river depth will affect the timing and duration of the development.

2. Shipping market

In general, the mechanism behind market cycles is very simple. According to Stopford (2000, pp.44), a shipping market cycle is a coordinator between supply and demand. The supply and demand model of economics is often used as a tool for analyzing market cycles. Most of the maritime economists accept that the shipping market is driven by a competitive process in which demand and supply determine the freight rate. On the demand side, the most important factor behind a shipping cycle is the business cycle of the world economy. Booming world economy increases the demand for transportation and, when the economy goes into recession, the world trade usually drops and the goods transportation eventually is reduced. Another class of factors influencing demand is sudden economic shocks like the oil crisis and wars. These events are unpredictable by nature, but still very important (Stopford, 2002).

The main cause of cyclicality in the supply side is the new shipbuilding cycle. Depending on the state of the shipbuilding market, the time lag between ordering a vessel and the delivery of it may range from one up to 3 or even 4 years. In the extreme shipyard market conditions of the 1970s, delivery times of 4-5 years were common (Stopford, 2002). Zannetos (1966) and Serghiou (1982) argue that ship-owners commonly overestimate economic opportunities when freight rates are rising, and order too many ships with a lag of about 6 months from the freight rate peak. That long delivery time implies that an unexpected upward jump in demand may leave freight rates high for some time until yards are able to deliver a sufficiently large number of new vessels. So the rate of investment in new tonnage is in most shipping markets volatile (Tvedt, 2003).

There has been a growing literature on asset valuation in the maritime industry that, inspired by the general finance literature, use continuous time price processes as a basis for deriving valuation models now (Tvedt, 2003). The earliest attempts at modeling were made by Tinbergen (1932), Koopmans (1939), Eriksen and Norman (1976), Charemza and Gronicki (1981), and Strandenes and Wergeland (2002). After Lucas's (1976) critique, rational expectations models that derive aggregate macroeconomic equations from the micro behavior of rational agents have become the standard. Also influential in the field, Beenstock and Vergottis (1993) employed the modern developments in dynamic macroeconomics and econometric theory to develop their econometric model of world shipping. Besides the inability of most structural models to outperform statistical models, economists have been suspicious of "black-box" type methodologies that do not take into account the ability of agents to learn rationally and adapt their optimal policies dynamically (Dikos, 2005).

The use of system dynamic models has not been common practice in the field of maritime economics, and especially in problems related to container shipping. The reasons for avoiding this approach may only be guessed, but, as Veenstra and Ludema (2003) argue, there are other commonly established research approaches, mostly based on econometric methods. In the beginning of the 1970s, Coyle (1977) conducted a study using system dynamics in order to analyze the design of an integrated oil supply system. The study was carried out for a major oil company, which already had effective processes for managing shipping operations. Dikos et al (2006) design a system-dynamics model for Niver Lines. The study was based on the situation prevailing in the oil industry at that time, which most of the oil company's required tanker capacity was controlled either by direct ownership or long time-charter contracts, while spot charters were only used to fill the gaps in seasonal demand. In all the models demand is decided by the world economy which is the big system.

This paper tempts to research the ship industry from a new point of the development of the terminal. As we know, the expansion of a terminal's capacity should be suitable for the growing of the goods, which means that we can use the expansion of the terminal's capacity to substitute the exogenous demand's change roughly. The substitution is reasonable when making research in the container transportation in the Yangtze, for the transportation is booming from now on.

3. System-dynamics approach

A system is a number of components integrated into a complex entity, and system analysis simply means the consideration of the entity rather than the separate consideration of individual components. The systems approach can be defined as an organized, efficient procedure for representing, analyzing and planning complex systems. It is a comprehensive, problem-solving methodology that involves two main steps: the rational and creative structuring of both quantitative and qualitative knowledge, mainly in the form of models, to represent problems; and the development of analytical techniques through which the problem can be analyzed and solved. System dynamics, a member of the family of systems approaches, provides a systematic framework for modeling and understanding a number of transport issues (Khaled *et al*, 1994).

In theory, the system-dynamics approach is a structural system with an architecture that incorporates cause and causality relations and provides a user-friendly interface for conducting sensitivity analyses. Furthermore, it does not require external calculations and allows users to incorporate their assessments on several external variables and fundamental relationships. Finally, it provides a framework for including feedback loops and nonlinear effects (Dikos *et al*, 2006).

From a manager's point of view, we tried to design a model that would contribute to the implementation of managerial practices in reality. System-dynamics modeling has the advantage of allowing the users to model the direct impact of changes in the market and dealing with the nonlinear problem with the feedback loops easily. System-dynamics problems suggest how the environment can act upon the system and contain feedback loops. In feedback situations, X affects Y, and Y in turn affects X, perhaps through a chain of causes and effects. One can not study the link between X and Y and, independently, the link between Y and X and predict how the system will behave. Only the study of the whole system as a feedback system will lead to correct results. Feedbacks are of two kinds (Sterman, 2000):

1. Self-reinforcing or positive feedback (Fig.2(a)), such as stock-market bubbles, compound interest, or breeding rabbits, accelerates growth or accelerates to a collapse.
2. Goal-seeking or negative feedback (Fig.2(b)), in which discrepancy induces corrective action to return the system to a target state or a long-term equilibrium.

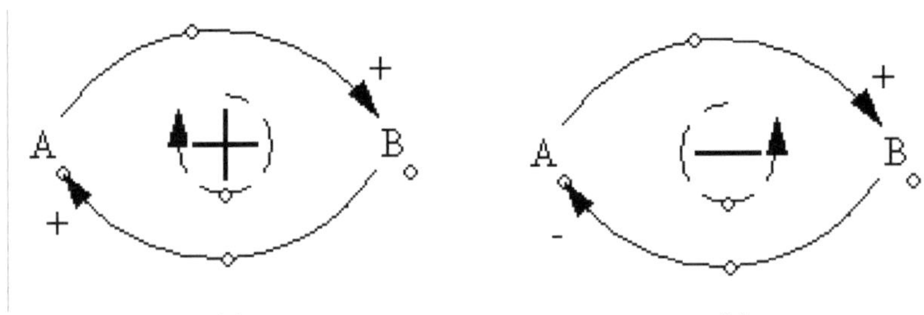

Fig. 2. (a) positive feedback (b) negative feedback

System-dynamics methods improve our understanding of the relationship between cause and effect and of the counterintuitive effects of delays and feedbacks. An industrial system is a complex multiple-loop interconnected system (basic loop as Fig.3) (Forrester, 1992). Decisions are made at multiple points throughout a system. Each resulting action generates information that may be used at several but not at all decision points. Feedback loops form the central structures that control change in all systems (Richardson, 1991). Likewise, feedback loops are the organizing structure around which system dynamics models are constructed.

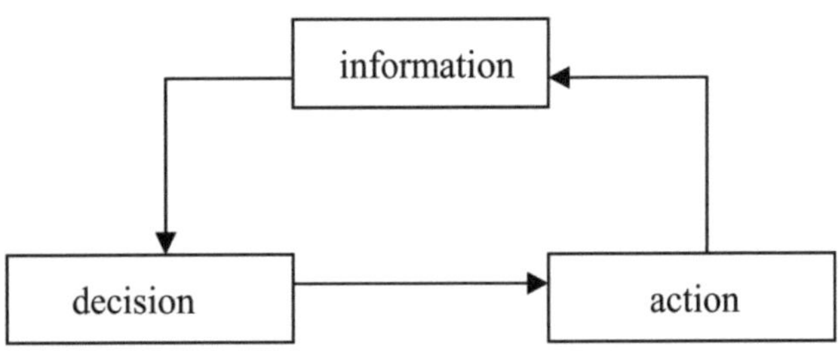

Fig. 3. Basic decision and information feedback
(Source: Forrester, 1992)

System dynamics provide a qualitative and quantitative environment for modeling complex decision-making environments. I try to use system dynamics depending on my ability to design a changeable-draft container shipment from Chongqing Terminal with some loops, feedbacks, and decisions for analyzing the shipping investment.

4. Containerized transport market of the Yangtze

4.1 The development of containerized transport market of the Yangtze

In the eighties of the 20th century, 17 domestic-trade container courses opened in China concentrated on the coastal course and range of the Yangtze-Jiangsu Province Section course mainly. The transported amount of containers by the waterway and port throughput increases progressively at the average speed of 5% every year. From the Transportation Annual Bulletin in China 2004, the waterway container port throughput of our country finished 9.5 ten thousand TEU in 1985, the goods weighed 26 ten thousand tons, among them there are only 5.5 ten thousand TEU in the water way carrier of the Yangtze. In 1990, the waterway container port throughput of our country finished 7.3 ten thousand TEU, the goods weighed 20 ten thousand tons, among them the waterway delivery container traffic volume of the Yangtze accounts for 4.8 ten thousand TEU. By 1995, with the high-speed development of national economy, the domestic coastal container market increases fast, having driven the development of waterway containerized transport of the Yangtze too, the waterway container port throughput of the Yangtze River finishes 16 ten thousand TEU, the goods weigh 51 ten thousand tons. Since entering 21st century, as fast development of the regional economy of the Yangtze River Delta and our country implement the develop-the-west strategy, the waterway containerized transport of the Yangtze River has entered fast developing period. In 2003, the whole throughput of port container in the Yangtze River has already been up to 140 ten thousand TEU (Table 1).

year	1985	1990	1995	2003
Inboard-trade containers by Water in China	9.5	7.3	20	400
Containers by the Yangtze	5.5	4.8	16	140

Source: http://www.chineseshipping.com.cn/statdata

Table 1. Containers transported in the Yangtze(ten thousands TEU)

From 1985 to 1990, the container demand was very low and most of them were abroad. At that time, terminals along the Yangtze were not suitable for handling containerized goods and no larger container vessels in the Yangtze can be chosen. If there were the inland containerized goods, the goods owners had to use the barges and pushers to transport them to Shanghai , which would take a lot of time. So most of owners preferred to transporting their goods to Hong Kong or Guangzhou by train and by this way the traffic cost was lower than to Shanghai. After 1995, the economy in Shanghai and Yangtze River Delta developed quickly. The government gave a great support for the construction of the Shanghai terminal and more and more foreign ship lines opened container courses. Then the container transportation in China increase quickly.

Container transportation in upstream part of the Yangtze River is a new focus in inland transportation of China, and China plans to boost shipping along the Yangtze River as a way to develop its western hinterland. On April 12, in Shanghai, the Yangtze Business Network 2007 is the first such event to lure investors to develop terminals long the so-called "Golden Waterway", which stretches 6,300 kilometers through seven provinces and the municipalities of Shanghai and Chongqing. So the container terminal of Chongqing plays an important role in the development of container transportation of the Yangtze River. According to the report of Shipping trade community 2004, Chongqing terminal has finished 92 thousand TEU in 2003, and it is estimated that its capacity will reach 700 thousand TEU in 2010 (Liu, 2005).

4.2 The hydrographical condition of the Yangtze

With the development of the economy in the middle and western part of China, more and more goods must be transported to the eastern China and to abroad from Chongqing terminal. But the original natural environment of the River, especially upstream part with a lot of riffles and low depth of water, is not suitable for bigger vessels to sail. According to the newly hydrographical investigation of the Yangtze River by CCS in 2004, the depth along the upstream part is different at different voyage passage because after the construction of Three-Gorge Dam, the water reserved in the reservoir can affect the depth and speed of the whole upstream part water remarkably. In general, we can divide the whole river into four ranges named natural part above dam, reservoir, between dams (Three-Gorge Dam and Ge-Zhou Dam), and natural part below dam. Meanwhile, the whole serving year can be divided into three periods named low, middle and high because the season will also affect the hydrographical condition such as depth and speed of fluid (Table 2-5). So once the vessel sail across the Three-Gorge, operation and design of the vessel must take the complicated environment mentioned above into consideration firstly. In the paper the container ship will sail from Changqing to Nanjin (distance: 1887km), through the Three-Gorge.

period	low	middle	high
days	90	65	210
depth	<2.6	2.6~3.5	>3.5

Table 2. speed and depth of parts in three periods (depth: m)

period	low			
part	above	reservoir	between	below
speed	0.608	0.608	1.215	3.232
distance	0	490	38	1359

Table 3. speed and distance of parts in low period (speed of fluid: km/h, distance: km)

period	middle			
part	above	reservoir	between	below
speed	5.12	2.097	4.193	4.405
distance	0	490	38	1359

Table 4. speed and distance of parts in middle period (speed of fluid: km/h, distance: km)

period	high			
part	above	reservoir	between	below
speed	7.64	3.736	7.471	5.836
distance	195	295	38	1359

note: "above" refers to natural part above dam; "between" refers to between two dams; "below" refers to natural part below dam.
Source: Report of hydrographical condition of the Yangtze River by CCS in 2004

Table 5. speed and distance of parts in high period (speed of fluid: km/h, distance: km)

5. Model of the changeable-draft container ship from Chongqing container terminal

Due to several general factors such as investment decisions and delayed production as well as case-specific reasons such as varying depth, ranges and not enough container ships available, new container ships should be built which could change the draft according to the varying depth of the fluid, because this kind of vessels could make good use of the water depth to transport the goods as much as possible. The key question is that the days of each period are not fixed because the hydrographical conditions change every year. If the low period lasts for a long time, ship should reduce the TEU every trip and the whole throughput of the terminal will be less. This will affect the traffic volume of the whole year, which will make the freight rate vary in the market and change the investment decision of the ship-owners. In the paper a system dynamics model concerning of the issue of the new building of changeable-draft container ships has been designed which links future container shipment to the new capacity-enlargement decisions.

As a start point in the simulation, the total transportation capacity is based on the data mentioned above (92 thousand TEU at the Chongqing terminal in 2003), when there are 9 container ships whose capacity is 144TEU available (Liu, 2005). Assuming the trade is transporting containers from Chongqing to Nanjing (Fig.1), these 9 ships would have a combined container capacity of 38 thousand TEU per month in general, which can have 30 roundtrip voyages in a month. During the low depth period, the ship should load less TEU, and during the high depth period, it should load more. Since it is a complex issues and subject to many reality operation things, but for modeling purposes it is assumed that varying days of the different period will increase the total transport volume to 82 thousand TEU per month[1].

The days that low period and high period last for have a great effect on the container ship capacity named total available container ship capacity in Fig.4. When the varying depth is taken into account, the total container ship capacity will be limited, but there still is a limitation of the increase of ship capacity. The maximum of the total container ship capacity will be equal to the design capacity of Chongqing terminal in the future.

---

[1] In the research paper of standard type vessels in the Yangtze River and Three-Gorge Reservoir by Wuhan University of Technology, 2004, if the low period lasts for 3 months at the depth of 2.6m and the high period lasts for 7 months at the depth of 3.5m, the total transportation volume of the whole year is equal to 2.2 times volume of the ship serves at 3m depth for 12 months.

Since the container ship in the market at present can not fulfill the container transportation demand, new ships must be built. As we know, shipbuilding needs a few years before newly constructed capacity is delivered into the market. In the simulation 2 years delay is adopted for although 2 years may be overoptimistic in today's shipbuilding market, but it is adequate for modeling purposes which is mainly to analyze the characteristics of a system in which pattern of increase container ship capacity goes. In the model, the initial capacity of Chongqing terminal is set to 92 thousand TEU per year, which is the terminal's true capacity when it was taken into operation in 2003 (Liu, 2005). From the programming of the Ministry Communications of China, the total capacity of Chongqing container terminal will reach 700 thousand TEU per year in 2010 (Liu, 2005). So the terminal capacity expands in steps of 21 thousand TEU and 40 thousand TEU per year after 5 years and 3 years from the beginning of operations in 2003[2]. Then the final capacity of the terminal is 702 thousand TEU per year in the model, which is assumed to last for 5 years.

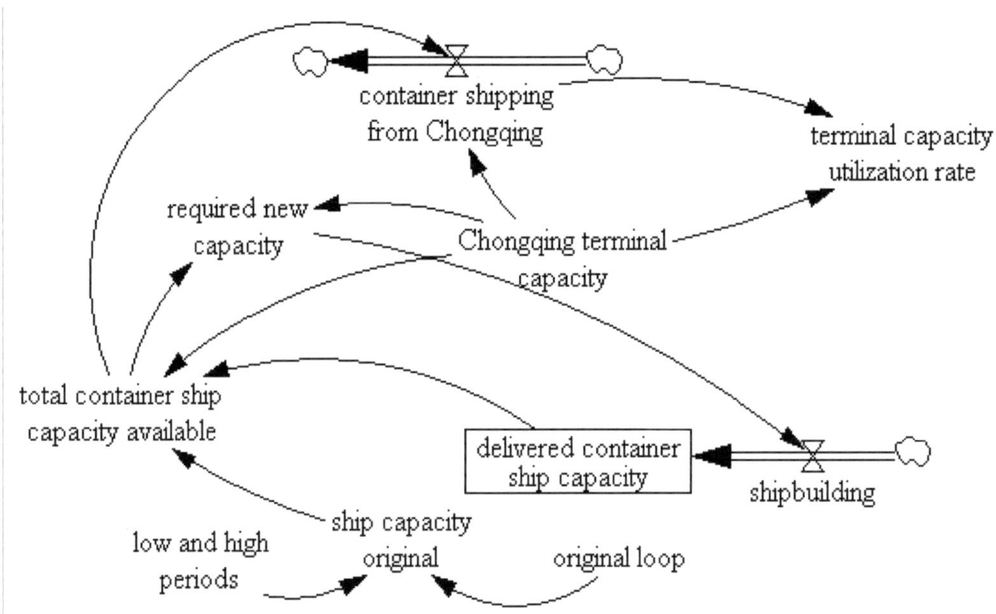

Fig. 4. System dynamics model for the container shipment of the Chongqing terminal

The equations used in the simulation model as follows:

(01) Delivered container ship capacity = INTEG(shipbuilding,0)
Units: Ten thousand TEU per year

(02) Final Time = 50
Units: Year

(03) Ship capacity original = Original loop (low and high periods)
Units: Dmnl

(04) Initial Time = 0
Units: Year

---

[2] Website of the Ministry Communications of China: http://www.moc.gov.cn/

(05) Container shipping from Chongqing = IF THEN ELSE(Chongqing terminal capacity>total container ship capacity available, total container ship capacity available, Chongqing terminal capacity)
Units: Ten thousand TEU per year
(06) Chongqing terminal capacity = 9.2+step(21,5)+step(40,2)
Units: Ten thousand TEU per year
(07) Required new capacity = Chongqing terminal capacity-total container ship capacity available
Units: Ten thousand TEU per year
(08) Shipbuilding = DELAY FIXED(required new capacity, 2, 0)
Units: Ten thousand TEU per year
(09) Terminal capacity utilization rate = container shipping from Chongqing/Chongqing terminal capacity
Units: percent
(10) SAVEPER = TIME STEP
Units: Year [0,?]
The frequency with which output is stored
(11) TIME STEP = 1
Units: Year [0,?]
The time step for the simulation
(12) Total available container ship capacity = IF THEN ELSE (ship capacity original*8.2/9*12+delivered container ship capacity>Chongqing terminal capacity, Chongqing terminal capacity, ship capacity original*8.2/9*12+delivered container ship capacity)
Units: Ten thousand TEU per year
(13) Low and high periods = 1,3,5,7,11
Units: month

The model assumes that the total volume of containers to be shipped from the Chongqing terminal cannot exceed the capacity of the terminal and the terminal capacity utilization rate is the ratio of the actual volume of container shipping from Chongqing terminal and the existing export capacity of the terminal, which can show the effect of the terminal actual operation and whether the existing capacity is suitable for the demand expansion.

6. Result analyses

The simulation runs under the five kinds of distribution in the days of the low period and high period condition. That is the low period will last for 1 month, 3 months, 5 months, 7 months and 11 months, and the high period will last for 11 months, 7 months, 5 months, 3 months and 1 month corresponding, for the total of the low and high period should be 10 months and the middle period lasts for 2 months in general. In the simulation the whole time is set to 50 years in order to make the patterns' tendency more visible using 25 years on the *x*-axis and the results are in Fig.5-7.

From Fig.5, it is obvious that the container ship capacity needed exactly follows the increase of the Chongqing terminal capacity, no matter what the distribution of the low and high period is. The supply of the container ship capacity should increase infinitely theoretically for all suitable-sized vessels in China may be used in the container trade, but the model is designed from the terminal points of view, so there is the limitation which the maximum of the ship capacity expansion is the final design capacity of the terminal in the model. Nearly in all the scenarios it takes about seven years before the capacity of vessels reaches the terminal's final capacity under the developing speed of the construction of the terminal. In all the scenarios except 1 month low, the new building delay forces the capacity to overshoot the goal level before corrective measures are taken in Fig.4. At this time the freight rate surely is at the peak and will go downward later. The high level of deliveries of the ship also is the trigger for increased deliveries and the ship-owner should consider carefully when he wants to invest at this moment.

The relationship between different ratio of the low and high periods and the deficits in available vessel capacity ultimately gives the push of ship building. In the case of 1 month low, the depth maintain the high level nearly the whole year, the existing vessels could hold as more containers as possible, so the new building demand of the container ships is lower than other scenarios. Oppositely, the incentive for new building construction is the high freight rates caused by capacity deficits because of the insufficient supply of the container ships.

The number of container ships to be constructed can be obtained from the simulated new container ship building pattern in Fig.6. With the real capacity of 82 thousand TEU 9 ships per month, a simulated new-built capacity of 47 ten thousand TEU per year can be translated to nearly 5 new 144TEU container ships (47/(8.2*12/9)), which could fully cover the transport demand although in the long low depth period.

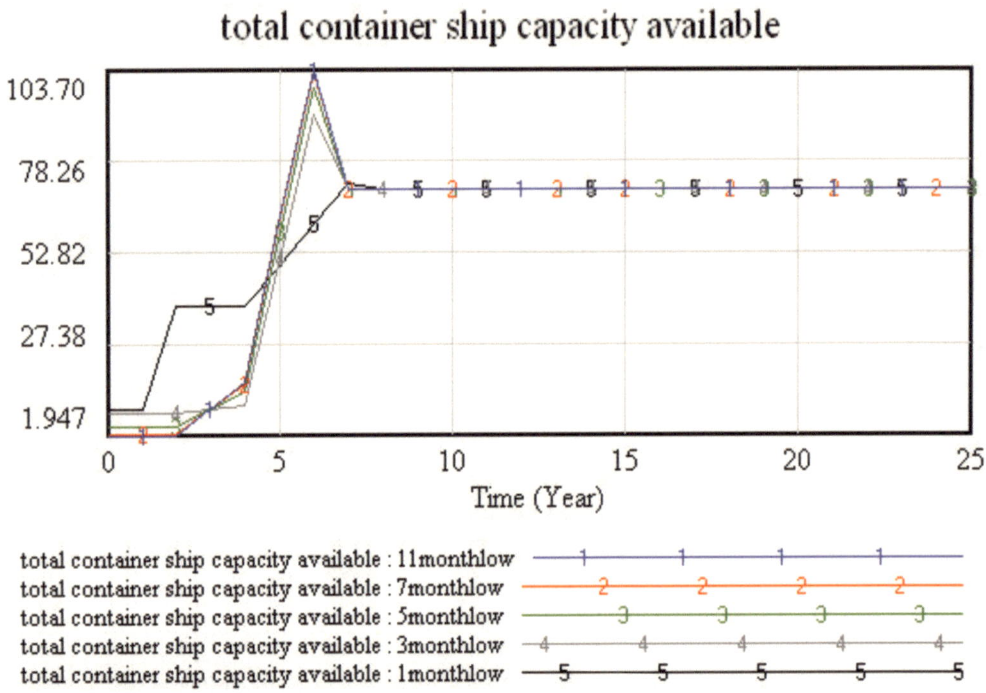

Fig. 5. Container ship capacity per year in different simulation scenarios

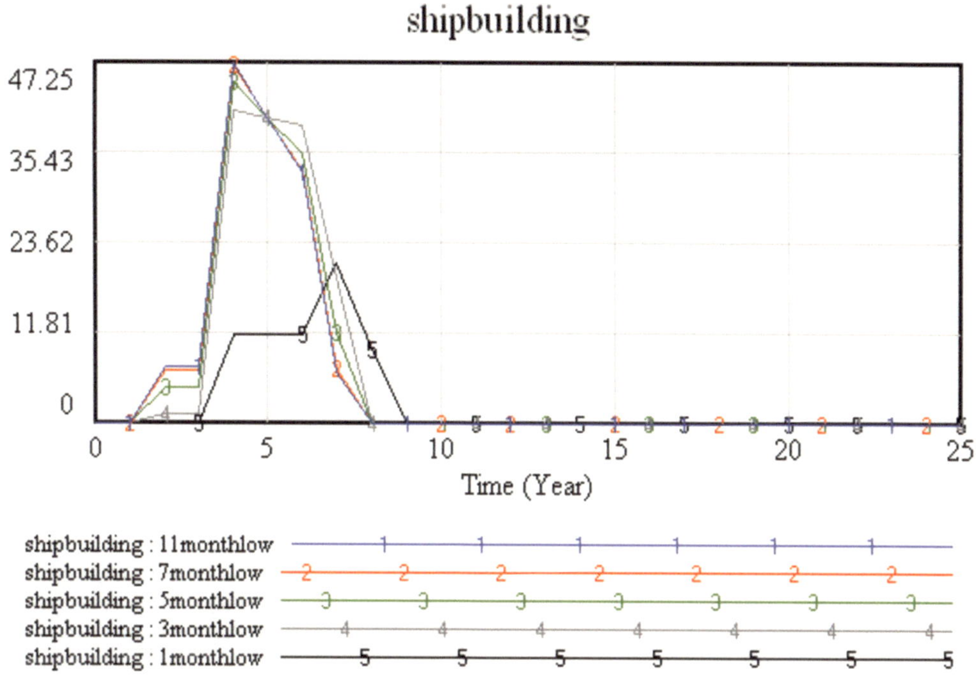

Fig. 6. New container ship building pattern in different simulation scenarios

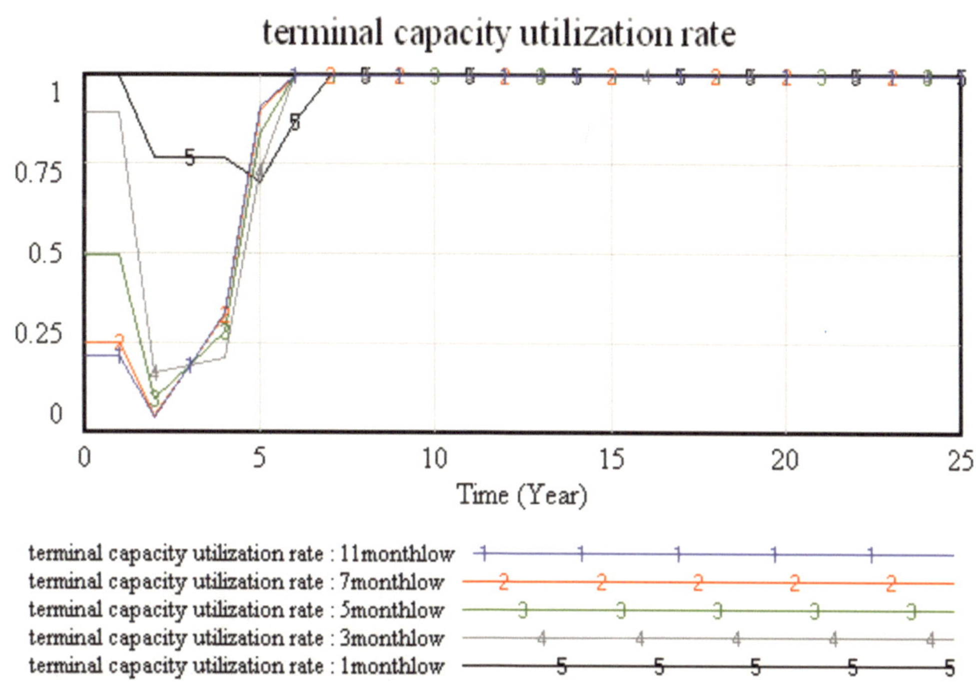

Fig. 7. Chongqing terminal utilization rate in different simulation scenarios

The way by which different ratio of the low and high period and the ship building delay affect the container transported from the Chongqing terminal is also showed in Fig. 7. At the beginning of the simulation, the terminal's utilization rate is not limited by ship capacity. But with the time goes on, the ship capacity could not satisfy the quick increase of the containers and the utilization rate of terminal capacity falls to a very low level, even to 10% in 11 month low scenario. Then the construction of new ships makes up the low level of terminal capacity utilization nearly after 7 or 8 years.
In the simulation, since a key factor is the delay time of the new ship building, a sensitivity analysis was done by changing the time from 2 years to 1, 3 and 5 years. From the result of the analysis, the patters of the behavior in container ship capacity, new ship building and terminal utilization rate in different scenarios were nearly the same as the figures given above. The only difference is that it takes either a litter shorter or longer time before the ship capacity reaches the desired level. During the all analysis, the most important factor is the ratio of the low and high periods distribute.

7. Conclusions

The system dynamics simulation gives the developing patterns of the container ship capacity and the terminal capacity under different hydrographical conditions of the Yangtze. The result of the simulation shows that the ship capacity expansion is incentive by the deficit supply and the occasional water depth. If new ship building is only encouraged by them, the container ship fleet growth will be slow, which will induce the low terminal utilization rate for a long time. The Three-Gorge Dam Project will be finished completely in 2008. At that time, the fluid condition of the upstream in the Yangtze will change which will be more suitable for the large draft vessels. On the other side, from the simulation, it is obvious that the new ship building delay will make the oversupply for some time in the market. So there are some investment risks. In order to guarantee adequate ship capacity from the beginning of the terminal operations, new container ships order should be made well in advance.
From the change of the river hydrographical condition, changeable-draft container ships are needed. From the development of the Chongqing terminal, new ship capacity is needed for the capacity deficit in the market. But in practice, the long-term chartering agreements between shippers and ship-owners without some certainty on freight rates will put some risks on the investment of the new ship building. The rough simulation in the paper gives the general patterns of some behavioral factors. There are some other works needed to research further on this base, such as the containers demand decided by the business should be considered for the pattern of demand's behavior in the market surges usually if the research time is long. But in this paper there is the background of the booming demand of the container transportation in the Yangtze, the tendency of the demand is going up, so it is reasonable to use the expansion of the terminal's capacity in the rough model. Also the investment decision of the government to the terminal and ship building industry and the pollution of the ship industry to the river are the factor affected the ship growing because all of them are included in the big system. If we want the whole system to be working in a good circle behavior, the elements taken into consideration should be as much as possible.

8. Acknowledgements

This paper is part of research financed by the European Commission Asia-link Program (Project no. VN010). Partners in this project are CICAT-Delft University of Technology, Wuhan University of Technology, Vietnam Maritime University and University of Antwerp-Department of Transport and Regional Economics.

9. References

Beenstock, M., A. Vergottis., *Econometric Modeling of World Shipping (International Studies in Economic Modeling)*, Chapman and Hall, London, UK, 1993.

Charemza, W. and Gronicki, M., An econometric model of world shipping and shipbuilding. *Maritime Policy & Mannagement*, 1981, 10(1), pp.21-30.

Coyle, RG, *Management System Dynamics*, John Wiley & Sons Ltd: London, 1977.

Devanney, J., F. Fischer, *Marine Decisions Under Uncertainty*, MIT Lecture Series, MIT Press, Cambridge, MA,1971.

Dikos,G. and Papadatos, P. M. The case of tanker freight rate dynamics, *Proceedings of the IAME 2005 Congress*, Cyprus.

Dikos,G., Marcus, H. S., Papadatos, P. M. and Papakonstantinou, V., Niver Lines: A System-Dynamics Approach to Tanker Freight Modeling, *Interfaces*, 2006,36(4), pp.326-341.

Eriksen, I. E. and Norman, V. D., Econometric model for tanker companies. *Institute of Shipping Reaearch*, Norwegian School of Economics and Business Adiminstration, Bergen,1976.

Jay W. Forrester, Policies, decisions and information sources for modeling, *European Journal of Operational Research*, 1992(59), pp.42-63.

Jostein Tvedt, Shipping market models and the specification of freight rate processes, *Maritime Economics & Logistics*,2003(5),pp.327-346.

Khaled A. A., Michael G. H. B., System Dynamics Applicability to Transportation Modelling, *Transpn. Res.-A*, 1994 (28)(5),pp.373-400.

Koopmans, T. C., *Tanker Freight Rates and Tankship Building*, 1939

Richardon, G.P., *Feedback Thought in Social Science and Systems Theory*, University of Pennsylvania Press, Philadelphia, PA,1991.

Serghiou, SS, Serghios, S and Zannetos, ZS. The level and structure of single voyage freight rates in the short run, *Transportation Science*, 1982(16), pp.19-44.

Strandenes, S.P. Economics of the Markets for Ships in C. Th. Grammenos editor. *The handbook of Maritime Economics and Business*. 2002

Sterman, J. D., Business Dynamics. *Systems Thinking and Modeling for a Complex World*, McGraw-Hill, New York, 2000.

Stopford, M., *Maritime Economics*. Routledge, London, UK, 2002.

Tinbergen, J., Scheepsbouwruimet en vrachten. *De Nederlandse Conjunctuur*, 1934 March, pp.23-35

Veenstra, AW and Ludema, MW, Cyclicality in the oil tanker shipping industry. *Conference Paper* Presented in September 2003, Riga, Latvia, Rotterdam School of

Economics/Centre for Maritime Economics and Logistics: The Netherlands, 2003.

Zannetos, ZS. *The Theory of Oil Tankship Rates.* The MIT Press: MA USA, 1966.

Zhuyuan Liu, The development analysis of the main container terminals in China in 2010, *Water Transportation Digest*, 2005(2), pp.8-13. (in Chinese).

7

Integrating Economic and Ecological Impact Modelling: Dynamic Processes in Regional Agriculture under Structural Change

Heikki Lehtonen
MTT Agrifood Research Finland / Economics
Finland

1. Introduction

Water quality has long been an important part of agricultural policy debate in Finland because agricultural activities are responsible for a significant part of nutrient load of surface waters. Changes in agricultural production, its input and land use intensity, as well as regional concentration of production, are seen as primary drivers of agricultural water pollution. Despite the theoretical fact that decreasing production linked agricultural subsidies should decrease input use intensity and volume of agricultural production, no or little decrease has been observed in agricultural water pollution in Finland during the last 15 years (Ekholm et al. 2007). This observation, despite the fact that nitrogen surplus has decreased by 42 % and phosphorous surplus by 65 % in Finland 1995-2006, has been a disappointment since ambitious targets have been set for water quality improvements and significant agri-environmental subsidies have been paid for farmers in order to reach the targets (Turtola, 2007). Ekholm et al. (2007) conclude that simultaneous changes in agricultural production (e.g. regional specialisation) and in climate may also have counteracted the effects of agri-environmental measures. The actions to reduce agricultural loading might have been more successful had they focused specifically on the areas and actions that contribute most to the current loading. Such conclusions and the apparent need for integrated modelling of agricultural economy, structural change in agriculture, and consequent impacts on nutrient leaching, are the main motivation for the modelling efforts presented and discussed in this study. Climate change concerns, both mitigation and adaptation, as well links between agricultural production, climate change and biodiversity, further increase the need for consistent integrated analysis. We present an approach designed for combined analysis of agricultural production and markets, nutrient leaching and water quality. While our emphasis here is in agriculture and water quality, the basic set-up, i.e. the relationship between changing agriculture (production) and environment is rather general.

Improvement in surface water quality has been so far the main objective of agri-environmental policy in Finland (Valpasvuo-Jaatinen et al. 1997). The quality of surface waters can be linked to agricultural production through estimating surplus of nutrients, which in turn provides indicator of potential runoff of nutrients. However, the actual nutrient runoff from a given parcel is only partly explained by estimated nutrient surplus in that parcel as there are many exogenous and stochastic factors which affect the amount of actual runoff including the weather, topography and soil characteristics.

Moreover, the relationship between nutrient surpluses and agricultural production is more complex than merely analysing individual farm management practices, such as fertilisation and crop yield levels for each crop. Changes in agricultural production may be linked to production specialisation, technological change and market feedback through prices, which also determines production intensity and the use inputs in production. Hence, if analysis focus only on individual crops or production lines then it may be difficult to identify important cause-effect linkages. There has been considerable changes in agricultural production, including the changing agricultural management practices, the increased use of fertilizers and pesticides, the increase of sub-surface drainage and enlarged field parcels, as well as the reduction of wintertime plant cover on farmland in the last 30–40 year (Tiainen & Pakkala 2000, 2001; Tiainen et al. 2004) Since grasslands providing wintertime plant cover have diminished, it is widely recognised that changes in livestock production are very decisive in terms of farmland biodiversity and nutrient runoff (Pykälä 2000). Hence, changes in nutrient runoff from agriculture seem to be linked to overall changes in agriculture.

Partial analyses focusing on individual production lines, which compete on the same regional land and labour resource, may not always provide a sound basis for policy recommendations. Especially regional changes in agriculture may not be driven by technical change and other (such as managerial abilities of farmers) developments in individual production lines alone, but also by comparative advantage of regions and farms. Hence a sector level analysis, entailing the overall change in agriculture, is needed when evaluating changes in the regional development of agricultural production, as well as when evaluating the potential to reduce nutrient runoff from agricultural sector. For example, the national supports and agri-environmental payments are very significant in Finland.

Aim in this paper is to show how the challenges of dynamic modelling of regional agricultural production and structures can be modelled in a way that not only provides (1) a consistent picture of agricultural changes with respect to overall markets and policies, but provides also (2) a major platform for integrated economic-ecological modelling of nutrient leaching impacts and for analysis how both agricultural production and nutrient leaching are impacted by agricultural and agri-environmental policies at regional scales.

We examine these modelling challenges by presenting and motivating the structure of a dynamic regional sector model of Finnish agriculture (DREMFIA; Lehtonen, 2001), which has been tailored to facilitate consistent integration between physical field scale and catchment scale nutrient leaching models. In addition to analyses of production and income effects of agricultural policies (Lehtonen 2004, 2007), this model has been earlier employed to assess the effects of alternative EU level policy scenarios on the multifunctional role of Finnish agriculture (Lehtonen et al. 2005, 2006). The integrated analysis of agricultural policy changes on agriculture, nutrient leaching and water quality have already been reported in Bärlund et al. (2005), Lehtonen et al. (2007), as well as in Rankinen et al. (2006). In this paper the role of economic modelling is given a particular emphasis and hence we approach the challenge of dynamic integrated modelling from the point of view of dynamic multiregional modelling of agricultural sector. In fact, we feel that the crucial role of economic modelling in the economy-ecology model integrations has not been sufficiently addressed in the literature, including the references mentioned above. For example, the capability of an economic model to take into account biological processes and physical nutrient flows, consistently both at farm and sector level, are important. In other words, the consistent model integration seem to require validation of the economic models not only in terms of monetary values (as is the standard practice), but also in terms of nutrients, their flows and utilisation in agriculture.

The rest of this paper is organised as follows. In the following section some of the previous studies that have used economic modelling for analysing the cost-effectiveness of alternative policy measures to reduce nutrient runoff from agriculture are briefly reviewed. We then present the main challenges in dynamic modelling of regional agriculture and its nutrient leaching. This is followed by presentation of the agricultural sector model and its tailored features facilitating integrated modelling. Finally, we discuss and conclude on the theoretical consistency and empirical feasibility of the presented approach.

2. Review of literature

We start by reviewing briefly some recent studies that have analysed the effectiveness and cost-effectiveness of different policy measures to reduce nutrient runoff from agriculture.

Mapp et al. (1994) analyse regional water quality impacts of limiting nitrogen use by broad versus targeted policies in five regions within the Central High Plains. Broad based policies analysed include: (i) limitations on the total quantity of nitrogen applied (total restriction) and (ii) limitations on per-acre nitrogen applications (per-acre restriction). Targeted policies analysed include: (iii) limits on the quantity of nitrogen applied on soils prone to leaching (soil targeted restriction) and (iv) specific irrigation systems (system-targeted restriction). Their results show that targeted policies provide greater reduction in environmental damage for each dollar reduction in net farm income, that is, targeted policies are more cost-effective than broad policies. Among the targeted policies nitrogen restrictions differentiated on production systems outperform nitrogen restrictions on soil types.

Vatn et al. (1997) developed an interdisciplinary modelling approach named ECECMOD to analyse the regulation of non-point source pollution from agriculture. They analyse the impacts of following policy scenarios on losses of nitrogen, phosphorus and soil: (i) 100% tax on nitrogen in mineral fertilisers, (ii) 50% arable land requirement on catch crops/grass cover, and (iii) a per hectare payment for spring tillage. The nitrogen tax induces both reduced fertiliser levels, more clover in the leys and better utilisation of nitrogen in manure. However it does not have any effect on soil or phosphorus losses. Requirement for catch cropping reduces all categories of losses and losses of nitrates are reduced twice as much as in the tax regime. Subsidising spring tillage has a stronger effect on soil losses than the catch crop regime, but it has insignificant effect on nitrate leaching. Tax on nitrogen is the least costly measure per ha and per kg reduced N leached, catch crops are more costly but they have positive effects on erosion and phosphorus losses as well. If the focus is exclusively on erosion then spring tillage is the least costly measure.

Johansson and Kaplan (2004) investigate the regional interaction of agri-environmental payments and water quality regulation (a carrot-and-stick approach) in animal and crop production setting by using the U.S. Regional Agricultural Sector Model (USMP), which maximises profits from livestock, poultry and crop production in the presence of agri-environmental payments and nutrient standards. Crop and animal production choices are linked to edge-of-field environmental variables using the Environmental Policy Integrated Climate Model (EPIC). The results show that meeting nutrient standards would result in decreased levels of animal production, increased prices for livestock and poultry products, increased levels of crop production, and water quality improvements. The impacts of nutrient policies are not homogeneous across regions; in regions with relatively less cropland per ton of manure produced these impacts are more pronounced. Moreover, their results indicate that there may be important environmental trade-offs relating to nutrient standards. For example, by requiring the spread of manure at no greater than agronomic rates result in increased leaching of nitrogen to groundwater as well as increased runoff of soil particles and pesticides to surface water in some areas.

Our approach here is a modelling strategy that integrates a national-level multi-regional agricultural sector model (Lehtonen 2001, 2004) with a region-specific field-scale or catchment scale nutrient leaching models (Tattari *et al.* 2001, Rankinen et al. 2006). The integrated analysis is challenging, because the agricultural production and its economy both at national and regional level has to be combined with sets of factors that influence water quality. Hence the policy relevant objective of this kind of modelling is to show to which extent different policies, both agricultural and environmental, may influence nutrient leaching which is determined at the practices and processes at the local level.

A similar, but not identical integrated agri-environmental modelling approach was used by Schou *et al.* (2000). They used a sector-level economic model in calculating economically rational changes in variable factors of production as a response to changing policy. The resulting prices and quantities of inputs and outputs were then utilised in different farm level economic models and in nutrient leaching models in order to calculate nutrient loads and their abatement costs for different soil types. The approach was seen convenient in combining the strengths of detailed bottom-up-based environmental analysis with the opportunities of aggregate top-down-based policy descriptions and economic modelling of agricultural production. However, the econometric sector level model used was not considered appropriate in evaluating effects of relatively large changes in prices or policy. The farm-level models based on statistical databases were static in the sense that no long-term adjustment mechanisms, like technology-inducing effects of price changes, or potential for cost-saving in the longer run, were modelled.

3. Challenges in modelling technical and structural changes in multi-regional economic models

The literature reviewed above suggests that both regional and dynamic aspects are relevant when evaluating environmental effects of agricultural policies. The regional dimension is vital in any deeper analysis of environmental effects which are often regionally specific and varying. Dynamics is important because of technical and structural change, and because of significant re-allocations of production between regions over time.

Modelling investments and technical change in sector level models, however, is difficult due to farm heterogeneity. Applying explicit farm level dynamic optimisation on many representative farms located in a number of regions with distinct support levels and other characteristics, for example, would be a difficult task, especially if the investment decisions are linked to product price changes. Various difficulties of explaining aggregate level investments using (stochastic) farm level dual dynamic models of investment (which address both uncertainty and irreversibility simultaneously) becomes clear in the studies of Pietola (1997) and Sckokai (2004), for example. Hence alternative approaches trying to combine the most relevant drivers of structural change may provide valuable aspects and viewpoints.

Activity analysis is a traditional and straightforward practice of modelling endogenous technical change in optimisation models: introduce alternative production activities with different linear (or why not non-linear) input-output-combinations and then let the model endogenously choose the optimal technique (Hazell & Norton 1986, p. 149). However, there are reasons which make such bottom-up approach problematic in analysis of structural change. First, free choice of technology means that farmers are assumed to be perfectly informed on the production techniques and capable of selecting and adopting the most profitable technique. This is an over-optimistic assumption given the diversity of Finnish farms in terms of production costs and the fact that large scale production techniques have been adopted only recently. Furthermore, if only few representative farms are used as supplying agents in the model, the linear activity analysis approach, which selects always a single most profitable technique, fails to explain co-evolution of several competing techniques. In reality, several techniques co-exist since one technique does not fit all farms.
Activity analysis rules out sunk cost behaviour and out-off-equilibrium movements typical for agriculture. Irreversibility of investments as well as uncertainty and sunk costs make it problematic to assume sudden shifts in technology, or shifts independent of earlier investments, in response to changes in economic conditions. Applying activity analysis in a sector model simulating competitive markets means that maximisation of consumer and producer surplus directly steer the technology choices of representative farms. Since large scale production techniques have been used only by a small sub-set of farms in Finland, such an assumption must be considered an exaggeration of the common knowledge and the efficiency of the markets. The same kind of problems are related to different non-linear specifications, such as smooth nested production functions (such as CES) specifying substitution between labour and capital at macro level (top-down approach). One may put under question the empirical content and validity of the calibrated substitution elasticities, and the assumption that they stay constant over time. Advantages and shortcomings of the bottom-up and top-down-approaches are obvious and well known, as well as the difficulties in combining the both approaches (Frei et al. 2003 and Sue Wing 2006).
Without going to the very details in the reasoning of technical change in economics, it is merely stated here that the dynamic reality of structural change in agriculture is poorly represented by static models, independent if they include bottom-up or top-down specifications of technical change. In a dynamic context one alternative to activity analysis approach and to macro-level substitution-based production functions is the concept of technology diffusion. Models of technology diffusion describe the progressive distributional change in the spread of different production techniques (Hagedoorn 1989, p.120, Karshenas & Stoneman 1995, p.263), i.e. the process how the most profitable techniques become wide-spread over time. The pattern of diffusion follows the description of the process of innovation and imitation with a few originators and a growing number of imitators or followers. This pattern of diffusion is generally pictured as a sigmoid (S-curve). In the early phase of the diffusion number of users of the new technique (or share of capital stock embodied in the new technique) increases rather slowly. There may be practical and technical difficulties related to the adoption of the new technique. If the first adopters are able to solve the problems and find the technique relatively profitable compared to the other techniques, other firms get interested in the adoption and the number of adopters increase. This, in turn, results to a spread of information and knowledge of the new technique, and

the number of adopters will grow faster. Those firms which gain the greatest benefits of the new technique most probably make the first investments in the new technique. In the later phase of the diffusion process, however, the growth rate in the number of adopters decreases because not all potential adopters have the same incentives (the profit motive) or costs of adoption. Some potential adopters remaining face relatively severe constraints for adoption and thus the rate of growth in the number of adopters decreases (Hagedoorn 1989, p. 121).

Sue Wing & Anderson (2007) model accumulative gains and dynamics of capital and economic growth in a dynamic recursive multi-regional computable general equilibrium model. Even though the general equilibrium set-up of recursive dynamic modelling includes a larger number of dimensions (such as migration) they conclude environmental applications, such as economic analysis related greenhouse gas emission abatement, as one of the most promising application areas of the model. Hence modelling the dynamics and drivers of regional economic changes are likely to provide useful analysis and insight in a number of issues related to interrelationships between economic dynamics and environment.

4. Economic model

4.1 General features

The dynamic regional sector model of Finnish agriculture (DREMFIA) is a dynamic recursive model simulating the development of the agricultural investments and markets from 1995 up to 2020 (Lehtonen 2001, 2004). The underlying hypothesis in the model is profit maximising behaviour of producers and utility maximising behaviour of consumers under competitive markets. According to microeconomic theory, this leads to welfare maximising behaviour of the agricultural sector. Decreasing marginal utility of consumers and increasing marginal cost per unit produced in terms of quantity lead to equilibrium market prices which are equal to marginal cost of production on competitive markets. Each region specialises to products and production lines of most relative profitability, taking into account profitability of production in other regions and consumer demand. This means that total use of different production resources, including farmland, on different regions are utilised optimally in order to maximise sectoral welfare, taking into account differences in resource quality, technology, costs of production inputs and transportation costs (spatial price equilibrium; Takayama & Judge 1971, Hazell & Norton 1986).

The model consists of two main parts: (1) a technology diffusion model which determines sector level investments in different production technologies; and (2) an optimization routine simulates annual price changes (supply and demand reactions) by maximizing producer and consumer surplus subject to regional product balance and resource (land and capital) constraints (Fig. 1). The major driving force in the long-term is the module of technology diffusion. However, if large changes take place in production, price changes, as simulated by the optimization model, are also important to be considered. The investment model and resulting production capacity changes is however closely linked to market model determining production (including land use, fertilisation, feeding of animals, and yield of dairy cows, for example), consumption and domestic prices. Our market model is a typical spatial price equilibrium model (see *e.g.* Cox & Chavas 2001), except that no explicit supply functions are specified, *i.e.* supply is a primal specification).

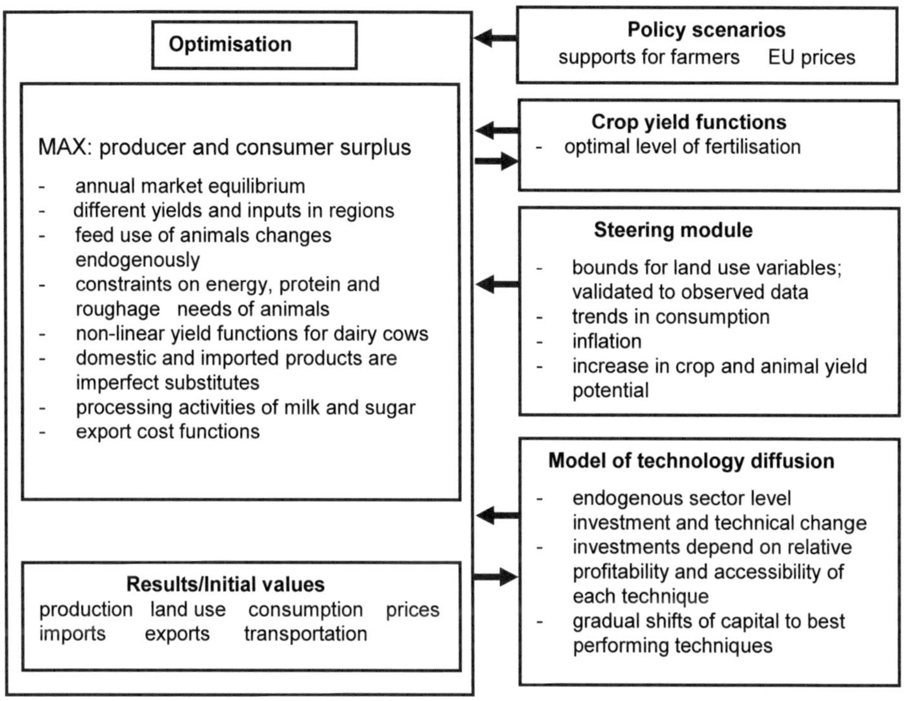

Fig. 1. Basic structure of DREMFIA sector model

Contrary to comparative static models, often used in agricultural policy analysis, current production is not assumed to represent an economic equilibrium in the DREMFIA model. The endogenous investments and technical change, as well as the recursive structure of DREMFIA model implies that incentives for changes in production affect production gradually in subsequent years, i.e. all changes do not take place instantaneously. The current situation in agricultural production and markets may include incentives for changes but these changes cannot be done immediately due to fixed production factors and animal biology. Hence, the continuation of current policy may also result in changes in production and income of farmers. However, the production in DREMFIA model will gradually reach a long-term equilibrium or steady state if no further policy changes take place.

Four main areas are included in the model: Southern Finland, Central Finland, Ostrobothnia (the western part of Finland), and Northern Finland. Production in these is further divided into sub-regions on the basis of the support areas. In total, there are 18 different production regions (Fig. 2), including 3 small catchment areas, of size 4 - 6 000 hectares, which match exactly the spatial aggregation of the bio-physical nutrient leaching models (see ch. 5 below). This allows a regionally disaggregated description of policy measures and production technology. The final and intermediate products move between the main areas at certain transportation cost. The most important products of agriculture are included in the DREMFIA model. Hence, the model provides a complete coverage of land use and animal production, which compete on production resources.

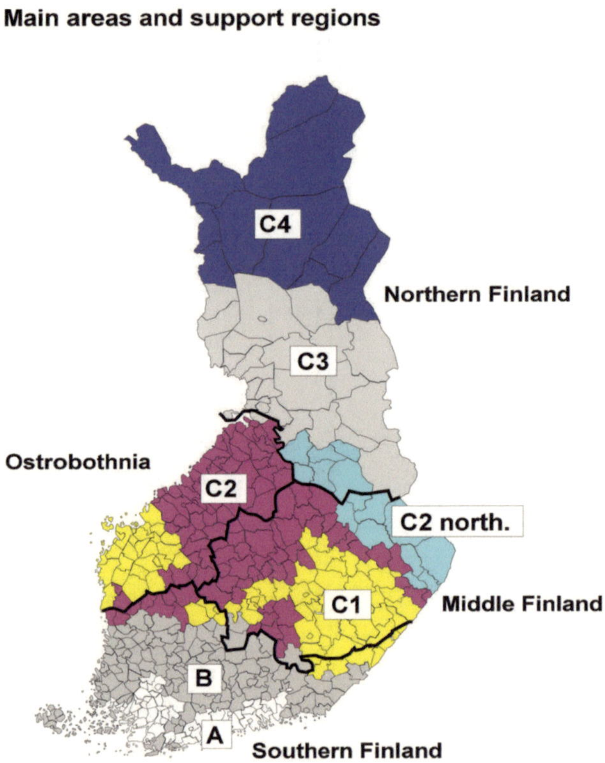

Fig. 2. Regional disaggregation of the DREMFIA sector model. There are 4 main regions split up by subsidy zones (A, B, C2-C4) and small catchments.

4.2 Technology diffusion, investments and technical change

The purpose of the technology diffusion sub-model is to make the process of technical change endogenous. This means that investment in efficient technology is dependent on the economic conditions of agriculture such as interest rates, prices, support, production quotas and other policy measures and regulations imposed on farmers. Changing agricultural policy affects farmers' revenues and the money available for investment. Investment is also affected by public investment supports. The model for technology diffusion and technical change presented below follows the main lines of Soete & Turner (1984). The choice of this particular diffusion scheme is further motivated in Lehtonen (2001). While the set-up of Dremfia model is rather neo-classical (competitive markets simulated by maximisation of consumer and producer surplus), the model of technology diffusion allows at least temporary movements out of equilibrium path and can be therefore considered close to the core of evolutionary economics paradigm (Nelson & Winter 2002).

Let us assume that there is a large number of farm firms producing a homogenous good. Different technologies with different production costs are used and firms can be grouped on the basis of their technology. The number of technologies is N. Each technology uses two groups of factors of production, variable factors, such as labour (L), and fixed factors, such as capital (K). Variable factors of production may also include land rent, particularly if agricultural land can be rented on a short-term basis, or opportunity cost of land, so that crucial issue of competition for land can be included in the analysis. A particular production technique is labelled α. The rate of return on capital for firms using the α technique, under assumption of fixed exogenous input prices (w), is

$$r_\alpha = \frac{Q_\alpha - wL_\alpha}{K_\alpha}. \tag{1}$$

The surplus available for investment—Q_α - wL_α (Q_α is the total revenue on the α technique)—is divided between all firms using the α technique. $f_{\beta\alpha}$ is the fraction of investable surplus transferred from α technique to β technique. This transfer will take place only if the rate of return on the β technique is greater than the rate of return on the α technique, *i.e.* $r_\beta > r_\alpha$. The total investable surplus leaving α technique for all other more profitable techniques is

$$\sum_{\beta: r_\beta > r_\alpha} f_{\beta\alpha} \sigma r_\alpha K_\alpha, \tag{2}$$

where $\sigma < 1$ is the savings ratio (constant). To make the model soluble, a form of $f_{\beta\alpha}$ has to be specified. Two crucial aspects about diffusion and adaptation behaviour are included: first, the importance of the profitability of the new technique, and secondly, the risk, uncertainty and other frictions involved in adopting a new technique. The information about and likelihood of adoption of a new technique will grow as its use becomes more widespread with a growth in cumulated knowledge of farmers.

To cover the first point, $f_{\beta\alpha}$ is made proportional to the fractional rate of profit increase in moving from technique α to technique β, *i.e.* $f_{\beta\alpha}$ is proportional to $(r_\beta - r_\alpha)/ r_\alpha$. The second point is modelled by letting $f_{\beta\alpha}$ be proportional to the ratio of the capital stock in the β technique to the total capital stock (in a certain agricultural production line), *i.e.* K_β/K. If β is a new innovation then K_β/K is likely to be small and hence $f_{\beta\alpha}$ is small. Consequently, the fraction of investable surplus transferred from α to β will be small. Combining these two assumptions, $f_{\beta\alpha}$ can be written as

$$f_{\beta\alpha} = \eta' \frac{K_\beta}{K} \frac{(r_\beta - r_\alpha)}{r_\alpha}, \tag{3}$$

where η' is a constant. A similar expression can be written for $f_{\alpha\beta}$. The total investment to α technique, after some simplification, is

$$I_\alpha = \sigma r_\alpha K_\alpha + \eta (r_\alpha - r) K_\alpha = \sigma (Q_\alpha - wL_\alpha) + \eta (r_\alpha - r) K_\alpha \tag{4}$$

where r is the average rate of return on all techniques. The interpretation of this investment function is as follows. If η were zero then (4) would show that the investment in the α technique would come entirely from the investable surplus generated by the α technique. For $\eta \neq 0$ the investment in the α technique will be greater or less than the first term, depending on whether the rate of return on the α technique is greater than r. This seems reasonable. If a technique is highly profitable, then it will tend to attract investment and conversely if it is relatively less profitable, investment will decline.

Assuming depreciations, the rate of change in capital invested in α technique is

$$\frac{dK_\alpha}{dt} = [\sigma r_\alpha + \eta(r_\alpha - r) - \delta_\alpha]K_\alpha, \tag{5}$$

where δ_α is the depreciation rate of α technique. If there is no investment in α technique during some time period, the capital stock K_α decreases at the depreciation rate. To summarise, the investment function (4) is an attempt to model the behaviour of farmers whose motivation to invest is greater profitability but nevertheless will not adopt the most profitable technique immediately, because of uncertainty and various other retardation factors. Total investment is distributed among the different techniques according to their profitability and accessibility. The most efficient and profitable technique, which requires a large scale of production, is not equally accessible for all farmers and, thus, farmers will also invest in other techniques which are more profitable than the current technique. When some new and profitable technique becomes widespread, more information is available about the technique and its characteristics, and farmers invest in that technique at an increasing rate.

Three dairy techniques (representing α techniques) and corresponding farm size classes have been included in the DREMFIA model: farms with 1-19 cows (labour intensive production), farms with 20-49 cows (semi-labour intensive production), and farms with 50 cows or more (capital intensive production). Let us briefly show the calibration of the diffusion model to the official statistics of farm size structure. Parameter σ has been fixed to 1.07 which means that an initial value 0.85 (*i.e.* farmers re-invest 85% of the economic surplus on fixed factors back into agriculture) has been scaled up by 26% which is the average rate of investment support for dairy farms in Finland. The η (fixed to 0.77) is then used as a calibration parameter which results in investments which facilitate the ex-post development of dairy farm structure and milk production volume. The chosen combination of the parameters σ and η (1.07:0.77) is unique because it calibrates the farm size distribution to the observed farm size structure in 2003 (a new combination is chosen each year when new information on farm size structure has been obtained). Choosing larger σ and smaller η exaggerates the investments on small farms, and choosing smaller σ and larger η exaggerates the investments on large farms. Choosing smaller values for both σ and η result in too low investment and production levels, and choosing larger values for both σ and η results in overestimated investment and production levels, compared to the ex post period.

The investment function (1) shows that the investment level is strongly dependent on capital already invested in each technique. This assumption is consistent with the conclusions of Rantamäki-Lahtinen *et al.* (2002) and Heikkilä *et al.* (2004), *i.e.*, farm investments are strongly correlated with earlier investments, but poorly correlated with many other factors, such as liquidity or financial costs. Other common features, except for the level of previous investments of investing farms, were hard to find. Hence, the assumption made on cumulative gains from earlier investments seems to be supported by empirical findings.

4.3 Recursive programming model

The optimization routine is a spatial price equilibrium model which provides annual supply and demand pattern, as well as endogenous product prices, using the outcome of the previous year as the initial value. Production capacity (number of animal places available, for example), which is an upper boundary for each production activity (number of animals) in each region, depends on the investment determined at a sub-model of technology diffusion.

The use of feed is a decision variable, which means that animals may be fed using an infinite number of different (feasible) feed stuff combinations. This results in non-linearities in balance equations of feed stuffs since the number of animals and the use of feed are both decision variables. There are equations ensuring required energy, protein and roughage needs of animals, and those needs can be fulfilled in different ways. The use of concentrates and various grain-based feed stuffs in dairy feeding, however, is allowed to change only 5-10 % annually due to biological constraints and fixed production factors in feeding systems. Concentrates and grain based feed stuffs became relatively cheaper than silage feed in 1995 because of decreased grain prices and CAP payments for grain. The share of concentrates and grain has increased, and the share of roughage, such as silage, pasture grass and hay, has gradually decreased in the feeding of dairy cows. There has also been substitution between grain and concentrates (in the group of non-roughage feeds), and between hay, silage and pasture grass (in the group of roughage feeds). The actual annual changes in the use of different feed stuffs have been between 5-10%, on the average, but the overall substitution between roughage and other feed stuffs has been slow: the share of concentrates and grain-based feed stuffs in the feeding of dairy cows has increased by 1% annually since 1994.

Feeding affects the milk yield of dairy cows in the model. A quadratic function is used to determine the increase in milk yield as more grain is used in feeding. Genetic milk yield potential increases exogenously 110-130 kilos per annum per cow (depending on the region). Fertilization and crop yield levels depend on crop and fertilizer prices via empirically validated crop yield functions.

There are 18 different processed milk products, many of which are low fat variants of the same product, in the model as well as the corresponding regional processing activities. There are explicit skim milk and milk fat balance equations in the model. In the processing of 18 milk products, fixed margins representing the processing costs are used between the raw material and the final product. This means that processing costs are different for each milk product, and they remain constant over time in spite of gradually increasing inflation. In other words, it is assumed that Finnish dairy companies constantly improve their cost efficiency by developing their production organisation, by making structural arrangements (shutting down small scale processing plants) and substituting capital for labour (enlarging the processing plants), for example. Such development has indeed taken place in Finland in recent years.

All foreign trade flows are assumed to be to and from the EU. It is assumed that Finland cannot influence the EU price level. Armington assumption is used (Armington 1969). The demand functions of the domestic and imported products influence each other through elasticity of substitution. Since EU prices are given the export prices are assumed to change only because of frictions in the marketing and delivery systems. In reality, exports cannot grow too rapidly in the short run without considerable marketing and other costs. Hence, the transportation costs of exports increase (decrease) from a fixed base level if the exports increase (decrease) from the previous year. The coefficients of the linear export cost functions have been adjusted to smooth down the simulated annual changes in exports to the observed average changes in 1995–2004. In the long-term analysis the export costs play little role, however, since they change only on the basis of the last year's exports. Hence the exports prices, (the fixed EU prices minus the export costs), change only temporarily from fixed EU prices if exports change. This means that Finland cannot actually affect EU price level. In fact the export specification is asymmetric to the specification of import demand. Export prices may be only slightly and temporarily different from EU average prices while the difference between domestic and EU prices may be even significant and persistent, depending on the consumer preferences. According to Jalonoja and Pietola (2004), there seems to be a significant time lag before Finnish potato prices move close to steady state equilibrium after shocks in EU prices. A unit root of domestic price process was found to be statistically significant which indicates that domestic price changes are rather persistent.

The export price changes due to changing export volume are relatively small and temporary compared to changes in domestic prices which are dependent on consumer preferences. In terms of maximizing consumer and producer surplus, this means that exports may fluctuate a lot and cause temporary and relatively small changes in export prices (through export costs), while the difference between domestic and average EU prices may be more or less persistent, depending on the consumer preferences. Hence, in addition to the import specification, the export specification explains why the domestic prices of milk products, as well as the producer prices of milk, remain at a higher level than the EU average prices even if Finland is clearly a net exporter of dairy products.

4.4 Links between technology diffusion and land use competition

Let us briefly discuss the role of land competition here since agricultural land is almost always required if livestock investments are to be made. Already nitrate directive of the European Union restricts the amount of nitrogen fertilisation to the maximum value of 170 kg N/ha per year. Environmental permits, required for large scale livestock production units, may pose more stringent conditions for a farm, implying more land area for manure spreading. Agri-environmental subsidy scheme in Finland poses significantly stricter requirements for manure spreading since not only nitrogen fertilisation level but also phosphorous fertilisation is given upper limits, as a condition for agri-enviromental subsidies. This phosphorous fertilisation limit is particularly compelling for pig and poultry farms since the phosphorous content of manure of pigs and poultry animals is significantly higher than that of bovine animals.

The price of land, affected consistently by all production activities regionally, is provided as shadow values of the regional land resource constraint. In earlier years land competition was not very intense in Finnish agriculture due to abundancy of farmland with respect to the quantity of regional animal production, i.e. due to low level of regional concentration of animal farms and and animal numbers. However in the last 10 years land competition has intensified, especially in areas where animal production has significantly increased (Lehtonen & Pyykkönen 2005). For this reason coupling the technology diffusion model with market simulating optimisation model provides a consistent treatment of land resource competition. When shadow price of regional land resource constraint is fed as an input price to the technology diffusion model, profitability of livestock investments decrease in those regions where land price (endogenous to the programming model) is high, while livestock investments become relatively more profitable in regions where land prices are low. Such connections to factors market, often demanded by agricultural economists in recent years (Chavas, 2001), provide an explanation why the increase in intensive animal production regions have decelerated due to land scarcity and high land prices, while animal production still exist in less productive regions. In technology diffusion model one may also include technological variations (biogas plants and methods how to fraction phosphorous out of manure to be spred on farmland) which may change the relative profitability of investments in different production techniques. This kind of options have not been included in the Dremfia model yet. Implementing a link between land prices between technology diffusion model and programming model however provides one more possibility to validate the simulated development path of regional animal production and land use to the observed ex-post development. Furthermore, regional feed use of animals, also endogenous in the programming model affects the land area required by animal production, hence a part of land scarcity costs can be avoided by changing feed use.

4.5 Trade of milk quotas

Milk quotas are traded within three separate areas in Finland. Within each quota trade area the sum of bought quotas must equal to the sum of sold quotas. In the model the support regions A, B and BS is one trade area (Southern Finland), support region C1 and C2 another trade area (Middle Finland - consisting of both Central Finland and Ostrobothnia regions in the model), and support areas C2P, C3 and C4 constitute a third region (Northern Finland). The price of the quota in each region is determined by the shadow value of an explicit quota trading balance constraint (purchased quotas must equal to sold quotas within the quota trading areas consisting of several production regions in the model, defined separately for each quota trading area. A depreciation period of five years is assumed, i.e. the uncertainty of the future economic conditions and the future of the quota system rule out high prices. Additional quotas and final phase-out of the EU milk quota system can be taken into account in a straightforward manner.

4.6 Risk specification

Ignoring risk-averse behaviour in farm planning models often leads to results that bear little relation to the decisions farmer actually makes (Hazell & Norton, 1986: 80). In studying climate change impacts on agricultural production it is essential to implement risk into the optimization models, rather than operate them assuming risk neutrality. Furthermore, including risk in optimisation models is relatively straightforward technically.
Several techniques have been developed to incorporating risk-averse behaviour in mathematical programming models. We adopted the mean-variance analysis with dynamic recursive sector model to explicitly include crop risks into estimates of land use changes in Finland. In classical mean-variance-model we maximize the utility function with positive risk aversion coefficient. If X is a vector of the different activities (amount of n), the vector of the land use of different crops is $(x_1, x_2, \ldots, x_n)$ and P is vector of the prices of different crops $(p_1, p_2, \ldots, p_n)$.
The model maximizes the utility function:

$$Max\ u = E[PQ] - cX - \Phi V[PQ]^{1/2}, \qquad (6)$$

where $E[PQ]$ is the expected profit (price vector multiplied with quantity vector Q), c is the unit cost of the activity (e.g. euros/ha), Φ is the positive risk averse parameter and V the variance operator. This can be written:

$$Max\ u = P^* E[y]X - cX - \Phi[X'\Omega X]^{1/2}\ , \tag{7}$$

where P^* is the expected price, y yield, Ω is covariance matrix between profits of the different activities. The target function u is maximized with resource constraint as matrix A contains the resource use, like availability of land and working ours at peak working period:

$$AX <= b \tag{8}$$

If the expected return per hectare is denoted:

$$r^* = P^* E[y] \tag{9}$$

we have:

$$Max\ u = r^*X - cX - \Phi[X'\Omega X]^{1/2} \tag{10}$$

In the optimum, the utility gained from the additional unit of activity equals with marginal costs. For a risk-averse farmer the possibility for the lower profits than expected is the additional cost. Increasing the activity produces additional costs determined by the risk parameter. These costs are positive if the profit of the activity correlates positively with the profits of the other activities and negative if the profit of the activity correlates negatively with the profits of the other activities. For example if the profit of certain crop correlates negatively with the profits of other crops, the variance of the total profit decreases.

The empirical estimation of the risk attitude parameters is difficult. Quadratic utility functions can't be summed up, so we are not able to calculate the mean value of the risk attitude parameters measured from different entrepreneurs and the groups of entrepreneurs. In addition the values of the risk attitude parameters depend substantially on definition of the optimization model and the mean prices. In empirical work the values of the risk attitude parameters are often calibrated so that the resulting model outcome is close to the realized production. The problem is that realized situation in a certain year or mean of the several years may not necessarily represent the economical equilibrium (Hardaker & Huirne, 1997:187-189; Coyle, 1992).

The variance-covariance matrixes of the crop contribution margins are calculated on the regional basis since there are 18 production regions in the DREMFIA model. We have used the regional data of crop yields from 1995 - 2006, product and input prices and agricultural subsidies from the official statistics. The use of inputs per hectare in different regions is already defined and validated to farm taxation data and farm level production costs calculations made by rural advisory services[1]. Hence the variance-covariance matrices we have produced fit the DREMFIA -model specifications but may not be usable in a context of some other input specification and aggregations. For example, we have fully included labour costs of farm family to production costs, which is more appropriate in long-term analysis than in short-term analysis.

[1] We have used input specification and aggregation of Pro Agria –organisation (www.proagria.fi) which is a central coordinating body of rural advisory services in Finland.

The calculation of matrixes shows that wheat, rye, malt barley and oilseeds have higher own variances than barley, oats and mixed grain which are mainly cultivated for feed use. The variances of wheat, rye, malt barley and oilseeds further grow towards the north. These crops of high variances also correlate positively with each other. This is understandable since feed crops are substitutes and also global cereals markets usually change cereals prices in the same direction. Also if crop yields are low due to weather, pests etc., the yield reducing factors tend to have similar impacts on all cereals. However, there tend to be large intra-annual variations in weather and yields between different regions, while the input and output prices are largely uniform since they are determined at global and EU markets. Consequently, while profitability covariance terms differ, they are almost all positive, there are only few negatively correlating crops in the northern areas of Finland, but areas under these crops are quite insignificant. Clearly positive covariance terms mean that risks cannot be significantly lowered through multicropping. However, the risk specification can provide an endogenous explanation for the fact that some crops are not only cultivated in southern most favourable regions but also in few other regions as well. Most importantly the risk terms in the objective function mitigate the tendency of the programming model to over-specialisation (discussed by Hazell & Norton 1984). Hence corner solutions typical for linear programming can be avoided[2], i.e. land use is not sensitive for small differences in prices, which is important when evaluating land use and environmental impacts, such as nutrient leaching of policies. The robustness of the policy impacts however should be routinely tested for sensitivity for input and output prices.

Risk aversion behaviour of farmers as well as changing patterns of crop and revenue risks are increasingly relevant in the changing climate. Simple expansion of risk based on observed covariance matrices (for example, by changing the risk aversion coefficient in eq. (7) and (10) may produce misleading results. Crop growth simulation models (Boogard et al. 1998) and their new versions tailored for climate change simulations could serve to create artificial realisations of crop yields and hence covariance matrices. Such a work, however, is computationally demanding in time scales of 50 or more years.

5. Integration to field scale and catchment scale nutrient leaching models

The outcome of the Dremfia model, i.e. numbers of animals, their manure to be spread on fields, chemical fertilisation, as well as land use variables (hectares of different crops) can be fed in physical field (Tattari et al. 2001) and catchment scale models in a relatively straightforward way.

However, the field scale nutrient leaching models are rich in biophysical detail. The field scale nutrient leaching model ICECREAM (Tattari et al. 2001), for example, has been developed to simulate water, soil loss and phosphorus (P) and nitrogen (N) transport in the unsaturated soil of agricultural land. The model is based on field scale simulations, but the

[2] While corner solutions are not possible for feed crops (due non-linear relations between feeding, meat and milk yields, market prices affected by Armington -specification and regional balance equations, the risk terms essentially eliminate the possible sensitivity of bread grain and malting barley production, not strongly affected by non-linearities in the model, on exogenous input or output price changes.

model results have been aggregated using typical soil-crop-slope combinations to small catchment scale to describe transport from agricultural land (Rekolainen et al. 2002).
To assess the environmental impacts of the agricultural policy scenarios, for example, the results of the field-scale simulations with ICECREAM have been up-scaled (Lehtonen et al. 2007). The relevant soil-crop-slope combinations form a simulation matrix of 6 soil types, 11 crop types and 9 field slopes, i.e., 594 single simulations. These results are averages of annual sums of, e.g., leached nitrate-N over the simulation period, here 10 years. The parameters to characterise soil properties and crop development are equal in both simulated areas, but the meteorological conditions are typical for each region. The model response to the (land use, fertilisation) input from the DREMFIA model is obtained by weighing the ICECREAM matrix by the percentage of each soil-crop-slope combination in each catchment for each year.
While the ways to integrate Dremfia output to nutrient leaching models depend on the technical set-up as well as the problem (i.e. unique solutions may not exist), one should note that the deeper integration of the models is done already inside Dremfia. In fact, the actual municipality (catchment) level disaggregations of the nutrient leaching model ICECREAM is introduced in Dremfia, which means that extra regions are added to the DREMFIA model. In this the rich datasets of cultivation and land use history of the region , collected for the validation of the nutrient leaching models such as ICECREAM or INCA (Rankinen et al.), can be utilised. For example, in Lehtonen et al. (2007) some penalty functions were developed for wheat yields in Yläneenjoki catchment, if wheat area exceeded the historical maximum. However individual soil types and field slopes, included in the nutrient leaching models, cannot be included in Dremfia except further increasing the number of dimensions and decision variables in the optimisation model. That, in turn, increases computational burden, and is also rather demanding in terms of crop fertilisation response functions included in Dremfia: not the same type of response functions can be assumed for crops on all soils. Crop growth simulation models (Boogard et al. 1998) could serve in creating artificial response functions. Such an approach, however, requires a considerable simulation work already in the case 5-10 few crops and soil types.

6. Conclusion

The presented research method is crucially based on the cumulative gains in the process of gradually increasing farm size at the local level. Small initial farm size, or any significant interruption in the process of farm size growth and improved labour efficiency, may lead to increased regional concentration of production over time. This means that agriculture at weaker agricultural areas will deteriorate while production at the national level can be considered more competitive if the concentration development is not intervened. The multi-regional sector model presented and discussed in this study explains increasing concentration of production in some particular areas. This development is confirmed by observed patterns of production concentration.
It must be recognised that the production development, and hence the development of regional production level and structure as well, is dependent on the exogenous parameters of the DREMFIA model, like the opportunity cost of labour, inflation of input prices, and general interest rate. Since the exogenous variables are the same in all policy scenarios, however, they are not likely to affect the relative changes in production development between the policy scenarios.

One can conclude that the diffusion models combined with recursive-dynamic optimisation model of agricultural sector provide analytically simple but not easily applicable approach in modelling aggregate investments and technical change. In principle the combination of the models provides a dynamic view of agricultural development and structural change without many complications prevalent in econometric approaches resulting from dynamics and a large number of dimensions in regional sector level models. However, the difficulty lies in the combination and coupling between diffusion and optimisation models. Concerning the particular diffusion scheme one can find a unique set of parameter values which explain ex- post structural development. However, since changes in market prices affect investments, the parameters of the diffusion models are conditional on the particular market module specification and its regional dis-aggregation and cannot be validated independently. Nevertheless the overall direction and magnitude of the production changes seem to be robust to minor changes in the diffusion model parameters.

On the other hand the optimisation approach employed in the market model facilitate explicit treatment of physical quantities, description of inputs (kg/ha, animal), and their substitution (such as imperfect substitution between chemical fertiliser and manure used as fertiliser; utilisation for plants). This makes the approach suitable for integrations and interdisciplinary research. Furthermore, the richness of the optimisation approach also lies in duality, i.e the use of dual variables (shadow prices) of explicit resource constraints and balance equations (interpreted as prices). Hence the approach taken can be made efficient in terms of utilisation of different kind of data used in validation. In practical terms, the model and its components need to be tuned to the data, and there are many options for that in optimisation approach.

Increasing model complexity and size by including endogenous investments and technical change in the economic model does not necessarily obscure economic logic. Rather, such an approach may provide a better understanding of dynamics and directions of future development. Nevertheless, one needs to keep in mind the simplification made in the construction of the technology diffusion model. The fact that current investments are best explained by previous investments is a major determinant of the model results. This simplification made it possible to employ a simple model of technology diffusion and keep the model structure clear and understandable.

If it turns out in the future that the earlier investments do not lower the threshold of new investments, or that only little economies of scale will be attained when enlarging farm size, then the self-enforcing pattern of technical change is overestimated in the DREMFIA model. In that case the future production development is less dependent on agricultural policy than outlined in this study. On the other hand, if the economies of scale will be higher than anticipated on the basis of farm level bookkeeping data, the future production levels, regional concentration of production, and environmental effects are underestimated.

7. References

Boogaard, H. L., C.A. van Diepen, R.P. Rötter, J.M. Cabrera, and H.H. van Laar, 1998. User's guide for the WOFOST 7.1 crop growth simulation model and Control Center 1.5, Alterra, Wageningen, The Netherlands, 143 pp.

Bärlund, I., Lehtonen, H. & Tattari, S. 2005. Assessment of environmental impacts following alternative agricultural policy scenarios. Water Science and Technology, vol. 51, issue 3-4 (March-April 2005) pp. 117-125.

Cox, T.L. & Chavas, J.-P. 2001. An Interregional Analysis of Price Discrimination and Domestic Policy Reform in the U.S. Dairy Sector. *American Journal of Agricultural Economics* 83: 89–106.

Chavas, J-P. 2001. Structural Change in Agricultural Production. In: B. Gardner and G. Rausser (editors.). Handbook of Agricultural Economics, Vol. 1, Ch. 5, 263-285, Elsevier Science B.V.

Coyle, B. 1992. Risk Aversion and Price Risk in Duality Models of Production: A Linear Mean-Variance Approach. American Journal of Agricultural Economics, Vol. 74, No. 4 (Nov., 1992). P. 849-859.

Ekholm P., Granlund, K., Kauppila, P., Mitikka, S., Niemi, J., Rankinen, K., Räike, A., Räsänen, J. 2007. Influence of EU policy on agricultural nutrient losses and the state of receiving surface waters in Finland. *Agricultural and Food Science* Vol. 16 (2007), No. 4, p. 282-300. http://www.mtt.fi/afs/pdf/mtt-afs-v16n4p282.pdf

Frei, C.W., Haldi, P-A and Sarlos, G. (2003). Dynamic formulation of a top-down and bottom-up merging energy policy model. *Energy Policy* 31, 1017-1031

Hagedoorn, J. (1989), The Dynamic Analysis of Innovation and Diffusion. Pinter Publishers 1989. 197 p.

Hardaker, J., Huirne, R., Anderson, J. & Lien, G. 1997: Coping with Risk in Agriculture. Second edition. CAP Publishing. USA.

Hazell, P. & Norton, R. 1986. Mathematical programming for economic analysis in agriculture. MacMillan, New york, USA. 400 p.

Heikkilä, A-M, Riepponen, L. & Heshmati, A. 2004. Investments in new technology to improve productivity of dairy farms. Paper presented in 91st EAAE seminar "Methodological and Empirical Issues of Productivity and Efficiency Measurement in the Agri-Food System", Rethymno, Greece, September 24-26, 2004.

Jalonoja, K., Pietola, K. 2004. Spatial integration between Finnish and Dutch potato markets. Acta agriculturae Scandinavica. Section C Food economics 1, 1, April 2004: 12-20.

Johansson, R.C. and Kaplan, J.D. 2004. A carrot-and-stick approach to environmental improvement: marrying agri-environmental payments and water quality regulations. *Agricultural and Resource Economics Review* 33: 91-104.

Karshenas, M. and Stoneman, P. 1995, Technological Diffusion. In: Stoneman, P. (ed.), Handbook of the Economics of Innovation and Technological Change, p. 265-297.

Lehtonen, H. 2001. Principles, structure and application of dynamic regional sector model of Finnish agriculture. Academic dissertation. MTT Publications 98. Helsinki, Finland.

Lehtonen, H. 2004. Impacts of de-coupling agricultural support on dairy investments and milk production volume in Finland. *Acta Agriculturae Scandinavica, Section C: Food Economics* 1: 46-62.

Lehtonen, H., Aakkula, J. & Rikkonen, P. 2005. Alternative Policy Scenarios, Sector Modelling and Indicators: A Sustainability Assessment. *Journal of Sustainable Agriculture, Vol. 26: Issue 4 (August 2005).*

Lehtonen, H., Pyykkönen, P. 2005. Maatalouden rakennekehitysnäkymät vuoteen 2013 (Structural change in Finnish agriculture up to 2013). MTT:n selvityksiä 100: 40 s., 1 liite. An English abstract is included. http://www.mtt.fi/mtts/pdf/mtts100.pdf

Mapp, H.P., Bernardo, D.J., Sappagh, G.J., Geleta, S. and Watkins, K.B. 1994. Economic and environmental impacts of limiting nitrogen use to protect water quality: a stochastic regional analysis. *American Journal of Agricultural Economics* 76: 889-903.

Nelson, R.R., Winter, S.G., 2002. Evolutionary theorizing in economics. *The Journal of Economic Perspectives* 16 (2), 23–46.

Pietola, K. 1997. A generalised model of investment with an application to Finnish hog farms. Agricultural Economics Research Institute, Finland. Publications 84. 113 p.

Rankinen, K., Kenttämies, K., Lehtonen, H. & Nenonen, S. 2006: Nitrogen load predictions under land management scenarios for a boreal river basin in northern Finland. *Boreal Environment.Research* 11: 213–228.

Rantamäki-Lahtinen, L., Remes, K. & Koikkalainen, K., 2002. The investment and production plans in Finnish bookkeeping farms. Agrifood Research Finland, Economic Research (MTTL), Working Papers 4/2002, 6-40.

Rekolainen S., Salt C.A., Bärlund I., Tattari S. and Culligan-Dunsmore M., 2002. Impacts of the management of radioactively contaminated land on soil and phosphorus losses in Finland and Scotland. *Water, Air, Soil Pollut.*, 139, 115-136.

Shou J.S., Skop E. and Jensen J.D., 2000. Integrated agri-environmental modelling: a cost-effectiveness analysis of two nitrogen tax instruments in the Vejle Fjord watershed, Denmark. *J. Environ. Manage.*, 58, 199-212.

Sckokai, P. 2004. Modelling impacts of agricultural policies on farm investments under uncertainty: The case of arable crop regime. Paper presented in OECD workshop on de-coupling in Paris 3-4 June 2004. http://www.oecd.org/dataoecd/14/27/34996395.pdf

Soete, L. and R. Turner. 1984. Technology diffusion and the rate of technical change. *Economic Journal* 94: 612-623.

Sue Wing, I. 2006. The synthesis of bottom-up and top-down approaches to climate policy modelling: Electric power technologies and the cost of limiting US CO_2 emissions. *Energy Policy* 34:3847-3869.

Sue Wing, I., & W.P. Anderson 2007. Modeling Small Area Economic Change in Conjunction with a Multiregional CGE Model, in R.J. Cooper, K.P. Donaghy and G.J.D. Hewings (eds.), *Globalization and Regional Economic Modeling*, Springer-Verlag (Advances in Spatial Science).

Tattari S., Bärlund I., Rekolainen S., Posch M., Siimes K., Tuhkanen H.-R. and Yli-Halla M., 2001. Modelling sediment yield and phosphorus transport in Finnish clayey soils. *Trans. ASAE*, 44 (2), 297-307.

Tiainen, J. & Pakkala, T. 2000. Population changes and monitoring of farmland birds in Finland. In: *Linnut-vuosikirja 1999*. BirdLife Suomi. Helsinki, Finland. p. 98-105.

Tiainen, J. & Pakkala, T. 2001. Birds. In: Pitkänen, M. and Tiainen, J. (eds.). *Biodiversity of Agricultural Landscapes in Finland. BirdLife Finland Conservation Series* (No3.). Helsinki, Finland. p.33-50.

Tiainen, J., Kuussaari, M., Laurila, I.P. & Toivonen, T. (eds) 2004. *Elämää pellossa - Suomen maatalousympäristön monimuotoisuus.* Edita Publishing Oy, Helsinki. 366 p.

Turtola, E. 2007. Preface. Agricultural and Food Science Vol. 16 (2007), No. 4, p. 279-281. http://www.mtt.fi/afs/pdf/mtt-afs-v16n4p279_preface.pdf

8

Advanced Simulation for Semi-Autogenous Mill Systems: A Simplified Models Approach

José Luis Salazar[1], Héctor Valdés-González[1] and Francisco Cubillos[2]
[1]*Universidad Andres Bello, Facultad de Ingeniería, Escuela de Industrias, Santiago*
[2]*Universidad de Santiago de Chile, Departamento de Ing. Química, Santiago*
Chile

1. Introduction

Modelling and simulation of semi-autogenous (SAG) mills are valuable tools for helping to design control laws for a given application and subsequently to optimise its performance and process control. SAG mills (see Figure 1) are presently one of the most widely used alternatives in the field of mineral size reduction as a result of their advantages such as higher processing capacity, lower physical space requirements, and lower investment and maintenance costs, as compared to conventional circuits (Salazar, et al., 2009).
Due to the size of SAG mills, pilot plants are usually used for research purposes to improve the control strategies. In cases where a pilot-scale is not available for test, simulations using models based on data from a wide range of full-scale plants are helpful and can significantly reduce risks for process control purposes. Simulations also provide an additional and very valuable crosscheck against the pilot results (Morell, 2004).

Fig. 1. Typical semi-autogenous (SAG) mills

This chapter presents a dynamic simulator of a semi-autogenous grinding operation deduced from first principles coupled to an on-line parameter estimation scheme able to simulate industrial operations for future control purposes. The proposed procedure for simulation purposes is as follows: Model equations are based on a conventional non-stationary population balance approach to develop the necessary dynamic model of the semi-autogenous mill operation. The presented models are able to predict the time-evolution of key operating variables such as product flow rate, level charge, power-draw,

load position and others, as functions of other important variables such as mill rotational speed and fresh feed characteristics. The set of ordinary differential equations was solved using MATLAB/SIMULINK as a graphic programming platform, a useful tool for understanding the grinding process.
Additionally, this work presents results using dynamic simulations from a 1700 t/h copper–ore mill showing the effectiveness of the system to track the dynamic behaviour of the variables.
The remainder of this chapter is organised as follows. Theory about specific models for SAG mill processes is presented in section 2. Simulations for the prescribed application are presented in section including the results using MATLAB/SIMULINK. The main conclusions of the chapter are provided in the final section, as well as ideas about future industrial applications of this work.

2. Models for semi-autogenous mills

Essentially, the modelling exercise consists in formulating non steady-state material balances in the milling equipment, along with force conservation relations and hydraulic considerations. The methodology used in this study has already been established by Magne (Magne et al., 1995) and Morrell (Morrell, 2004) and involves formulating particle inventories for each particle size inside the mill. The input variables are: water flow rate, mineral flow rate and size distribution, grinding media flow rate and the mill critical speed. The model output variables are: power-draw, load level, ball load, mineral discharge rate and size distribution, water discharge rate, ball throughput, bearing pressure, pebble throughput, and toe and shoulder angles of the internal load.

2.1 SAG mill model

The particles fed to the mill are ground in the milling chamber and subsequently downloaded into the discharge zone, where, according to a classification probability, they are either returned to the milling chamber for further grinding or become part of the mill output stream. For modelling purposes the mill is divided in two zones according to the process taking place (Fig. 2). The first zone encompasses the milling chamber where the particle reduction process is identified and modelled. In the second, the output zone, the material is internally classified and the final product is discharged. To complete the system

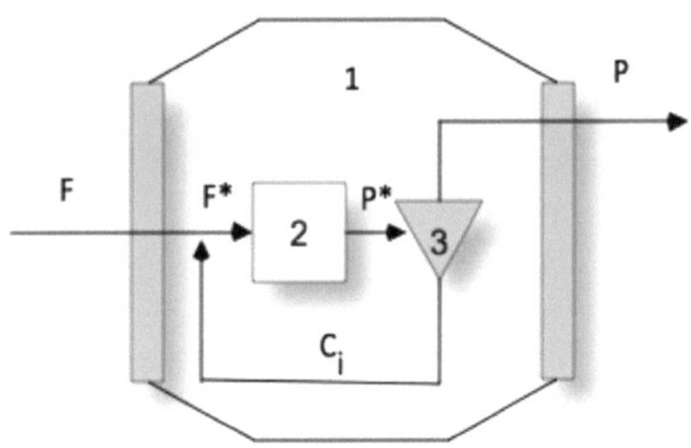

Fig. 2. Schematic representation of a SAG mill. (1) Mill. (2) Grinding Chamber. (3) Internal classifier

description it is necessary to consider the relationship between the feed stream and mill charge level. This relationship is known as the transport rate and is probably the least developed aspect in models proposed so far (Apelt et al., 2002 a,b).

2.2 Transport and water balance

The fictitious flow P* (Fig. 2.) that represents the amount of mineral in the internal charge that is handled by the classification grate or internal classification, is the representation of the mineral transport proposed by Magne (Magne et al., 1995). Several experimental studies have found the following rather unsatisfactory correlation of P* with the mass of the mineral retained in the mill W:

$$P^{*} = 29 \cdot W^{0,5} \tag{1}$$

Where W is in tonnes (t) and P* in t/h.

2.3 Water balance

The following equation represents the experimental variation of the internal water load, $W_W(t)$, as a result of changes in input and output water flow rates, F_W and P_W (t/h), the latter being estimated by $P_W = C_W \cdot W_W$ (Magne et al., 1995):

$$\frac{dW_w}{dt} = F_a - C_w \cdot W_w \tag{2}$$

The parameter C_W (h^{-1}), water output, has been correlated to the mass of mineral in the mill, W, according to the following relation (Magne et al., 1995):

$$C_w = \exp\left(64.41 - 19.56\ln(W) + 1.55\left(\ln(W)\right)^2\right) \tag{3}$$

The proposition that the classification system always allows particles of a size less than X_m to pass (Fig. 3) is the basis for the development proposed by Morrell (Morrell, 2004), who, like Magne (Magne et al, 1995), considers that particles less than this size behave like water in the grinding chamber, i.e. all particles with less than a certain size pass through the grate with the same classification efficiency.

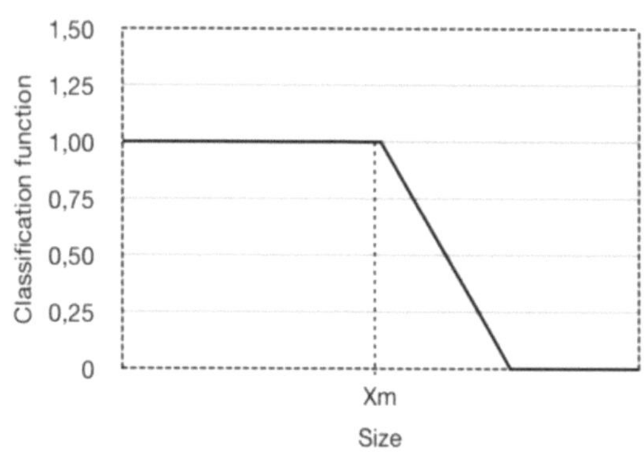

Fig. 3. Classification function against particle size

This discharge function, constant for sizes less than X_m and defined as d_m, is directly related to the flow of discharge of the pulp by the size of the mill, p_i, and the mass of the particles in the internal charge of the mill, w_i, according to:

$$d_m = \frac{\sum_m p_i}{\sum_m w_i} \tag{4}$$

In order to determine this discharge function, Morrell (Morrell, 2004) considers two effects. The first is the flow via grinding media interstices, and the second considers the flow via the slurry pool (where present). In addition, the contributions of Latchireddi (Latchireddi, 2002) have allowed this proposition to be studied in large-scale pilot models and to determine the influence of the design and the geometry of the mill pulp lifters. The results of the correlation between the fill level and discharge flow can be seen in the following general equation:

$$J = \eta \gamma^{n_1} A^{n_2} J_b^{n_3} \phi^{n_4} Q^{n_5} D^{n_6} \tag{5}$$

Where:
J is the net fractional slurry hold-up inside the mill;
A is the fractional open area;
J_b is the fractional grinding media volume;
ϕ is the fraction of critical speed;
Q is the slurry discharge flowrate;
γ is the mean relative radial position of the grate holes;
η is the coefficient of resistance, which varied depending on whether flow was via the grinding media interstices or the slurry pool (where present); and
n_1-n_6 are the models parameters.
The value of γ is a weighted radial position, which is expressed as a fraction of the mill radius and is calculated using the formula:

$$\gamma = \frac{\sum r_i a_i}{r_m \sum a_i} \tag{6}$$

Where a_i is the open area of all holes at a radial position r_i, and r_m is the radius of the mill inside the liners.
Latchireddi's (Latchireddi, 2002) contribution can be seen in the parameters n_i and η from equation (6) which shows the effect of the design of the pulp lifter. These were modeled according to:

$$n_i = n_g - k_i e^{(-k_j \lambda)} \tag{7}$$

Where:
n_g are the parameter values for the grate-only condition;
λ is the depth of the pulp lifter expressed as a fraction of mill diameter; and
k_i and k_j are constants.

For large-scale mills, the pulp discharge flow can be determined by combining equations (4) and (5) as follows:

$$d_m = \frac{Q}{J} \tag{8}$$

The calculation procedure can be transformed in an iterative numerical sequence.
A numerical approximation of the proposal by Gupta & Yan (Gupta & Yan, 2006) shows the product flow (m^3/h) from equation (5) as separate from the flow of the fluid through the zone of grinding medium (equation 9) and the flow from the pool zone (equation 10).

$$Q_M = 6100\,\gamma^{2,5} A\, J_H^{\,2}\, j^{-1,38} D^{0,5} \quad J_H < J_{MAX} \tag{9}$$

$$Q_t = 935\gamma^2 A\, J_S D^{0,5} \quad J_S = J_P - J_{MAX}, J_P > J_{MAX} \tag{10}$$

Where:
γ is the mean relative radial position of the grate apertures;
A is the total area of all apertures (m^2);
ϕ is the fraction of the critical speed of the mill;
D is the mill diameter (m);
Q_M is the volume flow rate through the grinding media zone (m^3/h);
Q_t is the volume flow rate of slurry through the pool zone, (m^3/h);
J_H is the net fraction of slurry hold-up within the interstitial spaces of the grinding media;
J_S is the net fractional volume of slurry in the slurry pool;
J_{MAX} is the maximum net fraction of slurry in the grinding zone; and
J_P is the net fraction of the mill volume occupied by pulp.

2.4 Internal classification and power-draw

For the internal classifier (Fig. 2.), the balance is carried out by defining a classification efficiency vector, c_i (fraction), which includes two effects: one produced by the mill's internal grate and the other by the pulp evacuation system (Magne et al., 1995). Thus, c_i is defined by:

$$1 - c_i = \frac{p_i}{p_i^*} \tag{11}$$

Where:
p_i is the product flow rate from the mill and p_i^* is the product flow rate from the grinding chamber (fictitious flow).
For each size class i, the mill chamber feed flow rate, f_i^* (t/h), is obtained by adding the mill feed flow rate, f_i (t/h), to the internal recirculation flow rate (Fig. 2.):

$$f_i^* = f_i + c_i p_i^* \tag{12}$$

Under experimental considerations (Magne et al., 1995) it is possible to find the following expression of the classification efficiency vector, where x_i is the size of particle, c_f is the solid pulp percentage and β is a parameter.

$$c_i = \psi\beta(x_i M)^{\beta-1}\exp\left(-\psi(x_i M)^{\beta}\right) + \frac{1}{1+\left(\frac{x_i}{x_{50}}\right)^z} \tag{13}$$

$$\psi = \exp\left(-13.12\ln(c_f) - 6.61\right) \tag{14}$$

$$M = \exp\left(16.53\ln(c_f) + 5.54\right) \tag{15}$$

For each size class i, Magne's (Magne et al, 1995) proposed model relates the mass variation in the milling chamber (Fig. 2) to the feed flow rate to the grinding chamber, f_i^* (t/h), to the product flow rate from the grinding chamber, p_i^* (t/h), and to the comminution kinetics, as follows:

$$\frac{dw_i}{dt} = f_i^* - p_i^* - K_i w_i - (K_i - K_{i-1})\sum_{l=1}^{i-1} w_l \tag{16}$$

Where K_i (h^{-1}) denotes the effective parameter (corresponding to S_i in conventional grinding) and w_i is the weight of size i particles in the mill charge (t).
The effective parameter, K_i is defined as the fraction of specific power supplied to the mill:

$$K_i = K_i^E \frac{M_p}{W} \tag{17}$$

Where K_i^E is defined as the specific grinding rate constant (t/kWh), M_p is the power-draw (kW) and W the total ore weight in the chamber (t). The equation used to predict the power consumed by the mill (power-draw), M_p, is based on a modification of Bond's Law (Austin, 1990):

$$M_p = K_p D^{2.5} L(1 - A\cdot J)\left(\frac{W}{V}\right)\phi_c\left[1 - \frac{0.1}{2^{9-10\phi_c}}\right] \tag{18}$$

Where D (m) and L (m) are the mill dimensions, V (m^3) is the mill effective volume, and K_p and A are parameters. The ratio between the internal load mass and the mill volume, (W/V), is related to the percentage of mill capacity by the following equation:

$$\frac{W}{V} = (1-\varepsilon_b)J\rho_s(1+w_c) + 0.6J_b\left(\rho_b - \rho_s(1+w_c)\right) \tag{19}$$

Where ε_b is the porosity of the mill internal load (void fraction), ρ_s (t/m^3) and ρ_b (t/m^3) are the density of mineral and balls respectively, w_c is the mill water/mineral mass ratio, and J_b (fraction) is the ball weight fraction.
Assuming that the mill chamber behaves like a perfectly mixed reactor (Whiten, 1974), p_i^* can be related to particle size i mill charge by:

$$p_i^* = w_i\left(\frac{P^*}{W}\right) \tag{20}$$

Where P* is the contribution of the total internal flow rate to the product stream (t/h). The relation between P* and W can be obtained assuming that there is no recycling of fines from the internal classifier. This assumption simplifies the mass balance equation and allows the calculation of P* on the basis of the product flow rate of fine particles, p_n (t/h), and the mass of fines in the internal charge, $w_n(t)$, as shown in equation (21):

$$P^* = W\left(\frac{p_n}{w_n}\right) \tag{21}$$

From equations (12), (16), and (21), the following expression is then obtained for the dynamic mass balance of size i particles in the milling chamber:

$$\frac{dw_i}{dt} = -\left(\frac{P^*}{W}\right)(1-c_i)w_i - K_i w_i - (K_i - K_{i-1})\sum_{l=1}^{i-1} w_l + f_i \tag{22}$$

As in equation (16), Morrell's (2004) proposal for the comminution process gives a similar relationship as follows:

$$\frac{dw_i}{dt} = f_i - p_i + \sum_{j=1}^{i} r_j w_j a_{ij} - r_i w_i \tag{23}$$

$$p_i = d_i w_i \tag{24}$$

Where r_i is a the breakage rate of particles of size i, d_i is the discharge rate of particles of size i and a_{ij} is the breakage distribution function.
The breakage rate function, r_i, can be obtained using data fitting techniques or full-scale mills with the general form being as follows:

$$Ln(r_i) = k_{i1} + k_{i2} J_b D_b + k_{i3}\varphi + k_{i4} J \tag{25}$$

Where D_b is make-up ball size, φ is the mill rotational rate and $k_{i1\text{-}i4}$ are constants. The breakage distribution function, a_{ij}, is obtained via the specific comminution energy, E_{cs} (kWh/t) and the t_{10} parameters estimated, used to generate a size distribution. This equation is:

$$t_{10} = A\left(1 - e^{-b \cdot E_{cs}}\right) \tag{26}$$

Where A and b are parameters of rock breakage.
The mill power-draw studied by Morrell (Morrell, 2004) is similar to that used by Austin (Austin, 1990) and considers the individual power requirements for the cylindrical section and the conical sections. The mill power, P_m (kW), is then the sum of the net power, P_{net} (kW) and the no load power, P_{nl} (kW). Thus:

$$P_m = P_{net} + P_{nl} \tag{27}$$

$$P_{nl} = 1.68 D^{2.05}\left(\phi_c\left(0.667 L_{cone} + L_{cyl}\right)\right)^{0.82} \tag{28}$$

$$P_{net} = 7.98D^{2.5}L_e\rho_s J\left(\frac{5.97\phi_c - 4.43\phi_c^{\ 2} - 0.985 - J}{\left(5.97\phi_c - 4.43\phi_c^{\ 2} - 0.985\right)^2}\right)\phi_c\left(1 - \left(1 - 0.954 + 0.135J\right)e^{-19.52(0.954+0.135J-\phi_c)}\right) \quad (29)$$

$$L_e = L\left(1 + 2.28J\left(1 - J\right)\frac{L_d}{L}\right) \quad (30)$$

Where L_d (m) is the medium size of the final section of the conical zone, and L_{cone} and L_{cyl} are the sizes (m) of the conical and cylindrical sections of SAG mill.

2.5 Grinding media, bearing pressure and load position

The mass of grinding media inside the chamber is determined by a mass balance considering the ball replacement rate and the metal consumption rate; this latter parameter is proportional to the mass of mineral in the mill (Salazar et al., 2009):

$$\frac{dW_b}{dt} = F_b - \chi\left(W + W_b\right) \quad (31)$$

Where W_b is the ball mass (t) in the mill, F_b the ball replacement rate (t/h), χ a ball wear constant (h^{-1}) and W the total internal mineral load (t).
The bearing pressure, P_b (psi) is estimated as a linear function of the total weight of the milling chamber (balls, water and mineral) as shown in equation (32) (Salazar et al., 2009), where α and λ are fitted parameters. The load position is expressed in terms of toe and shoulder angles, which are calculated by relations (33 to 35) (Apelt et al., 2001):

$$P_b = \alpha + \lambda\left(W + W_w + W_b\right) \quad (32)$$

$$\theta_T = 2.5307\left(1.2796 - J\right)\left(1 - e^{-19.42(\phi-\phi_c)}\right) + \frac{\pi}{2} \quad (33)$$

$$\theta_s = \frac{\pi}{2} - \left(\theta_T - \frac{\pi}{2}\right)\left(\left(0.3386 + 0.1041\phi_c\right) + \left(1.54 - 2.5673\phi_c\right)J\right) \quad (34)$$

$$\phi = 0.35\left(3.364 - J\right) \quad (35)$$

Where θ_T is the toe angle (radians), θ_S the shoulder angle (radians).

3. Simulation

3.1 SAG in Matlab-Simulink

The numerical solution of the set of algebraic–differential equations (model) described in the previous section, is obtained through a system in MATLAB/SIMULINKTM (Figure 3). Simulink is a programming system structured in blocks, which allows the solution of differential equations as well as the programming of user-blocks through S-functions. This feature, together with the possibility of using Matlab's specific toolboxes, makes it a powerful platform for the development of prototypes. The present model can be seen as a more complex simulation block compatible with this simulation strategy in (Salazar et al., 2009).

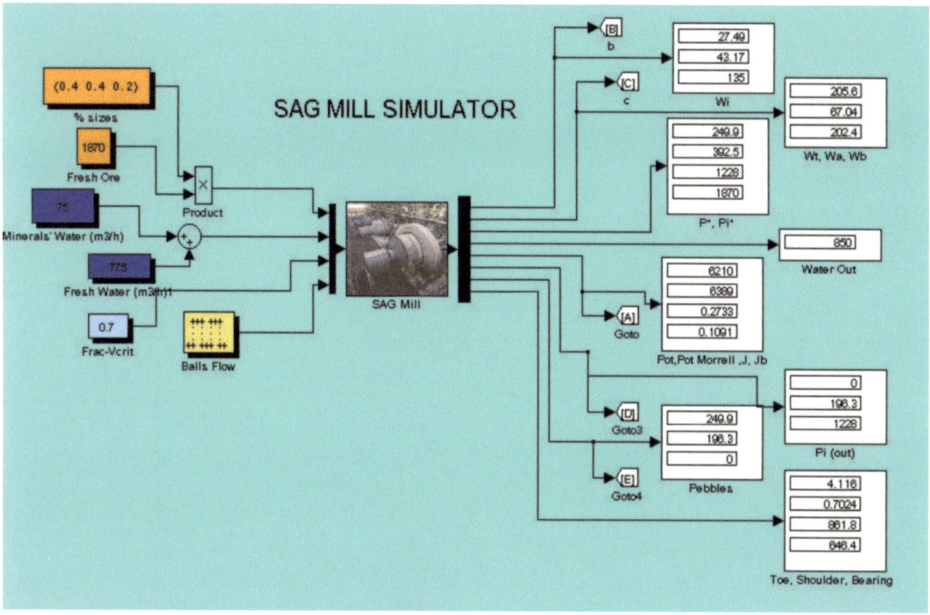

Fig. 3. SAG mill simulator in Matlab-Simulink

3.2 Results

An example of the simulation results is presented in Figs. 4 to 7. These figures respectively show the response of the power-draw and the fill level for the Magne approach (Magne et al., 1995) in Figures 4 and 5, and for the Morell approach (Morrell, 2004) in Figures 6 and 7. The results are the product of 10% flow change related to the nominal operation conditions (1700 t/h).

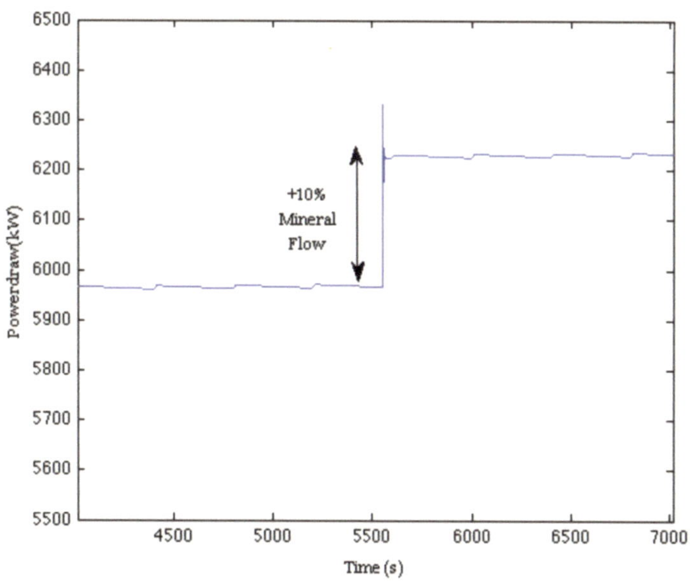

Fig. 4. Magne's model power-draw response

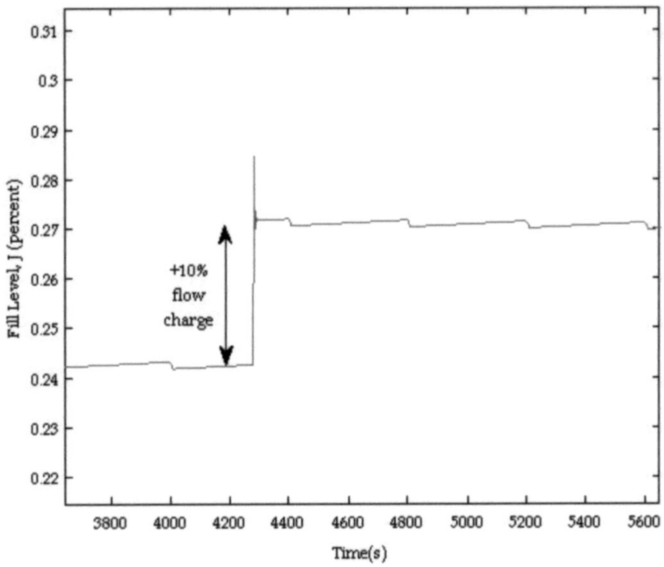

Fig. 5. Magne's model fill level response

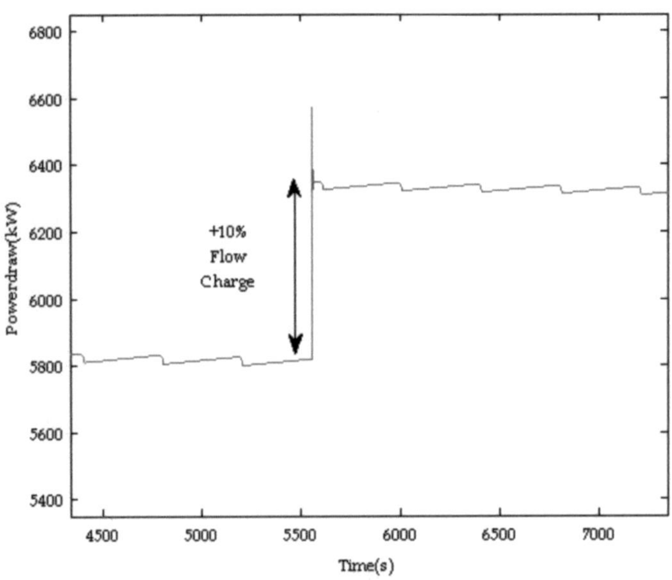

Fig. 6. Morell's model power-draw response

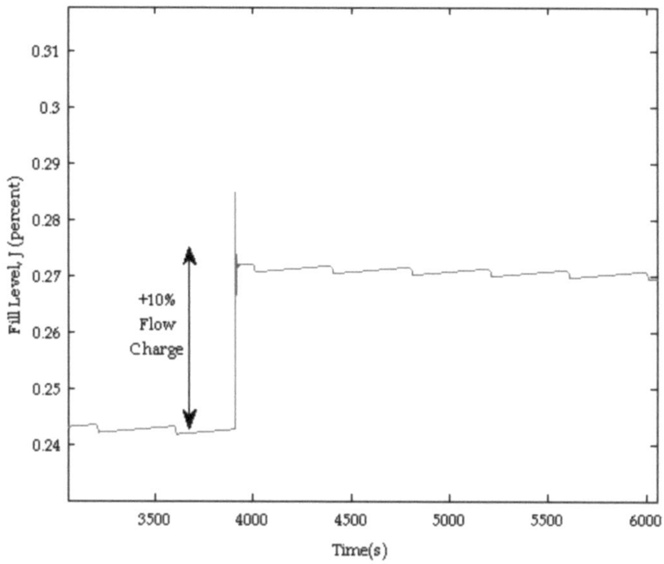

Fig. 7. Morell's model fill level response

4. Conclusion

Advanced simulation for semi-autogenous mill systems has been presented in the context of a simplified models approach that incorporated developments of (Magne et al., 1995) and Morrell (Morrell, 2004) among the others. A main focus has also been a comparison of these two models. This comparison showed that both models provided good predictive capability of two very important process variables, power draw and fill-level, especially under the same simulation conditions.

It is interesting to note that despite differences in the theoretical background for these approaches, the results of dynamic simulations under industrial operational conditions are similar. Thus, these results validate adequately the comminution process in the SAG mill, and in the future, these models could be combined for industrial purposes. With these results we believe that is possible to scale-up from pilot plant simulation and to optimise existing circuits for process control purposes using combinations of these models to reduce risks and improve performance.

5. Acknowledgment

The authors wish to acknowledge the support provided by *FONDECYT* (Project 1090062) and UNAB (project DI 4709/R).

6. References

Apelt, T.A.; Asprey, S.P. & Thornhill, N.F. (2001). Inferential measurement of SAG mill parameters. *Minerals Engineering*, 14 (6), 575–591.

Apelt, T.A.; Asprey, S.P. & Thornhill, N.F. (2002a). Inferential measurement of SAG mill parameters II: state stimulation. *Minerals Engineering*, 15 (12), 1043–1053.

Apelt, T.A.; Asprey, S.P. & Thornhill, N.F. (2002b). Inferential measurement of SAG mill parameters III: inferential models. *Minerals Engineering*, 15 (12), 1055–1071.

Austin, L.G. (1990). A mill power equation for SAG mills. *Minerals and Metallurgical Processing*, 7, 57–62.

Gupta, A. & D. Yan. (2006). *Mineral processing design and operation: an introduction*, Elsevier Science Ltd, ISBN 0-444-51636-7, 978-0-444-51636-7, Netherland.

Latchireddi, S. (2002). *Modelling of the performance of grates and pulp lifters in autogenous and semi autogenous mills*, Queensland, Australia. Ph.D.

Magne, L.; Amestica, R.; Barría, J. & Menacho, J. (1995). Modelización dinámica de molienda semiautógena basada en un modelo fenomenológico simplificado. *Revista de Metalurgia Madrid*, 31(2), 97-105.

Morrell, S. (2004). A new autogenous and semi-autogenous mill model for scale-up, design and optimisation. *Minerals Engineering*, 17 (3), 437-445.

Salazar, J.L.; Magne, L.; Acuña, G.& Cubillos, F. (2009). Dynamic modelling and simulation of semi-autogenous mills. *Minerals Engineering*, 22 (1), 70-77.

Whiten, W.J. (1974). A matrix theory of comminution machines. *Chemical Engineering Science*, 29 (2), 589-599.

9

Dynamic Modelling Predictions of Airborne Acidification of Polish Terrestrial Ecosystems

Wojciech Mill
Institute of Environmental Protection
Poland

1. Introduction

Once the Protocol to Abate Acidification, Eutrophication and Ground-level Ozone adopted in Gothenburg in 1999 has entered into force the process of its review started. According to the Protocol statements the adequacy of its obligations and the progress made towards the achievements of its objectives are the basic subjects of this review. Recent scientific findings mainly achieved form the effect-oriented activities of the Working Group on Effects (WGE), a sub-body of the Convention on Long-range Transboundary Air Pollution (CLRTAP), show that a considerable reduction of geographical extent and magnitude of excess acidification would be achieved in 2010 due to the sulphur and nitrogen emission cuts determined by the Protocol obligations (Working Group on Effects, 2004). Nevertheless still some areas also in Poland will remain under the permanent ecological risk resulting from the exceedance of critical loads of acidity. This means that current Protocol commitments are insufficient to prevent these areas from further acidification of ecosystems in a long-term scale and that additional measures are required to protect them. Another important question that the Protocol review answered, addressed to areas where critical loads are not exceeded, was when ecosystems will recover in response to the agreed emission reductions. The both questions may only be answered using a dynamic approach to estimate the response of ecosystems to changes in atmospheric acid deposition thus dynamic models are considered the most appropriate practical tools. A number of dynamic models to simulate acidification of soils and surface waters have been developed, tested and successfully applied to specific integrated monitoring sites in various countries but for a pan-European scale application a new Very Simple Dynamic (VSD) model has been elaborated suitable to support the integrated assessment of emission reduction scenarios (Posch et al., 2003). The VSD model was applied to assess the Polish terrestrial ecosystems soil chemistry reaction and consequently the damage and recovery time delays due to changing acid deposition.
Dynamic modelling calculations were done for six distinct terrestrial habitats (Table 1).
The spatial resolution applied is determined by 1 km^2 grid squares which contains 1 ha or more of the habitat.

2. From steady-state to dynamic approaches

Critical load concept supporting the Gothenburg Protocol is based on a steady-state approach where critical loads are constant depositions that an ecosystem can be exposed to

Ecosystem	EUNIS code	Area km^2	No of grid cells	Percentage of receptor area
Broad-leaved forest	G1	16056	30153	17.8%
Coniferous forest	G3	48398	88151	53.6%
Mixed forest	G4	23107	42992	25.6%
Natural grasslands	E	577	1145	0.6%
Moors and heath land	F	78	128	0.1%
Mire, bog and fen habitats	D	2114	3956	2.3%
	Total	**90330**	**166524**	**100.0%**

Table 1. Ecosystems subject to dynamic modelling calculations

with no damage to its functioning and structure in a long-term perspective. Thus, this concept refers to situation where equilibrium between a given deposition and biochemical status of an ecosystem is reached. A mathematical model has been constructed to reflect quantitatively the considered relations (UBA, 2004)

The model is based on the following mass balance equation:

$$S_{dep} + N_{dep} = BC_{dep} + BC_w - Bc_u + N_u + N_i + N_{de} - ANC_{le} \tag{1}$$

where:

S_{dep} – total S deposition
N_{dep} – total N deposition
BC_{dep} – base cation deposition
BC_w - base cation weathering
Bc_u – base cation uptake
N_i - long-term net immobilization of N in soil organic matter
N_u - net removal of N in harvested vegetation
N_{de} - flux of N to the atmosphere due to denitrification
ANC_{le} – leaching of acid neutralizing capacity

All quantities are given in eq $ha^{-1}yr^{-1}$. BC=Ca+Mg+K+N and Bc=Ca+Mg+K

Because sulphur and nitrogen simultaneously contribute to acidification and nitrogen sinks cannot compensate incoming sulphur acidity due to partial consumption by immobilization and denitrification, a function of critical loads of acidity must be considered of the following shape (Figure 1).

This function is defined by the three quantities:

$CL_{max}S$ - maximum critical load of sulphur, which is the maximum tolerable sulphur deposition in case of zero deposition of nitrogen:

$$CL_{max}S = BC_{dep} + BC_w - Bc_u - ANC_{le(crit)} \tag{2}$$

Where:

$$ANC_{le(crit)} = -Q \cdot (([Al]_{crit} / K_{bibb})^{\frac{1}{3}} + [Al]_{crit}) \tag{3}$$

Q - precipitation surplus [$m^3 ha^{-1} yr^{-1}$]
K_{gibb} - gibbsite equilibrium constant
$[Al]_{crit}$ - critical aluminium concentration in the soil solution

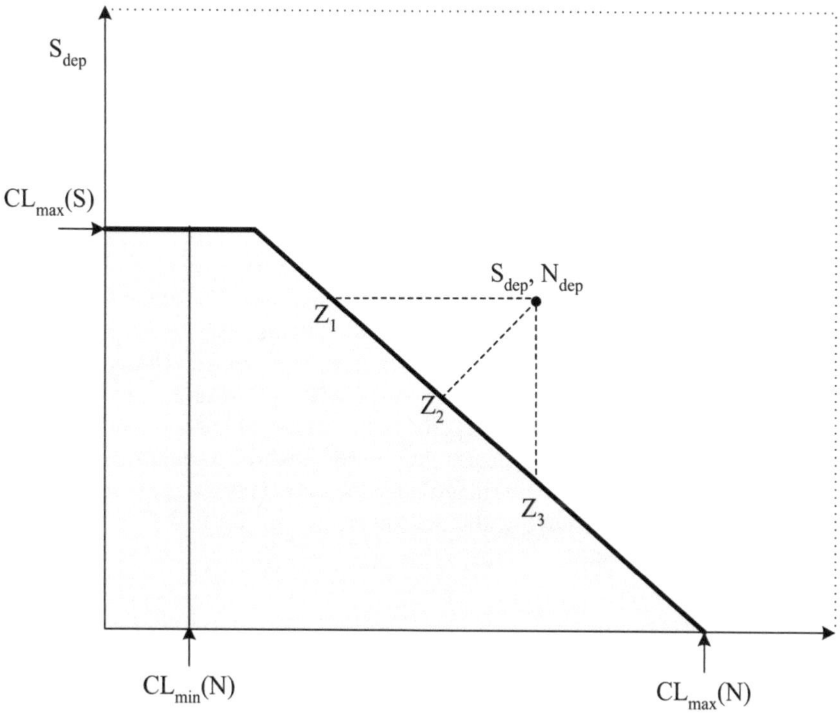

Fig. 1. The critical load function of acidity

$CL_{min}N$ - minimum critical load of nitrogen, which equals to long-term net removal, immobilization and denitrification of nitrogen in soil:

$$CL_{min}N = N_i + N_u + N_{de} \quad (4)$$

$CL_{max}N$ - maximum critical load of nitrogen is the harmless maximum deposition of nitrogen in case of zero sulphur deposition:

$$CL_{max}N = CL_{min}N + \frac{CL_{max}S}{1 - f_{de}} \quad (5)$$

where f_{de} is the denitrification fraction, a site-specific quantity.
However, in reality the equilibrium can practically not be kept due to processes delaying for decades the ecosystems reaction to relatively fast deposition changes. A dynamic model identifies the magnitude of critical loads excedances and areas where they occur and provides information on time of both the damage and recovery delay as well as determines target loads, e.g. the maximum deposition allowed to reach a certain ecological goal within a fixed time horizon. To perform these functions the model structure bridges the steady-state critical load approach with dynamic interpretation of ecological processes in a way that any dynamic model output has to be coherent with results from critical loads calculations. This

consistency is also required by the integrated assessment model RAINS (Alcamo et al., 1990) to evaluate cost effective and technically feasible emission reduction scenarios.
A Very Simple Dynamic (VSD) soil acidification model has been developed (Posch et al., 2003) to provide national scientific communities, acting within the effect-oriented program of the WGE, with a modelling tool of less possible input data requirements.

3. The VSD model concept

The VSD model concept is based on a set of mass balance equations replicating the change over time of the total amount of base cations and nitrogen in soil solution, in response to the temporal changes of atmospheric deposition of acidifying compounds. Consequently, the soil solution chemical status in VSD is interpreted as a product of the net element input from the atmosphere i.e. deposited minus uptaken minus immobilized mass, and the geochemical processes occurring in the soil i.e. CO_2 equilibrium, weathering of carbonates and silicates and cation exchange. The cation exchange mechanism between the liquid phase and the soil exchange complex is described by the Gains-Thomas or Gapon exchange equations. The exchangeable cations considered are: base cations (Ca+Mg+K), aluminium and protons. Soil water transport is simplified by assuming complete mixing of the element flux within one homogenous soil layer of a fixed thickness. Only vertical water transport is considered. The basic output of the VSD model are predicted concentration changes of considered chemical components of the soil water, leaving the soil layer, mostly limited to the root zone. The forecasting time-step is one year.

4. Critical loads database

The recently updated critical load database (Mill & Schlama, 2008) for Polish forest and semi-natural ecosystems was applied. Three parameters of the critical load function for acidity i. e. $CL_{max}S$, $CL_{min}N$ and $CL_{max}N$ have been derived using the Simple Mass Balance model (UBA, 2004) and were addressed to forest and semi-natural ecosystems as the most widespread sensitive receptor of sulphur and nitrogen deposition in Poland. The applied spatial resolution for mapping critical loads and their exceedance was based on a 1x1 km grid cell. Accordingly 166524 single sites were subject to modelling. The long-term average values of input parameters to calculate critical loads were derived from national or single site measurements. Data from 1468 I-level and 148 II-level forest monitoring sites provided the main input to calculations (Wawrzoniak & Małachowska, 2006). From this monitoring soil physical and chemical property, base cation depositions and vegetation parameters were derived. Default values of denitrification fraction, nitrogen immobilization, and gibbsite equilibrium constants have been obtained through an extensive review of existing literature data or adopted from the Manual for Modelling and Mapping (UBA, 2004). For mineral/organo-mineral soils dominating in the considered ecosystems the critical chemical threshold $[Al]_{crit}$= 0.2 eq · m^{-3} was used.
Geostatistical smoothing techniques were used to generate interpolated critical load maps of 1x1 km grid resolution from monitoring sites maps.

5. VSD model database

In addition to data already existing in the critical load database parameters characterizing the cation exchange process and nitrogen balance have been derived and inserted into the

VSD model database. These are soil bulk density, cation exchange capacity CEC, base saturation, exchangeable cation fractions and C/N ratio. All of the data are based on the II-level forest monitoring records (Wawrzoniak & Małachowska, 2006) assigned to the following four soil horizons: O - 0.05 m, A/E - 0.10 m, B - 0.30 m and C - 0.40 m. While VSD is a single-layer model the input data were averaged over the entire rooting zone of 0.5 m depth. These parameters (except C/N ratio) multiplied by soil layer thickness produce the pool of exchangeable cations.

Cation exchange constants based both on the Gaines-Thomas and Gapon exchange reactions were adopted form the Manual for Dynamic Modelling of Soil Response to Atmospheric Deposition (Posch et al., 2003). Historic sulphur and nitrogen deposition sequences contained in the VSD model were applied.

6. Results and discussion

The basic calculation runs were preceded with a preliminary step aimed at the exclusion from further calculations all these sites where critical loads are not exceeded in 2010 and the adopted chemical criterion is not violated. There is no need to calculate target loads for such sites. This operation resulted in a decrease of the total number of 166524 sites gathered in the national database to 48721 sites for which further tests were performed. Table2 summarizes the VSD model results with three possible cases distinguished.

STATUS	Target Year					
	2030		2050		2100	
Ecosystems safe in target year	9208	18.9 %	9403	19.3%	9574	19.7%
Target load function exists	38855	79.8 %	39172	80.2%	39147	80.4%
Target load not feasible	658	1.4 %	146	0.5%	0	0.0%

Table 2. Number and percentage of forest sites assigned by the VSD model to three situations characteristic for dynamic response of forest soil chemistry to changing acid deposition

Ecosystem safe in a target year is a one for which critical load is not exceeded and the chemical criterion is not violated. As can be seen from the above table 18.9% forest sites in 2030 to 19.7% in 2100 are safe in the considered target years when acid deposition remains at the level corresponding to the Gothenburg Protocol obligations.

The next step in the model calculations was to find sites which are safe in a given target year with background deposition determined by EMEP MSC-W i. e. the lowest possible deposition caused by non-anthropogenic emissions only. This group of sites appeared to be the biggest making up to approximately 80% of all processed sites.

The third group of sites selected from the database by the VSD model is composed of sites for which target loads are not feasible i.e. the chemical criterion cannot be reached in the target year even at depositions reduced to background values. There are 1.4 % of such sites for the target year 2030 and 0.5 % for 2050 while for 2100 it is not the case.

Figures 2 to 4 show how the dynamic characteristic is spatially distributed over the Polish terrestrial ecosystems in the considered time horizons.

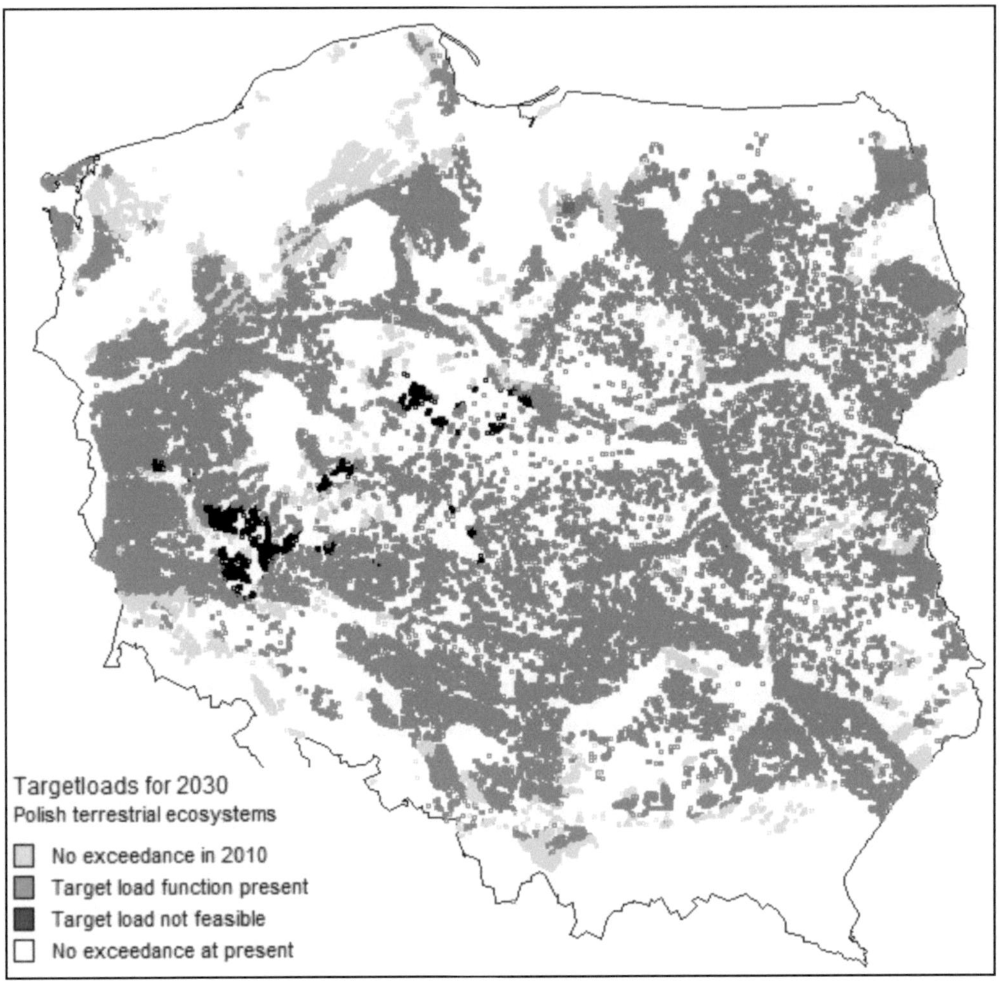

Fig. 2. Spatial distribution of results of target load calculations for 2030

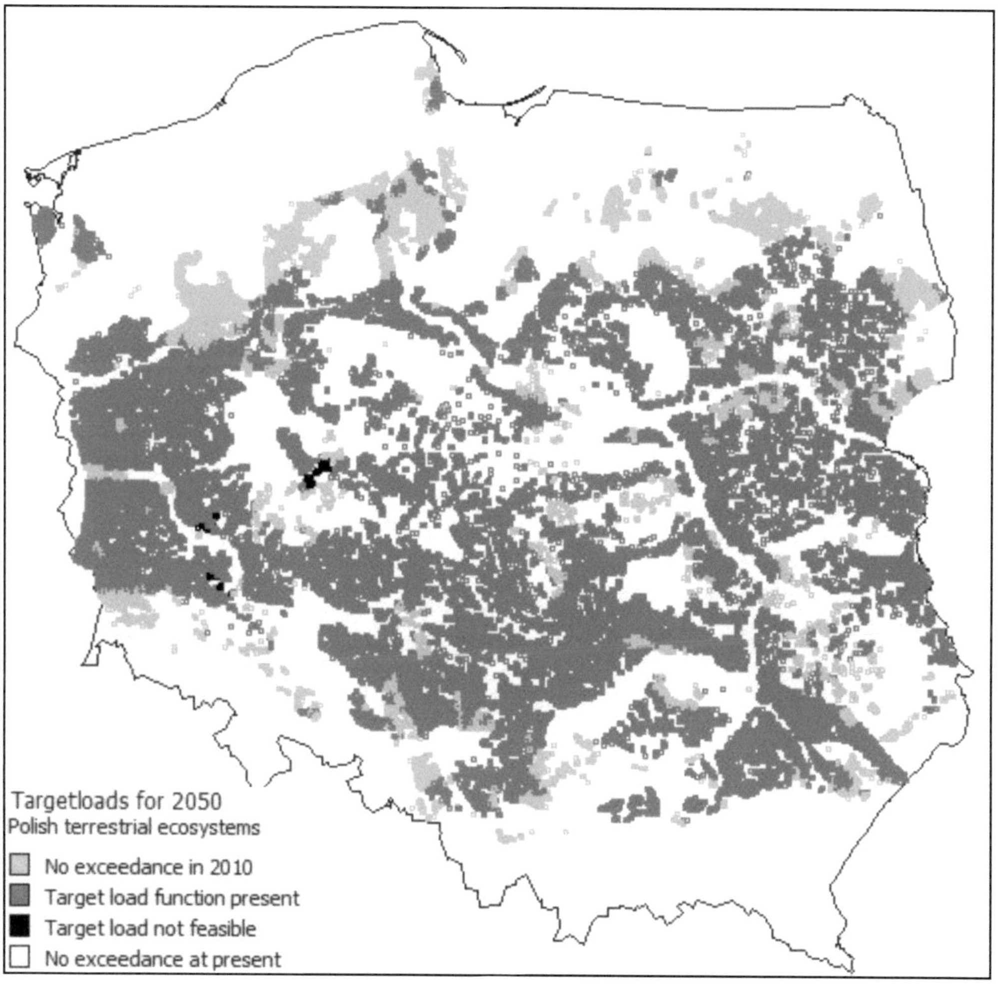

Fig. 3. Spatial distribution of results of target load calculations for 2050

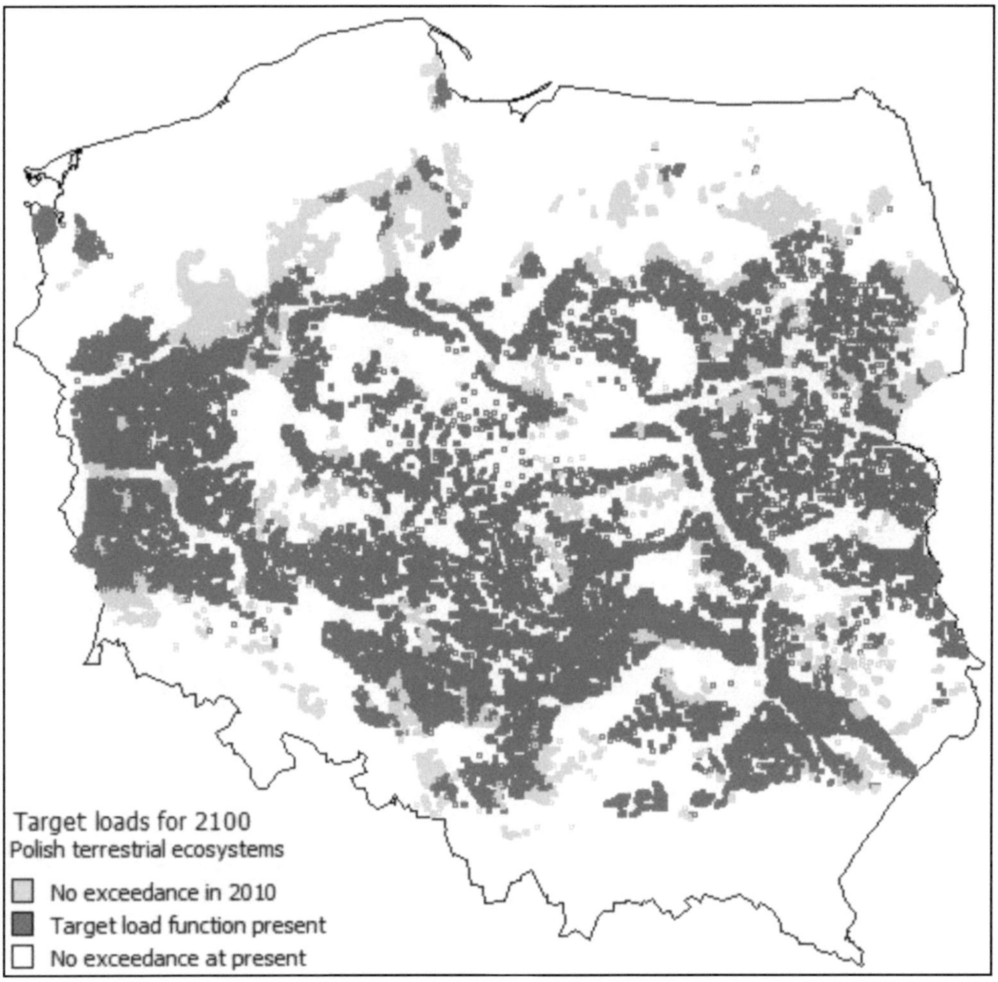

Fig. 4. Spatial distribution of results of target load calculations for 2100

Sites for which no exceedance in the three target years has been identified with the deposition of 2010 mainly occupy the northern and southern parts of the country being the less sensitive to acid deposition. The biggest central part is taken by sites for which target load functions exist for the all considered target years. Sites for which target loads does not exist because the chemical criterion cannot be met are located in the most sensitive areas partly in central but mainly in the west-southern part of Poland.
Calculations of recovery and damage delay times in the period 2010 - 2100 were based on the sulphur and nitrogen deposition scenarios for 2010 resulting from the Gothenburg Protocol. Table 3 presents the number and contribution of sites for which relevant delay times were identified as well as contribution of sites in which recovery or damage took place before 2010 and after 2100.

	2010-2100			2010<		>2100	
RDT	712	1.46%	**Recovered**	8821	18.11%	14	0.03%
DDT	4928	10.11%	**Damaged**	15861	32.55%	18385	37.74%

Table 3. Number and percentage of forest sites for which recovery (RDT) and damage (DDT) delay times were identified and contribution of sites in which recovery or damage took place before 2010 or after 2100

Only for 11.6% of the analyzed sites recovery or damage may occur within the considered time span being constantly exposed after 2010 to acid deposition resulting from the Gothenburg Protocol. Recovery from violated soil chemical criterion is possible for 1.46% of sites while damage may happen to about 10% of sites until 2100.
Sites for which damage may take place before 2010 or after 2100 contribute by about 70% to the total number of sites under consideration. Compared to this only ca. 18% of sites may recover before 2010 while after 2100 practically none of them.

7. Conclusions

The dynamic model predictions indicate that although the implementation of the Gothenburg Protocol will substantially reduce the Polish forest ecosystems area under excess acid deposition, still considerable parts of forests remain at potential risk resulting from the violation of the adopted chemical criterion for soils. This indicates that further sulphur and nitrogen emission reduction beyond the Protocol's obligations have to be considered within its intended review.

8. Acknowledgement

The author acknowledges the support of the Polish Ministry of Environment and the National Fund of Environmental Protection and Water Management.

9. References

Alcamo, J., Shaw, R. & Hordijk, L. (editors) (1990). *The RAINS Model of Acidification – Science and Strategies in Europe*, Kluwer Academic Publisher, Dordrecht, The Netherlands

Mill, W.& Schlama, A. (2008). *Updated Critical Loads and Parameters for Dynamic Modelling – Polish NFC report to CCE*, Institute of Environmental Protection, Warsaw

Posch, M., Hettelingh, J-P. & Sllotweg J. (editors) (2003). *Manual for Dynamic Modelling of Soil Response to Atmospheric Deposition,* RIVM Report 259101012, Bilthoven, The Netherlands

UBA (2004). *Manual on Methodologies and Criteria for Mapping Critical Loads and Levels and Air pollution Effects, Risks and Trends,* Federal Environmental Agency (Umweltbundesamt), Texte 52/04, Berlin

Wawrzoniak, J.& Małachowska, J. (editors) (2006). *Stan uszkodzenia lasów w Polsce w 2005 roku na podstawie badań monitoringowych (Report on forest damages in Poland in 2005 based on monitoring research),* Biblioteka Monitoringu Środowiska, Warszawa

Working Group on Effects (2004). *Review and assessment of air pollution effects and their recorded trends.* Working Group on Effects, Convention on Long-range Transboundary Air Pollution, National Environment Research Council, United Kingdom

10

Toward the Formulation of a Realistic Fault Governing Law in Dynamic Models of Earthquake Ruptures

Andrea Bizzarri
Istituto Nazionale di Geofisica e Vulcanologia – Sezione di Bologna
Italy

1. Introduction

Dynamic earthquake models can help us in the ambitious understanding, from a deterministic point of view, of how a rupture starts to develop and propagates on a fault, how the excited seismic waves travel in the Earth crust and how the high frequency radiation can damage a site on the ground. Since analytical solutions of the fully dynamic, spontaneous rupture problem do not exist (even in homogeneous conditions), realistic and accurate numerical experiments are the only available tool in studying earthquake sources basing on Newtonian Mechanics. Moreover, they are a credible way of generating physics-based ground motions. In turn, this requires the introduction of a fault governing law, which prevents the solutions to be singular and the crack tip and the energy flux to be unbounded near the rupture front.

Contrary to other ambits of Physics, Seismology presently lacks knowledge of the *exact* physical law which governs natural faults and this is one of the grand challenges for modern seismologists. While for elastic solids it exists an equation of motion which relates particle motion to stresses and forces through the material properties (the scale-free Navier-Cauchy's equation), for a region undergoing inelastic, brittle deformations this equation is presently missed and scientists have yet to fully decipher the fundamental mechanisms of friction.

The traction evolution occurring during an earthquake rupture depends on several mechanisms, potentially concurrent and competing one with each other. Recent laboratory data and field observations revealed the presence, and sometime the coexistence, of thermally-activated processes (such as thermal pressurization of pore fluids, flash heating of asperity contacts, thermally-induced chemical reactions, melting of rocks and gouge debris), porosity and permeability evolution, elasto-dynamic lubrication, etc.

In this chapter we will analyze, in an unifying and comprehensive sketch, all possible chemico-physical mechanisms that can affect the fault weakening and we will explicitly indicate how they can be incorporated in a realistic governing model. We will also show through numerical simulations that simplified constitutive models that neglect these phenomena appear to be inadequate to describe the details of the stress release and the consequent high frequency seismic wave radiation. In fact, quantitative estimates show that in most cases the incorporation of such nonlinear phenomena has significant effects, often dramatic, on the dynamic rupture propagation, that finally lead to different damages on the free surface.

Given the uncertainties in the relative weight of the various competing processes, the range of variability of the value of some parameters, and the difference in their characteristic time and length scales, we can conclude that the formulation of a realistic governing law still requires multidisciplinary efforts from theoretical models, laboratory experiments and field observations.

2. Dynamic models of earthquake ruptures

2.1 The fault system

A fault can be regarded as the surface, or more properly the volume, where non-elastic processes take place. In Figure 1 we report a sketch illustrating the most widely accepted model of a fault, which is also considered in the present chapter. It is essentially based on the data arising from a large number of field observations and geological evidence (e.g., Chester & Chester, 1998; Sibson, 2003).

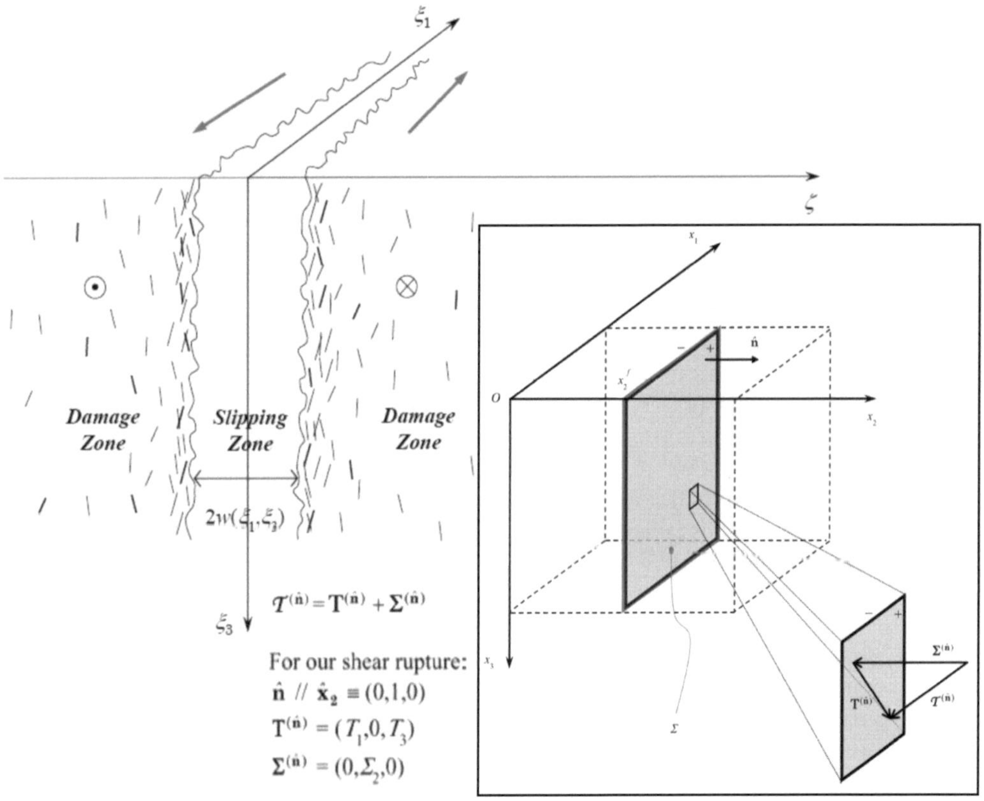

Fig. 1. Sketch representing the fault structure suggested by geological observations. The slipping zone of thickness $2w$ is surrounded by highly fractured damage zone and finally by the undamaged host rocks. The inset panel illustrates the mathematical representation of the fault model adopted in the numerical simulations discussed in the present chapter.

Many recent investigations on the internal structure of fault zones reveal that coseismic slip on mature fault often occurs within an ultracataclastic, gouge-rich and possibly clayey zone (the foliated fault core), generally having a thickness of the order of few centimeters. The fault core, which typically is parallel to the macroscopic slip vector, is surrounded by a cataclastic damage zone, which can extend up to hundreds of meters. This region is composed of highly fractured, brecciated and possibly granulated materials and it is generally assumed to be fluid-saturated. Outside the damage zone we have the host rock, basically composed of undamaged materials (e.g., Wilson *et al.*, 2003).

Observations tend to suggest that the slip is accommodated along a single, nearly planar surface, the prominent slip surface (pss) – sometime called principal fracture surface (pfs) – which generally has a thickness of the order of millimeters (Rice & Cocco, 2007). When the breakdown process is realized (i.e., the traction is degraded down to its kinetic, or residual, level), the fault structure reaches a mature stage and the slip is concentrated in one (or sometime two) pss, which can be in the middle or near one border of the fault core (symmetric or asymmetric disposition, respectively; see Sibson, 2003). The localization to that narrow slip zone generally takes place at the early stages of the deformation. Moreover, field observations from exhumed faults indicate that fault zones grow in width by continued slip and evolve internally as a consequence of grains size reduction (e.g., Engelder, 1974). As we will see in the following of the chapter, the fault zone width, which is a key parameter for many phenomena described below, is difficult to be quantified, even for a single fault and it exhibits an extreme variation along the strike direction.

2.2 The constitutive law

The second ingredient necessary to solve the elasto-dynamic problem is represented by the introduction of a governing model which ensures a finite energy flux at the rupture tip and describes the traction temporal evolution. As an opposite of a fracture criterion – which is simply a binary condition that specifies whether there is a rupture at a given fault point and time – a governing (or constitutive) law is an analytical relation between the components of stress tensor and some physical observables. Following the Amonton's Law and the Coulomb-Navier criterion, we can relate the magnitude τ of the shear traction vector $\mathbf{T}^{(\hat{\mathbf{n}})}$ to the effective normal stress on the fault $\sigma_n{}^{eff}$ through the well known relation:

$$\tau = \left\| \mathbf{T}^{(\hat{\mathbf{n}})} \right\| = \mu \sigma_n{}^{eff}, \tag{1}$$

μ being the (internal) friction coefficient and

$$\sigma_n{}^{eff} = \left\| \boldsymbol{\Sigma}^{(\hat{\mathbf{n}})} \right\| = \sigma_n - p_{fluid}{}^{wf} \tag{2}$$

In equation (1) an additional term for the cohesive strength C_0 of the contact surface can also appear on the right-hand side. In equation (2) σ_n is the normal stress (having tectonic origin) and $p_{fluid}{}^{wf}$ is the pore fluid pressure on the fault.

Once the boundary conditions (initial conditions, geometrical settings and material properties) are specified, the value of the fault friction τ fully controls the metastable rupture nucleation, the further (spontaneous) propagation (accompanied by stress release, seismic wave excitation and stress redistribution in the surrounding medium), the healing of slip and finally the arrest of the rupture (i.e., the termination of the seismogenic phase of the rupture), which precedes the re-strengthening interseismic stage. With the only exception of post-seismic and interseismic phases of the seismic cycle, all the above-mentioned stages of the rupture process are accounted for in fully dynamic models of an earthquake rupture, provided that the exact analytical form of the fault strength is given. The possibility to explicitly include all the previously-mentioned physical processes that can potentially occur during faulting is a clear requisite of a realistic fault governing law. In the light of this, equation (1) can be rewritten in a more comprehensive form as follows (generalizing equation (3.2) in Bizzarri & Cocco, 2005):

$$\tau = \tau\,(w_1O_1, w_2O_2, \ldots, w_NO_N) \tag{3}$$

where $\{O_i\}_{i=1,\ldots,N}$ are the physical observables, such as cumulative fault slip (u), slip velocity modulus (v), internal variables (such as state variables, Ψ; Ruina, 1983), etc.. (see Bizzarri & Cocco, 2005 for further details). Each observable can be associated with its evolution equation, which is coupled to equation (3).

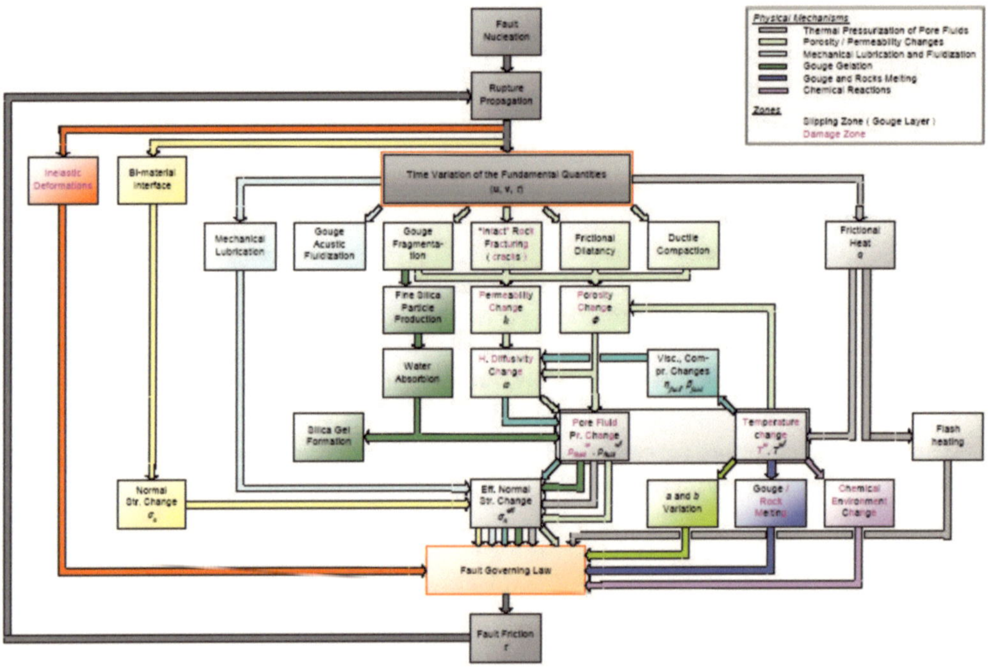

Fig. 2. Scheme of the mechanisms potentially occurring within the cosesimic time scale. Each color path represent a distinct phenomenon. Processes occurring in the slipping zone are written in black; processes potentially involving the damage zone are written in purple.

In Figure 2 we present in a unifying sketch all phenomena that can potentially occur during a faulting episode and that can lead to changes to the fault traction. In the following sections we will follow each single color path, which identifies a specific mechanism.

It is unequivocal that the *relative* importance of each single process (represented by the weights $\{w_i\}_{i=1,\ldots,N}$ in equation (3)) can change depending on the specific event we consider. Therefore it would be very easily expected that not all independent variables O_i will appear in the expression of fault friction for all natural faults. Moreover, each phenomenon is associated with its own characteristic length and duration (spatial and temporal characteristic scale) and it is controlled by some parameters, some of whom are sometime poorly constrained by observational evidences. As we will discuss in the following of the chapter, the difference in the length (and time) scale parameters of each chemico-physical process potentially represents a theoretical and computational complication in the effort to include different mechanisms in the governing law.

2.3 The numerical approach

Unless some explicit, restrictive hypotheses are introduced (e.g., assuming a constant rupture speed, neglecting inertial effects, considering homogeneous condition in the seismogenic region of interest) it is not possible to obtain closed-form analytical solutions of the elasto-dynamic problem. As a consequence, fully dynamic, spontaneous (i.e., with not prior-assigned rupture speed), realistic (i.e., structurally complex) models of earthquakes require the exploit of numerical codes. In some situations free surface topography, anisotropy, non-planar interfaces, spatially variable gradients of velocity, density and quality factors are necessary ingredients for a faithful description of the real-world events. We can regard computer simulations as a type of experimental approach in the case of conditions that can be not reproduced in laboratory experiments of intact rock fracturing and/or sliding friction on pre-exsisting surfaces.

The overall requirement for a numerical code is to satisfy the three basic properties: *i*) the consistency of the discretized (algebraic) equations with respect to the original differential equations, *ii*) the stability and *iii*) the convergence of the numerical solution. The goodness of the obtained synthetic solution has to be validated through a systematic comparison against other numerical solutions, obtained independently and with different numerical algorithms (e.g., Bizzarri *et al.*, 2001; Harris *et al.*, 2009). Another essential feature of a numerical code is represented by the computation requests (or the computational efficiency), expressed in terms of memory requirements and CPU time. The latter can be successfully reduced by the utilization of optimized mathematical libraries and parallelization paradigms, such as MPI and OpenMP.

In the literature (see for instance Moczo *et al.*, 2007 for a review) several numerical codes have been used to simulate dynamic earthquake ruptures, some of them belonging to the class of boundary elements approaches (boundary elements (BE), boundary integral equation methods (BIEM)), as well as to the class of domain methods (finite differences (FD), finite elements (FE), spectral elements (SE) and pseudospectral elements (pSE), combined (hybrid) FD and FE).

The results of the numerical experiments presented and discussed in the following of the present chapter have been obtained by using the FD, conventional grid code described in detail in Bizzarri & Cocco (2005). They refer to a strike slip fault, as illustrated in the inset panel of Figure 1. The adopted numerical code – which is under continuous development – is 2nd-order accurate in space and in time, OpenMP-parallelized, it contains various absorbing boundary conditions (in order to minimize spurious numerical pollutions arising from the reflection at the borders of the computational domain) and includes the free surface condition. It also fully manages the time-weakening friction (fault traction is released over a finite time interval), the slip-dependent laws (either linear and non linear), various formulations of the rate- and state-dependent friction laws (including regularizations at low slip velocities). Moreover, it also incorporates the thermal pressurization of pore fluids (see section 3.1), the flash heating of asperity contacts (section 3.2), porosity and permeability variations (sections 4.1 and 4.2). The fault boundary conditions is implemented by using the Traction-at-Split-Node (TSN) technique, which has been proved to be one of the most accurate numerical schemes to incorporate the non elastic response of the fault. Finally, the code can handle multiple faults, in order to simulate stress interaction and fault triggering phenomena (e.g., Bizzarri & Belardinelli, 2008).

3. Thermally activated processes

3.1 Thermal pressurization of pore fluids

The role of fluids and pore pressure relaxation on the mechanics of earthquakes and faulting is the subject of an increasing number of studies, based on a new generation of laboratory experiments, field observations and theoretical models. The interest is motivated by the fact that fluids play an important role in fault mechanics; they can affect the earthquake nucleation and the earthquake occurrence (e.g., Sibson, 1986; Antonioli *et al.*, 2006), they can trigger aftershocks (Nur & Booker, 1972 among many others) and they can control the breakdown process through the so-called thermal pressurization phenomenon (Bizzarri & Cocco, 2006a, 2006b and references therein). Here we will focus on the coseismic time scale, but we want to remark that pore pressure can also change during the interseismic period, due to compaction and sealing of fault zones.

The temperature variations caused by frictional heating,

$$T^{w}(\xi_1,\zeta,\xi_3,t)=T_0+\frac{1}{4\,c\,w(\xi_1,\xi_3)}\int_0^{t-\varepsilon}\mathrm{d}t'\left\{\mathrm{erf}\left(\frac{\zeta+w(\xi_1,\xi_3)}{2\sqrt{\chi(t-t')}}\right)-\mathrm{erf}\left(\frac{\zeta-w(\xi_1,\xi_3)}{2\sqrt{\chi(t-t')}}\right)\right\}\tau(\xi_1,\xi_3,t')v(\xi_1,\xi_3,t') \quad (4)$$

(Bizzarri & Cocco, 2006a; χ is the thermal diffusivity, c is the heat capacity of the bulk composite and erf(.) is the error function), heats both the rock matrix and the pore fluids; thermal expansion of fluids is paramount, since thermal expansion coefficient of water is greater than that of rocks. The stiffness of the rock matrix works against fluid expansion, causing its pressurization. Several *in situ* and laboratory observations show that there is a large contrast in permeability (k) between the slipping zone and the damage zone: in the damage zone k might be three orders of magnitude greater than that in the fault core (see also Rice, 2006). As a consequence, fluids tend to flow in the direction perpendicular to the fault. Pore pressure changes are associated to temperature variations caused by frictional heating, temporal changes in porosity and fluid transport through the equation:

$$\frac{\partial}{\partial t}p_{fluid} = \frac{\alpha_{fluid}}{\beta_{fluid}}\frac{\partial}{\partial t}T - \frac{1}{\beta_{fluid}\Phi}\frac{\partial}{\partial t}\Phi+\omega\frac{\partial^2}{\partial\zeta^2}p_{fluid} \quad (5)$$

where α_{fluid} is the volumetric thermal expansion coefficient of the fluid, β_{fluid} is the coefficient of the compressibility of the fluid and ω is the hydraulic diffusivity, expressed as:

$$\omega \equiv \frac{k}{\eta_{fluid}\Phi\beta_{fluid}} \quad (6)$$

η_{fluid} being the dynamic fluid viscosity and Φ the porosity, which potentially can evolve through the time. The solution of equation (5), coupled with the Fourier's heat conduction equation, can be analytically determined and assumes the following form:

$$p_{fluid}^{\,w}(\xi_1,\zeta,\xi_3,t) = p_{fluid_0} + \frac{\gamma}{4\,w(\xi_1,\xi_3)} \int_0^{t-\varepsilon} \mathrm{d}t' \left\{ -\frac{\chi}{\omega-\chi}\left[\mathrm{erf}\left(\frac{\zeta + w(\xi_1,\xi_3)}{2\sqrt{\chi(t-t')}}\right) - \mathrm{erf}\left(\frac{\zeta - w(\xi_1,\xi_3)}{2\sqrt{\chi(t-t')}}\right)\right] + \right.$$
$$+ \frac{\omega}{\omega-\chi}\left[\mathrm{erf}\left(\frac{\zeta + w(\xi_1,\xi_3)}{2\sqrt{\omega(t-t')}}\right) - \mathrm{erf}\left(\frac{\zeta - w(\xi_1,\xi_3)}{2\sqrt{\omega(t-t')}}\right)\right]\}\{ \tau(\xi_1,\xi_3,t')v(\xi_1,\xi_3,t') +$$
$$\left. - \frac{2\,w(\xi_1,\xi_3)}{\gamma}\frac{1}{\beta_{fluid}\Phi(t')}\frac{\partial}{\partial t'}\Phi(\xi_1,\zeta,\xi_3,t') \right\} \tag{7}$$

(Bizzarri & Cocco, 2006b). In previous equations p_{fluid0} is the initial pore fluid pressure (i.e., $p_{fluid0} \equiv p_{fluid}(\xi_1,\zeta,\xi_3,0)$) and $\gamma \equiv \alpha_{fluid}/(\beta_{fluid}c)$. In (7) the term involving Φ accounts for compaction or dilatation and it acts in competition with respect to the thermal contribution to the pore fluid pressure changes. Additionally, variations in porosity will modify, at every time instant (see equation (6)), the arguments of error functions which involve the hydraulic diffusivity.

As a consequence of equations (1) and (2), it follows from equation (7) that variations in pore fluid pressure lead to changes in fault friction:

$$\begin{aligned} \tau &= \left[\mu_* + a\ln\left(\frac{v}{v_*}\right) + b\ln\left(\frac{\Psi v_*}{L}\right)\right]\sigma_n^{eff} \\ \frac{\mathrm{d}}{\mathrm{d}t}\Psi &= -\frac{\Psi v}{L}\ln\left(\frac{\Psi v}{L}\right) - \left(\frac{\alpha_{LD}\Psi}{b\sigma_n^{eff}}\right)\frac{\mathrm{d}}{\mathrm{d}t}\sigma_n^{eff} \end{aligned} \tag{8}$$

(Linker & Dieterich, 1992; a, b, L and α_{LD} are constitutive parameters and μ_* and v_* are reference values for friction coefficient and sliding velocity, respectively).

In their fully dynamic, spontaneous, 3-D earthquake model Bizzarri & Spudich (2008) showed that the inclusion of fluid flow in the coseismic process strongly alters the dry behavior of the fault, enhancing instability, even causing rupture acceleration up to super-shear rupture velocities for rheologies which do not allow this transition in dry conditions. For extremely localized slip (i.e., for small values of slipping zone thickness) or for low value of hydraulic diffusivity, the thermal pressurization of pore fluids increases the stress drop, causing a nearly complete stress release (Andrews, 2002; Bizzarri & Cocco, 2006b). It also changes the shape of the slip-weakening curve and therefore the value of the so-called fracture energy. This is important, since fracture energy, defined physically as the amount of energy (for unit fault surface) necessary to maintain an ongoing rupture which propagates on a fault, is recognized to be one of the most important parameter in the context of the physics of the earthquake source. It directly influences the earthquake dynamics, since its value controls the rupture propagation and its arrest and it affects the radiation efficiency.

In Figure 3 we report slip-weakening curves obtained in the case of Dieterich-Ruina law (Linker & Dieterich, 1992) for different vales of $2w$ and ω. In some cases (Bizzarri & Cocco, 2006b) it is impossible to determine the equivalent slip-weakening distance (in the sense Cocco & Bizzarri, 2002) and the friction exponentially decreases as recently suggested by several papers (Abercrombie & Rice, 2005; Mizoguchi *et al.*, 2007).

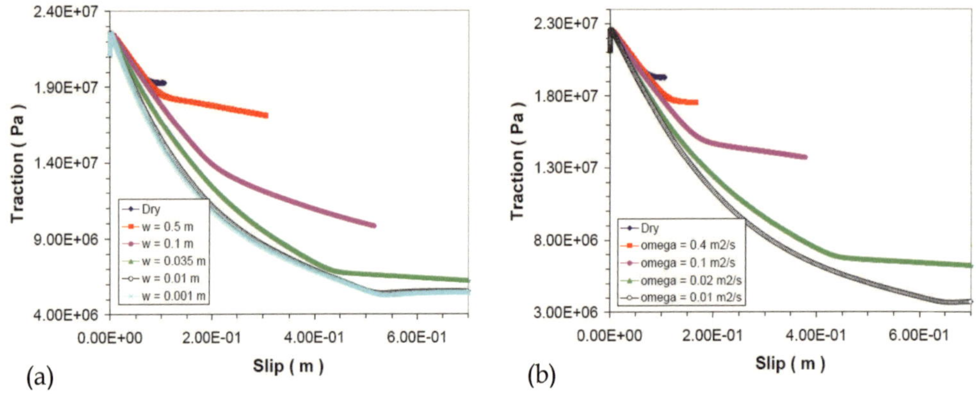

Fig. 3. Traction *versus* slip curves for wet faults obeying to equation (8). (a) Effect of different slipping zone thickness, $2w$. (b) Effect of different hydraulic diffusivities, ω. In all panels blue line refers to a fault where fluid migration is not allowed (i.e., dry faults where σ_n^{eff} is constant through the time).

3.2 Flash heating of asperity contacts

Another thermically-activated phenomenon is the flash heating (FH thereinafter; Tullis & Goldsby, 2003; Rice, 2006; Bizzarri, 2009) which might be invoked to explain the reduction of the friction coefficient μ from typical values at low slip rate (μ = 0.6–0.9 for almost all rock types; e.g., Byerlee, 1978) down to μ = 0.2–0.3 at seismic slip rate. It is assumed that the macroscopic fault temperature (T^{wf}) changes much more slowly than the temperature on an asperity contact, causing the rate of heat production at the local contact to be higher than average the heating rate of the nominal area. In the model, flash heating is activated if sliding velocity is greater than the critical velocity

$$v_{fh} = \frac{\pi\chi}{D_{ac}}\left(c\frac{T_{weak} - T^{wf}}{\tau_{ac}} \right)^2 \tag{9}$$

where τ_{ac} is the local shear strength of an asperity contact (which is far larger than the macroscopic applied stress), D_{ac} is its diameter and T_{weak} (near the melting point) is a weakening temperature at which the contact strength of an asperity begin to decrease. We want to remark that v_{fh} changes in time as macroscopic fault temperature T^{wf} does. When fault slip exceeds v_{fh} the governing equations are (Bizzarri, 2009):

$$\begin{aligned} \tau &= \left[\mu_* + a\ln\left(\frac{v}{v_*}\right) + \Theta \right] \sigma_n^{eff} \\ \frac{d}{dt}\Theta &= -\frac{v}{L}\left[\Theta + b\frac{v_{fh}}{v}\ln\left(\frac{v}{v_*}\right) + \left(1 - \frac{v_{fh}}{v}\right)\left(a\ln\left(\frac{v}{v_*}\right) + \mu_* - \mu_{fh} \right) \right] \end{aligned} \tag{10}$$

being μ_{fh} a reference value for friction coefficient at high slip velocities. For $v < v_{fh}$, the governing equations retain the classical form (Ruina, 1983):

$$\tau = \left[\mu_* + a \ln\left(\frac{v}{v_*}\right) + \Theta \right] \sigma_n^{eff}$$
$$\frac{d}{dt}\Theta = -\frac{v}{L}\left[b \ln\left(\frac{v}{v_*}\right) + \Theta \right] \tag{11}$$

We note that thermal pressurization of pore fluids and flash heating are inherently different mechanisms because they have a different length scale: the former is characterized by a length scale of the order of few micron (D_{ac}), while the length scale of the latter phenomenon is the thermal boundary layer ($\delta = (2\chi\, t_{pulse})^{1/2}$, where t_{pulse} is the duration of slip, of the order of seconds), which is ~ mm up to few cm. Moreover, while thermal pressurization affects the effective normal stress, flash heating causes changes only in the analytical expression of the friction coefficient at high slip rates. In both cases the evolution equation for the state variable is modified: by the coupling of variations is σ_n^{eff} for the first phenomenon, by the presence of additional terms involving v_{fh}/v in the latter.

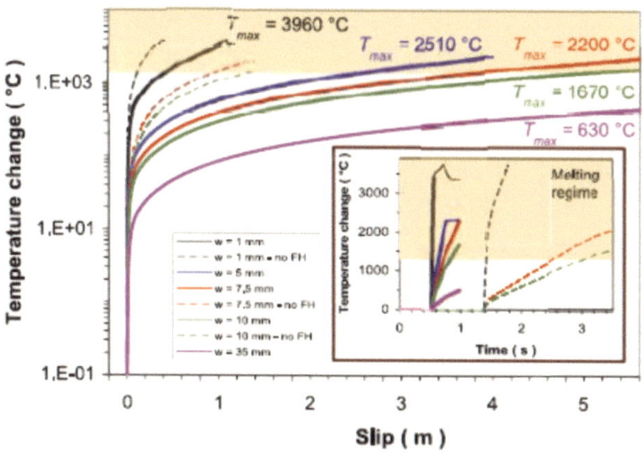

Fig. 4. Temperature change (computed from equation (4)) as a function of cumulative fault slip. The inset shows the time evolution of temperature change. Dashed lines refer to models without FH.

Numerical results of Bizzarri (2009) demonstrate that, compared to classical models where FH is neglected, the inclusion of FH considerably increases the degree of instability of the fault; the supershear rupture regime is highly favored, peaks in slip velocity are greater (nearly 50 times), as well as the stress drop (more than 3 times). Moreover, the fault traction exhibits larger weakening distances, leading to a greater (nearly 4 times) fracture energies. It is also found that for highly localized shear ($2w \leq 10$ mm for a in between 0.016 and 0.018) the modification of the governing law due to FH causes a fast re-strengthening, leading to a self-healing of slip. In self-healing cases, the strength recovery for increasing slip and slip velocity is quite similar to that previously obtained by Tinti *et al.* (2005) and it is such that the final traction is in a steady state and therefore it is not sufficient to originate a further failure event in absence of external loading. Finally, Bizzarri (2009) indicates that the FH increases the propensity of the fault to melt earlier and can not prevent it from occurring (see Figure 4): the decrease of the sliding resistance is counterbalanced by enhanced slip velocities (recall equation (4)). This results leaves us with the mystery of why actual evidence of melting is so rare.

3.3 Melting of gouge and rocks

As first pointed out by Jeffreys (1942), melting should probably occur during coseismic slip, typically after rocks comminution. Rare field evidence for melting on exhumed faults (i.e., the apparent scarcity of glass or pseudotachylytes, natural solidified friction melts produced during coseismic slip) generates scepticism for the relevance of melt in earthquake faulting. However, several laboratory experiments have produced melt, when typical conditions of seismic deformation are attained (Spray, 1995; Tsutsumi & Shimamoto, 1997). Moreover, as previously mentioned in section 3.1, it has been demonstrated by theoretical models that for thin slipping zones (i.e., $2w/\delta < 1$) melting temperature T_m can be easily exceeded in dynamic motion (Bizzarri & Cocco, 2006a, 2006b). Even if performed at low (2–3 MPa) normal stresses, the experiments of Tsutsumi & Shimamoto (1997) demonstrated significant deviations from the predictions obtained with the usual rate- and state-friction laws (e.g., Ruina, 1983). Fialko & Khazan (2005) suggested that fault friction simply follows the Coulomb-Navier equation (1) before melting and the Navier-Stokes constitutive relation, $\tau = \eta_{melt}\, v/(2w_{melt})$, after melting ($2w_{melt}$ being the thickness of the melt layer).
Nielsen *et al.* (2008) theoretically interpreted the results from high velocity ($v > 0.1$ m/s) rotary friction experiments and derived the following relation expressing the fault traction in steady state conditions when melting occurs:

$$\tau = {\sigma_n^{eff}}^{1/4} \frac{K_{NEA}}{\sqrt{R_{NEA}}} \sqrt{\frac{\ln\left(\frac{2v}{v_m}\right)}{\frac{2v}{v_m}}} \tag{12}$$

where K_{NEA} is a dimensional normalizing factor, R_{NEA} is the radius of the sample and v_m is a characteristic slip rate.

3.4 Chemical environment changes

It is known that fault friction can be influenced also by chemical environment changes. Chemical analyses of gouge particles formed in high velocity laboratory experiments by Hirose & Bystricky (2007) showed that dehydration reactions (i.e., the release of structural water in serpentine) can take place. Moreover, recent experiments on Carrara marble performed by Han *et al.* (2007) showed that thermally activated decomposition of calcite (into lime and CO_2 gas) occurs from a very early stage of slip, in the same temporal scale as the ongoing and enhanced fault weakening. Thermal decomposition weakening may be a widespread chemico-physical process, since natural gouges commonly are known to contain sheet silicate minerals. The latter can decompose, even at lower temperatures than that for calcite decomposition, and can leave geological signatures of seismic slip (Han *et al.*, 2007), different from pseudotachylytes. Presently, there are no earthquake models where chemical effects are incorporated within a governing equation. We believe that some efforts will be spent to this goal in the next future.

4. The importance of porosity and permeability

4.1 Temporal evolution of porosity

The values of permeability (k), porosity (Φ) and hydraulic diffusivity (ω) play a fundamental role in controlling the fluid migration and the breakdown processes on a seismogenic wet fault. During an earthquake event the frictional sliding tends to open (or dilate) cracks and pore spaces (leading to a decrease in pore fluid pressure), while normal traction tends to close (or compact) cracks (therefore leading to a pore fluid pressure increase). Stress readjustment on the fault can also switch from ineffective porosity (i.e., closed, or non-connected, pores) to effective porosity (i.e., catenary pores), or *vice versa*. Both ductile compaction and frictional dilatancy cause changes to k, Φ and therefore to ω. It is clear from equation (11) that this leads to variations to p_{fluid}^{wf}.

Starting from the theory of ductile compaction of McKenzie (1984) and assuming that the production rate of the failure cracks is proportional to the frictional strain rate and combining the effects of the ductile compaction, Sleep (1997) introduced the following evolution equation for the porosity:

$$\frac{\mathrm{d}}{\mathrm{d}t}\Phi = \frac{v\,\beta_{cp}\mu_*}{2w} - \frac{\sigma_n^{eff\,n}}{C_\eta(\Phi_{sat} - \Phi)^m} \tag{13}$$

where β_{cp} is a dimensionless factor, C_η is a viscosity parameter with proper dimensions, n is the creep power law exponent and m is an exponent that includes effects of nonlinear rheology and percolation theory. Equation (13) implies that porosity can't exceeds a saturation value Φ_{sat}.

As noticed by Sleep & Blanpied (1992), frictional dilatancy is associated also with the formation of new voids, as well as with the intact rock fracturing (i.e., with the formation of new tensile micro-cracks). In fact, it is widely accepted that earthquakes result in a complex mixture of frictional slip processes on pre-existing fault surfaces and shear fracture of initially intact rocks. This fracturing will cause a change in porosity; fluid within the fault zone drains into these created new open voids and consequently decreases the fluid pressure. The evolution law for the porosity associated with the new voids is (Sleep, 1995):

$$\frac{\mathrm{d}}{\mathrm{d}t}\Phi = \frac{v\,\beta_{ov}\mu}{2w} \tag{14}$$

where the factor β_{ov} is the fraction of energy that creates the new open voids.

Sleep (1997) also proposed the following relation that links the increase of porosity to the displacement, which leads to an evolution law for porosity:

$$\frac{\mathrm{d}}{\mathrm{d}t}\Phi = \frac{v\,\Phi\,\alpha_{fluid}\,\tau}{2wc} \tag{15}$$

Finally, Segall & Rice (1995) proposed two alternative relations for the evolution of Φ. The first mimics the evolution law for state variable in the Dieterich-Ruina model (Beeler *et al.*, 1994 and references therein):

$$\frac{\mathrm{d}}{\mathrm{d}t}\Phi(\xi_1,\zeta,\xi_3,t) = -\frac{v}{L_{SR}}\left[\Phi(\xi_1,\zeta,\xi_3,t) - \varepsilon_{SR}\ln\left(\frac{c_1 v + c_2}{c_3 v + 1}\right)\right] \tag{16}$$

where ε_{SR} and L_{SR} are two parameters representing the sensitivity to the state variable evolution (in the framework of rate- and state-dependent friction laws) and a characteristic length–scale, respectively, and $\{c_i\}_{i=1,2,3}$ are constants ensuring that Φ is in the range [0,1]. In principle, ε_{SR} can decrease with increasing effective normal stress, but at the present state we do not have detailed information about this second–order effect.

The second model, following Sleep (1995), postulates that Φ is an explicit function on the state variable Ψ:

$$\Phi(\xi_1,\zeta,\xi_3,t)=\Phi_*-\varepsilon_{SR}\ln\left(\frac{\Psi v_*}{L_{SR}}\right) \tag{17}$$

Φ_* being a reference value, assumed to be homogeneous over the whole slipping zone thickness.

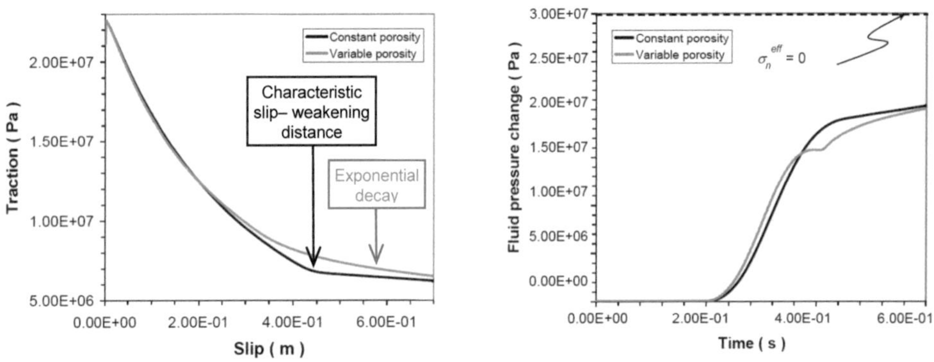

(a) (b)

Fig. 5. Comparison between solutions of the thermal pressurization problem in case of constant (black curve) and variable porosity (as in equation (17); gray curve). (a) Traction vs. slip curve. (b) Traction evolution of the effective normal stress.

Considering the latter equation, coupled with (7), and assuming as Segall & Rice (1995) that the scale lengths for the evolution of porosity and state variable are the same, we have that, even if the rupture shape, the dynamic stress drop and the final value of σ_n^{eff} remain unchanged with respect to a corresponding simulated event in which a constant porosity was assumed, the weakening rate is not constant for increasing cumulative slip. Moreover, the equivalent slip–weakening distance becomes meaningless. This is clearly visible in Figure 5, where we compare the solutions of the thermal pressurization problem in cases of constant (black curve) and variable porosity (grey curve).

All the equations presented in this section clearly state that porosity evolution is concurrent with the breakdown processes, since it follows the evolution of principal variables involved in the problem (v, τ, σ_n^{eff}, Ψ). However, in spite of the above–mentioned profusion of analytical relations, porosity is one of the biggest unknowns in the fault structure and presently available evidence from laboratory, and from geological observations as well, do not allow us to discriminate between different possibilities. Only numerical experiments performed by coupling one of the equations (13) to (17) with (7) can show the effects of different assumption and suggest what is the most appropriate. Quantitative results will plausibly give some useful indications for the design of new laboratory experiments.

4.2 Permeability changes

As mentioned above, changes in hydraulic diffusivity can be due not only to the time evolution of porosity, but also to variations of permeability. k is known to suffer large variations with type of rocks and their thermo-dynamical state (see for instance Turcotte & Schubert, 1982) and moreover local variations of k have been inferred near the fault. Several laboratory results (e.g., Brace *et al.*, 1968) supported the idea that k is an explicit function of σ_n^{eff}. A reasonable relation (Rice, 1992) is:

$$k = k_0 \, e^{-\frac{\sigma_n^{eff}}{\sigma_*}} \tag{18}$$

where k_0 is the permeability at zero effective normal stress and σ_* is a constant. For typical changes in σ_n^{eff} expected during coseismic ruptures we can guess an increase in k at least of a factor 2 within the temporal scale of the dynamic rupture. In principle, this can counterbalance the enhancement of instability due to the fluid migration out of the fault. This is particularly encouraging because seismological estimates of the stress release (almost ranging from about 1 to 10 MPa; e.g., Aki, 1972) do not support the evidence of a nearly complete stress drop, as predicted by numerical experiments of thermal pressurization.
Another complication may arise from the explicit dependence of permeability on porosity and on grain size d. Following one of the most widely accepted relation, the Kozeny-Carman equation (Kozeny, 1927), we have:

$$k = K_{KC} \frac{\Phi^3}{(1 - \Phi)^2} d^2 \tag{19}$$

Previous equation therefore states that gouge particle refinement and temporal changes in Φ, such as that described in equations (13) to (17), affect the value of k.
As in the case of porosity evolution, permeability changes also occur during coseismic fault traction evolution and consequently equations (18) or (19) can be easily incorporated in the thermal pressurization model (i.e., coupled with equation (7)).

5. Elasto–dynamic lubrication

Another important effect of the presence of pore fluids within the fault structure is represented by the mechanical lubrication (Sommerfeld, 1950; Ma *et al.*, 2003). In the model of Brodsky & Kanamori (2001) an incompressible fluid obeying the Navier-Stokes equations flows around the asperity contacts of the fault, without leakage, in the direction perpendicular to the fault surface. In absence of elastic deformations of the rough surfaces, the fluid pressure in the lubrication model is:

$$p_{fluid}^{(lub)}(\xi_1) = p_{res} + \frac{3}{2}\eta_{fluid} V \int_0^{\xi_1} \frac{w^* - w(\xi_1')}{\left(w(\xi_1')\right)^3} \, d\xi_1' \tag{20}$$

where p_{res} is the initial reservoir pressure (which can be identified with quantity p_{fluid}^{wf} of equation (7)), V is the relative velocity between the fault walls ($2v$ in our notation), $w^* \equiv w(\xi_1^*)$, where ξ_1^* is such that $(dp_{fluid}^{(lub)}/d\xi_1)|_{\xi_1=\xi_1^*} = 0$, and ξ_1 maps the length of the lubricated zone $L^{(lub)}$. Qualitatively, $L^{(lub)}$ is equal to the total cumulative fault slip u_{tot}.

Interestingly, simple algebra shows that if the slipping zone thickness is constant along the strike direction also the lubrication pore fluid pressure is always equal to p_{res}.
The net result of the lubrication process is that the pore fluid pressure is reduced by an amount equal to the last member of equation (20). This in turn can be estimated as

$$P^{(lub)} \cong 12\eta_{fluid} v \frac{r u_{tot}^{2}}{(<2w>)^{3}} \tag{21}$$

where r is the aspect ratio constant for roughness and $<2w>$ is the average slipping zone thickness. Therefore equation (2) is then rewritten as:

$$\sigma_n^{eff} = \sigma_n - p_{fluid}^{wf} - P^{(lub)}. \tag{22}$$

The fluid pressure can also adjust the fault surface geometry, since

$$2w(\xi_1) = 2w_0(\xi_1) + u^{(lub)}(\xi_1), \tag{23}$$

where $2w_0$ is the initial slipping zone profile and $u^{(lub)}$ is elasto-static displacement caused by lubrication. Equation (23) can be approximated as

$$<2w> = <2w_0> + \frac{P^{(lub)} L}{E} \tag{24}$$

E being the Young' s modulus. $u^{(lub)}$ is significant if $L^{(lub)}$ (or u_{tot}) is greater that a critical length, defined as (see also Ma *et al.*, 2003):

$$L_c^{(lub)} = 2<2w_0>\left(\frac{<2w_0>E}{12\eta_{fluid} v r}\right)^{\frac{1}{3}}; \tag{25}$$

otherwise the slipping zone thickness does not widen. If $u_{tot} > L_c^{(lub)}$ then $P^{(lub)}$ is the positive real root of the following equation

$$P^{(lub)}\left(<2w_0> + \frac{P^{(lub)} u_{tot}}{E}\right)^{3} - 12\eta_{fluid} v r u_{tot}^{2} = 0. \tag{26}$$

It is clear from equation (22) that lubrication contributes to reduce the fault traction (and therefore tends to increase the fault slip velocity, which in turn further increases $P^{(lub)}$, as stated in equation (21)). Moreover, if the lubrication increases the slipping zone thickness, then it will reduce asperity collisions and the contact area between the asperities (which in turn will tend to decrease $P^{(lub)}$, as still expressed by equation (21)).
In many papers it has been generally assumed that when effective normal stress vanishes then material interpenetration and/or tensile (i.e., mode I) cracks (Yamashita, 2000) develop, leading to the superposition during an earthquake event of all three basic modes of fracture mechanics (Atkinson, 1987; Petit & Barquins, 1988). An alternative mechanism that can occur when σ_n^{eff} falls to zero, if fluids are present in the fault zone, is that the frictional stress of contacting asperities described by the Amonton's Law (1) becomes negligible with respect to the viscous resistance of the fluid and the friction can be therefore expressed as

$$\tau = \frac{<2w>}{u_{tot}} P^{(lub)} \tag{27}$$

which describes the fault friction in the hydrodynamic regime. Depending on the values of total cumulative fault slip and fault slip velocity, in equation (27) $P^{(lub)}$ is alternatively expressed by (21) or by the solution of (26). For typical conditions ($<2w_0>$ = 1 mm, E = 5 x 10^4 Pa, v = 1 m/s, u_{tot} = 2 m, r = 10 x 10^{-3} m), if the lubricant fluid is water (η_{fluid} = 1 x 10^{-3} Pa s), then $u_{tot} < L_c^{(lub)}$ and (from equation (21)) $P^{(lub)} \cong 4.8 \times 10^4$ Pa. Therefore the lubrication process is negligible in this case and the net effects of the fluid presence within the fault structure will result in thermal pressurization only. On the contrary, if the lubricant fluid is a slurry formed form the mixture of water and refined gouge (η_{fluid} = 10 Pa s), then $u_{tot} > L_c^{(lub)}$ and (from equation (26)) $P^{(lub)} \cong$ 34.9 MPa, which can be a significant fraction of tectonic loading σ_n. In this case hydro-dynamical lubrication can coexist with thermal pressurization; in a first stage of the rupture, characterized by the presence of ample aqueous fluids, fluids can be squeezed out of the slipping zone due to thermal effects. In a next stage of the rupture, the gouge, rich of particles, can form the slurry with the remaining water; at this moment thermal pressurization is not possible but lubrication effects will become paramount. This is an example of how two different physical mechanisms can be incorporated in a single frictional model.

6. Bi–material Interfaces

Traditional and pioneering earthquake models (see for instance Brace & Byerlee, 1966) simply account for the reduction of the frictional coefficient from its static value to the kinetic frictional level, taking the effective normal stress constant over the duration of the process. Subsequently, Weertman (1980) suggested that a reduction in σ_n during slip between dissimilar materials can influence the dynamic fault weakening. Considering an asperity failure occurring on a bi-material, planar interface separating two uniform, isotropic, elastic half-spaces, Harris & Day (1997) analytically demonstrated that σ_n can change in time. On the other hand, a material property contrast is not a rare phenomenon in natural faults: Li *et al.* (1990) and Li & Vidale (1996) identified some strike–slip faults where one side is embedded in a narrow, fault parallel, low-velocity zone (having width of a few hundred of meters). At the same time several authors (Lees, 1990; Michael & Eberhart-Phillips, 1991) inferred the occurrence of significant velocity contrasts across faults, generally less than 30%.

Even if Renardy (1992) theoretically demonstrated that Coulomb frictional sliding is unstable if occurs between materials with different properties, there is not a general consensus about the importance of the presence of bi-material interface on natural earthquakes (Ben–Zion, 2006 *versus* Andrews & Harris, 2005). More recently, Dunham & Rice (2008), showed that spatially inhomogeneous slip between dissimilar materials alters σ_n^{eff} (with the relevant scale over which poro-elastic properties are to be measured being of order the hydraulic diffusion length, which for large earthquakes is mm to cm). Moreover, it is known that the contrast in poro-elastic properties (e.g., permeability) across faults can alter both σ_n and p_{fluid} (while the elastic mismatch influences only σ_n).

7. Characteristic lengths and scale separation

It has been previously mentioned that each nonlinear dissipation process that can potentially act during an earthquake rupture has its own distance and time scales, that can be very different from one phenomenon to another. The difference in scale lengths, as well as the problem of the scale separation, can represent a limitation in the attempt to simultaneously incorporate *all* the mechanisms described in this chapter in a single constitutive model.

We have previously seen that thermal pressurization (section 3.1) can coexist with mechanical lubrication (section 5) as well as with porosity (section 4.1) and permeability evolutions (section 4.2). The same holds for flash heating and thermal pressurization. This simultaneous incorporation ultimately leads to numerical problems, often severe, caused by the need to properly resolve the characteristic distances and times of each single process. The concurrent increase in computational power and the development of new numerical algorithms can definitively assist us in this effort.

In Table 1 we report a synoptic view of the characteristic length scales for the processes described in the present chapter. Two important lengths (see Bizzarri *et al.*, 2001) involved in the breakdown process, are the breakdown zone length (or size, X_b) and the breakdown zone time (or duration, T_b). They quantify the spatial extension, and the time duration, of the cohesive zone; in other words they express the amount of cumulative fault slip, and the elapsed time, required to the friction to drop, in some (complicated) way, from the yield stress down to the residual level.

Process	*Characteristic distance*	*Typical value*
	Scale length	
Macroscopic decrease of fault traction from yield stress to residual level	d_0	~ few mm in the lab
	X_b	~ 100 of m
Temporal evolution of the state variable in the framework of the rate- and state-dependent friction laws	L	~ few μm in the lab
Thermal pressurization (section 3.1)	$2w$	≤ 1 cm
	$\delta = (2\chi\, t_{pulse})^{1/2}$	~ few cm
Flash heating (section 3.2)	D_{ac}	~ few μm
Gouge and rocks melting (section 3.3)	$2w_{melt}$	~ 100 of μm in the lab
Porosity evolution (section 4.1): - equations (13) to (15) - equations (16) and (17)	 $2w$ L_{SR}	 ≤ 1 cm assumed to be equal to L

Table 1. Synoptic view of the characteristic lengths of the processes described in the chapter.

Another open problem is related to the difficulty to move from the scale of the laboratory (where samples are of the order of several meters) up to the scale of real faults (typically several kilometer long). A large number of the phenomena described above have been measured in the lab: this raises the problem of how to scale the values of the parameters of the inferred equations to natural faults.

It is apparent that both geological observations and improvements in laboratory machines are necessary elements in the understanding of earthquake source physics and in the capability to reproduce it numerically.

8. Summary and conclusions

The dynamic modelling of an earthquake rupture on a fault surface is extremely challenging not only from a merely numerical point of view, but also because of the lack of knowledge of the state of the Earth crust and of the law which describes the earthquake physics.

In this chapter we have described a large number of physical mechanisms that can potentially take place during a faulting episode. These phenomena are macroscopic, in that the fundamental variables (i.e., the physical observables) describing them have to be regarded as macroscopic averages (see also Cocco *et al.*, 2006) of the solid-solid contacts properties. As a result, the fault friction, expressed analytically in terms of a governing law, does not formally describe the stress acting on each single asperity, but the macroscopic average of the stress acting within the slipping zone (see Figure 1). Unlikely, a link between the microphysics of materials, described in terms of lattice or atomic properties, and the macrophysical description of friction, obtained from stick-slip laboratory experiments, is actually missed. On the other hand, we can not expect to be able to mathematically describe (either deterministically or statistically) the evolution of all the surface asperities and of all micro-cracks in the damage zone.

Recent laboratory experiments and geological investigations have clearly shown that different dissipative processes can lead to the same steady state value of friction. In the simple approximation which considers only one single event on an isolated fault, some authors claim that the slip dependence is paramount (Ohnaka, 2003). On the other hand, the explicit dependence of friction on sliding velocity (Dieterich, 1986) is unquestionable, even at high slip rates (Tsutsumi & Shimamoto, 1997). In fact, in the literature there is a large debate (see for instance Bizzarri & Cocco, 2006c) concerning the most important dependence of fault friction. Actually, the problem of what is (are) the dominant physical mechanism(s) controlling the friction evolution (i.e., the quantitative estimate of the weights w_i in equation (3)) is still unsolved. Given this fact, we have to regard Figure 2 as a schematic representation of the logical links existing between the different phenomena. It is clear that in a realistic situation only a few colour paths will survive; the scope of that diagram is to emphasize the degree of complexity of the rupture process, which contains more ingredients than the so-called first-order observables (such as slip, slip velocity and state variable(s)).

We believe that seismic data presently available are not sufficient to clarify what specific mechanism is operating (or dominant) during a specific earthquake event. The inferred traction evolution on the fault, as retrieved from seismological records (e.g., Ide & Takeo, 1997), gives us only some general information about the average weakening process on an idealized mathematical fault plane. Moreover, it is affected by the unequivocal choice of the source time function adopted in kinematic inversions and by the frequency band limitation in data recording and sometime could be inconsistent with dynamic ruptures. On the other hand, we have seen in previous sections that we do not have any physical basis to neglect *a priori* the insertion of additional physical and chemical mechanisms in the analytical expression of a fault governing equation. The first reason is that, compared to results obtained by adopting a simplified (or in some sense idealized) constitutive relation, numerical experiments from models where additional physical mechanisms are accounted for show a significant, often dramatic, change in the dynamic stress drop (and therefore in the resulting ground motions), in the distance over which it is realized, in the so-called fracture energy and in the total scalar seismic moment. The second reason is that, as we have shown (recall the effects of gouge and rocks melting and those of hydro-dynamic lubrication), the inclusion of different mechanisms in some case requires a modification of its classical analytical expression.

As a future perspective, it would be intriguing try to compare synthetics obtained by assuming that one particular physical mechanism is paramount with respect to the others, in order to look for some possible characteristic signatures and specific features in the solutions. The next step would eventually be try to envisage such features in real seismological data.

The above-mentioned approaches are not mutually exclusive and the contributes from each field can lead to the answer of the following key questions: 1) what are the predictions arising from different mathematical and physical descriptions of rupture dynamics that can be observed in the real world?, and 2) what can data illuminate us about earthquake faulting?

In the present chapter we have underlined that some different, nonlinear, chemico-physical processes can potentially cooperate, interact, or even compete one with each other. We have also seen that in most cases we are able to write equations describing them and we have explicitly indicated how they can be incorporated into a fault constitutive model. It is clear that in order to reproduce quantitatively the complexity of the inelastic and dissipative mechanisms occurring on a fault during a failure event a "classical" constitutive relation appears to be nowadays inadequate. To conclude, we are inclined to think that only a multidisciplinary approach to source mechanics, which systematically combines results from accurate theoretical models, advanced laboratory experiments, field observations and data analyses, can hopefully lead in the future to the formulation of a realistic and consistent governing model for real earthquakes. This is an ambitious task of great urgency, and it has to be pursued in the next future.

9. Acknowledgements

The author would like to thank Emily Brodsky, Renata Dmowska, Eric Dunham, Yann Klinger, Chris Marone, Jim Rice and Paul Spudich for fruitful discussions.

10. References

Abercrombie, R. E., & J. R. Rice (2005), Can observations of earthquake scaling constrain slip weakening?, *Geophys. J. Int.*, Vol. 162, pp. 406-424

Aki, K. (1972), Earthquake mechanism, *Tectonophys.*, *13*, pp. 423-446

Andrews, D. J. (2002), A fault constitutive relation accounting for thermal pressurization of pore fluid, *J. Geophys. Res.*, Vol. 107, No. B12, 2363, doi: 10.1029/2002JB001942

Andrews, D. J., & R. A. Harris (2005), The wrinkle-like slip pulse is not important in earthquake dynamics, *Geophys. Res. Lett.*, Vol. 32, L23303, doi: 10.1029/2005GL023996

Antonioli, A., Belardinelli, M. E., Bizzarri, A., & Vogfjord, K. S. (2006). Evidence of instantaneous dynamic triggering during the seismic sequence of year 2000 in south Iceland. *J. Geophys. Res.*, Vol. 111, B03302, doi: 10.1029/2005JB003935

Atkinson, B. K. (1987), *Fracture Mechanics of Rock*, Academic, San Diego, CA

Beeler, N. M., T. E. Tullis, & J. D. Weeks (1994), The roles of time and displacement in the evolution effect in rock friction, *Geophys. Res. Lett.*, Vol. 21, No. 18, pp. 1987–1990

Ben-Zion, Y. (2006), A comment on "Material contrast does not predict earthquake rupture propagation direction" by R. A. Harris and S. M. Day, *Geophys. Res. Lett.*, Vol. 33, L13310, doi: 10.1029/2005GL025652

Bizzarri, A (2009), Can flash heating of asperity contacts prevent melting?, *Geophys. Res. Lett.*, Vol. 36, L11304, doi: 10.1029/2009GL037335

Bizzarri, A., & M. E. Belardinelli (2008), Modelling instantaneous dynamic triggering in a 3-D fault system: application to the 2000 June South Iceland seismic sequence, *Geophys. J. Int.*, Vol. 173, pp. 906–921, doi: 10.1111/j.1365-246X.2008.03765.x

Bizzarri, A. & Cocco, M. (2005). 3D dynamic simulations of spontaneous rupture propagation governed by different constitutive laws with rake rotation allowed. *Annals of Geophysics*, Vol. 48, No. 2, pp. 279–299

Bizzarri, A., & M. Cocco (2006a), A thermal pressurization model for the spontaneous dynamic rupture propagation on a three-dimensional fault: 1. Methodological approach, *J. Geophys. Res.*, Vol. 111, B05303, doi: 10.1029/2005JB003862

Bizzarri, A., & M. Cocco (2006b), A thermal pressurization model for the spontaneous dynamic rupture propagation on a three-dimensional fault: 2. Traction evolution and dynamic parameters, *J. Geophys. Res.*, Vol. 111, B05304, doi: 10.1029/2005JB003864

Bizzarri, A., & M. Cocco (2006c), Comment on "Earthquake cycles and physical modeling of the process leading up to a large earthquake", *Earth Planets Space*, Vol. 58, pp. 1525-1528

Bizzarri, A., M. Cocco, D. J. Andrews, & E. Boschi (2001), Solving the dynamic rupture problem with different numerical approaches and constitutive laws, *Geophys. J. Int.*, Vol. 144, pp. 656–678

Bizzarri, A., & P. Spudich (2008), Effects of supershear rupture speed on the high-frequency content of S waves investigated using spontaneous dynamic rupture models and isochrone theory, *J. Geophys. Res.*, Vol. 113, B05304, doi: 10.1029/2007JB005146

Brace, W. F., & J. D. Byerlee (1966), Stick-slip as a mechanism for earthquakes, *Science*, Vol. 153, No. 3739, pp. 990-992

Brace, W. F., Walsh, J. B., & W. T. Frangos (1968), Permeability of granite under high pressure, *J. Geophys. Res.*, Vol. 73, No. 6, pp. 2225-2236

Brodsky, E. E., & H. Kanamori (2001), Elastohydrodynamic lubrication of faults, *J. Geophys. Res.*, Vol. 106, No. B8, pp. 16,357–16,374

Byerlee, J. D. (1978), Friction of rocks, *Pure Appl. Geophys.*, Vol. 116, pp. 615–626

Chester, F. M., & J. S. Chester (1998), Ultracataclasite structure and friction processes of the Punchbowl fault, San Andreas system, California, *Tectonophys.*, Vol. 295, pp. 199–221

Cocco, M., & A. Bizzarri (2002), On the slip-weakening behavior of rate and state-dependent constitutive laws, *Geophys. Res. Lett.*, Vol. 29, No. 11, doi: 10.1029/2001GL013999

Cocco, M.; Spudich, P. & Tinti, E. (2006). On the mechanical work absorbed on faults during earthquake rupture, In: *Earthquakes Radiated Energy and the Physics of Faulting*, Vol. 170, R. Abercrombie, A. McGarr, H. Kanamori & G. Di Toro (Eds.), pp. 237-254, Geophysical Monograph Series, American Geophysical Union, Washington DC, USA, doi: 10.1029/170GM24

Dieterich, J. H. (1986), A model for the nucleation of earthquake slip, *Earthquake Source Mechanics, Geophysical Monograph*, Vol. 37, *Maurice Ewing Series*, 6, S. Das, J. Boatwright & C. H. Scholz (Eds.), *Am. Geophys. Union*, Washington D. C., pp. 37–47

Dunham, E. M., & J. R. Rice (2008), Earthquake slip between dissimilar poroelastic materials, *J. Geophys. Res.*, Vol. 113, B09304, doi: 10.1029/2007JB005405

Engelder, J. T. (1974), Cataclasis and the generation of fault gouge, *Geol. Soc. Amer. Bull.*, Vol. 85, pp. 1515–1522

Fialko, Y., & Y. Khazan (2005), Fusion by the earthquake fault friction: stick or slip? *J. Geophys. Res.*, Vol. 110, B12407 doi: 10.1029/2005JB003869

Han, R., Shimamoto, T., Hirose, T., Ree, J.-H., & J.-i. Ando (2007), Ultralow friction of carbonate faults caused by thermal decomposition, *Science*, Vol. 316, pp. 878–881

Harris, R. A., & S. M. Day (1997), Effects of a low-velocity zone on a dynamic rupture, *Bull. Seism. Soc. Am.*, Vol. 87, pp. 1267–1280

Harris, R. A., Barall, M., Archuleta, R., Aagaard, B., Ampuero, J.-P., Bhat, H., Cruz-Atienza, V. M., Dalguer, L., Dawson, P., Day, S. M., Duan, B., Dunham, E. M., Ely, G., Kaneko, Y., Kase, Y., Lapusta, N., Liu, Y., Ma, S., Oglesby, D., Olsen, K. B., Pitarka, A., Song, S., & E. Templeton (2009), The SCEC/USGS dynamic earthquake rupture code verification exercise, *Seism. Res. Lett.*, Vol. 80, No. 1, pp. 119–126, doi: 10.1785/gssrl.80.1.119.

Hirose, T., & M. Bystricky (2007), Extreme dynamic weakening of faults during dehydration by coseismic shear heating, *Geophys. Res. Lett.*, Vol. 34, L14311, doi: 10.1029/2007GL030049

Ide, S., & M. Takeo (1997), Determination of constitutive relations of fault slip based on seismic wave analysis, *J. Geophys. Res.*, Vol. 102, No. B12, pp. 27,379–27,391

Jeffreys, H. (1942), On the mechanics of faulting, *Geological Magazine*, Vol. 79, pp. 291–295

Kozeny, J. (1927), Über kapillare leitung des wassers in boden, *Sitzungsber Akad. Wiss. Wien Math. Naturwiss. Kl.*, Abt. 2a, pp. 136,271–306 (In German)

Lees, J. M. (1990), Tomographic P-wave velocity images of the Loma Prieta earthquake asperity, *Geophys. Res. Lett.*, Vol. 17, pp. 1433–1436

Li, Y.-G., Leary, P., Aki, K., & P. Malin (1990), Seismic trapped modes in the Oroville and San Andreas fault zones, *Science*, Vol. 249, pp. 763–766

Li, Y.-G., & J. E. Vidale (1996), Low-velocity fault-zone guided waves: numerical investigations of trapping efficiency, *Bull. Seism. Soc. Am.*, Vol. 86, pp. 371–378

Linker, M. F., & J. H. Dieterich (1992), Effects of variable normal stress on rock friction: observations and constitutive equations, *J. Geophys. Res.*, Vol. 97, No. B4, pp. 4923–4940

Ma, K.-F., Brodsky, E. E., Mori, J., Ji, C., Song, T.-R. A., & H. Kanamori (2003): Evidence for fault lubrication during the 1999 Chi-Chi, Taiwan, earthquake (Mw 7.6), *G. Res. Lett.*, Vol. 30, No. 5, 1244, doi: 10.1029/2002GL015380

McKenzie, D. P. (1984), The generation and compaction of partially molten rock, *J. Petrol.*, Vol. 25, pp. 713-765

Michael, A. J., & D. Eberhart-Phillips (1991), Relations among fault behavior, subsurface geology, and three-dimensional velocity models, *Science*, Vol. 253, pp. 651-654

Mizoguchi, K., Hirose, T., Shimamoto, T., & E. Fukuyama (2007), Reconstruction of seismic faulting by high-velocity friction experiments: An example of the 1995 Kobe earthquake, *Geophys. Res. Lett.*, Vol. 34, L01308, doi: 10.1029/2006GL027931

Moczo, P., Robertsson, J. O. A., & Eisner, L. (2007). The finite-difference time-domain method for modelling of seismic wave propagation, *Avances in Geophysics*, Vol. 48, Chapter 8, pp. 421-516

Nielsen, S., Di Toro, G., Hirose, T., & T. Shimamoto (2008), Frictional melt and seismic slip, *J. Geophys. Res.*, Vol. 113, B01308, doi: 10.1029/2007JB005122

Nur, A., & J. Booker (1972), Aftershocks caused by pore fluid flow?, *Science*, Vol. 175, pp. 885-887

Ohnaka, M. (2003). A constitutive scaling law and a unified comprehension for frictional slip failure, shear fracture of intact rocks, and earthquake rupture. *J. Geophys. Res.*, Vol. 108, No. B2, 2080, doi: 10.1029/2000JB000123

Petit, J. P., and M. Barquins (1988), Can natural faults propagate under mode II conditions?, *Tectonics*, Vol. 7, pp. 1243-1256

Renardy, Y. (1992), Ill-posedness at the boundary for elastic solids sliding under Coulomb-friction, *J. Elasticity*, Vol. 27, No. 3, pp. 281-287

Rice, J. R. (1992), Fault stress states, pore pressure distributions, and the weakness of the San Andreas Fault, in *Fault Mechanics and Transport Properties in Rocks (the Brace Volume)*, B. Evans & T.-F. Wong (Eds.), Academic Press, San Diego, CA ,pp. 475-503

Rice, J. R. (2006), Heating and weakening of faults during earthquake slip, *J. Geophys. Res.*, Vol. 111, No. B5, B05311, doi: 10.1029/2005JB004006

Rice, J. R., & Cocco, M. (2007). Seismic fault rheology and earthquake dynamics, In: *Tectonic Faults: Agents of Change on a Dynamic Earth*, M. R. Handy, G. Hirth & N. Hovius (Eds.), pp. 99-137, MIT Press, Cambridge, MA, USA

Ruina, A. L. (1983), Slip instability and state variable friction laws, *J. Geophys. Res.*, Vol. 88, No. B12, pp. 10,359-10,370

Segall, P., & J. R. Rice (1995), Dilatancy, compaction, and slip instability of a fluid-infiltrated fault, *J. Geophys. Res.*, Vol. 100, No. 101, pp. 22,155-22,171

Sibson, R. H. (1986), Brecciation processes in fault zones: inferences from earthquake rupturing, *Pure Appl. Geophys.*, Vol. 124, pp. 169-175

Sibson, R. H. (2003), Thickness of the seismic slip zone, *Bull. Seism. Soc. Am.*, Vol. 93, No. 3, pp. 1169-1178

Sleep, N. H. (1995), Ductile creep, compaction, and rate and state dependent friction within major fault zones, *J. Geopys. Res.*, Vol. 100, No. B7, pp. 13,065-13,080

Sleep, N. H. (1997), Application of a unified rate and state friction theory to the mechanics of fault zones with strain localization, *J. Geophys. Res.*, Vol. 102, No. B2, pp. 2875-2895

Sleep, N. H. & M. L. Blanpied (1992), Creep, compaction and the weak rheology of major faults, *Nature*, Vol. 359, 687-692

Sommerfeld, A. (1950), *Mechanics of Deformable Bodies*, Academic Press, San Diego, CA

Spray, J. (1995), Pseudotachylyte controversy; fact or friction?, *Geology*, Vol. 23, pp. 1119-1122

Tinti, E., Bizzarri, A., and M. Cocco (2005), Modeling the dynamic rupture propagation on heterogeneous faults with rate- and state-dependent friction, *Ann. Geophysics*, Vol. 48, No. 2, pp. 327-345.

Tullis, T. E., & Goldsby D. L. (2003). Flash melting of crustal rocks at almost seismic slip rates, *Eos Trans. AGU*, Vol. 84, No. 46, Fall Meet. Suppl., Abstract S51B-05

Turcotte, D. L. & Schubert, G. (1982). *Geodynamics*, John Wiley and Sons, New York, USA

Tsutsumi, A., & T. Shimamoto (1997), High-velocity frictional properties of gabbro, *Geophys. Res. Lett.*, Vol. 24, pp. 699-702

Yamashita, T. (2000), Generation of microcracks by dynamic shear rupture and its effects on rupture growth and elastic wave radiation, *Geophys. J. Int.*, Vol. 143, pp. 395-406

Weertman, J. (1980), Unstable slippage across a fault that separates elastic media of different elastic constants, *J. Geophys. Res.*, Vol. 85, No. B3, pp. 1455–1461

Wilson, J. E., Chester, J. S., & F. M. Chester (2003), Microfracture analysis of fault growth and wear processes, Punchbowl Fault, San Andreas system, California, *J. Struct. Geol.*, Vol. 25, pp. 1855-1873

11

Dynamic Modelling of a Wind Farm and Analysis of Its Impact on a Weak Power System

Gastón Orlando Suvire and Pedro Enrique Mercado
Instituto de Energía Eléctrica – Universidad Nacional de San Juan
Argentina

1. Introduction

Wind power generation is considered the most economic viable alternative within the portfolio of renewable energy resources. Among their advantages are the large number of potential sites for plant installation and the rapidly evolving technology with many suppliers offering from the individual turbine set to even turnkey projects. On the other hand, wind energy projects entail high initial capital costs and, in operation, a lack of controllability on the discontinuous or intermittent resource. In spite of these disadvantages, their incorporation is growing steadily, a fact that is making the utilities evaluate the various influencing aspects of wind power generation onto power systems.

Throughout the world there are large scarcely populated areas with good wind power potential where the existing grids are small or weak, due to the small population. A typical example is the large expanse of the Argentine Patagonia, with small cities clustered on the coastal areas and the Andean valleys. In these areas the capacity of the grid can very often be a limiting factor for the exploitation of the wind resource. One of the main problems concerned with wind power and weak grids is the voltage fluctuations. Several factors contribute to the voltage fluctuations in the terminals of a wind turbine generator (Suvire & Mercado, 2006; Slootweg & Kling, 2003; Ackermann, 2005; Chen & Spooner, 2001; Mohod & Aware, 2008; Smith et al., 2007): the aerodynamic phenomena, i.e., wind turbulence, tower shadow, etc.; the short-circuit power at the connection points; the number of turbines and the type of control. Besides, wind turbines may also cause voltage fluctuations in the grid if there are relatively large current variations during the connection and disconnection of turbines. With these aspects in mind, it turns necessary to ponder the information stemming from models that simulate the dynamic interaction between wind farms and the power systems they are connected to. Such models allow performing the necessary preliminary studies before connecting wind farms to the grid.

The purpose of this chapter is to show by means of simulations the voltage fluctuations caused by a wind farm in a weak power system. A model for dynamic performance of wind farms is presented, which takes into account the dynamic behaviour of an individual wind turbine and the aggregation effect of a wind farm (i.e., the larger the wind farm, the smoother the output waveforms). In addition, the wind speed model and wind turbine models are briefly presented. Validation of models and simulations of the interactions between the wind farm and the power system are carried out by using SimPowerSystems of SIMULINK/MATLAB™.

2. Wind system model

The main subsystems in a wind system model are the wind, the turbine and the farm. Fig. 1 shows this general structure with its main composing models.

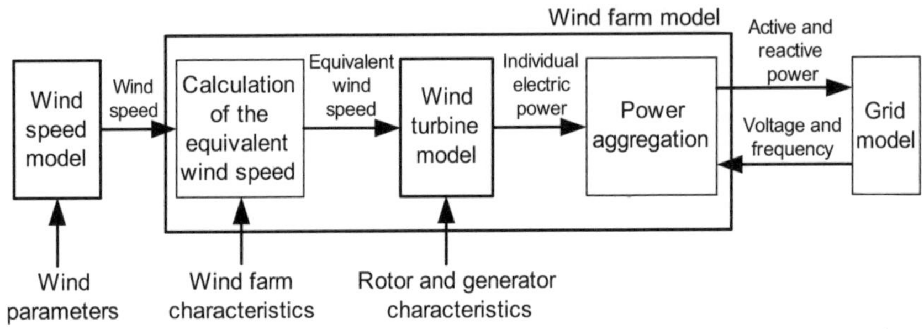

Fig. 1. General structure of a wind system model

From left to right, the wind speed model produces a wind speed sequence whose parameters are chosen by the user according to the wind pattern of the region. Then, the equivalent wind speed for the individual turbines is calculated using both the wind speed and the wind farm characteristics. The equivalent wind speeds are used to calculate the electric power generated by individual turbines, using the wind turbine model and both rotor and generator characteristics. The electric power outputs of the individual turbines are added using the power aggregation block. Thus, the total power of the wind farm injected to the power system is found.

2.1 Wind speed model

In the long-term range, i.e., for consideration over days and weeks, macro-meteorological influences dominate the wind speed. In the short-term range from several seconds up to minutes, fluctuations of particular interest here occur, e.g., in the form of wind gusts. In the medium time range the wind speed can be viewed as more or less stationary (Hassan & Sykes, 1985; Welfonder et al., 1997). As a result, mean values and mean standard deviations of the wind speed can be determined over a range of hours. In the process, the fluctuations of this mean wind speed and the superimposed short-term wind-speed fluctuations can be examined and modelled, independent of each other. The research on wind power conversion systems, especially the development of control solutions, involves the modelling of wind speed as a random process. Wind speed is considered as consisting of two elements (Nichita et al., 2002; Leithead et al., 1991): a slowly varying mean wind speed of hourly average; and a rapidly varying turbulence component. Since this chapter is focused on voltage fluctuations caused by wind generation, only the rapidly varying turbulence component is modelled and a mean wind speed is considered constant throughout the observation period. This component is modelled by a normal distribution with a null mean value and a standard deviation that is proportional to the current value of the mean wind speed. The block diagram of Fig. 2 is used as the referential base for modelling the wind speed behaviour (Welfonder et al., 1997).

The source for wind speed variation is assumed to be normally distributed white noise caused by a generator of random numbers. The output signal thus obtained shows the null mean value and a normalized standard deviation equal to one.

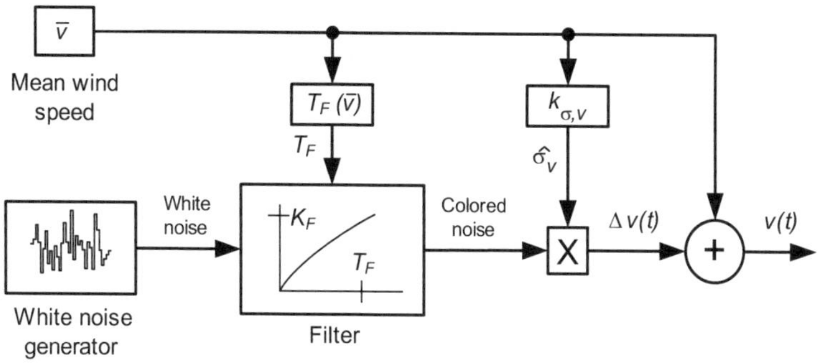

Fig. 2. Model for simulating the wind speed behaviour

However, since the wind speed $v(t)$ cannot change abruptly (because of physical reasons), but rather continuously, the white noise is smoothed using a properly designed signal-shaping filter with transfer function $H_F(j\omega)$. This way, it is transformed into a colored noise. The signal-shaping filter used in the model has a gain K_F and a time constant T_F. With a gain K_F of this shaping filter adapted to the filter time constant T_F, the standard deviation of the colored noise signal turns to be equal to one as well. The fluctuating part of the wind speed $\Delta v(t)$ is obtained by multiplying this normalized colored noise signal and the respective wind speed dependent standard deviation $\hat{\sigma}_v$. Then, the respective mean speed $\bar{v}$ is added to this value. The characteristics of the artificial wind speed signals determined in this way are dependent on the wind parameters.

The mean wind speed and the standard deviation are linearly related with the constant $k_{\sigma,v}$

$$\hat{\sigma}_v = k_{\sigma,v} \cdot \bar{v} \tag{1}$$

$k_{\sigma,v}$ is found experimentally and it depends on the characteristics of the place. Typical values of $k_{\sigma,v}$ are 0.1...0.15 for the coastal and offshore sites and 0.15...0.25 for the cases where the site topography is more important.

If the transfer function of the shaping filter is specified according to (Welfonder et al., 1997), e.g.

$$H_F(j\omega) = \frac{K_F}{(1 + j\omega T_F)^{5/6}} \tag{2}$$

then, a very good correspondence between the measured and the simulated values is obtained. The amplification factor K_F is computed on the condition that the colored noise from the filter has a standard deviation value equal to one. This condition is set by the following relationship between K_F and T_F.

$$K_F = \sqrt{\frac{2\pi}{B\left(\frac{1}{2}, \frac{1}{3}\right)} \frac{T_F}{T}} \tag{3}$$

where T is the sampling period and B is the beta function, also called the Euler integral of the first kind.

The time constant T_F of the shaping filter is chosen as:

$$T_F = \frac{L}{V} \tag{4}$$

where L is the turbulence length scale and it depends on the site characteristics. Typical values of L are 100...200m for coastal and offshore sites and 200...500m in cases where site topography is more important.

2.2 Wind turbine model

The produced electrical power from wind turbines does not have the same behaviour in terms of variation as the wind. Wind turbines are dynamic generators with several components that influence the power conversion from the wind. The dynamics of the wind turbine filter out the high frequency power variations but it also includes new components due to its dynamics itself.

Wind turbines can in most cases be represented by a generic model with its main parts: the rotor and the generation system. These model elements are presented below.

Rotor

The turbine rotor reduces the air speed and at the same time transforms the absorbed kinetic energy of the air into mechanical power, P_{MECH}. The mechanical power of the wind turbine is given using the following equation:

$$P_{MECH} = \frac{1}{2}\rho A v^3 C_P(\lambda, \beta) \tag{5}$$

where ρ is the air density, A the area swept by the rotor, v is the wind speed, C_P is the power coefficient, β is the blade angle of the wind turbine, and λ is the tip-speed ratio, which is defined by:

$$\lambda = \frac{\omega_{turb} R}{V} \tag{6}$$

where ω_{turb} is the turbine rotational speed and R is the rotor radius.

The power coefficient C_P depends on the aerodynamic characteristics of the wind turbine. The following generic equation can be used to model C_P (Siegfried, 1998):

$$C_P(\lambda, \beta) = 0.5\left(\frac{116}{\lambda_i} - 0.4\beta - 5\right)e^{-\frac{21}{\lambda_i}} \tag{7}$$

where

$$\lambda = \frac{\omega_{turb} R}{V} \tag{8}$$

It may be noted that C_P is a highly nonlinear power function of λ and β, where λ in turn is dependent of the turbine rotational speed and the wind speed.

Generation System

There are different types of generation system. According to the rotational speed of the rotor, wind generation systems can be classified into two types: fixed-speed systems and variable-speed systems (Slootweg & Kling, 2003; Jenkins et al., 2000).

Fixed-speed systems

In fixed-speed machines, the generator, usually of induction with squirrel-cage rotor, is directly connected to the grid. The frequency of the grid establishes the rotational speed of the generator. The slow rotational speed of the turbine's blades is transmitted to the generator by means of a gear box.
Squirrel-cage induction generators always require reactive power. Thus, the use of reactive power is always provided by capacitors so as to reach a power factor close to one.
Fixed-speed systems have the advantage of simplicity and low cost and the disadvantage of requiring reactive power supply for the used induction generators. Fig. 3 shows a model of fixed-speed systems for wind turbines. This model consists mainly of the squirrel-cage induction generator and the compensating capacitors. For the generator, standard models of this type of machine are usually employed.

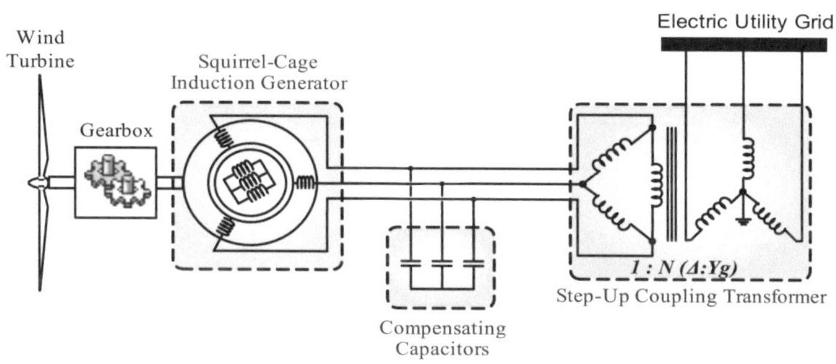

Fig. 3. Fixed-speed systems

Variable-speed systems

Variable-speed systems usually use power electronics to connect the generator with the grid, what makes it possible to uncouple the rotational speed of the rotor from the frequency of the grid, hence, allowing the rotational speed of the rotor to depend only on the speed of the wind. Since power is transmitted through power electronic converters, there is significant electric loss. However, there are some important advantages using variable speed, such as: a better energy exploitation; a decrease in mechanical loss, which makes possible lighter mechanical designs; and a more controllable power output (less dependent on wind variations). In variable-speed systems, wind turbines mainly use some of the following generating systems:

a. Direct-driven synchronous generator

In this system, the generator is completely uncoupled from the grid by means of power electronic converters connected to the winding of the stator and so, it does not need a gear box to connect to the grid. On the grid's side, the converter used is a voltage source converter. On the generator's side, it can be a voltage source converter or rectifier diodes. Fig. 4 shows a model of this type of generating system.

b. Doubly-fed induction generator (wound rotor)

In these systems, the excitation windings of the generator are fed with an external frequency through an ac/dc/ac converter; in this way, the rotor speed can be uncoupled from the electric frequency of the system. This variable-speed system have the advantage over direct-driven synchronous generators of using power electronic converters that can be reduced in size, owing to the fact that these can only be found in the circuit of the rotor. However, these systems have the disadvantage of necessarily requiring a gear box for the connection to the grid, what can reduce reliability. Fig. 5 shows a model of this type of generating system.

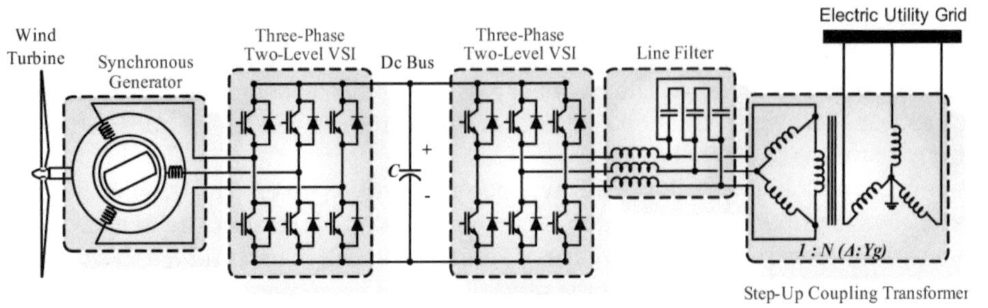

Fig. 4. Variable-speed system with direct-driven synchronous generator

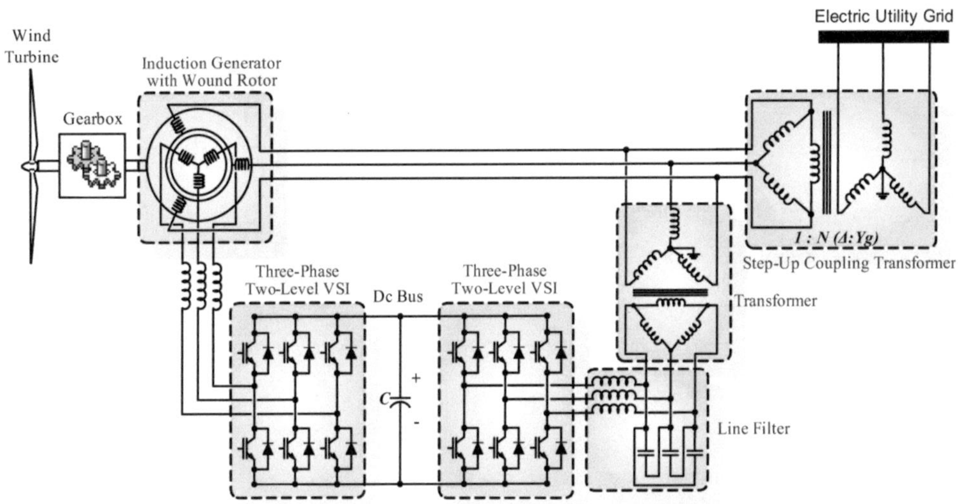

Fig. 5. Variable-speed system with doubly-fed induction generator

2.2.1 Simplified model of fixed-speed wind turbines

The wind turbine topology used in this study is the type of the fixed-speed wind turbine. This turbine type is equipped with an induction generator (squirrel cage or wound rotor) that is directly connected to the grid. Detailed models for wind turbines are complex, with differential equations requiring much computational work. For certain studies (e.g., power system dynamics) these models can not be applied, which calls instead for simplified models. The development of simplified models implies a compromise between, on the one hand, making substantial simplifications to reduce the computational load and, on the other hand, keeping the necessary adequacy to allow predicting the influence of wind power on the dynamic behaviour of the system. A simplified equivalent model for power behaviour of a typical fixed-speed wind turbine is presented below, based on an equivalent transfer function developed in (Soens et al., 2005; Delmerico et al., 2003).

For fixed values of mean wind speed, the entire system is assumed to be linear and, thus, can be approximated by a simple transfer function. This transfer function must be a first order low-pass filter for low wind speeds (i.e., a value below the rated wind speed) and a higher order function for high wind speeds (higher values than the rated wind speed) (Soens et al., 2005; Delmerico et al., 2003). Rated wind speed is the wind speed for which the turbine generates its rated power. Fig. 6 shows the model used. The input of the function is the available wind speed. The output is the turbine's power available for electricity generation. Considering the upper part of Fig.6, the wind speed is low-pass filtered and converted into power using the turbine's power curve. The time constant of the low-pass filter depends on the average wind speed. For this simplified model, it is assumed constant. The power curve of the wind turbine is depicted in Fig. 7.

The power curve has an upper limit for the output power, which is equal or near the rated power (i.e., 1pu). The upper input of the summator in Fig. 6 remains nearby at 1pu for high wind speeds. The effect of wind speed fluctuations at rated power operation is taken into account by a second transfer function (lower part of Fig. 6).

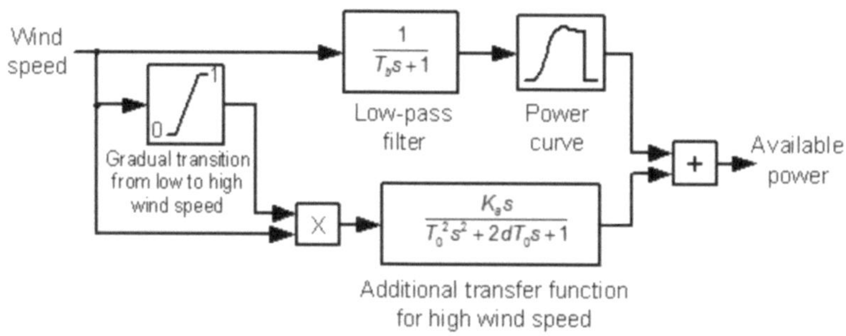

Fig. 6. Equivalent Transfer Function for the wind turbine model

The simplified model contains a gradual transition between the low wind speed and the high wind speed region. For wind speeds below 90% of rated wind speed, the transfer function for high wind speeds is not regarded (factor 0). For wind speeds above 100% of rated wind speed, the transfer function for high wind speeds is fully taken into account (factor 1). A linear interpolation is used for the intermediate wind speeds.

The parameters of the equivalent transfer function were obtained through simulations. The output of the equivalent transfer function was compared with the output of the detailed model of a wind turbine included in the library of the SimPowerSystems/Simulink. In this way, adjustments were progressively made on the parameters of the equivalent function until obtaining a good fit between both models.

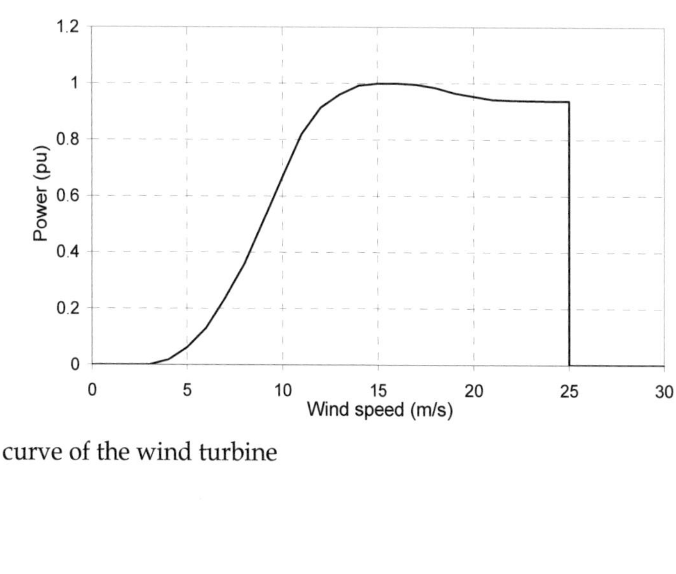

Fig. 7. Power curve of the wind turbine

2.3 Wind farm model

The mathematical model used for the wind farm behaviour in power systems is presented in this section. Typically, the number of wind turbines in a wind farm is high. In fact, a large wind farm can feature hundreds of wind turbines. Therefore, only for wind farm projects it is necessary to analyze in detail the entire generating facility, with each wind turbine represented individually.

In studies where the objective is to verify the influence of the wind farm on the electrical system, the model of every individual turbine of the wind farm would need excessively long processing times and a very robust computational infrastructure. In such studies, the wind farm is represented by an equivalent model from the viewpoint of the electrical system (Pavinatto, 2005; Pálsson et al., 2004; Pöller & Aechilles, 2003).

The simplest way to represent the wind farm is to model the entire farm as an equivalent single wind turbine (Pálsson et al., 2004). This approach assumes that the power fluctuations from each wind turbine are all equal throughout the farm. This assumption, however, does not reflect reality, because the power fluctuations of a wind farm are relatively smaller than those of a wind turbine. Another way to model the wind farm is through a detailed modelling of the farm and considering factors such as the coherence and the correlation of wind turbulence as the presented in (Rosas, 2003; Sørensen et al., 2007). These models imply a heavy load of mathematical modelling and sizable hardware to process them. The model presented in this work takes into account the aggregation effect of the wind farm using an equivalent for the wind added to groups of wind turbines in the farm (Pavinatto, 2005). The model thus conformed renders a good approximation of the behaviour of the wind farm, from the electric system viewpoint. As an advantage, the need for computational resources is reduced.

In order to take into account the aerodynamic effects associated to the layout of wind turbines in the farm, the scheme of Fig. 8 has been considered. The wind turbines of the first row of M turbines take a part of the kinetic energy of the wind. Therefore, the wind speed for the second row is reduced, and so on in the following rows. This speed decrease is illustrated in Fig. 9.

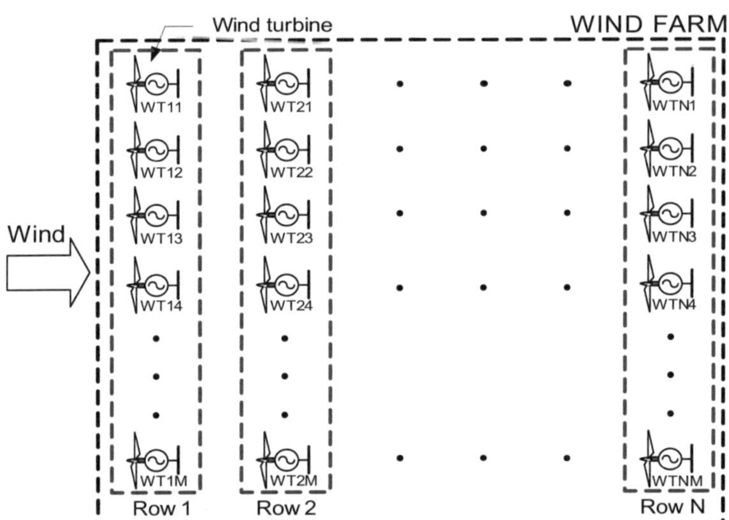

Fig. 8. Layout of a typical wind farm

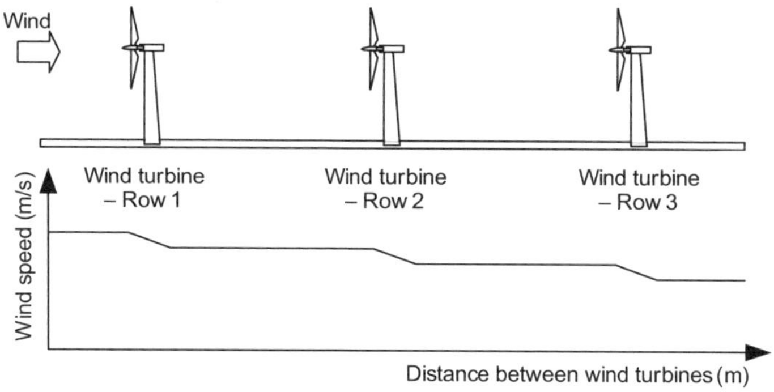

Fig. 9. Decrease of the wind speed due to the aerodynamic shadow effect of a turbine upon the following one

Reference (Frandsen et al., 2004) presents several methods to quantify this wind speed decrease. Typically, this speed reduction as the wind passes through the farm is characterized by the general pattern of Fig. 10.

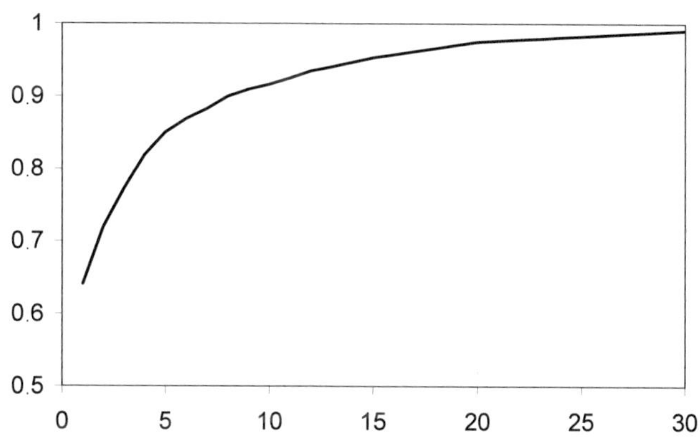

Fig. 10. Comparison of wind speed in two rows of wind turbines

In addition to the phenomenon of wind speed reduction, the effect of a temporary delay in the variations of the wind speed in these turbines is a contributing factor as well. That is, the turbines of the second row experience the wind speed variations of first row after a certain time, called the propagation time, which depends on the wind speed and the separating distance between turbines.

2.3.1 Calculation of the equivalent wind speed

For calculations, each row of turbines is considered as a single equivalent turbine, subjected to the effects from the wind speed decrease and propagation time. Equations (9) to (11) are used for modelling the wind speed on each turbine row (Pavinatto, 2005; Pálsson et al., 2004). The time series of wind speed for the first row is as follows:

$$v_{eq\_s}(t) = \bar{v} + \frac{v(t) - \bar{v}}{\sqrt{M}} \tag{9}$$

where $v_{eq\_s}(t)$ is the time series of the equivalent wind speed for the first row; $v(t)$ is the wind speed simulated in modeling; $\bar{v}$ is the mean wind speed (for ten minutes, in this case) and M is the number of wind turbines for each row.
For the consecutive rows, the following expression is used:

$$v_{eq\_sk}(t,k) = \left[v_{eq\_s}\left(t+t_p\right)\right]a_r^{k-1} \tag{10}$$

$$t_p(k) = \frac{D(k-1)}{\bar{v}} \tag{11}$$

where k is the row number; $v_{eq\_sk}(t,k)$ is the series of values of the equivalent wind speed for row k; a_r is the coefficient that represents the reduction effect of the wind speed; $t_p(k)$ is the propagation time for row k, and D is the separating distance between rows in the farm.
The series of wind speed obtained for each row is applied to the dynamic simplified model of the wind turbine presented before.

2.3.2 Power aggregation

The output power of the wind turbine is multiplied by the number of wind turbines of the row, M. Thus, the total power of the row is obtained (P_{WT}). Finally, the corresponding values for the N rows are added up to attain the total power generated by the wind farm (P_{WF}). The overall structure of the wind farm model is presented in Fig. 11.

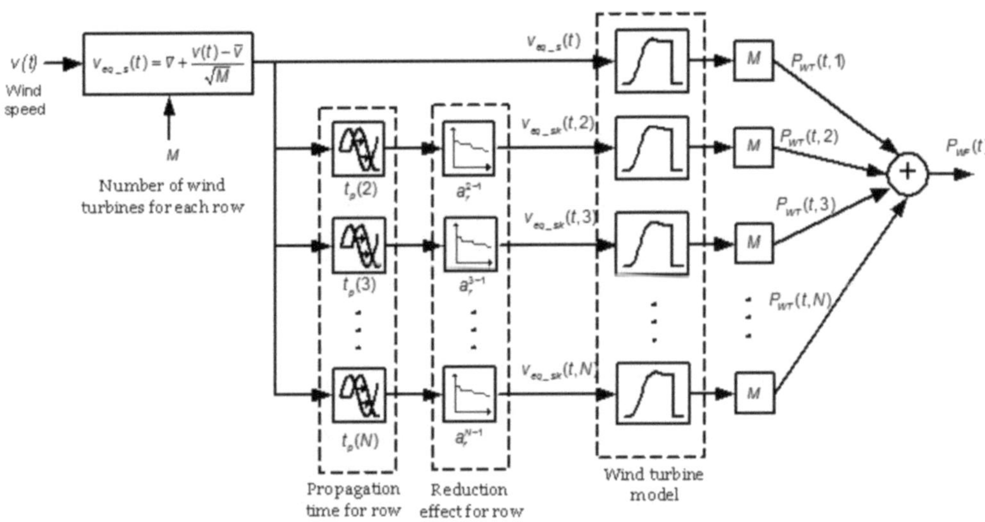

Fig. 11. Overall structure of the wind farm model

3. Test system

The test system to evaluate the interaction of the wind farm with the power system is shown in Fig. 12 as a single-line diagram. Such a system features a substation, represented by a Thevenin equivalent with a short circuit power of 100MVA, which feeds a transmission network operating at 132kV/50Hz.

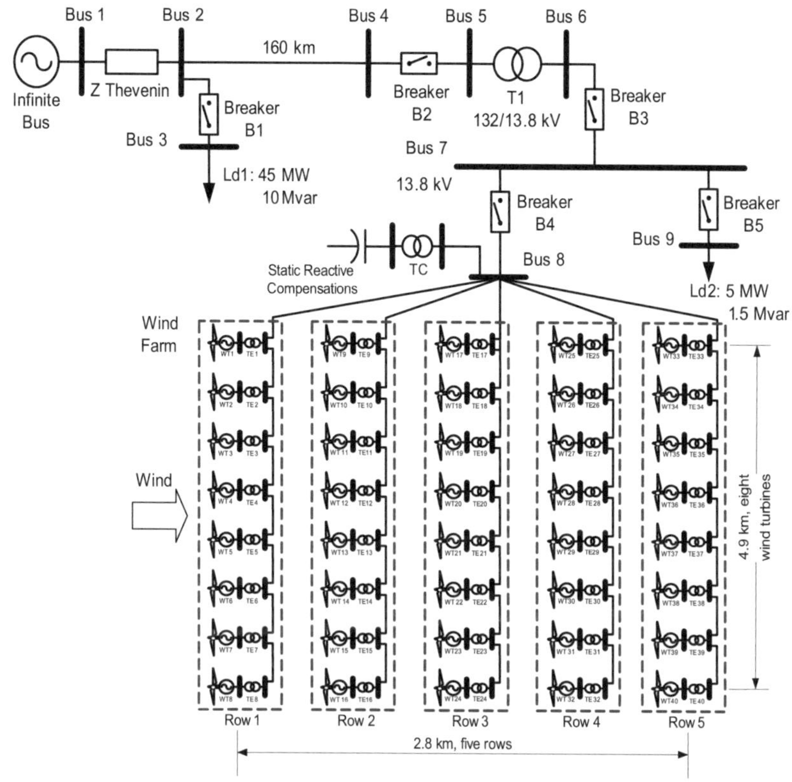

Fig. 12. Test system

Sets of loads are connected to bus 3 (Ld1: 45MW, 10Mvar) and at bus 9 (Ld2: 5MW, 1.5Mvar). A 160km transmission line links, through a 132/13.8kV transformer, the load Ld2 and the wind farm to the substation. The wind farm consists of five rows with eight wind turbines each. The distance between two neighbour turbines and between two consecutive rows is 700m. The wind turbines use a fixed-speed system; and their power curve is shown in Fig. 7. The rated power of each wind turbine is 1.5MW. Therefore, the forty-turbine wind farm has 60MW rated power. Each wind turbine is connected to the grid through an induction generator with squirrel-cage rotor. The demand of reactive power from the wind farm is supplied by capacitors so as to reach a close-to-one power factor. The capacitor banks feature five sections, one per each turbine row. Now, for simplicity in the figure the sections are represented by a single capacitor.

4. Simulation results

4.1 Wind speed and wind farm

This section shows the main results of the models described, mainly of the wind speed model and wind farm model. Fig. 13 shows a profile of wind speed, generated using the model of Fig. 2. Chosen parameters in the algorithm are: $L = 200$m, $k_{\sigma,v} = 0.15$ with a sampling period of $T = 1$s. The wind model is applied with three mean values for wind speed, $\bar{v}_1$ = 4m/s, $\bar{v}_2$ = 10m/s, and $\bar{v}_3$ = 16m/s, and for a time period of 10min. Fig. 13 shows the increase of fluctuation amplitudes for growing mean wind speed.

A mean wind speed of 10m/s was chosen for showing the simulation results of the wind farm model. This wind profile is regarded the impinging wind on the first row. Fig. 14 shows the equivalent wind speed for each row of wind turbines. When comparing the wind speed $\bar{v}_2$ = 10m/s of Fig. 13 with the wind speed of the row 1 of Fig. 14, it can be noted a reduction of wind turbulence in the wind speed of row 1 of Fig. 14. This reflects the non-coincidence of power fluctuations in all turbines of the same row. Moreover, in Fig. 14, a reduction is noted on the wind speed for all rows, and a time delay of wind speed fluctuations among rows.

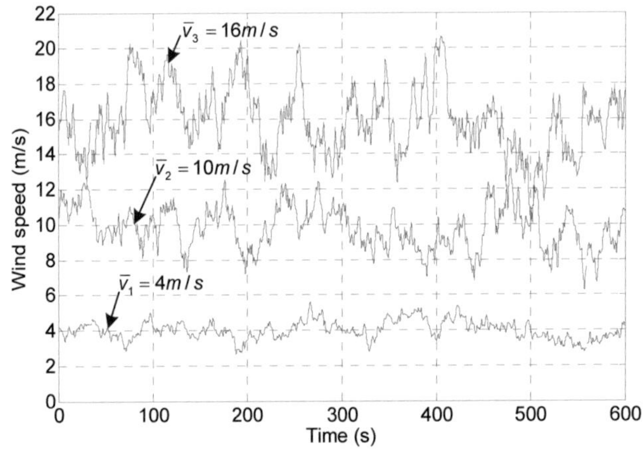

Fig. 13. Profiles of the generated wind speed, for different values of mean speed: $\bar{v}_1$ = 4m/s, $\bar{v}_2$ = 10m/s, and $\bar{v}_3$ = 16m/s

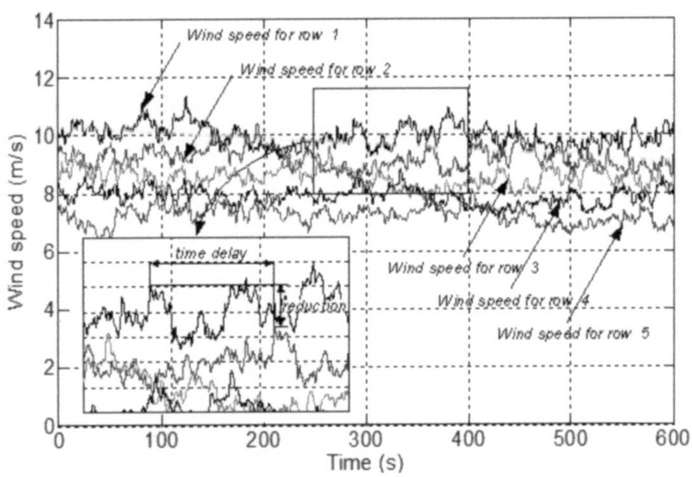

Fig. 14. Equivalent wind speed for each row of the wind farm

Fig. 15 shows the active power generated by each row and the total active power delivered by the wind farm. Fig. 16 shows the reactive power produced by the wind farm and compensated by a capacitors bank for a mean wind speed of 10m/s. In Fig. 15, an important fluctuation of the active power delivered by the wind farm can be noted. This fluctuation of active power is transmitted into the grid via the transmission line, which may cause problems not only at the connection point of the wind farm but also at other points of the system.

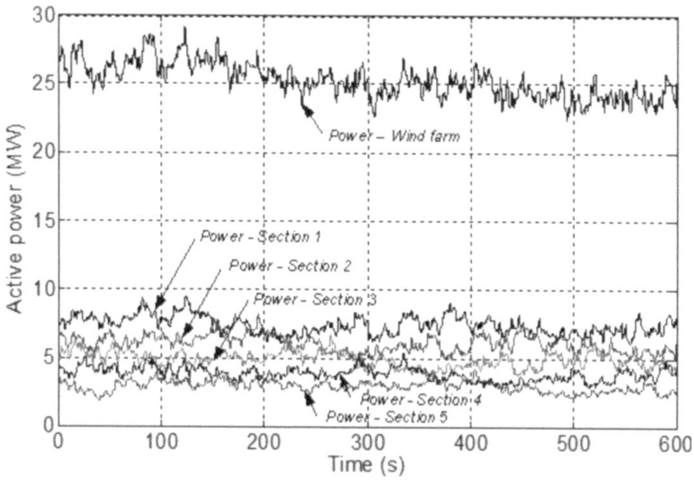

Fig. 15. Active power generated by the wind farm and by each row of wind turbines

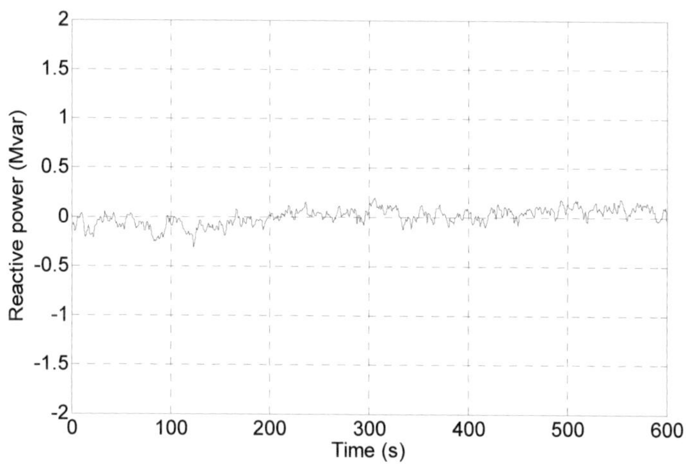

Fig. 16. Reactive power generated by the wind farm and the capacitors bank

4.2 Impacts of wind power on the power system

This section studies the impacts of the wind farm on the power system of Fig. 12. For this, case studies that represent different operating states of the wind farm are simulated. The behaviour of the voltage is observed at bus bars of the wind farm and at loads. First, an analysis is made on the wind farm operating with two mean wind speeds. Finally, the effects are studied when contingencies arise in the farm.

4.2.1 Wind farm operating with mean wind speeds of 10 m/s and 6 m/s

Two cases are simulated with the wind farm operating with all wind turbines connected. One of them has a mean wind speed of 10m/s and the other has mean wind speed of 6m/s.

In the first case, the power through the line flows from the wind farm to the substation. With a value of 10m/s of mean wind speed, the wind farm injects into the grid both the active and reactive power as shown in Fig. 15 and in Fig. 16, respectively. Since the load is constant; the same power fluctuations injected by the wind farm are transmitted along the transmission line to the rest of the system. In the second case, with a mean wind speed of 6m/s, the power through the line flows from the substation to the wind farm bus; because the power injected by the wind farm cannot supply the entire demand at bus 7. Fig. 17 shows both the active and the reactive power injected by the wind farm, with a mean operating wind speed of 6m/s. In this case, the capacitors bank compensates the reactive power for a mean wind speed of 6m/s, rendering the system with a null average reactive power.

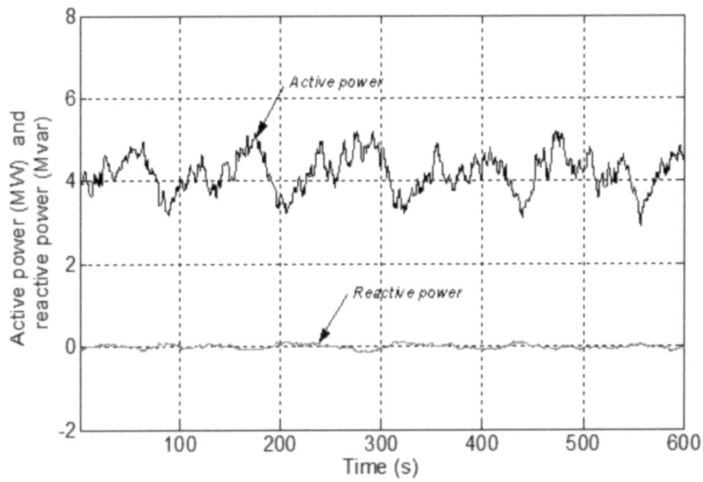

Fig. 17. Active and reactive power injected by the wind farm with a mean wind speed of 6m/s

As mentioned above, the power injections of the wind farm are transmitted to the entire system through the transmission line. These power injections may cause certain problems at different points in the grid. This is most likely to happen in a weak system as the one discussed in this chapter. Fig. 18 and Fig. 19 show the voltage at two buses of the system: at bus 7 (13.8kV), where the wind farm is connected, and where the load is present; and at bus 2 (132kV), at the other end of the transmission line, where load is also present. Figs. 18 and 19 show, respectively, the voltage for the wind farm operating with a mean wind speed of 10m/s and 6m/s.

The figures show that both simulated cases experience marked voltage fluctuations, even when the farm operates with a mean wind speed of 6 m/s and injecting relatively little power to the grid. Besides, for both cases, these voltage fluctuations take place not only at the connection point of the wind farm but also at bus 2 on the other end of the line. The reason for this is that it is a relatively weak system and that it has a low short circuit power at bus 2.

Finally, when the wind farm operates with a mean wind speed of 10m/s, it may be noted that the voltage is above the desired value of 1 pu at bus 7. This is mainly due to the injection of a large power flow at a point where the load is relatively small.

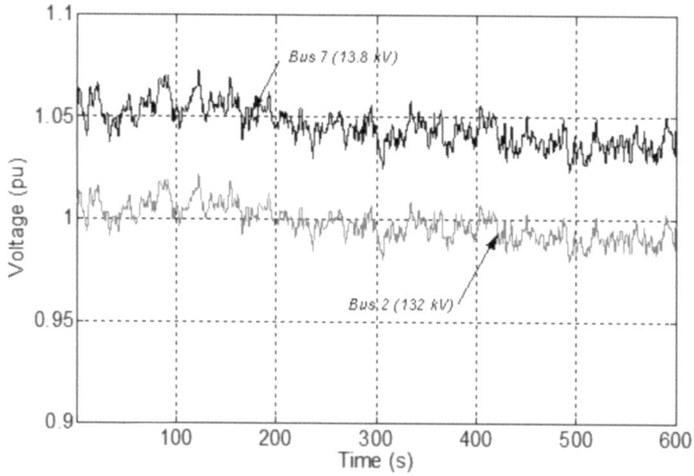

Fig. 18. Voltage at bus 2 and bus 7 for the wind farm operating with a mean wind speed of 10m/s

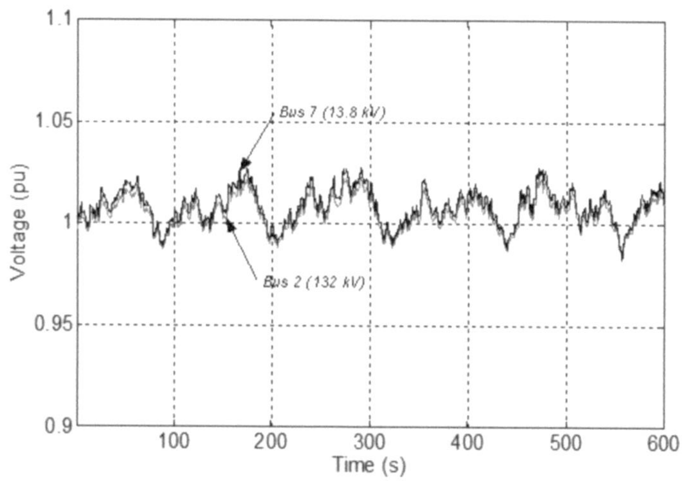

Fig. 19. Voltage at bus 2 and bus 7 for the wind farm operating with a mean wind speed of 6m/s

4.2.2 Contingencies in the wind farm

This section discusses two cases for a wind farm system introducing contingencies into the grid. In both cases simulated, a mean wind speed of 10m/s is used.

The first case simulates the gradual connection of eight wind turbines with their respective capacitors banks. At first, it is considered that the wind farm is operating with four of the five rows of Fig. 12. Then, the fifth row is added by gradually connecting by pairs its eight turbines at: t = 150s, t = 250s, t = 350s and t = 450s. When connecting each pair, the corresponding capacitors for reactive power compensation are gradually connected as well; in four steps every 15s. Fig. 20 shows, respectively, the active and reactive power injected to the grid.

In the second case, a fault is simulated for one turbines row which causes the disconnection of the row's eight wind turbines. First, a normal operation is considered, i.e., the wind farm with the forty wind turbines connected. In t = 30s a fault is produced (a short circuit between one phase and ground) in the line that links row 1 with bus 8. Then, at t = 30.1s, the fault is cleared by disconnecting this row of eight turbines from the system. Fig. 21 shows the active and reactive power injected by the wind farm in such a case. It can be seen that the reactive power has a mean value around zero before and after the fault occurrence. This is explained by the fact that, when row 1 is disconnected, the capacitors bank that compensates such row gets disconnected as well.

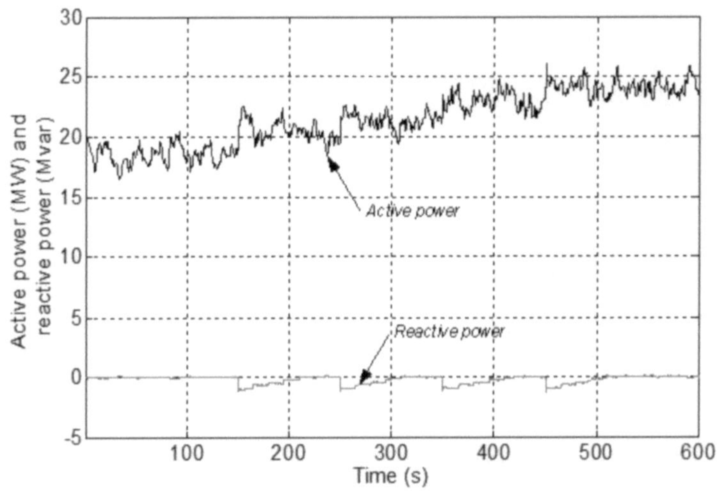

Fig. 20. Active and reactive power injected by the wind farm when the wind turbines are connected

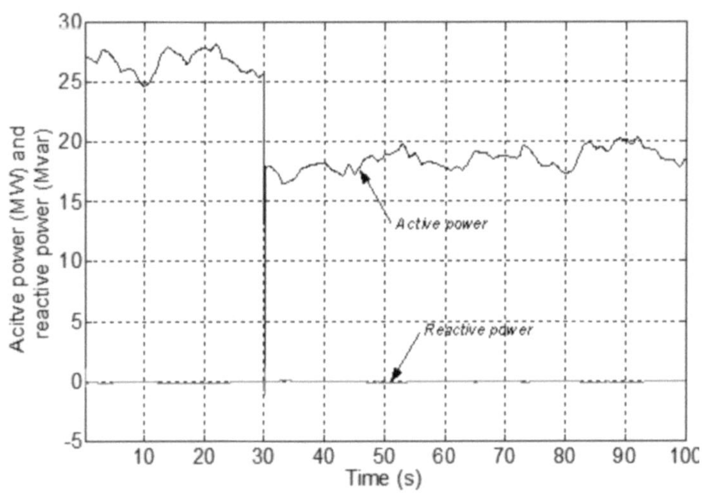

Fig. 21. Active and reactive power injected by the wind farm when a fault inside the farm occurs

These fluctuations of active and reactive power are passed into the system, causing voltage fluctuations at the various buses. Fig. 22 and Fig. 23 show the voltage at bus 7 and at bus 2 for both simulations. In the first case (Fig. 22), voltage fluctuations caused by wind turbulence are noted. In addition, a voltage increase due to the connection of wind turbines is also noted.

In the second case (Fig. 23), it can be noted that when the fault occurs, the voltage at bus 2 and bus 7 falls sharply to values near zero. After clearing the fault and disconnecting the eight wind turbines of row 1, the voltage at both buses remains with lower value than the one existing before the fault arose.

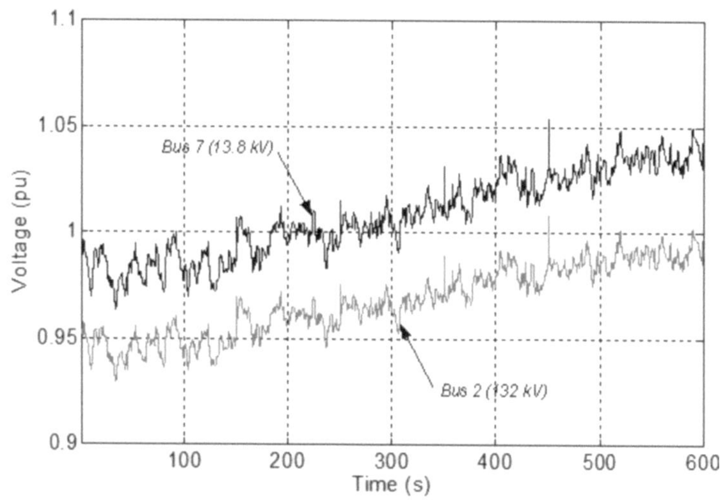

Fig. 22. Voltage at bus 2 and bus 7 for connection of wind turbines

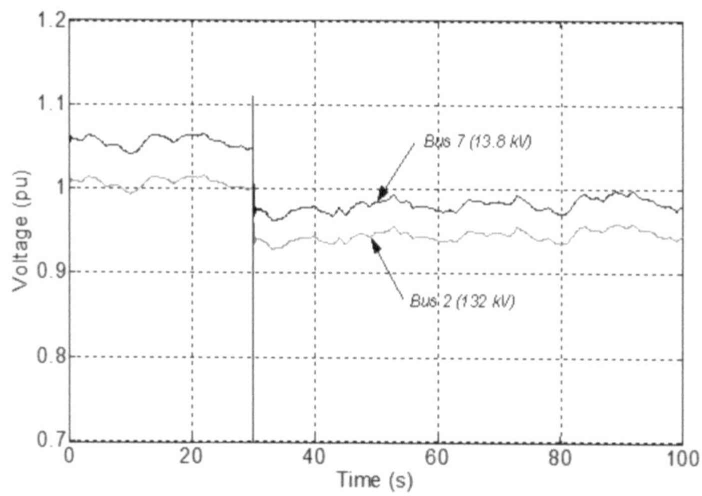

Fig. 23. Voltage at bus 2 and bus 7 for a fault inside the wind farm

Finally, and taking into account all the cases analyzed, it can be concluded that the power fluctuations injected by the wind farm with fixed-speed wind turbines cause significant voltage fluctuations. It was observed that, for this weak power system here studied, these voltage fluctuations take place not only at the point of connection of the wind farm but also at other buses of the system. These voltage fluctuations are mainly caused by wind turbulence and, obviously, are increased when contingencies arise in the system, such as when connecting the turbines or when faults occur. Therefore, the insertion of a wind farm with fix-speed wind turbines into a weak power system introduces significant problems as regards the quality of the voltage levels delivered to the consumers. Voltages with so poor quality could cause malfunction of equipments and significant losses, depending on the type of consumer load.

5. Conclusions

In this chapter, the model aspects and the impact of wind power onto a weak power system have been described. A wind system model was presented that takes into account factors such as a rapidly varying turbulence component of the wind and the aerodynamic effects associated to the layout of wind turbines throughout the farm. A test system was used and case studies for different instances of wind farm operation were analyzed, aiming at evaluating the interaction of the wind farm with the power system.

The results here obtained have shown that the incorporation of the wind farm with fix-speed wind turbines into a weak power system introduces important problems in the quality of voltage. Therefore, in order to insert the wind farm into a weak power system would call for incorporating additional means and equipment to improve the voltage quality rendered to the costumers. Among the different solutions that could be resorted to, more compensation from local reactive and voltage support devices, such as capacitors, SVCs, etc. should be considered. And for faster voltage fluctuations, synchronous static compensators could be used, such as DSTATCOM devices. Better solutions are obtained if these static compensators incorporate devices for energy storage and fast response, such as flywheels, SMES systems or supercapacitors. These devices with storage capacity not only allow controlling the reactive power but also the active power which can make the wind farm deliver a smoother power output to the grid.

6. References

Ackermann, T. (2005). *Wind Power in Power systems*. John Wiley & Sons, Ltd, ISBN 0-470-85508-8 (HB), England.

Chen, Z. & Spooner, E. (2001). Grid Power Quality with Variable Speed Wind Turbines. *IEEE Transactions on Energy Conversion*, vol. 16, N° 2, pp 148-154, June 2001.

Delmerico, R.W.; Miller, N.; Price, W.W. & Sanchez-Gasca, J.J. (2003). Dynamic Modelling of GE 1.5 and 3.6 MW Wind Turbine-Generators for Stability Simulations, *IEEE Power Engineering Society PES General Meeting*, 13-17, July 2003, Toronto, Canada.

Frandsen, S.; Barthelmie, R.; Pryor, S.; Rathmann, O.; Larsen, S. & Højstrup, J. (2004). Analytical Modeling of Wind Speed Deficit in Large Offshore Wind Farms.

European Wind Energy Conference & Exhibition, pp. 6-11, London, Nov. 2004, England.

Hassan, U. & Sykes, D.M. (1985). Wind structure and statistics. *Wind Energy Conversion Systems*, Ch. 2. Prentice Hall, New York.

Jenkins, N.; Allan, R.; Crossley, P.; Kirschen, D. & Strbac, G. (2000). *Embedded Generation*, The Institution of Electrical Engineers, ISBN 978-0-85296-774-4, England.

Leithead, W.E.; De la Salle, S. & Reardon D. (1991). Role and Objectives of Control for Wind Turbines. *IEE Proceedings*, vol. 138, Pt.C, N° 2, pp.135-148.

Mohod, S.W. & Aware, M.V. (2008). Power Quality Issues & It's Mitigation Technique in Wind Energy Generation. *IEEE Harmonics and Quality of Power*, September 2008.

Nichita, C.; Luca, D.; Dakyo, B. & Ceanga, E. (2002). Large band simulation of the wind speed for real time wind turbine simulators. *IEEE Transactions on Energy Conversion*, vol. 17, N° 4, 2002.

Pálsson, M.; Toftevaag, T.; Uhlen, K.; Norheim, I.; Warland, L. & Tande, J. O. G. (2004). Wind Farm Modeling for Network Analysis - Simulation and Validation. *European Wind Energy Conference & Exhibition*, pp. 134-138, Nov. 2004, England.

Pavinatto, E. (2005). Ferramenta para Auxílio à Análise de Viabilidade Técnica da Conexão de Parques Eólicos à Rede Elétrica. *Tese de Mestrado, COPPE/UFRJ*, Rio de Janeiro, Brasil, 2005.

Pöller, M. & Aechilles, S. (2003). Aggregated Wind Park Models for Analysing Power System Dynamics. *4th International Workshop on Large Scale Integration of Wind Power an Networks for Offshore Wind-Farms*, Billund, Denmark.

Rosas, P. (2003). Dynamic Influences of Wind Power on the Power System. *PhD thesis, Ørsted•DTU, Section of Electric Power Engineering*, March 2003.

Siegfried Heier. (1998). *Grid Integration of Wind Energy Conversion Systems*, John Wiley & Sons Ltd, 1998, ISBN 0-471-97143-X, New York, USA.

Slootweg, J.G. & Kling, W.L. (2003). Is the Answer Blowing in the Wind? *IEEE Power & Energy magazine*, pp 26-33, November/December 2003.

Smith, J.C.; Milligan, M.R. & DeMeo, E.A. (2007). Utility Wind Integration and Operating Impact State of the Art. *IEEE Transaction on Power System*, vol. 32, N°.3, pp.900-907, August 2007.

Soens, J.; Driesen, J. & Belmans, R. (2005). Equivalent transfer function for a variable speed wind turbine in power system dynamic simulations. *International Journal of Distributed Energy Resources*, vol. 1 num. 2, pp. 111-133, Apr.-Jun. 2005.

Sørensen, P.; Cutululis, N.A.; Vigueras - Rodriguez, A.; Jensen, L.; Hjerrild, J.; Donovan M.H. & Madsen, H. (2007). Power Fluctuations from Large Wind Farms, *IEEE Trans on Power Systems*, vol. 22, N° 3, 958-965, 2007.

Suvire, G. O. & Mercado, P. E. (2006). Impacts and alternatives to increase the penetration of wind power generation in power systems. *X SEPOPE (X Symposium of specialists in electric operational and expansion planning)*, Florianopolis, May 2006, Brasil.

Welfonder, E.; Neifer, R. & Spanner, M. (1997). Development and experimental identification of dynamic models for wind turbines. *Control Eng. Practice*, vol. 5, N° 1, pp. 63–73, 1997.

12

Optimal Design of a Multifunctional Reactor for Catalytic Oxidation of Glucose with Fast Catalyst Deactivation

Zuzana Gogová[1], Jiří Hanika[1] and Jozef Markoš[2]
[1]*Institute of Chemical Process Fundamentals AS CR, v. v. i., Rozvojová 135, CZ-165 02 Prague 6,*
[2]*Institute of Chemical and Environmental Engineering, Slovak University of Technology, Radlinského 9, 812 37, Bratislava,*
[1]*Czech republic,*
[2]*Slovakia*

1. Introduction

Oxidations of organic compounds in liquid phase by oxygen have been applied for years in many important industrial and waste water treatment processes. There are several variants of technical design of these processes - ranging from homogeneous through heterogeneous to biotechnological routes. As an example, the process of gluconic acid production by glucose oxidation can be arranged in all of these variants.

Bioprocesses are usually carried out in aqueous media at ambient temperature and atmospheric pressure in the presence of living microorganisms and their enzymatic apparatus (e.g. Aspergillus niger), or by using pure enzymes (glucose oxidase and catalase), (Sikula, et al. (2006), (2007)). In the former case, the biomass represents a solid phase in the reaction system, whereas in the latter case, the reaction system is homogeneous - liquid. Some drawbacks are also inherent with the bioprocesses - e.g. strong sensitivity of microorganisms to impurities present in the reaction system, losses of the substrate transformed to carbon dioxide or utilized for the microorganisms growth, low solubility of oxygen in the reaction system owing to the presence of ionic salts and nutrients (e.g. glucose) with a high rate of oxygen consumption by the microorganisms on the other hand, frequent occurrence of non-newtonian hydrodynamic properties of biomass suspension, foam formation, etc. For such bioprocesses, gas-lift reactors (known as air-lift reactors) (GLRs) are often used for their capability of delivering oxygen to the growing culture at a sufficient rate, while maintaining low shear stress.

Heterogeneous catalyst application to the oxidation process is advantageous compared to homogeneous catalytic systems with respect to simpler separation of a catalyst from the reaction mixture by filtration. At the heterogeneous variant however, a catalyst selection and its optimization is one of the crucial points to be considered. Another one is the reactor type selection and its design (estimation of the geometry and the size of the reactor selected). Neither the authors' experience, nor literature search provide many generalizations on selection of a reactor type for which a counter-example could not be thought up. An open mind and good ideas are probably more important here than any generalization. Furthermore, because of complexity in scale dependency of various reactor selection criteria, the authors incline to agree with the statement of Bisio & Kabel (1985) : „*You cannot design a reactor until you have selected its type, and you cannot know if your type selection was wise until you have designed it*". Thus, the selection - design optimization is an iterative procedure, the "building blocks" of which may use dynamic models to various extents.

Heterogeneously catalyzed wet air oxidation of glucose (Glc) to gluconic acid (Glcac) in aqueous alkaline solution serves as a model reaction. Palladium on activated carbon commercial catalyst enables to run the reaction selectively at ambient conditions. On an industrial scale, biotechnological routes of Glcac production currently prevail over the catalytic one. This is mainly because of the Glcac broad utilization in the food industry. The other reason is a problem with activity of the catalysts used. Pt-group catalysts suffer from gradual reversible deactivation due to an action of oxygen during the reaction course.

One way to overcome the problem leads through the catalyst optimization. Recently, good activity, selectivity and long-term stability were reported for supported gold catalysts (Biella, et al. (2002), Comotti, et al. (2006), Thielecke, et al. (2007)).

Another approach to solve the problems with the catalyst activity deals with the process and/or reactor optimization. It is based on correct choice of a reactor type for a chemical process, the reactor well-suited design and on setting an appropriate mode of the reactor operation. These are the crucial aspects for maximizing the technological output.

The text is focused on solving the problem with the catalyst unstable activity through the reactor / reaction step optimization. Optimization of continuous stirred tank reactor (CSTR) and gas-lift reactor (GLR) productivity through the gas feed modulation is attempted. For any input operational conditions the task is to find conditions of the highest possible productivity of the reactors, i.e. to find conditions where the reaction and reactivation times are shared optimally, so that neither any time is wasted in prolonged activation process, nor is an insufficient activation time provided.

Beneficial effect of composition modulation on a CSTR performance is demonstrated. The catalyst activity can be maintained long-term steady by periodically alternating the gas feed composition. In the case of CSTR, period length and the period split represent independent variables. They both can be varied independently within one CSTR unit of a given construction. It is demonstrated here that for any period length always a split value exists, where the maximum reactor productivity is achieved. By connecting the points of optimal split for every period length, trajectory of the maximal CSTR productivity is obtained.

GLR was selected as the reactor type suitable to carry out the model reaction in. A GLR natural operation enables the catalyst to be periodically exposed to reaction and activation conditions, in the riser and downcomer sections of the GLR, respectively. Such reactors are in their nature multifunctional. In a GLR both, the period length and the split value are bound with geometry of the GLR given. Therefore only one geometrical optimum exists for given set of input operational conditions. The maximal GLR productivity is guaranteed only in this geometrical optimum, because the residence time in riser (reaction time) and the residence time in downcomer (activation time) are only here shared optimally.

1.1 The model reaction kinetics

Glucose (Glc) wet air oxidation over palladium on activated carbon catalyst is used as the model reaction. It takes place in three-phase medium. Advantage of the catalyst is its ability to catalyze the reaction selectively towards gluconic acid (Glcac) at mild conditions. Its

drawback is fast deactivation during the oxidation reaction, when oxygen forms surface oxides or penetrates from the topmost Pd layer to subsurface layer forming subsurface oxide (Simmons, et al. (1991), Lundgren, et al. (2002), Ketteler, et al. (2005)). These Pd-O phases are less active compared to chemisorbed oxygen (oxygen adsorbed above the first metallic layer), and will be referred to as those responsible for change in the catalyst activity. This deactivation was proved reversible (Vleeming, et al. (1997)).
Activation and reactivation of the catalyst is based on reduction of the catalyst active sites. Glucose is good reduction agent to pre-reduce the catalyst. Existence of optimal activation times depending on the reaction mixture composition was observed (see Gogová & Hanika (2009,a) for details).
Equations (1) and (2) form the kinetic model of the model reaction (Gogová & Hanika (2009,b)). They describe mathematically processes of the main surface reaction, the catalyst deactivation and the catalyst reactivation. Change in the catalyst activity is described through a change in fractional coverage by inactive oxygen species, θ_{so}.

$$\dot{\xi}_w = \frac{k_w c_{Glc}\sqrt{c_O}(1-\theta_{so})^2}{(1+K_{Glc}c_{Glc}+K_{Glcac}c_{Glcac})(1+K_O\sqrt{c_O})^2} \tag{1}$$

$$\frac{d\theta_{so}}{dt} = \rho_c W^L(\dot{\xi}_D - \dot{\xi}_A) = \rho_c W^L\left(\frac{k_D\sqrt{c_O}(1-\theta_{so})^2}{(1+K_O\sqrt{c_O})} - \frac{k_A\theta_{so}(1-\theta_{so})}{(1+K_O\sqrt{c_O})}\right) \tag{2}$$

This kinetic model applies all the time except when oxygen concentration in the liquid phase approaches zero. Then the reaction and reactivation mechanism changes: inactive oxygen species (responsible for the catalyst deactivation) take over the function of the chemisorbed oxygen in the main surface reaction. When the mechanism changes, its mathematical description also changes, and equations (3) and (4) apply as the kinetics model instead of equations (1) and (2).

$$\dot{\xi}_w = k_w^+ c_{Glc}\theta_{so}(1-\theta_{so}) \tag{3}$$

$$\frac{d\theta_{so}}{dt} = \rho_c W^L(\dot{\xi}_D - \dot{\xi}_A) = \rho_c W^L k_A\theta_{so}(1-\theta_{so}) \tag{4}$$

Expressions of the lumped rate and adsorption constants of equations (1) - (4) are listed in Table 1.

Rate and adsorption constant	Dimension	Value
k_w	$[m^{4.5}kg^{-1}mol^{-0.5}s^{-1}]$	0.00313
K_{Glc}	$[m^3mol^{-1}]$	0.0169
K_O	$[m^{1.5}mol^{-0.5}]$	4.50
K_{Glcac}	$[m^3mol^{-1}]$	0.384
k_D	$[m^{1.5}mol^{-0.5}kg^{-1}s^{-1}]$	0.00612
k_A	$[kg^{-1}s^{-1}]$	0.00518
k_w^+	$[m^3kg^{-1}s^{-1}]$	$5.47\ 10^{-5}$

Table 1. Parameters of equations (1) - (4), (Gogová & Hanika (2009,b)).

In the kinetic model (equations (1) and (2) or alternatively (3) and (4)), the change in the catalyst activity is expressed through the change in the fractional coverage by inactive oxygen species, θ_{so}. Relation between θ_{so} and the activity is explained below.
Relative activity of the catalyst at time t is defined as the ratio of the reaction rate at time t and reaction rate on a fresh catalyst at the same concentrations and temperature:

$$a(t) = \frac{\dot{\xi}_w(t)}{\dot{\xi}_w^0} \qquad [T,\bar{c}] = const. \tag{5}$$

Thus the relative activity is useful parameter that characterizes changes in the reaction rate as the catalyst deactivates, and it is obtained conveniently from the experimental results. The equation (5) applies to all deactivation processes, no matter if the rate equation is separable or not according to the concept of separability (Szépe & Levenspiel (1970), Butt & Petersen (1988)).
A rate equation is separable if it can be expressed as a product of two terms – the reaction rate on the fresh catalyst and the catalyst activity in the following form:

$$\dot{\xi}_w = \dot{\xi}_w^0(\bar{c})a(\alpha) \qquad [T] = const. \tag{6}$$

Active fraction α is defined as the ratio of the number of active sites per unit mass of the catalyst and the number of all sites, i.e. it gives for this case the following:

$$\alpha = (1 - \theta_{so}) \tag{7}$$

The rate equation (1) is separable. Combination of the equations (1), (6) and (7) gives the following relation between the catalyst activity and the active fraction:

$$a = (1 - \theta_{so})^2 = \alpha^2 \tag{8}$$

Thus the activity depends only on the amount of inactive oxygen species.

1.2 Reversible deactivation of the Pd/C catalyst

Figure 1 provides an insight into the findings made during the model reaction kinetics study. Several regions can be recognized there. Before each experiment in semi-continuous stirred tank reactor (SSTR), the catalyst was activated in the reactor by its reduction with Glc as a component of the reaction mixture in inert atmosphere. The reaction was started up replacing nitrogen flow by flow of nitrogen/oxygen mixture with the desired partial pressure of oxygen. Each experiment consisted of one or more consecutive oxidation runs. Between these oxidation runs the catalyst was reactivated in inert atmosphere with Glc.
The reaction rate at the beginning of the second reaction cycle in SSTR (full circles in Figure 1) is lower because of change in the reaction mixture composition during the first reaction cycle in the batch system (SSTR). To prove full reversibility of the Pd/C catalyst deactivation, the primary experimental data in Figure 1 were corrected for the reaction mixture composition change (empty circles in Figure 1). To serve this purpose, the Glc and Glcac concentrations at the reaction start-up were applied in the kinetic model (equations (1) and (2) with parameters of Table 1).
Figure 1 indicates possibility of improving the reactor performance by periodically exchanging the reaction and reactivation cycles. In the text below, this approach is analyzed

in process of selection and optimization of a target reactor suitable to carry out the model reaction in.

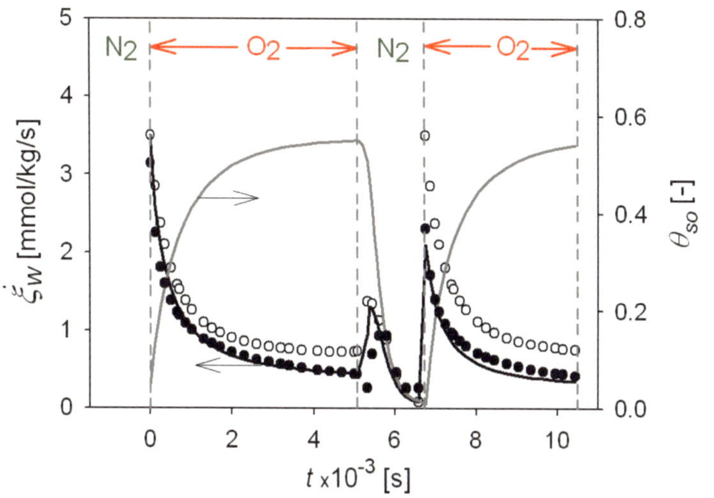

Fig. 1. Transient reaction rate and extent of the catalyst deactivation (represented by θ_{so}) during Glc oxidation in SSTR (reprinted from Gogová & Hanika (2009,b)). Primary experimental data (•); data recalculated for concentrations at the reaction start-up (o); lines – the SSTR experimental data predicted by the kinetics model. Conditions: SSTR; $c_{0,Glc}$ = 100.6 mol/m^3; $c_{0,Glcac}$ = 0 mol/m^3; ρ_c =1 kg/m^3; D_p = 45 μm; p_{O2} = 0.1 MPa; ω = 600 min^{-1}; T = 303 K; pH = 8.1; kinetic regime (i.e. negligible effect of internal and external diffusion).

1.3 Strategy for elimination of the catalyst deactivation

The advantage of the Pd/C catalyst is its ability to catalyze the model reaction efficiently at mild conditions maintaining high selectivity towards Glcac. Its drawback is fast deactivation during the oxidation reaction. In one hour the catalyst activity can drop to less than 40% of its original value depending on the reaction conditions. Although reversible, the deactivation rate presents a crucial problem for industrial implementation of the process.

This text is devoted to one of many strategies aimed to eliminate the problems with unstable activity of the catalyst. It leads through the process and/or reactor optimization. This approach deals with correct choice of a reactor type for a chemical process, the reactor well-suited design and with setting an appropriate mode of its operation. These are the crucial aspects for maximizing the technological output.

For process similar to the model one, Markusse, et al. (2001) found that the catalyst activity can be maintained steady by periodically switching between oxygen and nitrogen flow to a CSTR. In general, the term "periodic operation" refers to operation regimes in which one or more reactor parameters vary in time. Modulation of mostly composition and/or feed flow rate was researched by e.g.: Boelhouwer, et al. (2002), Silveston & Hanika (2002), Tukač, et al. (2003), Silveston & Hanika (2004), Liu, et al. (2008) etc., with the aim to improve chemical reactors performance through forcing the reactor to operate under transient rather than steady-state conditions. Silveston (1998) in his monograph pays attention to several catalytic processes operated in this way.

For the reaction of Glc oxidation by air over reversibly deactivating Pd catalyst, it was indicated in Figure 1 that CSTR productivity can be enhanced by the gas feed flow modulation. Beneficial effects of composition modulation on a CSTR performance were studied in Gogová & Hanika (2009,b) with the model reaction. The task was to share optimally the reaction and reactivation times within given period length, so that neither any time is wasted in prolonged activation process, nor an insufficient activation time is provided.

2. Dynamic operation of CSTR with feed periodic modulation

Possibility of improving the reactor performance by exchanging the reaction and reactivation cycles is indicated in Figure 1. For deeper insight into the model system behaviour under periodic mode of operation, the kinetic model (equations (1) and (2); or (3) and (4)) was implemented in mathematical model of a CSTR (equations 9-12) operating at constant Glc and Glcac concentrations in time and with varying volumetric flow rate of the liquid feed stream according to the value of immediate reaction rate, $\dot{\xi}_w$.

$$\dot{V}_f^L = \frac{W^L \rho_c \nu_{Glc} \dot{\xi}_w}{c_{Glc,f} X_{Glc}} \tag{9}$$

$$\frac{dc_O}{dt} = \frac{\dot{V}_f^L (c_{O,f}^L - c_O^L)}{W^L} + k_L a (c_O^* - c_O^L) + \nu_O \rho_c \dot{\xi}_w \tag{10}$$

$$\frac{d\theta_{so}}{dt} = \rho_c W^L (\dot{\xi}_D - \dot{\xi}_A) \tag{11}$$

with initial conditions:

$$t = 0: \quad c_O^L = c_O^{L,0} \quad \theta_{so} = \theta_{so}^0 \quad \dot{V}_f^L = \dot{V}_f^{L,0} \tag{12}$$

where c_{Glc} and c_{Glcac} are constant, and the expressions for $\dot{\xi}_w$, $\dot{\xi}_D$ and $\dot{\xi}_A$ are defined in equations (1) or (3) and (2) or (4), respectively. Inlet and outlet liquid volumetric flow rates are assumed to be equal, i.e. the liquid density is independent on the conversion degree. Inlet and outlet concentrations of oxygen in the CSTR gas streams are assumed identical. Therefore the above CSTR mathematical model consists of liquid phase material balances only.

The value of $k_L a$ was set constant and far enough from a region where G-L external diffusion affects the overall reaction rate (see Gogová & Hanika (2009,a) for details).

Oxygen saturation concentration in the liquid phase, c_O^*, was calculated according to data of Eya, et al. (1994) on oxygen solubility in Glc aqueous solutions, by using the following regression equation:

$$c_O^* = p_{O_2} (1.162 \cdot 10^{-5} - 2.380 \cdot 10^{-8} (c_{Glc} + c_{Glcac})^{0.69}) \tag{13}$$

The kinetics model (equations (1) and (2) or alternatively (3) and (4)) embedded in model of CSTR enables to separate the effect of the reagents concentrations from the effect of the change in the catalyst activity itself on deviation of the reaction rate in time. The CSTR model makes it possible to express the catalyst activity directly through the ratio of the immediate to the initial reaction rate (i.e. by using equation (5)), and reveals directly the progress in the extent of the catalyst deactivation, see Figure 3. Figure 2 illustrates the effect of varying oxygen partial pressure in the gas feed stream on performance of the CSTR operated under O_2/N_2 periodic mode.

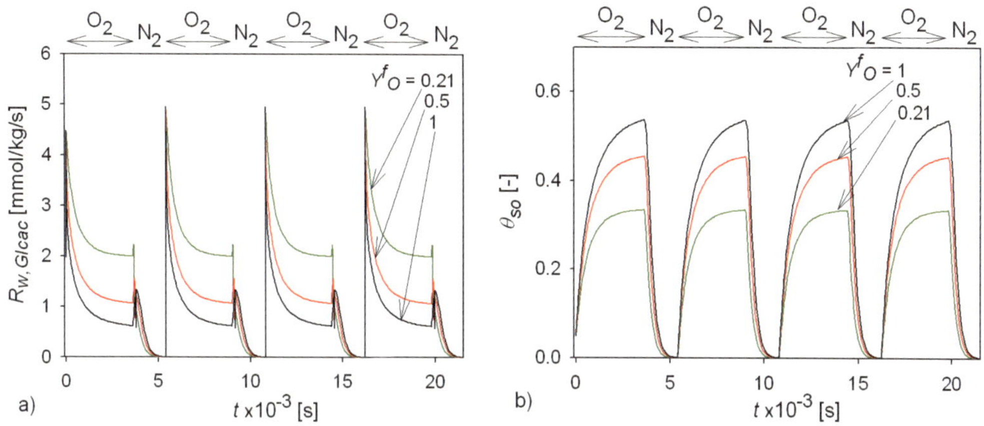

Fig. 2. Simulations of four reaction / reactivation cycles in CSTR operating in periodic O_2/N_2 mode for various oxygen molar fractions in the gas feed stream. Time course of a) immediate rate of Glcac formation, b) the catalyst fractional coverage by inactive oxygen species (reprinted from Gogová & Hanika (2009,b)). Conditions: t_R = 3600s; t_A = 1800s; ρ_c = 1kg/m³; W_R= 860 cm³; c_{Glc} = const.; X_{Glc} = 2%; $c_{Glc,f}$= 100 mol/m³; $c_{Glcac,f}$= 0.

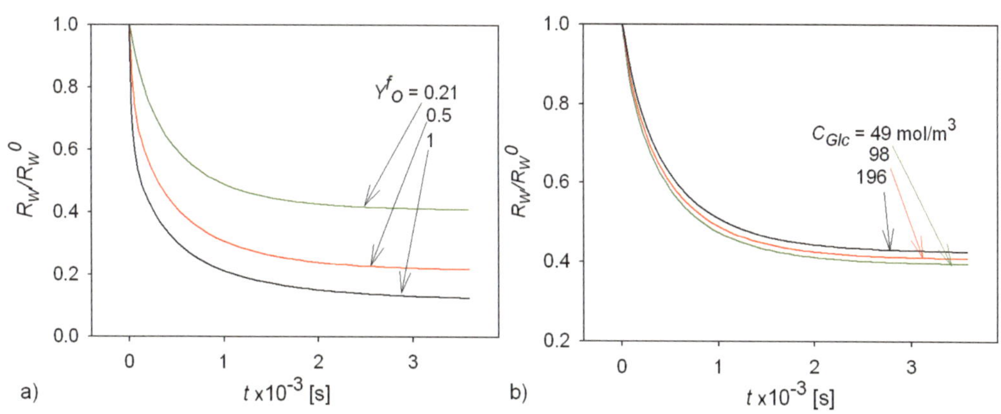

Fig. 3. Time course of the catalyst activity, expressed through ratio of the immediate to the initial rate of Glcac formation in CSTR as a function of a) oxygen molar fraction in the gas feed stream, b) Glc concentration in the reaction mixture (reprinted from Gogová & Hanika (2009,b)). The case „a)" corresponds to the conditions of the second reaction cycle of Fig. 2.

Figure 2a shows the rate of Glcac formation in time and Figure 2b reveals the progress in the catalyst fractional coverage by the inactive oxygen species, which stand behind the catalyst deactivation. It can be seen that in addition to the observed inhibition effect of oxygen on the Glc oxidation rate (Vleeming, et al. (1997), Gogová & Hanika (2009,a), (2009,b)), also the rate and the extent of the catalyst deactivation are influenced by oxygen concentration in the liquid phase. With its raise, both the θ_{so} steady-state value as well as the transient one increase (Figure 2b), and the catalyst's transient and steady-state activity decreases (Figure 3). Less important is the effect of Glc concentration in the reaction mixture on the catalyst deactivation extent (Gogová & Hanika (2009,b)).

2.1 Optimization of the CSTR under forced periodic operation

The CSTR operation was optimized in the conditions outlined above with equations (9) – (12), i.e. at constant Glc and Glcac concentrations in time and varying volumetric flow rate of the liquid feed stream according to the immediate reaction rate. The reactor is now operated under on-off periodic mode, i.e. with alternating cycles of switching on and off air feed stream. The catalyst reactivation in this case takes over in the oxygen-free intervals.
The period length is defined as a sum of reaction and reactivation times:

$$P = t_R + t_A \tag{14}$$

The split of period is the time the reaction takes in relation to the entire period length:

$$S = t_R / (t_R + t_A) \tag{15}$$

The reactor productivity is represented by cycle-time-averaged reaction rate, $\overline{\dot{\xi}}_w$, which is a reaction rate averaged over the entire period length:

$$\overline{\dot{\xi}}_w = \frac{1}{P}\int_{t_0}^{t_0+P} \dot{\xi}_w(t)dt \tag{16}$$

In case of CSTR, period length and the period split value represent independent variables. They both can be varied independently within one CSTR unit of a given (and constant) construction. Beneficial effect of the gas feed modulation on the CSTR performance is showed in Figure 4.
The catalyst activity can be maintained long-term steady by periodically alternating the reaction and activation periods of the catalyst operation. As can be seen in Figure 4, for any period length always a split value exists, where the maximal reaction rate is achieved. The CSTR optimization task was to find conditions that guarantee the highest reactor productivity at any period given. In other words, the optimal reaction-reactivation time-share had to be found within any given period length. The maximal CSTR productivity is only guaranteed in the split optimum, where no time is wasted in prolonged activation process, neither an insufficient activation time is provided. Figure 4 maps the CSTR performance for selected input conditions. By connecting the points of optimal split for every period length, trajectory of the maximal CSTR productivity is obtained. For illustration, the trajectory is highlighted in Figure 4.
In the direction of decreasing the values of *P* and *S* in Figure 4, the system approaches operation of such a hypothetical CSTR that runs without the periodic on-off mode, but with lower content of oxygen in gas feed stream (compared to oxygen content in the on-mode of the original system). In the opposite direction the system approaches operation of such CSTR that runs without reactivation of the catalyst and the cycle-time-averaged reaction rate

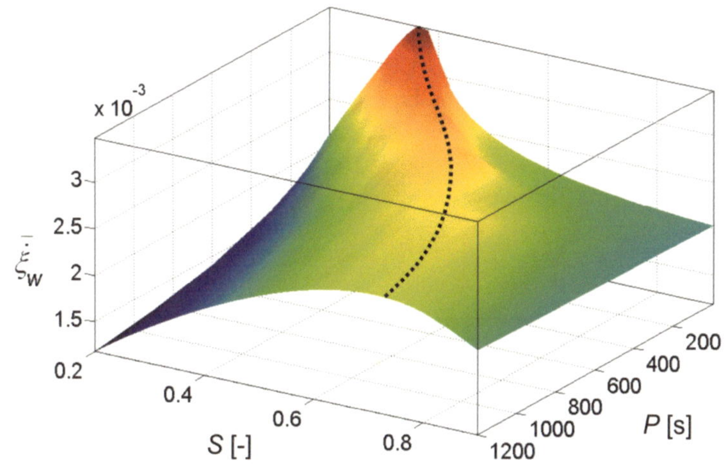

Fig. 4. Simulation of the model reaction run in CSTR operated under on-off periodic mode; cycle-time-averaged reaction rate as a function of period length and split value with trajectory of the CSTR maximal productivity (dots). (The model solution is only approximate in $P \rightarrow 0$, see the text below). (reprinted from Gogová & Hanika (2009,b)). Conditions: $\rho_c = 1 \mathrm{kg/m^3}$; $W_R = 860 \mathrm{cm^3}$; $Y_{O,f} = 0.21$; $c_{Glcac,f} = 0$; $X_{Glc} = 2\%$; $c_{Glc,f} = 100 \mathrm{mol/m^3}$.

approaches value of steady-state reaction rate of such system. It should be noted that the model solution in Figure 4 ought to be taken as an approximation in the region near P=0. A relation between the gas flow rate to the reactor and the gas holdup in it becomes important in this region. The model doesn't take it into account (see the model assumptions at the beginning of Section 2).

3. Multifunctional gas-lift reactor (GLR) employment

3.1 Characteristics of gas-lift reactors

What makes gas-lift reactors attractive for chemical and biotechnological applications is their relatively simple construction with possible segregation into various reaction zones, low and homogeneously distributed shear forces, good (and cheap) mixing with elimination of backmixing, and whole lots of possible design modifications.

Gas-lift reactor (GLR) consists of four main sections (see Figure 5): riser, gas-liquid separator, downcomer and bottom of the reactor. Operation of the GLR is relatively simple. It is based on spontaneous circulation of the reaction mixture along these four sections of the reactor as a result of difference in apparent density of the media present in riser and downcomer of the GLR. Successful application of these reactors to a specific (bio)chemical process is closely related with proper design of the reactor and on optimization of the mode of its operation.

However, in a GLR of a given construction (geometry), superficial gas velocity is the only independent variable that affects the entire hydrodynamics within the reactor - see the scheme in Figure 5, which documents the complexity of phenomena that occur in a GLR. Understanding of such hydrodynamic phenomena as gas hold-up, flow regimes or circulation velocity leads to more insight into the resulting mixing, heat and mass transfer.

Gas hold-up is the volumetric fraction of gas in the gas-liquid (G-L) or the gas-liquid-solid (G-L-S) dispersion. This phenomenon indicates a potential for mass transfer (higher gas hold-up = larger interfacial area) and the difference in gas hold-up between the riser and the downcomer is the driving force for liquid circulation. The **liquid velocity**, in turn, determines the residence times of the liquid in various zones of the reactor and controls important reactor parameters such as gas-liquid mass transfer, heat transfer, mixing and turbulence. For biochemical applications, oxygen mass transfer is one of the most important design parameters. Any shortage of oxygen significantly affects the process performance. Ideally, a reactor should have a maximum transfer rate, with efficient mixing, at minimum energy input.

When a GLR is employed for Glc production with living cultures, then quite contrary to the catalytic route, oxygen has to be present in riser, as well as in downcomer, to ensure living conditions all over the GLR circulation loop. But since the difference in the gas hold-up in riser and that in downcomer ($\varepsilon_{GR} - \varepsilon_{GD}$) represents the liquid circulation driving force, this requirement is only satisfied at the expense of decreased circulation velocity. Thus, an optimal ε_{GD} should be assured in the bioprocess by correctly designed separator of the reactor (Blažej, et al. (2004)).

The geometric design of GLR (scale of reactor, separator design, slightness of the reactor, ratio of cross-sectional areas of the downcomer and the riser etc.), the superficial gas velocity, pressure drop (friction) along the flow path and physical properties of the liquid phase have a strong influence on both the gas hold-up and the liquid velocity.

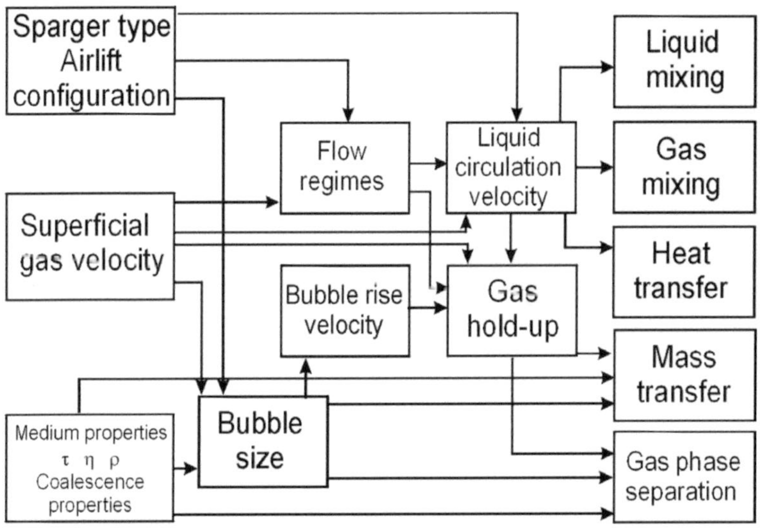

Fig. 5. Interrelated processes in a GLR (adopted from Blažej (2004)).

In a gas-lift (air-lift) reactor the hydrodynamics, transport and mixing properties, gas hold-up, interfacial areas and interphase mass transfer coefficients depend strongly on the prevailing flow regime. Following regimes occur in direction of increasing flow rate and can be deducted from both visual observation and gas hold-up:

Bubble flow (homogeneous flow regime): Small, spherical and equally sized gas bubbles that are distributed more or less uniformly over the column's cross section characterize this flow regime.

Churn turbulent (heterogeneous flow regime): Bubbles of widely varying size and shape can be observed as well as bubble coalescence and break-up.

Slug flow regime: With Newtonian media, this regime can be observed only at high superficial gas velocities and in airlift reactors with small riser diameter. Practical importance of slug regime is low. But if the liquid phase changes its physico-chemical properties during the process in such a way that the initially Newtonian behaviour changes into non-Newtonian (as a result of the biomass growth), then churn flow may transform into slug flow (see Godó, et al. (1999)).

3.2 Natural periodic operation of GLR

Gas-lift reactor (GLR) was selected as the reactor type suitable to carry out the model reaction in. GLR natural operation resembles the above mentioned forced periodic operation of the CSTR as follows: In GLR, the model reaction, as well as the catalyst reactivation proceeds within one multifunctional reactor unit. In principle, GLR operation is based on spontaneous circulation of the catalyst dispersion in liquid, which results from difference in apparent density of the reaction mixture present in riser and downcomer sections of the reactor. Therefore, if complete separation of the gas phase is ensured after the reaction media passes the riser where the main reaction (and the catalyst deactivation) takes part, the downcomer serves as reactivation zone of the reactor.

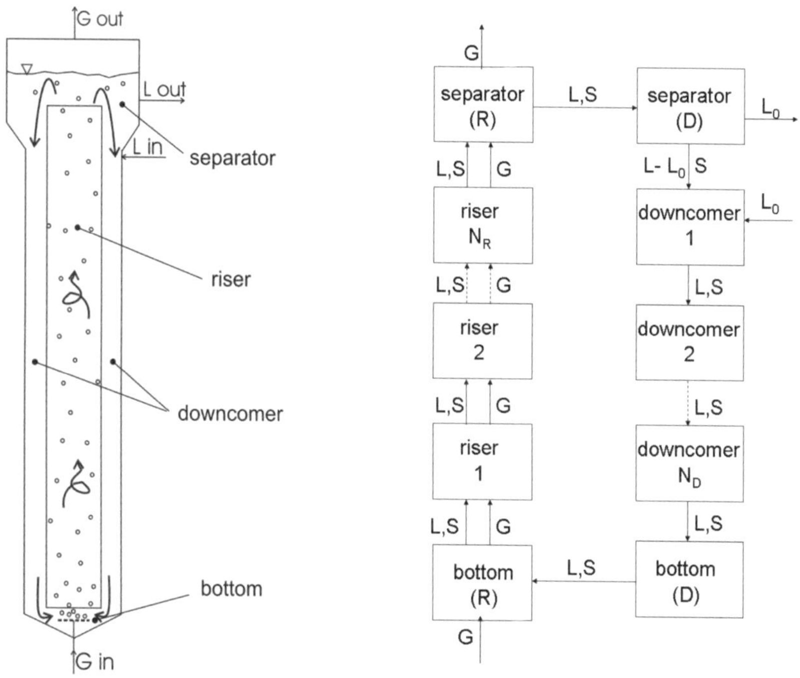

Fig. 6. Sketch of tanks-in-series model (right) linking hydrodynamics with kinetics that occur in the individual sections of continuously operating three-phase gas-lift reactor (left).

Kluytmans, et al. (2003) proposed application of GLR for reaction similar to the model one. To design the target three-phase GLR that would suit the reaction of Glc oxidation over the Pd/C catalyst, we constructed GLR mathematical model (see Gogová & Hanika (2009,c)) that is presented and applied in the following text. For any input operational conditions maximal productivity of the reactor is only guaranteed in the point of the target GLR optimal geometry. The GLR model proposed employs tanks-in-series mixing model sketched in Figure 6 to combine hydrodynamics of a real GLR (Bello, et al. (1984), Blažej, et al. (2004), Blažej, et al. (2004), Juraščík, et al. (2006), Sikula, et al. (2007), Sikula (2008), Sikula & Markoš (2008)) and the kinetics of the model reaction from Section 1.1. This GLR model is much simpler and a bit more realistic than that of Kluytmans, et al. (2003) who employed axial dispersion mixing model with hydrodynamics measured in small-scale 2D bubble-column reactor and considered intra-particle diffusion.

3.3 Modelling and optimization of the GLR productivity

Optimization of GLR productivity is attempted in the following couple of sections. In the case of GLR it is impossible to move along a trajectory of maximal productivity as was the case with the CSTR of Section 2.1, without reconstruction of the GLR itself, as both, the period length and the split value, are bound with geometry of the GLR given. Since both, the reaction and the reactivation times in GLR are set by the reaction mixture residence times in riser and downcomer of the GLR, respectively, only one geometrical optimum exists for given set of input conditions. The maximal GLR productivity is guaranteed only in this geometrical optimum. The optimization task in this case therefore is to find these geometrical optima for any set of input conditions.

GLR mathematical model was derived and applied to aid the target reactor design. The GLR model consists of two main parts (Figure 7). In the first one (hydrodynamics cycle), hydrodynamics and optimal geometry of the reactor is iteratively calculated. The second part (reactor performance cycle) uses the results of the first part, links them up with the model reaction kinetics and iteratively calculates the actual GLR steady-state performance.

Tanks-in-series model (as sketched in Figure 6) is employed in the second part of the GLR mathematical model to grasp the way of mixing in real GLR. Every tank of the tanks-in-series model is described by a set of nonlinear algebraic equations (NAE) linking hydrodynamics and kinetics that apply in the given section of GLR. Tanks-in-series and axial dispersion models are the most frequently used mixing models for GLRs. Both were applied recently for simulation of the biotechnological equivalent of the model reaction run in GLR (Znad, et al. (2004), Sikula, et al. (2006), (2007), Sikula & Markoš (2008)).

The following set of assumptions applies with the derived GLR mathematical model:

1. The GLR operates in steady state in the region of homogeneous bubbly flow.
2. The downcomer gas hold-up is zero; this is achievable by correct design of separator (Gogová, et al. (2002)).
3. The number of tanks that form riser and downcomer corresponds to the extent of axial dispersion in these sections. Plus, there are two tanks for each – the bottom and the separator. In the latter two tandems, the sizes of the individual twin tanks vary depending on the respective volumes taken up by either liquid (then they become a functional part of downcomer) or G-L dispersion (and then act as a part of riser).
4. Each of the tanks in series operates isothermally and is perfectly mixed.
5. The mathematical model combines description of the GLR hydrodynamics with the kinetics of the glucose oxidation reaction and the catalyst deactivation and reactivation.
6. The reactor operates at low Glc conversion, up to 10%. Then, according to Kunz & Recker (1995) assumption of 100% selectivity towards Glcac can be taken.

7. The Pd/C catalyst particles (45 μm) are assumed to be homogeneously dispersed in liquid phase. Then it is justifiable, for the mathematical description purpose, to accept a concept of pseudo-homogeneous reaction phase. However, apart from the liquid phase, the catalyst does not leave the reactor.
8. Constant liquid volumetric flow rate within the reactor sections is assumed, i.e. the liquid density is constant - independent on the conversion degree.

3.3.1 Algorithm for the GLR mathematical model solution

The GLR model is used to firstly aid the target GLR design for any given input conditions, and secondly, to predict steady state characteristics of the target reactor. The simulations presented were run by using commercial software Matlab.

Algorithm of the GLR mathematical model is sketched in Figure 7. The GLR model input adjustable parameters are: degree of Glc conversion, all the feed (and start-up) concentrations, the catalyst concentration, kinetics parameters, temperature (fixed, 30°C), atmospheric pressure (fixed), superficial gas velocity, number of tanks and basic geometrical parameters. The basic geometrical parameters (the reactor type - internal-loop gas-lift reactor (ILGLR), the GLR volume, its separator volume, its bottom height, the liquid height, the outer column diameter and the riser wall thickness) were adopted from experimental GLR, volume 40L (see Blažej, et al. (2004), Blažej, et al. (2004), Juraščík, et al. (2006), Sikula, et al. (2007), Sikula (2008), Sikula & Markoš (2008)). This particular reactor has been a source of many hydrodynamic correlations employed in the GLR model. Non-adjustable parameters have complex dependencies on the input adjustable ones. The procedure pictured in Figure 7 is applied to calculate them. See Gogová & Hanika (2009,c) for more details on the GLR mathematical model.

The one-tank model is an integral part of the GLR mathematical model (see Figure 7). It uses concept of one CSTR, which for the period of t_R operates as reactor (and the gas phase is being introduced to it) and for duration of t_A works as activator (with no gas introduced). In both of these cases, the liquid phase is being continuously introduced and discharged at a constant, cycle-time-averaged volumetric flow rate. (In this parameter the CSTR of the one-tank model differs from the CSTR optimized in Section 2).

The one-tank model serves to estimate a first approximation of the optimal split value (defined in Eq.(15)) for the target gas-lift reactor. At the optimal split, the target GLR productivity reaches its maximum (given by the cycle-time-averaged reaction rate). The S_{opt} value found by the one-tank model is only optimal for CSTR of the one-tank model (i.e. for conditions of ideal mixing), and therefore it is necessary to correct it for conditions given by hydrodynamics of the target reactor. The split correction takes the following aspects into account. In the GLR model, mixing in the target GLR was described by dividing riser into 7 + 2 tanks (one tank of bottom(R) and one tank of separator(R)) and downcomer into at least 7 + 2 tanks (one tank of bottom(D) and one tank of separator(D)). These values are based on experimentally determined local and overall Peclet numbers (Sikula (2008), Sikula & Markoš (2008)). Depending on the actual GLR geometry and hydrodynamics, the portion separator contributes to either riser or downcomer varies. One-tank model doesn't count with this variation, which therefore has to be included in the split correction, too. Different mixing in CSTR and GLR is closely related with different distribution of the reaction mixture components between reactor and activator modes of the one-tank model and that of tanks-in-series model. The split value is therefore corrected for formation of concentration profiles along the GLR, as well.

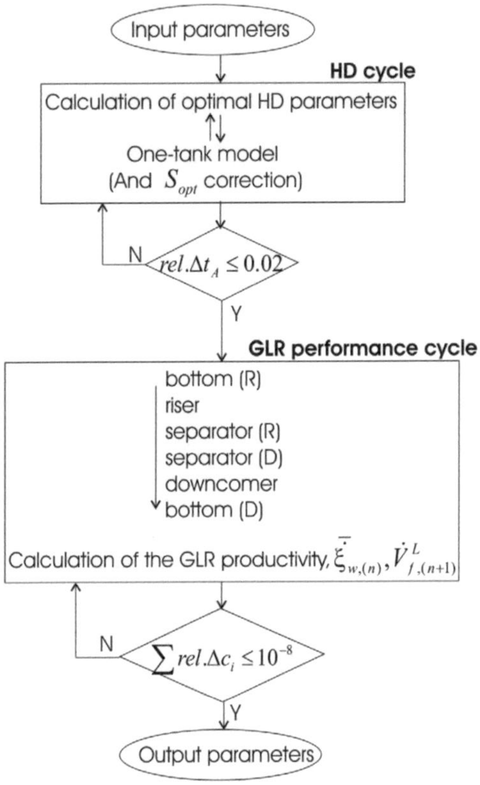

Fig. 7. Algorithm of GLR model for calculation of design and performance of the target GLR suited for the model reaction accompanied with the catalyst reversible deactivation. (reprinted from Gogová & Hanika (2009,c))

3.4 Optimal design of the target GLR

To optimize GLR productivity, optimal residence times in the riser and downcomer sections have to be found. Optimal value of split, S_{opt}, guarantees the GLR maximal productivity (represented by cycle-time-averaged reaction rate). By shifting the split value, the reaction-reactivation time-share changes, and so does the geometry parameter (downcomer-to-riser cross sectional area ratio, A_D/A_R) of the target GLR. This dependency is demonstrated in Table 3. The GLR productivity reaches maximum in conditions of its optimal geometry. It is the case "b" in Tab. 3 with the optimal split value. Increase in the S_{opt} of 20% triggers shift of A_D / A_R in such a way, that the reaction gets favoured at the expense of the catalyst activation. The cycle-time-averaged catalyst fractional coverage by inactive oxygen, $\bar{\theta}_{so}$, then settles on higher values (see Tab. 3, case c). Change in $\bar{\theta}_{so}$ indicates change in the catalyst activity. The higher the $\bar{\theta}_{so}$ is, the more the catalyst's activity drops (see Section 1.1). If the opposite trend is attempted, i.e. if the optimal split is 20% reduced, the activation gets favoured. But even though the catalyst is more active for the reaction (see the lower value of the cycle-time-averaged catalyst fractional coverage by inactive oxygen in Tab. 3, case a), the reaction time portion is not long enough to cover the overall time loss spent by the catalyst activation and the reactor productivity drops down again.

Case	$\bar{\dot{\xi}}_w$ [mol/kg/s]	$\bar{\theta}_{so}$ [-]	A_D/A_R [-]	D_R [m]	$D_{D,Eqv.}$ [m]
a) $0.8 \times S_{opt}$	0.00286	0.0658	1.6989	0.0909	0.1184
b) S_{opt}	0.00349	0.1332	0.8588	0.1084	0.1005
c) $1.2 \times S_{opt}$	0.00287	0.2380	0.4065	0.1236	0.0788

Table 3. Effect of deflection from the optimal split value. (reprinted from Gogová & Hanika (2009,c)). Simulation conditions: ILGLR; $N_R = N_D = 7$; $N_{Sep} = N_B = 2$; $U_{GR} = 0.04$ m/s; $P_W = 80$ %; $c_{f,Glc} = 100$ mol/m^3; $c_{f,Glcac} = 0$ mol/m^3; $Y_{f,O} = 0.21$; $X_{Glc} = 0.02$

Figure 8 shows effect of superficial gas velocity U_{GR} and molar fraction of oxygen in the gas feed stream $Y_{O,f}$ on the location of the GLR optimal geometry (plot a), which is where the maximum reactor productivity is achieved (plot b). Similar effect is showed in Figure 9 for various Glc liquid feed stream concentrations.

It can be seen in Fig. 8, that a change in $Y_{O,f}$ is compensated to large extent by change in A_D/A_R and the reaction rate responds only slightly to it. In the case of increasing Glc concentration (Fig. 9), the GLR productivity increases significantly (in the point of the GLR optimal geometry). As the Glc concentration rises up, the rate of the catalyst reactivation increases as a result of quicker consumption of oxygen. As a consequence, the downcomer zone of GLR, required for the catalyst reactivation, shrinks, too.

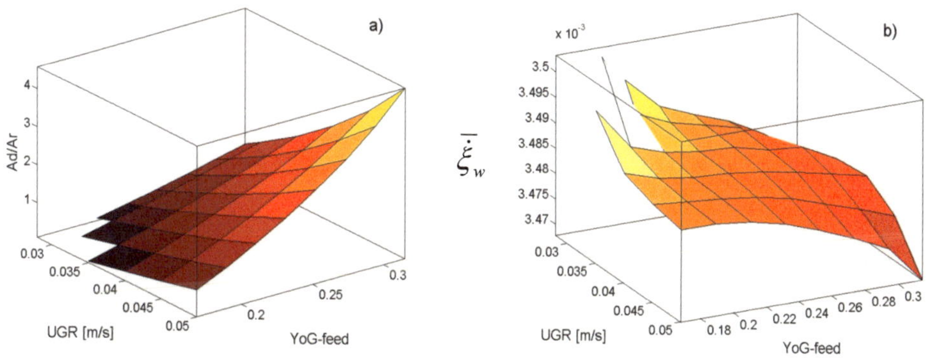

Fig. 8. Influence of oxygen concentration in the gas feed ($Y_{OG\text{-}feed}$) stream at various U_{GR} levels on a) location of the target GLR optimum geometry; b) cycle-time-averaged reaction rate in the point of optimal geometry. (reprinted from Gogová & Hanika (2009,c)). Conditions: $c_{Glc,f} = 100$mol/m^3; $c_{Glcac,f} = 0$; $X_{Glc} = 2$%; $N_R = N_D = 7$; $N_{Sep} = N_B = 2$; $P_W = 80$%.

It was found during the model reaction kinetics study that the reaction rate is inhibited by oxygen. Moreover, oxygen affects the extent of the catalyst deactivation. The variation range of oxygen content in gas feed stream is therefore limited. Figure 8 covers major part of the target GLR operational window in terms of U_{GR} and $Y_{O,f}$. In the region of low $Y_{O,f}$ and U_{GR} (Figure 8) or high $c_{Glc,f}$ and low U_{GR} (Figure 9) the catalyst reactivation is sufficient enough and the downcomer reaches only a couple of cm in diameter there. It gives raise the impression that even bubble column reactors (BC) can be used to carry out the reaction under these conditions. The impact of backmixing (characteristic for BCs) on the catalyst behaviour may, however, be detrimental. Another limitation in terms of the GLR operational window arises at high U_{GR}, where the riser diameter may become critically small. Here, the flow regime is more likely to change from homogeneous bubbly flow to slug flow (see a flow map in e.g. Shah, et al. (1982)).

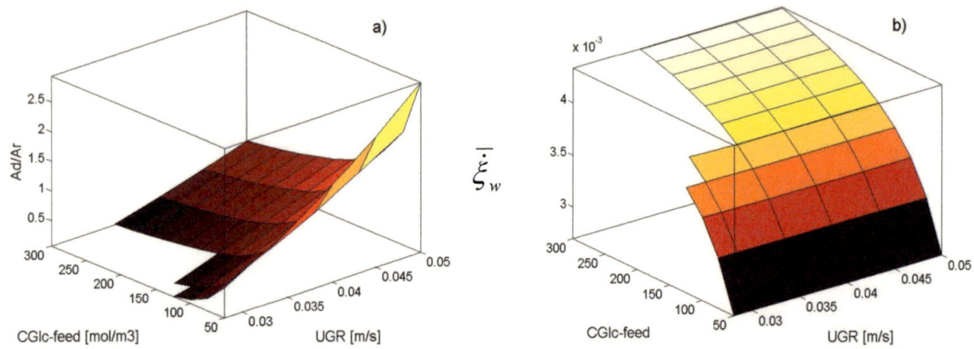

Fig. 9. Effect of glucose concentration in the liquid feed stream at various U_{GR} levels on a) location of the target GLR optimum geometry; b) cycle-time-averaged reaction rate in the point of optimal geometry. (reprinted from Gogová & Hanika (2009,c)). Conditions: $Y_{O,f}$ = 0.21; $c_{Glcac,f}$ = 0; X_{Glc} = 2%; N_R=N_D= 7; N_{Sep}=N_B= 2; P_W= 80%.

For the input operational parameters given by the points on the U_{GR} - $c_{i,f}$ and U_{GR} - $Y_{O,f}$ coordinates in Figures 8a and 9a, respectively, the 3D-plane of solutions represents the optimum geometry with the only possible reaction-reactivation time-share to achieve the highest possible cycle-time-averaged reaction rate in the target GLR. Every geometrical solution either above or below the optimum plane would lead to either too long or too short reactivation time, respectively. Any of these two deviations results in depression in cycle-time-averaged reaction rate compared to that achieved in GLR of optimal geometry.
As proved above, depending on the input conditions the optimum reaction-reactivation time-share varies and so does the optimum in the target GLR geometry, which is also reflected in the profiles of the reaction rate and the concentrations along the GLR. In Figure 10, calculated profiles of the actual concentrations and reaction rates along the circulation loop are presented for selected set of input parameters. Each symbol in Figure 10 represents one tank of the tanks-in-series within the loop (their abbreviations are for illustration marked at the top of the Figures 10a, b). The space time in Figure 10 is defined as follows:

$$\tau_{\Sigma k} = \frac{\sum_{j=1}^{k} W_j^L}{\dot{V}^L}; \qquad k = 1,2,\ldots,N_{tot} \tag{10}$$

The target GLR operates continuously. In the profiles, inlet and outlet points in the reactor are visible (compare with Figure 6). For the input conditions listed with Figure 10, the calculated reactor productivity (cycle-time-averaged reaction rate) is 3.49 mmol Glcac per 1 kg of the catalyst per second.
In Figures 11 and 12 calculated profiles of reaction rates and molar fraction of oxygen in the gas phase are shown along the GLR circulation loop. The arrows indicate the trends as the $Y_{O,f}$. (Figure 11) and $c_{Glc,f}$ (Figure 12) rise. Optimal geometry of the target reactor varies for varying input conditions (as shown in Figures 8 and 9), and thus the hydrodynamics and the residence times vary, too. Therefore, comparison of the profiles calculated for various input conditions is facilitated through normalized space times along the circulation loop.

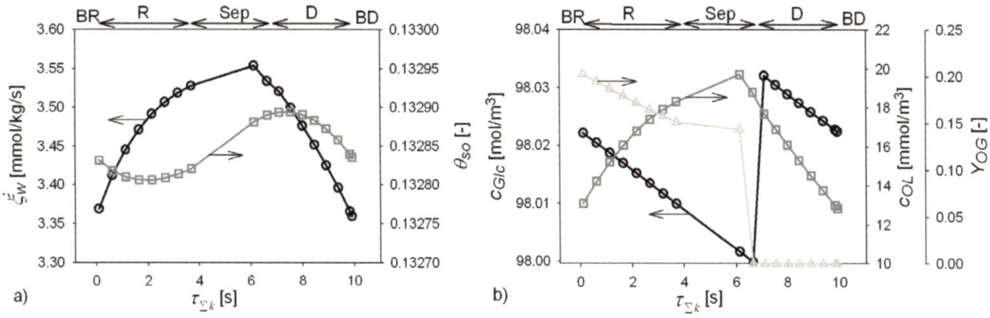

Fig. 10. Profiles of a) the actual reaction rates (circles) and the catalyst fractional coverage by inactive oxygen (squares); b) Glc (circles) and dissolved oxygen concentrations (squares) and molar fraction of oxygen in the gas phase (triangles); along the GLR circulation loop (reprinted from Gogová & Hanika (2009,c)). Conditions: $c_{Glcac,f}$ = 0; $c_{Glc,f}$ = 100mol/m^3; $Y_{O,f}$. = 0.21; X_{Glc} = 2%; U_{GR} = 0.04 m/s; N_R=N_D= 7; N_{Sep}=N_B= 2; P_W = 80%.

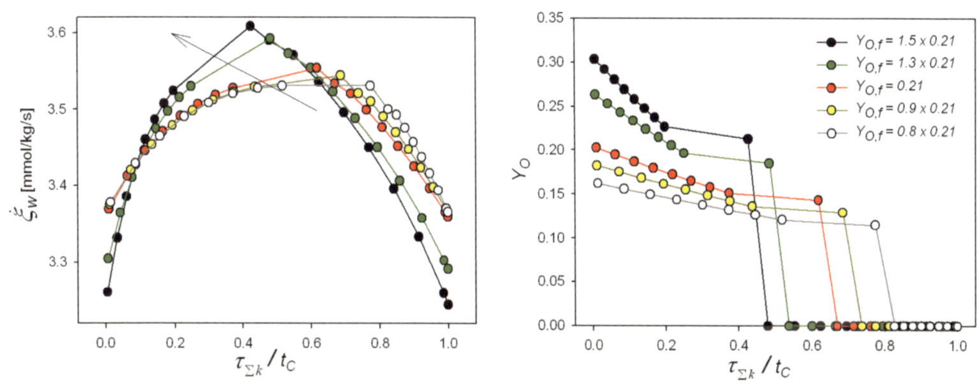

Fig. 11. Profiles of a) the immediate reaction rates, and b) oxygen molar fraction in the gas phase along the GLR circulation loop for various $Y_{O,f}$. (reprinted from Gogová & Hanika (2009,c)). Simulation conditions: $c_{Glcac,f}$ = 0; $c_{Glc,f}$ = 100mol/m^3; X_{Glc} = 2%; U_{GR} = 0.04 m/s; N_R=N_D= 7; N_{Sep}=N_B= 2; P_W = 80%.

Similarly to Figure 10, the maximum immediate reaction rate is achieved in separator(D) tank for every $Y_{O,f}$. (Figure 11) or $c_{Glc,f}$ (Figure 12). As the arrow in Figure 11a indicates, this value even increases with increase in $Y_{O,f}$., and shifts towards lower space times. At the same time, as the maximum immediate reaction rate in separator(D) tank rises with $Y_{O,f}$., the minimum reaction rate in the bottom tanks depresses. Therefore, quite contrary to the trend of immediate rate in the separator(D) tank, the cycle-time-averaged reaction rate decreases slightly as demonstrated in Figure 8b. The above mentioned shift towards lower space times on increasing $Y_{O,f}$. is given by shift in the optimal geometry of the target GLR towards higher A_D /A_R values (see Figure 8a and the rationale to it). The trends in Figure 11a are reflected by the profiles in Figure 11b - rising the $Y_{O,f}$. causes more prompt consumption of oxygen in riser (which corresponds with the steep increase in immediate reaction rate profile along riser - Figure 11a), but duration of this period decreases gradually.

Simulation results in Figure 12 show profiles of the immediate reaction rates and molar fraction of oxygen in the gas phase for various $c_{Glc,f}$. As the arrows indicate, increase in $c_{Glc,f}$ shifts the reaction rate towards higher values and at the same time, it shifts the residence times in downcomer tanks towards lower values (Figure 12a). Analogous trend is observable in the Y_O profiles (Figure 12b). This is in agreement with Figure 9 and the rationale given to it in the text above.

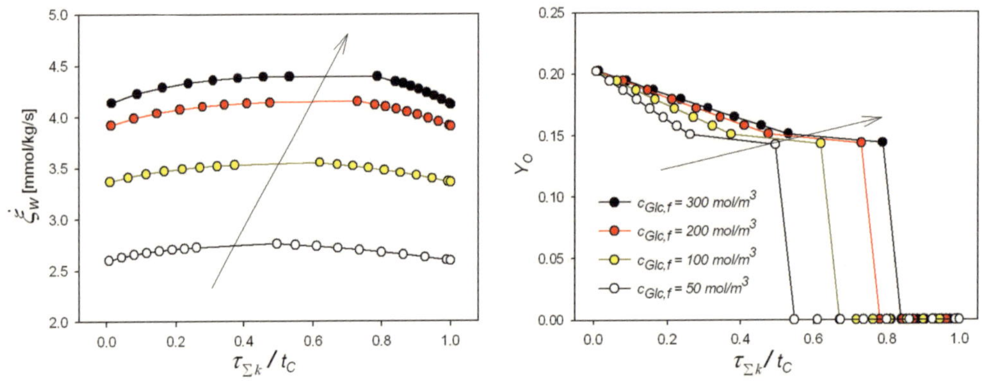

Fig. 12. Profiles of a) the immediate reaction rates, and b) oxygen molar fraction in the gas phase along the GLR circulation loop for various $c_{Glc,f}$ (reprinted from Gogová & Hanika (2009,c)). Simulation conditions: $c_{Glcac,f}$= 0; $Y_{O,f}$. = 0.21; X_{Glc} = 2%; U_{GR} = 0.04 m/s; N_R=N_D= 7; N_{Sep}=N_B= 2; P_W= 80%.

3.5 Practical aspects

The derived GLR mathematical model was used for computer aided design and optimization of a target multifunctional gas-lift reactor with the aim to solve the main problem of the model reaction - the catalyst unstable activity. Examples of such processes are e.g. wet air oxidation of waste waters or syntheses of chemical specialties. Glucose oxidation (in alkaline aqueous solution) with oxygen in the presence of a palladium catalyst was used as the case study. Application of GLR to this reaction system enabled simultaneous reaction in riser and the catalyst reactivation in downcomer section of the reactor.

The GLR model assumptions lean on the kinetics of the reaction and the catalyst deactivation. All the simulations assume homogeneous bubbly flow of the reaction mixture in riser, zero gas hold-up in downcomer and predict the system steady state operation. The isothermal tanks-in-series mixing model describes axial dispersion of the reaction mixture in the oxidation and the catalyst reactivation sections of the reactor. Hydrodynamic parameters of the GLR model were taken from pilot plant data (Blažej, et al. (2004), Blažej, et al. (2004), Juraščík, et al. (2006), Sikula, et al. (2007), Sikula (2008), Sikula & Markoš (2008)).

The GLR mathematical model proposed helps to overcome the problem with the catalyst unstable activity by appropriate calculation of the target GLR geometry for any given input operational conditions. Moreover, the model is capable of predicting optimal geometry of the target GLR, its maximal productivity and other steady state characteristics for reactions similar to the model one, i.e. for G-L-S oxidations with reversible deactivation of a catalyst due to an action of any substance present in the gas phase. The limitations are only given by meeting the ranges of GLR operational window as explained with Figures 8 and 9.

The GLR model derived is not limited to the model reaction only. It can easily be extended for other G-L-S oxidations with reversible deactivation of a catalyst due to an action of a substance present in the gas phase. The limitation here is given by at least partly overlapping the ranges of a GLR applicability (see the reasoning given with Figures 8 and 9 about the ranges of the model reaction operational window) with the new reaction requirements (set by the new reaction kinetics).

The proposed GLR model can also be extended to non-isothermal process conditions. In future, the area of the GLR model employment may be broadened for process scale-up and the reactor safe control. But, the experimental validation of the model solutions remains a challenge for the future research.

For the biotechnological routes of Glcac production, GLRs are also of interest due to several advantages that they offer over alternative bioreactors. However, a GLR design for the biotechnological applications is based on different policy, compared to the catalytic application. In the catalytic process the condition of zero gas hold-up in downcomer was directive for the reactor design. On the contrary, in the biotechnological application this condition is no longer relevant as the living conditions for the cell cultures involved have to be ensured all over the GLR circulation loop, i.e. oxygen has to be present in downcomer. Therefore, GLR correctly designed for a bioprocess should provide sufficient G-L mass transfer, and it should operate at an optimal gas hold-up in downcomer.

4. Conclusion

The model reaction chosen appears to be interesting, not only due to its versatility for the industrial applications, but also because it raises many chemico-engineering problems to be solved in unconventional ways. The main problem of the model reaction is fast but fully reversible deactivation of Pd catalyst due to an action of oxygen during the reaction course. Various approaches can be taken to get over the problem. In the work described in this chapter, the problem is tackled through a tailored selection, design and optimization of the catalytic reactor. For reasons explained below, gas-lift reactor (GLR) was selected as the target reactor suitable to carry out the model reaction in. It allows the reaction along with the catalyst reactivation proceed within one reactor unit. Such reactors are in their nature multifunctional.

Deeper insight into the catalyst deactivation is made by analyzing the model reaction behaviour under conditions of a continuous stirred tank reactor (CSTR) operation. Optimization of the CSTR productivity through the gas feed stream composition / flow modulation was attempted. Dynamic mathematical model of CSTR operating under on-off periodic mode was used to aid this task. In the periodic operation, enhancement of the overall reaction rate results from forcing the catalyst to operate under transient conditions. In CSTR, period length, as well as the period split value represent independent variables and can be varied independently within one CSTR unit of a given (and constant) construction. For any period length always a split value exists, where maximum reaction rate is achieved (see Figure 4). The optimization task was to find conditions that guarantee the highest reactor productivity at any period given. In other words, the optimal reaction-reactivation time-share had to be found within a given period length, where the maximum CSTR productivity is guaranteed, because in the period split optimum no time is wasted in prolonged activation process, neither insufficient activation time is provided. Figure 4 maps the CSTR performance for selected input conditions. Benefits of running the model reaction

under conditions of periodic exposure to oxidative and reductive environment were explored and a trajectory of maximal CSTR productivity was defined. A real production plant operational requirements and limitations decide about the position on this trajectory.
GLR (gas-lift reactor) natural operation resembles the above mentioned forced periodic operation of the CSTR as follows: In GLR, the main reaction, as well as the catalyst reactivation proceeds within one multifunctional reactor unit. In principle, GLR operation is based on spontaneous circulation of the catalyst dispersion in liquid, which results from difference in apparent density of the reaction mixture present in riser and downcomer sections of the reactor. Therefore, if complete separation of the gas phase is ensured after the reaction media passes the riser where the main reaction (and the catalyst deactivation) takes part, the downcomer serves as reactivation zone of the reactor. If economic aspects were considered, GLR natural periodic operation would be cheaper than the forced periodic operation of CSTR.
In GLR it is impossible to move along a similar trajectory of the highest reactor productivity (as was the case with CSTR) without reconstruction of the GLR itself. The period value is given by liquid circulation velocity, i.e. the time one circulation loop takes; and the split value is set by the given GLR geometry. Only one geometrical optimum exists for given set of input operational conditions. The maximal GLR productivity is only guaranteed in this geometrical optimum, because the residence time in riser (reaction time) and the residence time in downcomer (activation time) are only here shared optimally. The optimization task for this GLR case was to find the optimal geometry for any set of input conditions. The derived GLR mathematical model was used to aid design of target reactor for reaction of heterogeneously catalyzed glucose oxidation. The model helps to overcome the problem of the catalyst's fast reversible deactivation by appropriate calculation of the target GLR.
In this chapter presented theoretical analysis of the target reactor optimal design procedure also offers several extensions to the future research. It should firstly focus on experimental validation of the presented GLR mathematical model and after that on the model extension for non-isothermal reactions. This would make the GLR model a useful tool for a process scale-up and its safety control.
Another direction of subsequent research efforts might be a critical comparison of chemical and biotechnological oxidation routes for syntheses of chemical specialties. An objective confrontation would be valuable from the viewpoint of technical arrangement of the processes as well as from the viewpoint of the two processes economics.

5. Nomenclature

A	cross-sectional area (m^2)
a	relative activity of the catalyst (-)
c	concentration (mol m^{-3})
D	diameter (m)
D_p	catalyst particle diameter (m)
K	adsorption coefficients (see Table 1 for details and dimensions)
k	rate constants (see Table 1 for details and dimensions)
$k_L a$	volumetric mass transfer coefficient (s^{-1})

N	number of tanks (-)
P	period $P=t_R+t_A$ (s)
P_W	portion of separator volume that functionally contributes to riser (%)
p	pressure (Pa)
R_w	specific rate of formation / consumption (mol kg^{-1} s^{-1})
S	split $S=t_R/(t_R+t_A)$ (-)
T	temperature (K)
t	time (s)
t_C	cycle time (s)
U	superficial velocity (m s^{-1})
$\dot{V}$	volumetric flow rate (m^3 s^{-1})
W	volume (m^3)
X	conversion (%)
Y	molar fraction (-)

Greek symbols

α	active fraction (-)
ε	gas hold-up (-)
ν	stoichiometric coefficient (-)
θ_{so}	catalyst fractional coverage by inactive oxygen species (-)
ρ_c	catalyst concentration (kg m^3)
τ	space time (s)
$\dot{\xi}_{A(D)}$	specific activation (deactivation) rate (kg^{-1} s^{-1})
$\dot{\xi}_w$	specific reaction rate (mol kg^{-1} s^{-1})
ω	stirring frequency (min^{-1})

Subscript/superscript

0	initial, at t=0s
–	average; vector (with concentration)
*	saturated
A	activation; activator
B	bottom
D	downcomer; deactivation
Eqv	equivalent (with downcomer diameter)
f	feed
G	gas phase
Glc	glucose
$Glcac$	gluconic acid

i	i-th species
k	k-th tank
L	liquid phase
O	oxygen
opt	optimal
R	riser; reaction; reactor
Sep	separator
tot	total
w	related to the weight of the catalyst used
Σk	sum from bottom(R) tank to the k-th tank (with space time)

Abbreviations

B	bottom
CSTR	continuous stirred tank reactor
D	downcomer
G	gas phase
Glc	glucose
Glcac	gluconic acid
GLR	gas-lift reactor
HD	hydrodynamics
ILGLR	internal-loop gas-lift reactor
L	liquid phase
R	riser
S	solid phase
Sep	separator
SSTR	semi-continuous stirred tant reactor

6. References

Bello, R.A., Robinson, C.W. & Moo-Young, M. (1984). Liquid circulation and mixing characteristics of airlift contactors. *The Canadian Journal of Chem. Engng.* 62, 573-577.

Biella, S., Prati, L. & Rossi, M. (2002). Selective oxidation of D-glucose on gold catalyst. *J. Catal.* 206, 242-247; doi:10.1006/jcat.2001.3497.

Bisio, A. & Kabel, R.L. (1985). *Scaleup of chemical processes; Conversion from laboratory scale tests to successful commercial size design*. John Wiley & Sons.

Blažej, M. (2004). *Study of hydrodynamics and oxygen mass transfer in an airlift reactor, PhD Thesis,* Department of Chem. and Biochem. Engng., Slovak University of Technology in Bratislava.

Blažej, M., Juraščík, M., Annus, J. & Markoš, J. (2004). Measurent of mass transfer coefficient in an airlift reactor with internal loop using coalescent and non-coalescent liquid media. *J Chem Technol Biotechnol.* 79, 1405-1411; doi: 10.1002/jctb.1144.

Blažej, M., Kiša, M. & Markoš, J. (2004). Scale influence on the hydrodynamics of an internal loop airlift reactor. *Chem. Eng. and Processing* 43, 1519-1527; doi: 10.1016/j.cep.2004.02.003.

Boelhouwer, J.G., Piepers, H.W. & Drinkenburg, A.A.H. (2002). Advantages of forced non-steady operated trickle-bed reactors. *Chem. Eng. Technol.* 25, 647-650.

Butt, J.B. & Petersen, E.E. (1988). *Activation, deactivation and poisoning of catalysts.* Academic Press, Inc.

Comotti, M., Della Pina, C., Falletta, E. & Rossi, M. (2006). Aerobic oxidation of glucose with gold catalyst: Hydrogen peroxide as intermediate and reagent. *Adv. Synth. Catal.* 348(3), 313-316.

Eya, H., Mishima, K., Nagatani, M., Iwai, Y. & Arai, Y. (1994). Measurements and correlation of solubilities of oxygen in aqueous solutions containing glucose, sucrose and maltose. *Fluid Phase Equilibria* 94, 201-209.

Godó, Š., Klein, J., Polakovič, M. & Báleš, V. (1999). Periodical changes of input air flowrate - a possible way of improvement of oxygen transfer and liquid circulation in airlift bioreactors. *Chem. Eng. Sci.* 54, 4937-4943.

Gogová, Z., Čamaj, V., Hronec, M. & Stanček, F. (2002). *Device for conditions of chemical technologies and its application*, Patent No.: WO2004047980, EP1569747 (SK appl. No.: 1676/2002)

Gogová, Z. & Hanika, J. (2009,a). Reactivation of a palladium catalyst during glucose oxidation by molecular oxygen. *Chem. Pap.* 63(5), 520-526; doi: 10.2478/s11696-009-0053-3.

Gogová, Z. & Hanika, J. (2009,b). Dynamic modelling of glucose oxidation with palladium catalyst deactivation in multifunctional CSTR; Benefits of periodic operation. *Chem. Eng. J.* 150(1), 223-230; doi: 10.1016/j.cej.2009.02.020.

Gogová, Z. & Hanika, J. (2009,c). Model aided design of three-phase gas-lift reactor for oxidation accompanied with catalyst reversible deactivation. Chem. Eng. Technol. 32(12), 1929-1940; doi: 10.1002/ceat.200900191.

Juraščík, M., Blažej, M., Annus, J. & Markoš, J. (2006). Experimental measurements of the volumetric mass transfer coefficient by the dynamic pressure-step method in an internal loop airlift reactors of different scale. *Chem. Eng. J.* 125, 81-87; doi: 10.1016/j.cej.2006.08.013.

Ketteler, G., Ogletree, D.F., Bluhm, H., Liu, H., Hebenstreit, E.L.D. & Salmeron, M. (2005). In Situ Spectroscopic Study of the Oxidation and Reduction of Pd(111). *J.Am.Chem.Soc.* 127, 18269-18273; doi:10.1021/ja055754y.

Kluytmans, J.H.J., van Wachem, B.G.M., Kuster, B.F.M. & Schouten, J.C. (2003). Design of an Industrial-Size Airlift Loop Redox Cycle (ALRC) Reactor for Catalytic Alcohol Oxidation and Catalyst Reactivation. *Ind. Eng. Chem. Res.* 42, 4174-4185; doi: 10.1021/ie020916+.

Kunz, M. & Recker, C. (1995). A new continuous oxidation process for carbohydrates. *Carbohydrates in Europe* 13, 11-15.

Liu, G., Zhang, X., Wang, L., Zhang, S. & Mi, Z. (2008). Unsteady-state operation of trickle-bed reactor for dicyclopentadiene hydrogenation. *Chem. Eng. Sci.* 63, 4991-5002.

Lundgren, E., Kresse, G., Klein, C., Borg, M., Andersen, J.N., De Santis, M., Gauthier, Y., Konvicka, C., Schmid, M. & Varga, P. (2002). Two-Dimensional Oxide on Pd(111). *Phys. Rev. Lett.* 88(24); doi:10.1103/PhysRevLett.88.246103.

Markusse, A.P., Kuster, B.F.M. & Schouten, J.C. (2001). Platinum catalysed aqueous methyl-a-D-glucopyranoside oxidation in a multiphase redox-cycle reactor. *Catal. Today* 66, 191-197.

Shah, Y.T., Kelkar, B.G., Godbole, S.P. & Deckwer, W.D. (1982). Design parameters estimation for bubble column reactors. *AIChE Journal* 28(3), 353-379.

Sikula, I. (2008). *Modelling of fermentation in airlift bioreactor, PhD Thesis*, Department of Chem. and Biochem. Engng., Slovak University of Technology in Bratislava.

Sikula, I., Juraščík, M. & Markoš, J. (2006). Modeling of enzymatic reaction in an internal loop airlift bioreactor. *Chem. Pap.* 60(6), 446-453; doi: 10.2478/s11696-006-0081-1.

Sikula, I., Juraščík, M. & Markoš, J. (2007). Modeling of fermentation in an internal loop airlift bioreactor. *Chem. Eng. Sci.* 62, 5216-5221; doi: 10.1016/j.ces.2007.01.050.

Sikula, I. & Markoš, J. (2008). Modeling of enzymatic reaction in an airlift reactor using an axial dispersion model. *Chem. Pap.* 62(1), 10-17; doi:10.2478/s11696-007-0073-9.

Silveston, P.L. (1998). *Composition modulation of catalytic reactors.* Gordon and Breach Science Publishers.

Silveston, P.L. & Hanika, J. (2002). Challenges for the periodic operation of trickle-bed catalytic reactors. *Chem. Eng. Sci.* 57, 3373-3385.

Silveston, P.L. & Hanika, J. (2004). Periodic operation of three-phase catalytic reactors. *Canadian Journal of Chemical Engineering* 82, 1105-1142.

Simmons, G.W., Wang, Y., Marcos, J. & Klier, K. (1991). Oxygen Adsorption on Pd(100) Surface: Phase Transformations and Surface Reconstruction. *J. Phys. Chem.* 95, 4522-4528.

Szépe, S. & Levenspiel, O. (1970). Catalyst deactivation. *Chemical reaction Eng. Proc., 4-th Euro. Symp. Chem. React. Eng. Oxford.*

Thielecke, N., Vorlop, K.D. & Prusse, U. (2007). Long-term stability of an Au/Al_2O_3 catalyst prepared by incipient wetness in continuous-flow glucose oxidation. *Catal. Today* 122, 266-269; doi:10.1016/j.cattod.2007.02.008.

Tukač, V., Hanika, J. & Chyba, V. (2003). Periodic state of wet oxidation in trickle-bed reactor. *Catalysis Today* 79-80, 427-431.

Vleeming, J.H., Kuster, B.F.M. & Marin, G.B. (1997). Selective Oxidation of Methyl a-D-Glucopyranoside with Oxygen over Supported Platinum: Kinetic Modeling in the Presence of Deactivation by Overoxidation of the Catalyst. *Ind. Eng. Chem. Res.* 36, 3541-3553.

Znad, H., Báleš, V., Markoš, J. & Kawase, Y. (2004). Modeling and simulation of airlift bioreactors. *Biochemical Engineering Journal* 21, 73-81; doi: 10.1016/j.bej.2004.05.005.

13

Adiabatic Shear: Pre- and Post-critical Dynamic Plasticity Modelling and Study of Impact Penetration. Heat Generation in this Context

Patrice Longère[1] and André Dragon[2]
[1]*Université Européenne de Bretagne (UBS, LIMATB)*
[2]*Laboratoire de Mécanique et de Physique des Matériaux (CNRS, ENSMA)*
France

1. Introduction

Adiabatic Shear Banding (ASB) is recognized as a phenomenon of notable importance, being a failure precursor in the context of dynamic deformation for a large class of metals and alloys (in particular high-strength steels and alloys) and non-metals (polymers). Stemming from the pioneering work of Zener & Hollomon (1944), Recht (1964), extensive investigation - metallurgical and mechanical, experimental and theoretical -, and relevant literature have been devoted to the matter, see for instance numerous references given in the books by Bai & Dodd (1992), Wright (2002). These authors have attempted complementary syntheses of the field ranging from materials science oriented research to non linear mechanics issues. The special issue 'Shear Instabilities and Viscoplasticity Theories' of Mechanics of Materials published in 1994, including notably the papers by Mason et al. (1994), Nemat-Nasser et al. (1994), keeps also its topical importance. The seminal contribution by Marchand & Duffy (1988) should be cited as a major experimental work.

The emergence of ASB is attributed predominantly to the opposite influence of strain and strain rate hardening and thermal softening effects, respectively. Thermal softening is assumed to lead to a stage when the material can no longer harden and, in this way, looses its stability, making possible the formation of a localized discontinuity/failure mode. This is why many studies of instability inception are concerned, in this context, with perturbation analysis of the mechanical and thermal fields, see for instance Molinari & Clifton (1987). Very recent results regarding the ASB phenomenon bring out some finer points to the picture mentioned above. They tend to clarify the role of microstructural evolutions and point out a particular phase transition, namely dynamic recrystallization as a possible factor in the ASB generation (Rittel et al., 2008). Adiabatic shear mode requires that thermal conductivity effects be attenuated by a small deformation time, i.e. high strain rate involved. In such a way this mode is considered sometimes as 'a characteristics' of impact loading (Woodward, 1990).

Depending on the thermomechanical properties of the target material and on the intensity of loading, the penetration of a flat end projectile into, say, a hard steel plate can be accompanied by the formation of a ring shape intense (localized) shear zone inside the target. Intense shearing can lead to the development of adiabatic shear bands which are known as precursor of the ultimate dynamic plugging of the plate. In the present authors' opinion accurate prediction of the protection response during the target/penetrator interaction needs an advanced three-dimensional (3D) description of the behaviour of the structural materials containing adiabatic shear bands. The 3D TEVPD (for Thermo Elastic ViscoPlastic with Viscous Deterioration) constitutive model and the inherent numerical formalism, presented in this chapter, aim to describe the post-critical behaviour of a high strength metallic material in the presence of the ASB related evolution.

In the approach presented, ASB is considered as a specific anisotropic deterioration process. Some earlier tentatives in this direction are due to Pecherski (1988), and Perzyna and coworkers, see e.g. Perzyna (1990). The constitutive model presented here describes the thermo-elastic/viscoplastic behaviour of a sound material and the mechanical anisotropy, i.e. directional degradation of both elastic and viscoplastic moduli, induced by ASB in the framework of large elastic-plastic deformation. The model, particularly destined to deal with impacted structures, has been progressively elaborated in recent articles (Longère et al., 2003; 2005; 2009). It is applied to a genuine ballistic penetration problem for a target plate material, namely to the interaction between a fragment simulating projectile (FSP) and a semi-thick target metal plate.

Since thermal evolutions are crucial in the ASB related research, special importance has been given to the real-time monitoring of the temperature of impacted specimens, see e.g. Mason et al. (1994), Kapoor & Nemat-Nasser (1998), Rittel (1999), Rosakis et al. (2000). These works have led to a better understanding of the thermomechanical conversion phenomena, notably to the fraction of the plastic work rate converted into heat, corresponding to inherent dissipative nature of plastic deformation. Despite of widespread, crude practice assuming the inelastic heat fraction coefficient as a constant, there is now experimental evidence that it is not only strain but also strain-rate and possibly temperature dependent quantity. Based on this experimental work and some earlier modelling tentatives (Aravas et al., 1990; Zehnder, 1991; Rosakis et al., 2000), some present authors' recent contributions to the matter of the adiabatic heat evaluation viewed as an evolving process are synthesized in this chapter. It can be shown that the accuracy in the prediction of favourable conditions for the onset of plastic (ASB) localization is dependent strongly on the method retained for evaluating the fraction of effectively dissipated plastic work (i.e. converted into heat), see e.g. Longère & Dragon, 2009. Moreover, a methodology combining some aspects of dislocation theory in the domain of thermally activated deformation and the internal variable approach applied to thermo-elastic/viscoplastic behaviour is developed (Voyiadjis & Abed, 2006; Longère & Dragon, 2008); it allows for obtaining physically based inelastic heat fraction expressions. This contribution is summarized at the end of the chapter.

In such a way this chapter brings forward a threefold contribution relevant to the ASB process as a part of dynamic plasticity of high strength metallic materials. It is organized as follows:

i. A three-dimensional finite deformation model is first presented; the model is based on a specific scale postulate and devoted to cover a wide range of dissipative phenomena including ASB related material instabilities i.e. strong softening prefailure stage. The model and related indicator of the ASB onset are reviewed in Section 2.
ii. A ballistic penetration problem representing the dynamic interaction between an FSB-projectile and a target plate is rehearsed in Section 3. The three-dimensional numerical study shows the failure of the target occurring as a plugging event resulting from an adiabatic shearing process.

iii. An evaluation of the inelastic heat fraction under adiabatic conditions involving microstructure supported dynamic plasticity modelling is discussed in Section 4 in relation to the dynamic plastic (ASB) localization.

As an introduction to a very recent lecture on adiabatic shear localization, Rittel (Rittel, 2009) pointed out that 'so far, there is no clear connection between the profusion of microstructural observations and mechanical quantities, such as a critical strain for failure, so that the physical picture is still incomplete'. This chapter, summarizing some recent contributions of the authors to the field, embodied in the (i), (ii) and (iii) foregoing items, attempts to fill the gap regarding 'mechanical quantities', i.e. strictly speaking the thermomechanical insight into the 'physical picture' of ASB phenomenon and its salient engineering aspects.

2. Finite strain viscoplasticity model incorporating ASB-induced degradation

2.1 Context and basic concepts

In some engineering applications, notably those implying detailed analysis of consecutive phases for impacted metallic structures (see e.g. Stevens & Batra, 1998, Martinez et al., 2007) and high speed machining (see e.g. Molinari et al., 2002, Burns & Davies, 2002) with the predominant failure mechanism triggered by adiabatic shear banding (ASB), a three-dimensional insight and treatment are desirable. They are scarce in the literature as the relative modelling should be rigorous enough and robust as well to incorporate and overcome local instabilities relative to inception and growth of ASB. Contrarily to fine, micromechanical and one-dimensional analyses encountered in many valuable studies (Bai (1982), Clifton et al. (1984), Molinari (1985,1997) and Klepaczko (1994)) what is searched here, in the context mentioned in the foregoing, is a 'larger scale' material response to dynamic loading. Some attempts by Perzyna and coworkers (see e.g. Perzyna (1990), Lodygowski & Perzyna (1997)) are directed towards such an alternative large-scale, three-dimensional modelling. The aim of the present contribution is clearly set in this perspective. The approach proposed is a phenomenological one - while many hypotheses are micromechanically motivated -, however the model outlined is not a micromechanical model strictly speaking. It is based on the choice of the reference representative volume element (RVE) whose length scale is much greater than the bandwidth (while many existing works, some of them cited above, consider in fact a length scale lower than the bandwidth). An approach accounting for salient physical features concerning the ASB formation and development at the actual (global) RVE scale, should obviously consider the following consequences:

- thermo-mechanical softening;
- ASB-induced material anisotropy (due to band orientation);
- specific finite strain kinematics including ASB-effect.

In the approach put forward, the evolution of the 'singular' dissipative processes (intervening inside the band cluster), contributing to macromechanical (global) softening is described via the evolution of a single internal variable, called ASB-intensity d. The softening behaviour, see e.g. its detailed analysis by Marchand & Duffy (1988) and Liao & Duffy (1998), is being considered as resulting from ASB-induced degradation, the density d characterises the state of the global material deterioration due to ASB as shown in Fig.1.

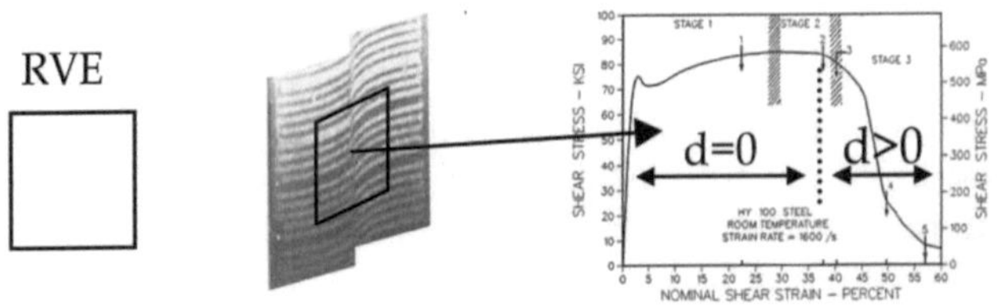

After Marchand & Duffy (1988)

Fig. 1. 'Large RVE' concept illustrated by Marchand and Duffy dynamic torsion experiment and consecutive global softening corresponding to growing density d according to the present model

In order to describe the state of anisotropic degradation of the material caused by the presence of ASB, a second order tensor, damage-like variable **D** is introduced. Its components are denoted as D_{ij} and are expressed by Eq.(1) below, where d^{α} and $\mathbf{n}^{\alpha}$ represent respectively the scalar density introduced above and the orientation for the band pattern α, see Fig.2.

$$D_{ij} = \sum_{\alpha} d^{\alpha} N_{ij}^{\alpha} \; ; \; N_{ij}^{\alpha} = n_i^{\alpha} n_j^{\alpha} \tag{1}$$

For a high strain rate plastic flow considered hereby the work done in plastic deformation (intrinsic dissipation) is converted largely to heat. The latter, if not conducted away as it is the case under the conditions at stake, leads to a high rise in temperature. In metals and alloys where the rate of thermal softening (a corresponding drop in stress) surpasses the rate of work hardening, deformation is seen to concentrate in narrow softened bands of adiabatic shear. This is a nowadays well-known mechanism of ASB inception and growth (Zener & Hollomon (1944), Recht (1964)). Consequently in the framework of the present model, the onset and further evolution of ASB are produced by thermal softening, respectively in the sound (non degraded) material during locally homogeneous plastic deformation and then inside the bands themselves, during evolving localization process. The intensity d^{α} includes thus information relative to temperature inside the band pattern α. Consider now a single band pattern (Fig.2, α=1) and recall that the adjective 'singular' applies to the process relevant to the ASB itself (inside the bands), and the adjective 'regular' for the processes outside the bands. With such a distinction, the current density d of the internal variable **D** depends on the 'singular' temperature T*, and can be thus written as:

$$d = d(T^*, \ldots) \tag{2}$$

The dots represent other possible singular arguments as it is further detailed.
The kinematic consequences of the presence of the shear band pattern (see Fig.2) are viewed as those of a 'super-dislocation' (or a 'super gliding system'). By generalizing, for the RVE-element considered, the kinematics of the crystalline plasticity, an ASB-induced supplementary ('singular') velocity gradient $\mathbf{L}^{d}$ (in addition to the one relevant to 'regular' plastic deformation outside the band, designated $\mathbf{L}^{p}$) is introduced as the result of the glide velocity $\dot{\gamma}^{\alpha}$ due to the band pattern α of the normal $\mathbf{n}^{\alpha}$ and with orientation $\mathbf{g}^{\alpha}$ (see Fig.2):

$$L_{ij}^{d} \propto \sum_{\alpha} \dot{\gamma}^{\alpha} g_i^{\alpha} n_j^{\alpha} \tag{3}$$

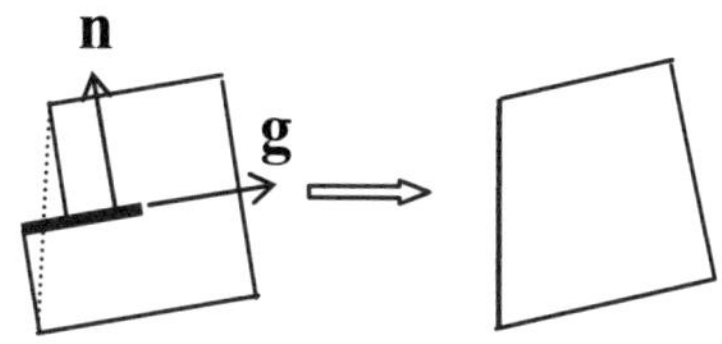

Fig. 2. Equivalent homogeneous volume element containing a family of band (α=1)

The partition of this ASB-induced velocity gradient $\mathbf{L}^d$ into symmetric and antisymmetric parts respectively leads to the corresponding strain rate $\mathbf{d}^d$ and spin $\boldsymbol{\omega}^d$ as follows:

$$\begin{cases} d_{ij}^{d} \propto \sum_{\alpha} \dot{\gamma}^{\alpha} M_{ij}^{\alpha} \; ; \; M_{ij}^{\alpha} = \left(g_i^{\alpha} n_j^{\alpha}\right)^{S} = \dfrac{1}{2}\left(g_i^{\alpha} n_j^{\alpha} + g_j^{\alpha} n_i^{\alpha}\right) \\ \omega_{ij}^{d} \propto \sum_{\alpha} \dot{\gamma}^{\alpha} T_{ij}^{\alpha} \; ; \; T_{ij}^{\alpha} = \left(g_i^{\alpha} n_j^{\alpha}\right)^{AS} = \dfrac{1}{2}\left(g_i^{\alpha} n_j^{\alpha} - g_j^{\alpha} n_i^{\alpha}\right) \end{cases} \tag{4}$$

The corresponding kinematics leads to further smoothing of the boundary discontinuity caused by the ASB as illustrated in Fig.2, as it is done in crystalline plasticity. Finally, two contributions to the inelastic strain rate of the equivalent homogeneous volume element can be distinguished: the 'regular' plastic strain rate, denoted $\mathbf{d}^p$, and the 'singular' one, $\mathbf{d}^d$. The total inelastic strain rate $\mathbf{d}^{dp}$ is defined as the sum of these two contributions:

$$d_{ij}^{dp} = d_{ij}^{p} + d_{ij}^{d} \tag{5}$$

The physical motivations and scale assumptions put forward in the foregoing are further developed in Sect.2.2. The complete constitutive model is given in Sect.2.3 in the specific three-dimensional, finite strain, elastic/viscoplastic and ASB-anisotropic degradation framework. The regular vs. singular dissipation terms are respectively designated and corresponding regular vs. singular heating parts specified.

The specific shock configurations for a hat shape structure (HSS) and ballistic penetration involving plugging failure mechanism have been chosen as examples of the application of the present model. The numerical results relevant to HSS configurations, leading to partial or complete banding (and subsequent failure) depending on the shock intensity, see Longère et al. (2005 and 2009), have been examined and compared with experimental data obtained by Couque (2003)$_{a,b}$. A tentative, ASB-induced local failure criterion is being inferred from the corresponding analysis and experimental evidence. The HSS problem investigation, not detailed in this chapter, was viewed as a stage towards genuine ballistic engineering problems where the ASB trajectories cannot be known a priori.

A particular problem of this kind is being dealt with in Sect.3.2, involving a fragment simulating projectile (FSP) and a semi-thick plate interaction. A three-dimensional numerical study is summarized for shock configurations below and above the ballistic penetration limit velocity V_{bpl}. The thermoelastic/viscoplastic/ASB deterioration model (TEVPD) employed allows for bringing out complex ASB-related history regarding impacted plate material. The history at stake consists in occurrence of two competing ASB deterioration mechanisms. The first one, starting earlier, involves a set of localized bands related potentially to punching failure. However, these bands arrest without crossing the plate thickness. It is shown that a new family of crossing bands appears, leading finally to expected plugging failure pattern.

It should be stressed that the thermomechanical TEVPD model, detailed earlier in Longère et al. (2003;2005), represents a specific, directly applicable alternative with respect to non-local modelling due to its proper scale postulate involving material length. The numerical simulations regarding various shock configurations for initial/boundary value problems are intended to put to the test the pertinence of the TEVPD model as a predictive tool for structural analysis involving shock/impact problems. In a sense they appear conclusive for the model legitimation and prospective improvements.

2.2 Physical motivations

Consider simple shear of a material element shown in Fig.3 (the pictures are due to Marchand & Duffy (1988)). Let us suppose the succession of events as follows implying ASB phenomenon where the last picture shows the near-failure stage (involving neither genuine damage nor fracture yet) of the element under adiabatic shear banding.

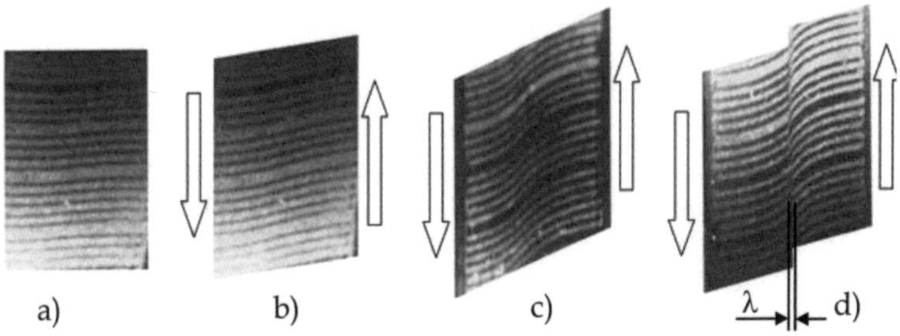

Fig. 3. Material element under dynamic shearing as observed by Marchand & Duffy (1988); a) Undeformed configuration ; b) Homogeneous shear deformation ; c) Weak localization ; d) ASB induced strong localization

The band width is designated λ, and the representative volume element (RVE) is assumed tentatively with a length equal to $\ell < \lambda$. To distinguish the process relevant strictly to the band deformation mechanisms from the process not relevant to the band, the first is henceforth called 'singular' process and the other is called 'regular' one. It is now supposed that the evolution of both processes can be described via the evolution of state variables such like relevant measures of elastic strain $\mathbf{e}^e$, temperature T, strain hardening p, damage (if any) δ, metallurgical state as f.ex. phase transformation (if any) ξ, and so on:

$$V_{regular} = \left(\mathbf{e}^e, T, p, \delta, \xi, ...\right) \text{ and } V_{singular} = \left(\mathbf{e}^{e}*, T*, p*, \delta*, \xi*, ...\right)$$

where $V_{regular}$ and $V_{singular}$ represent respectively the sets of 'regular' and 'singular' state variables. At an advanced stage of deformation, 'singular' elastic strain can be neglected, while a specific 'singular' variable describing intense shearing will be introduced further. We then have tentatively: $V_{regular} = \left(\mathbf{e}^e, T, p, \delta, \xi, ...\right)$ and $V_{singular} = \left(T*, p*, \delta*, \xi*, ...\right)$

Due to localization phenomena involved during the process of adiabatic shear banding, the 'singular' variables measured in any RVE located inside the band reach values which become progressively much greater than those of the 'regular' variables measured in any RVE located outside the band.

Instead of a description considering a 'small' representative volume element (RVE), i.e. whose length scale is lower than the bandwidth ($\ell < \lambda$), the more global insight is preferred here with a 'large' RVE, i.e. whose length scale is greater than the bandwidth ($\ell > \lambda$). In this aim in view, all the set of 'singular' variables (and respective dissipation effects), and notably the 'singular' temperature T*, are incorporated in the complementary (internal) variable d whose more general definition constitutes the subject of the following.

Such a phenomenological approach must account for physical features concerning in particular ASB formation and development and the consequences of the presence of bands at the RVE scale ($\ell > \lambda$) in terms of mechanical softening, structural anisotropy and additional kinematics.

In the present approach, the evolution of the 'singular' dissipative processes contributing to the macromechanical softening is described via the evolution of an internal variable called d^{α}, α designating a family of bands with the same orientation. The softening of the global RVE behaviour being considered as a form of mechanical degradation, the variable d^{α} characterises the global material deterioration under adiabatic shear banding. It is then a function of the 'singular' state variables and of the characteristic length λ^{α} of the band:

$$d^{\alpha} = d^{\alpha}\left(\lambda, V_{singular}\right) = d^{\alpha}\left(\lambda, T^*, p^*, \delta^*, \xi^*, \ldots\right) \tag{6}$$

An increase in the 'singular' temperature T* (the temperature inside the band) generates consequently increase in the magnitude of d^{α} without causing explicit increase of the 'regular' temperature T (the temperature outside the band), preserving the hypothesis of local adiabaticity.

In the same way, the structural anisotropy induced in the RVE ($\ell > \lambda$) by the presence of the bands is linked to the orientation $\mathbf{n}^{\alpha}$ of the band, through the orientation tensor $\mathbf{N}^{\alpha}=\mathbf{n}^{\alpha} \otimes \mathbf{n}^{\alpha}$.

The combination of d^{α} and $\mathbf{n}^{\alpha}$ allows for describing entirely the specific orthotropic mechanical degradation of the RVE under adiabatic shear banding. This combination is performed here through the definition of a 2nd order tensorial variable already introduced by (1), with the density d conveying singular deterioration mechanism as follows:

$$\mathbf{D} = \sum_{\alpha} d^{\alpha}.\mathbf{N}^{\alpha} \; ; \; d^{\alpha} = d^{\alpha}\left(\lambda, V_{singular}\right) = d^{\alpha}\left(\lambda, T^*, p^*, \delta^*, \xi^*, \ldots\right) ; \; \mathbf{N}^{\alpha} = \mathbf{n}^{\alpha} \otimes \mathbf{n}^{\alpha} \tag{7}$$

As already pointed in Sect.2.1, see Eq.(2), the current density d of the deterioration tensor **D** depends notably on the 'singular' temperature T*, i.e. d=d(T*,...), the dots signifying other arguments in $(7)_2$, see also Longère et al. (2003). As **D** quantifies adiabatic shear band-induced degradation of the RVE, this variable can be considered as a sort of 'deterioration' (or damage-like) variable.

In parallel, while **D** governs the anisotropic degradation, the kinematic consequence of the presence of the band, viewed as an idealized 'super-dislocation' within the representative volume, see Fig.2 and the comments above, is dealt with by incorporating the contribution (3) to the total inelastic velocity gradient $\mathbf{L}^{dp}$ such as

$$\mathbf{L}^{dp} = \mathbf{L}^{p} + \mathbf{L}^{d} \tag{8}$$

There are thus two contributions to the inelastic velocity gradient $\mathbf{L}^{dp}$: $\mathbf{L}^{p}$ relative to homogeneous 'regular' viscoplasticity, and $\mathbf{L}^{d}$, as mentioned above, resulting from adiabatic shear banding-induced 'singular' mechanism. The corresponding decomposition of the symmetric part of $\mathbf{L}^{dp}$, namely that of $\mathbf{d}^{dp}$, the inelastic strain rate, is given by (5) above.

2.3 Constitutive relations. Indicator for ASB-incipience

The actual modelling aims at describing the material behaviour not only during the first stage of locally homogeneous and weakly inhomogeneous deformation (stages 1 and 2 of Marchand & Duffy's curve, see Figs.1,3) but also during the phase of strong localization induced by the formation of ASB (stage 3 of Marchand & Duffy's curve, see Figs.1,3). The model should thus be robust enough to overcome local instabilities relative to inception and growth of ASB on mesoscale level.

Due to its specific scale background summarized above (Sect.2.2) by the inequality $\ell > \lambda$ and introduced in more detail in Longere et al. 2005 (Sect.1 of this reference), the model conveys implicitly a characteristic material length scale in its constitutive formulation. This implicit incorporation of the length scale becomes explicit when dealing with finite element (FE) implementation of the model and its application for structural analysis including ASB phenomena. The spatial FE discretization violating the foregoing scale level postulate is excluded. Some comments regarding this aspect and related mesh sensitivity problem are given later in Sect.3. In conclusion, the constitutive model detailed below remains apparently a local one while enfolding a scale postulate in its substructure; this represents a sort of compromise with respect to non-locality, clearly put forward in the present context by Abu Al-Rub & Voyiadjis (2006).

Based on irreversible thermodynamics with internal variables (see Coleman & Gurtin (1967), Meixner (1969) and Bataille & Kestin (1975)), the constitutive model, called TEVPD model for convenience (for 'thermoelastic/viscoplastic-deterioration'), is detailed below to be applied later in the context of high-velocity impact and penetration mechanics. Some simplifying assumptions, regarding notably strain and strain rate hardening description and small elastic strain, are made.

Kinematical considerations. The decomposition of the deformation gradient $\mathbf{F}$ as the product $\mathbf{F}=\mathbf{V}^e\mathbf{Q}\mathbf{F}^{dp}$ (see Fig.4), where $\mathbf{V}^e$ denotes the pure 'elastic' stretching ($\mathbf{F}^e=\mathbf{V}^e\mathbf{R}^e$, $\mathbf{R}^e$ the orthogonal 'elastic' rotation tensor), $\mathbf{Q}$ the rotation of anisotropy axes and $\mathbf{F}^{dp}$ the 'deterioration-plastic' i.e. inelastic deformation, allows further for following Eulerian kinematic decompositions:

$$d_{ij} = d^e_{ij} + d^{dp}_{ij} \quad ; \quad \omega_{ij} = W_{ij} + \omega^e_{ij} + \omega^{dp}_{ij} \tag{9}$$

where $\mathbf{d}$ is the total rate of strain tensor and $\boldsymbol{\omega}$ the spin tensor. The symbols $\mathbf{d}^e$ and $\boldsymbol{\omega}^e$ represent respectively the elastic rate of strain and spin, $\mathbf{W} = \dot{\mathbf{Q}}\mathbf{Q}^T$ the rotation rate of anisotropy axes and $\mathbf{d}^{dp}$ and $\boldsymbol{\omega}^{dp}$ respectively the inelastic rate of strain and spin. The inelastic terms include regular contributions and those due to ASB evolution, namely $\mathbf{d}^d$ and $\boldsymbol{\omega}^d$ introduced in (4). The objective corotational derivative $\overset{\nabla}{\mathbf{A}}$ of a 2nd order tensor $\mathbf{A}$ is given by (see e.g. Sidoroff & Dogui, 2001):

$$\overset{\nabla}{A}_{ij} = \dot{A}_{ij} - W_{ik}A_{kj} + A_{ip}W_{pj} \tag{10}$$

Assuming small elastic deformation and a weak contribution of the plastic ('regular') spin $\boldsymbol{\omega}^p$ with regard to the ASB-deterioration induced spin $\boldsymbol{\omega}^d$ (see Longere et al., 2003, for detailed argument) the rotation rate $\mathbf{W}$ is simplified as follows:

$$W_{ij} = \omega_{ij} - \omega^d_{ij} \tag{11}$$

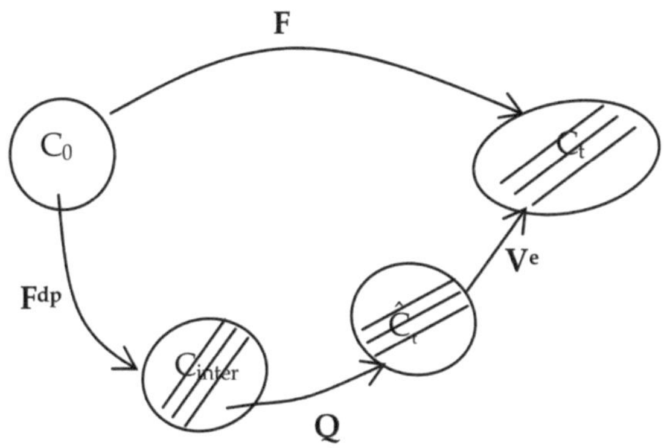

Fig. 4. Intermediate configuration and decomposition of the deformation gradient **F** in the presence of anisotropy; see also (Sidoroff & Dogui (2001))

Free energy and thermodynamic forces. In the model presented, involving 'large' RVE reference scale $\ell > \lambda$, the set of state variables referred to the actual configuration C_t is reduced to

$$V = \left(\mathbf{e}^e, T, p; \tilde{\mathbf{D}}\right)$$

with $\tilde{\mathbf{D}}$ representing a measure of the material deterioration in the current configuration due to 'singular' ASB related evolution. The tensor **D**, defined in the intermediate configuration, is 'transported' to the current one, the symbol $\tilde{\mathbf{D}}$ designating the tensor **D** transformed in this way, namely $\tilde{\mathbf{D}} = \mathbf{QDQ}^T$.
The set $\left(\mathbf{e}^e, T, p\right)$ corresponds exactly to the set of 'regular' state variables mentioned above while $\tilde{\mathbf{D}}$ embraces the 'singular' effects at the actual 'large' RVE scale. The tensor $\mathbf{e}^e$ represents here a spatial elastic strain measure, namely $\mathbf{e}^e=\ln(\mathbf{V}^e)$. As mentioned above, for the class of materials considered the hypothesis of small elastic strain is being assumed, i.e. ($V^e_{ij} \approx \delta_{ij} + \varepsilon_{ij}$ with $\varepsilon_{ij}\varepsilon_{ji} << 1$).
The thermo-elastic response of the anisotropic medium is supposed to be described by the specific free energy $\psi\left(\mathbf{e}^e, T, p; \tilde{\mathbf{D}}\right) = \psi^e\left(\mathbf{e}^e, T; \tilde{\mathbf{D}}\right) + \psi^p\left(T, p; \tilde{\mathbf{D}}\right)$ where the thermoelastic energy ψ^e and the stored energy ψ^p are assumed respectively in the form:

$$\begin{cases} \rho_0\psi^e = \dfrac{\lambda}{2} e^e_{ii} e^e_{jj} + \mu e^e_{ij} e^e_{ji} - \alpha K e^e_{ii} \Delta T - \rho_0 c_0 \left[T \ln\left(\dfrac{T}{T_0}\right) - \vartheta \right] - a e^e_{kk} e^e_{ij} \tilde{D}_{ji} - 2b e^e_{ij} e^e_{jk} \tilde{D}_{ki} \\ \rho_0\psi^p = R_\infty \left[p + \dfrac{1}{k} \exp(-kp) \right] \exp(-\gamma T) \exp\left(-d_1 \tilde{D}_{ii} - \dfrac{d_2}{2} \tilde{D}_{ij} \tilde{D}_{ji} \right) \end{cases} \tag{12}$$

where λ and μ represent Lamé elasticity coefficients, K is the bulk modulus ($K = \lambda + 2\mu/3$), α is the thermal expansion coefficient, ρ_0 the initial density, c_0 the heat capacity, $\vartheta = T - T_0$ the temperature rise, a and b the moduli related to elastic energy ASB-induced degradation and inducing a form of orthotropy. The elastic stiffness depends now on the constants λ, μ, a, b and on the actual form of $\tilde{\mathbf{D}}$. In the expression $(12)_2$ R_∞ is related to the saturation of hardening, k the plastic hardening parameter, γ the thermal softening parameter, d_1 and d_2 the deterioration (ASB) related softening constants.

The model, to be consistent with irreversible thermodynamic framework, should satisfy the Clausius-Duhem dissipation inequality. It is to be reminded that adiabatic conditions are assumed (no heat conduction). The intrinsic dissipation is expressed as follows (with respect to the current configuration):

$$D_{int} = \tau_{ij} d_{ji} - \rho_0 \left(\dot{\psi} + s\dot{T} \right) \geq 0$$

with τ designating the Kirchhoff stress tensor, s the local entropy.
The Gibbs relation and Clausius-Duhem inequality are further detailed as follows:

$$\rho_0 \dot{\psi} = -\rho_0 s\dot{T} + \tau_{ij} d^e_{ji} + r\dot{p} - \tilde{k}_{ij} \overset{\nabla}{\tilde{D}}_{ji} \; ; \; D_{int} = \tau_{ij} d^{dp}_{ji} - r\dot{p} + \tilde{k}_{ij} \overset{\nabla}{\tilde{D}}_{ji} \geq 0 \tag{13}$$

The thermo-elastic Kirchhoff stress tensor τ, the strain hardening thermodynamic force (affinity) r and the deterioration conjugate force $\tilde{\mathbf{k}}$ are classically derived from the thermodynamic potential $\psi\left(\mathbf{e}^e, T, p; \tilde{\mathbf{D}}\right)$ with respect to $\mathbf{e}^e$, p and $\tilde{\mathbf{D}}$:

$$\tau_{ij} = \lambda e^e_{kk} \delta_{ij} + 2\mu e^e_{ij} - \alpha K \Delta T \delta_{ij} - a\left(e^e_{mn} \tilde{D}_{nm} \delta_{ij} + e^e_{kk} \tilde{D}_{ij} \right) - 2b\left(e^e_{ik} \tilde{D}_{kj} + \tilde{D}_{ik} e^e_{kj} \right) \tag{14}$$

$$r = R_\infty \left[1 - \exp(-kp) \right] \exp(-\gamma T) \exp\left(-d_1 \tilde{D}_{kk} - \frac{d_2}{2} \tilde{D}_{kl} \tilde{D}_{lk} \right) \tag{15}$$

$$\tilde{k}_{ij} = a e^e_{kk} e^e_{ij} + 2b e^e_{ik} e^e_{kj} + R_\infty \left[p + \frac{1}{k} \exp(-kp) \right] \exp(-\gamma T) \exp\left(-d_1 \tilde{D}_{kk} - \frac{d_2}{2} \tilde{D}_{kl} \tilde{D}_{lk} \right) \left[d_1 \delta_{ij} + d_2 \tilde{D}_{ij} \right] \tag{16}$$

The form of entropy $s = -\partial\psi / \partial T$ is not detailed here, see Longère et al. (2003) for this item.
Regular heating and anisotropic deterioration including singular, ASB-induced heating, contribute to reduce the stress level $\boldsymbol{\tau}\left(\mathbf{e}^e, T; \tilde{\mathbf{D}}\right)$. Constants a and b contribute both to reduce Young's modulus, while b is alone responsible for the decrease of the shear modulus.
Hardening conjugate force $r\left(T, p; \tilde{\mathbf{D}}\right)$ increases during pure hardening but decreases with heating and further deterioration effects superposed on hardening, r is thus describing the competition between plastic hardening and thermal and ASB-induced softening effects.
The ASB induced deterioration conjugate force $\tilde{\mathbf{k}}\left(\mathbf{e}^e, T, p; \tilde{\mathbf{D}}\right)$ is the energy release rate with respect to $\tilde{\mathbf{D}}$. It includes a contribution from the reversible part ψ^e of the free energy, and another one from the stored energy ψ^p. The corresponding terms represent respectively elastic and stored energy release rates induced by the formation and development of ASB in the material (RVE). It is noteworthy that both contributions to the degradation conjugate force exist before ASB inception. A finite supply of energy release rate k_{inc} is indeed assumed to be necessary to activate the deterioration process. The threshold force k_{inc} is explicitly determined by the auxiliary analysis (see Sect.2.4).
Regular vs. singular heating. The dissipation in $(13)_2$ can be decomposed into a 'regular' term directly linked to plasticity and a 'singular' term resulting from the contribution of irreversible process involving ASB:

$$D_{int} = D_{reg} + D_{sing} \; ; \; D_{reg} = \tau_{ij} d^p_{ji} - r\dot{p} \; ; \; D_{sing} = \tau_{ij} d^d_{ji} + \tilde{k}_{ij} \overset{\nabla}{\tilde{D}}_{ji} \tag{17}$$

'Regular' heating $\dot{T}$ caused by plasticity outside the bands is then estimated from the relation established under the conventional adiabaticity assumption using $(17)_2$:

$$\rho_0 c_0 \dot{T} = \tau_{ij} d^p_{ji} - r\dot{p} \tag{18}$$

where c_0 represents the heat capacity.
By employing the inelastic heat fraction β, the relation (18) is reduced to:

$$\rho_0 c_0 \dot{T} = \beta \tau_{ij} d^p_{ji} \tag{19}$$

where β, depending on plastic strain, plastic strain rate and temperature (see Longère and Dragon, 2007) , is expressed by:

$$\beta = 1 - \frac{r\dot{p}}{\tau_{ij} d^p_{ji}} \tag{20}$$

The effects of 'singular' heating $\dot{T}^*$ localized inside the band cluster are included, by definition of the deterioration variable $\tilde{\mathbf{D}}$ (see $(7)_2$), in the scalar density $d(T^*,...)$, evolving with the ongoing deterioration. As a first approximation (neglecting thermomechanical coupling), one can write, using $(17)_3$:

$$\rho_0 c_0 \dot{T}^* \propto D_{sing} = \tau_{ij} d^d_{ji} + \tilde{k}_{ij} \overset{\nabla}{\tilde{D}}_{ji} \tag{21}$$

The temperature rise effects inside the ASB are indeed included in the 'singular' dissipation which is now represented by the product $D^D_{sing} = \tilde{k}_{ij} \overset{\nabla}{\tilde{D}}_{ji}$ in (21). The other singular term $D^{in}_{sing} = \tau_{ij} d^d_{ji}$ in (21) is due to the ASB contribution to the total inelastic strain. During the process of ASB induced degradation, the 'regular' part of dissipation decreases while the 'singular' part of dissipation increases.

Dissipation potential, yield function and evolution laws. The existence of viscous plastic and deterioration potentials of Norton-Perzyna's type is assumed in the form of a power law:

$$\phi^c_p = \frac{Y}{n+1} \left\langle \frac{F}{Y} \right\rangle^{n+1} \;;\; \phi^c_d = \frac{Z}{m+1} \left\langle \frac{F}{Z} \right\rangle^{m+1} \tag{22}$$

where Y and n represent viscous constants relative to plasticity, Z and m viscous constants relative to (time-dependent) degradation, the bracket $\langle x \rangle = \max(x,0)$.

A single yield function F that includes both plasticity and deterioration effects appears actually suitable to describe, via the generalized normality hypothesis, the evolution of corresponding variables:

$$F\left(\tau_{ij}, r, \tilde{k}_{ij}\right) = \hat{J}^s_2\left(\tau_{ij}, \tilde{k}_{ij}\right) - \left(R_0 + r\right) \;;\; \hat{J}^s_2\left(\tau_{ij}, \tilde{k}_{ij}\right) = \sqrt{\frac{3}{2} s_{ij} P_{ijkl}\left(\tilde{k}_{mn}\right) s_{kl}} \tag{23}$$

where $\mathbf{s}$ represents the deviatoric part of the Kirchhoff stress tensor, and $\mathbf{P}\left(\tilde{\mathbf{k}}\right)$ the 4th order tensor inducing deterioration-prompted anisotropy of the plastic flow, assumed in the following form:

$$P_{ijkl} = \frac{1}{2}\left(\delta_{ik}\delta_{jl} + \delta_{il}\delta_{jk}\right) + 2\sum_{q=2}^{N}\eta_q\left(\tilde{k}^{+}_{mn}\tilde{N}_{nm}\right)^q\tilde{M}_{ij}\tilde{M}_{kl} \tag{24}$$

In the same way as $\tilde{\mathbf{D}}$, the symbols $\tilde{\mathbf{M}}$ and $\tilde{\mathbf{N}}$ designate respectively the tensors **M** and **N** (see $(4)_1$ and $(1)_2$) transported from the intermediate configuration to the current one.
In order to preserve the continuity of stress at the onset of ASB induced degradation, the deterioration driving force $\tilde{\mathbf{k}}$ intervenes via the expression $\mathrm{Tr}\left(\tilde{\mathbf{k}}^{+}\mathbf{N}\right)$, the latter representing the difference between the current value $\mathrm{Tr}\left(\tilde{\mathbf{k}}\mathbf{N}\right)$ and the corresponding one at the incipience of degradation $k_{inc} = \mathrm{Tr}\left(\tilde{\mathbf{k}}\mathbf{N}\right)_{inc}$:

$$\tilde{k}^{+}_{ij}\tilde{N}_{ji} = \left\langle \tilde{k}_{ij}\tilde{N}_{ji} - k_{inc}\right\rangle \tag{25}$$

To determine k_{inc} an auxiliary analysis based on a perturbation method is conducted for a particular loading path. The function R_0 is expressed in a form similar to that of the hardening affinity except for the genuine hardening effect:

$$R_0 = R_{int}\exp(-\gamma T)\exp\left(-d_1\tilde{D}_{kk} - \frac{d_2}{2}\tilde{D}_{mn}\tilde{D}_{nm}\right) \tag{26}$$

where R_{int} represents an internal stress.
Applying the normality rule, evolution laws are derived from dissipation potentials:

$$d^{dp}_{ij} = d^{p}_{ij} + d^{d}_{ij} = \frac{\partial\phi^c_p}{\partial\tau_{ij}} = \Lambda^p\frac{\partial F}{\partial\tau_{ij}};-\dot{p} = \frac{\partial\phi^c_p}{\partial r} = \Lambda^p\frac{\partial F}{\partial r};\overset{\nabla}{\tilde{D}}_{ij} = \frac{\partial\phi^c_d}{\partial\tilde{k}_{ij}} = \Lambda^d\frac{\partial F}{\partial\tilde{k}_{ij}} \tag{27}$$

The respective multipliers governing viscoplasticity and viscous deterioration are expressed by

$$\Lambda^p = \left\langle\frac{\partial\phi^c_p}{\partial F}\right\rangle = \left\langle\frac{F}{Y}\right\rangle^n;\Lambda^d = \left\langle\frac{\partial\phi^c_d}{\partial F}\right\rangle = \left\langle\frac{F}{Z}\right\rangle^m \tag{28}$$

The corresponding rates are detailed below:

$$\begin{cases} d^p_{ij} = \dfrac{3}{2}\Lambda^p\dfrac{s_{ij}}{\hat{J}^s_2} \\ d^d_{ij} = 3\Lambda^p\dfrac{\sum_{q=2}^{N}\eta_q\left(\tilde{k}^{+}_{mn}\tilde{N}_{nm}\right)^q s_{kl}\tilde{M}_{kl}}{\hat{J}^s_2}\tilde{M}_{ij}\end{cases} \qquad \begin{cases} \dot{p} = \Lambda^p \\ \overset{\nabla}{\tilde{D}}_{ij} = \dfrac{3}{2}\Lambda^d\dfrac{\sum_{q=2}^{N}q.\eta_q\left(\tilde{k}^{+}_{mn}\tilde{N}_{nm}\right)^{q-1}\left(s_{kl}\tilde{M}_{kl}\right)^2}{\hat{J}^s_2}\tilde{N}_{ij}\end{cases} \tag{29}$$

The deterioration induced spin ω^d is deduced from (4) and $(29)_2$ as follows:

$$\omega^d_{ij} = 3\Lambda^p\frac{\sum_{q=2}^{N}\eta_q\left(\tilde{k}^{+}_{mn}\tilde{N}_{nm}\right)^q s_{kl}\tilde{M}_{kl}}{\hat{J}^s_2}\tilde{T}_{ij} \tag{30}$$

$\tilde{\mathbf{T}}$ is again (as is $\tilde{\mathbf{M}}$) the tensor **T** (see $(4)_2$) expressed in the actual configuration C_t.

The evolution laws (29) verify the collinearity of the 'regular' plastic strain rate $\mathbf{d}^p$ with the deviatoric part $\mathbf{s}$ of the Kirchhoff stress tensor, the collinearity of the 'singular' ASB-induced strain rate $\mathbf{d}^d$ with the orientation tensor $\tilde{\mathbf{M}} = [\tilde{\mathbf{g}} \otimes \tilde{\mathbf{n}}]^S$ (note that $\tilde{\mathbf{T}} = [\tilde{\mathbf{g}} \otimes \tilde{\mathbf{n}}]^{AS}$), according to (4), and finally the collinearity of the damage rate $\overset{\nabla}{\tilde{\mathbf{D}}}$ with the orientation tensor $\tilde{\mathbf{N}} = \tilde{\mathbf{n}} \otimes \tilde{\mathbf{n}}$ for conservative damage growth configuration considered here tentatively. On the other hand, the form of the polynomial in $\mathrm{Tr}(\tilde{\mathbf{k}}^+\tilde{\mathbf{N}})$, starting with the exponent q=2 (see $(29)_2$ and $(29)_4$), ensures the concomitance of the deterioration induced rates $\mathbf{d}^d$ and $\overset{\nabla}{\tilde{\mathbf{D}}}$. The adiabatic shear banding process which generates the supplementary inelastic strain rate $\mathbf{d}^d$ modifies the initial direction of the inelastic strain rate $\mathbf{d}^p$.

Auxiliary indicator for deterioration incipience. The constitutive model summarized above is completed by a deterioration incipience criterion based on a simplified analysis of material instability using the linear perturbation method. It is not detailed here, the reader can consult the references (Molinari, 1985, Longère et al., 2003, Longère & Dragon, 2007) for this approach. The auxiliary simplified analysis performed here is intended to help to establish ASB induced degradation incipience threshold and its form based on more pertinent indications than purely phenomenological formulation (see e.g. Batra & Lear, 2005, for phenomenological proposals). The general (three-dimensional) criterion obtained is as follows:

$$G\left(\tau_{ij}, r, \dot{p}; \frac{\partial r}{\partial p}, \frac{\partial r}{\partial T}\right) = \sqrt{3}\left|\tau_{res}\right| - \left(r - \frac{1}{n}Y\dot{p}^{\frac{1}{n}} + \rho_0 c_0\left(\frac{\partial r}{\partial p} / \left(-\frac{\partial r}{\partial T}\right)\right)\right) > 0 \qquad (31)$$

where $\tau_{res} = \mathrm{Tr}(\mathbf{s}\tilde{\mathbf{M}})$ represents the resolved shear stress for a loading path at stake, r the isotropic hardening conjugate force, $Y\dot{p}^{1/n}$ the strain rate-induced overstress, $\partial r / \partial p$ the plastic hardening and $\partial r / \partial T$ the thermal softening effects. In the present simplified analysis (see Longère et al. (2003) for further details), the deterioration process is actually assumed to run as soon as $G = 0$. The condition (31) must be interpreted as the auxiliary indicator for the deterioration process incipience leading to the determination of the deterioration conjugate force threshold $k_{inc} = \mathrm{Tr}(\tilde{\mathbf{k}}\tilde{\mathbf{N}})_{inc}$ in (25), for the stress-state τ.

3. Application: initial/boundary value problem involving dynamic shearing

3.1 Preliminaries: numerical procedure and HSS testing/simulation

This section aims at determining numerically the plugging conditions for an armour steel plate submitted to the impact of a fragment-simulating projectile (FSP). During the FSP/plate interaction, the ultimate failure of the plate is here preceded by adiabatic shear banding, as it is often the case with high strength steel plates.

Numerical procedure. The three-dimensional constitutive TEVPD model presented in Sect.2 has been implemented as 'user material' in the finite element code LS-DYNA®.

Integration of constitutive equations in the case of softening behaviour is not trivial, and there is no standard procedure. It is well-known that viscosity contributes to 'regularize' the boundary value problem but in the present case (strong localization induced by ASB formation) a complementary procedure was needed to overcome numerical locking in the context of explicit numerical scheme. The adaptive time step procedure adopted herein is based on the principle of the maximal strain increment and consists in sampling, i.e. partitioning, the 'global' time increment (the time increment determined by the code itself for integrating the equations of motion). By reducing the 'local' time increment (the time increment used for integrating constitutives equations), for the element concerned and not for the whole structure, it ensures numerical convergence and stability as stated by Kulkarni et al. (1995). This procedure leads to an equivalence with a damage-like model with a 'controlled rate', see e.g. Suffis et al. (2003), assuring that the $\tilde{\mathbf{D}}$-rate here tends never to infinity and that there is very limited (if any) mesh sensitivity effect for a post-localization stage (for some details regarding mesh dependency analysis see Longère et al. (2005)).

Experimental procedure. Prior to carrying out the ballistic penetration simulation, it is necessary to characterize the material behaviour of both the FSP and the plate under dynamic loading. In this aim in view, the FSP and the plate materials have been tested under compressive loading using the split Hopkinson pressure bar (SHPB) device. The plate material has also been tested under simple shear loading using the split Kolsky bar device. The experimental data have been used to determine the viscoplasticity (plastic flow, strain hardening, thermal softening) and ASB-deterioration related material constants of the present model. The set of constants has been validated by confronting experimental and numerical results obtained from the dynamic shearing of a hat shape structure (HSS) composed of the plate material. These dynamic shearing tests provide furthermore a failure criterion which is used in the simulation of the ballistic penetration problem. This criterion is interpreted here tentitatively in term of admissible deterioration state. The method consists practically in determining a critical value for the quantity $\mathrm{Tr}\tilde{\mathbf{D}}$, i.e. $\mathrm{Tr}\tilde{\mathbf{D}}_c$, for which the failure is observed experimentally. From the numerical viewpoint, as $\mathrm{Tr}\tilde{\mathbf{D}}$ reaches the value $\mathrm{Tr}\tilde{\mathbf{D}}_c$ in a finite element, the corresponding element is eroded, allowing for the formation/propagation of a crack.

3.2 Ballistic penetration problem. Numerical simulation

We are now examining the interaction between a fragment simulating projectile (FSP) and a semi-thick target metal plate regarding the engineering problem of ballistic penetration (see DeLuca et al. (1998) and Mahfuz et al. (2000), for applications involving FSP/composite material plate interaction). According to the relative value of the diameter (2R) of the FSP and the thickness (H) of the plate in relation to the FSP length and initial velocity, the expected failure mode of the plate is plugging (see Backman & Goldsmith (1978) and Woodward (1990) for exhaustive review of penetration induced phenomena) which is known to occur as the result of adiabatic shearing process. The penetration is indeed accompanied by the formation of annular adiabatic shear bands. In the case of a projectile harder than the plate, the progressively formed annulus of ASB and further fracture zone has a diameter equal to the initial diameter of the projectile and the failure mode is typically punching. In the case of a projectile and a semi-thick plate with a very close hardness, there is generally formation of a 'first' progressive annulus of ASB with a diameter equal to the initial diameter of the projectile followed by the formation of a 'second' progressive annulus of ASB with a diameter greater than the initial diameter of the projectile. The former, which forms early, does not cross entirely the thickness of the plate and is not responsible for the ultimate failure; the second annulus, which forms later, is due to the radial expansion of the projectile during deformation and is responsible for the ultimate failure. This process

characterizes the failure mode of plugging. This feature constitutes a major criterion that may discriminate various models and related numerical simulations of the penetration process and failure under plugging.
The discrete model used for numerical simulation via LS-DYNA computation code is shown in Fig.5. It is to be noted that no particular zone has been finely meshed because the ASB trajectory is supposed to be unknown. On the other hand, during the numerical simulation, no adaptive mesh refinement has been used.

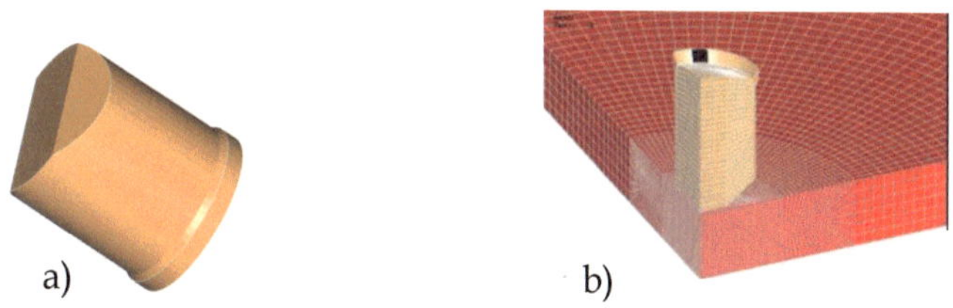

Fig. 5. Geometry and spatial discretization of the FSP and the plate; a) FSP geometry; **b)** Spatial discretization

The hard steel projectile material behaviour is modelled with Johnson and Cook law, see Johnson & Cook (1983), while the hard steel plate behaviour is described via TEVPD model, see Table 1 - the respective materials are different. An erosion criterion in term of critical cumulated plastic strain p_c has been applied to both the projectile and the plate. Concerning the plate a complementary erosion criterion in term of critical ASB-induced degradation state $\mathrm{Tr}\tilde{\mathbf{D}}_c$ has also been applied. The former is indeed very suitable for managing the boundary erosion at the FSP/plate interface at the impact (normal contact) and during the penetration (tangential contact). The latter is used for ASB-induced internal failure.
As mentioned previously, the values of material constants relative to the TEVPD model have been determined from compression and torsion dynamic tests and failure/erosion critical value $\mathrm{Tr}\tilde{\mathbf{D}}_c$ from HSS dynamic shearing tests. For confidentiality reason no value can be given.

$\rho_0 = 7800\ \mathrm{kg/m^3}$	$c_0 = 420\ \mathrm{J/kg.K}$	$E = 200\ \mathrm{GPa}$	$\nu = 0.33$	$\alpha = 1.e\text{-}6\ \mathrm{K^{-1}}$
$R_{int} = 920\ \mathrm{MPa}$	$R_{\infty} = 400\ \mathrm{MPa}$	$k = 10$	$\gamma = 1.1e\text{-}3\ ^{\circ}\mathrm{C^{-1}}$	$Y = 60\ \mathrm{MPa.s^{1/n}}$
$n = 6$	$a = 0$	$b = 15\ \mathrm{GPa}$	$d_1 = 0.05$	$d_2 = 0.05$
$\eta_2 = 0.12\ \mathrm{MPa^{-2}}$	$Z = 19\ \mathrm{MPa.s^{1/m}}$	$m = 2$		

Table 1. Plate material constants for numerical simulation (30 NiCrMo6-6 steel)

Fig.6 shows numerical diagrams of the plate for a configuration with a FSP initial velocity V_{FSP} equal to 95 % of the ballistic limit V_{bpl} (Fig.6a) and for a configuration with a FSP initial velocity V_{FSP} equal to 105% of V_{bpl} (Fig.6b). The numerical simulation including the TEVPD model for the plate is thus able to reproduce the plugging of the plate near the ballistic limit. We are now analysing the process which leads to failure. According to Fig.6 the projectile is subject to large deformation due to very close hardness of the plate and itself. Fig.6a shows two families of deteriorated FE bands: the early ones which are concentrated in an annulus with a diameter close to the initial diameter of the projectile and the late bands which are concentrated in an annulus with a diameter greater than the initial diameter of the projectile. The failure (erosion) following ASB-induced deterioration within the late bands occurs first inside the plate and propagates to the surface forming a macro-crack which leads for a higher velocity to plugging (see Fig.6b) - Mode II like crack propagation.

Fig. 6. Numerical views of the deformed plate ($\mathrm{Tr}\tilde{\mathbf{D}}$) for FSP initial velocity V_{FSP} lower a) and higher b) than the ballistic penetration limit velocity V_{bpl} (H=2R)

In order to evaluate the predictive ability of the model, a series of numerical tests of influence has been carried out. They concern first the influence of some TEVPD model constants, then the influence of the model for the plate, and finally the influence of the mesh size.

Influence of TEVPD model constant k. The first comparative study is devoted to the influence of the isotropic plastic hardening modulus k which appears explicitly in the expression of the isotropic hardening conjugate force r (15) and also in the deterioration incipience criterion (31) via r and its partial derivatives. In the sense that it describes the material hardening kinetics– the greater is k the faster the saturation stress is reached - the instability (and further localization) is anticipated or delayed depending on the magnitude of k. Some numerical simulations have shown that increasing k leads to decreasing of the shear strain at localization onset in the case of dynamic simple shear and to accelerating formation of crossing bands in the case of dynamic shearing of HSS.

According to Fig.7a, showing the deterioration map in the configuration with a low value of k, three families of bands appear. The family 1 is formed early, the family 2 after it and the family 3 ultimately. The family 1 has crossed the plate thickness and provokes a striction at the plate rear. The deformation localizes then in the striction zone while the other families of bands slacken their progression. In the configuration with a higher value for k (see Fig.7b), the families 1 and 2 are group together without crossing the plate thickness while the family 3 propagation is complete and yields to a striction at the plate rear. These two configurations show two types of localized deformation processes depending on the plate material and particularly its hardening ability. This statement shows that the boundary value problem involves both structural and material effects, the latter being less significant in the case of thin plates.

Influence of the model for the plate material. Engineering problems of ballistic penetration are often carried out employing the Johnson and Cook law, see Johnson & Cook (1983), as constitutive model. This application-oriented model describes the combined effects of strain hardening, thermal softening and plastic viscosity, but does not incorporate any anisotropic

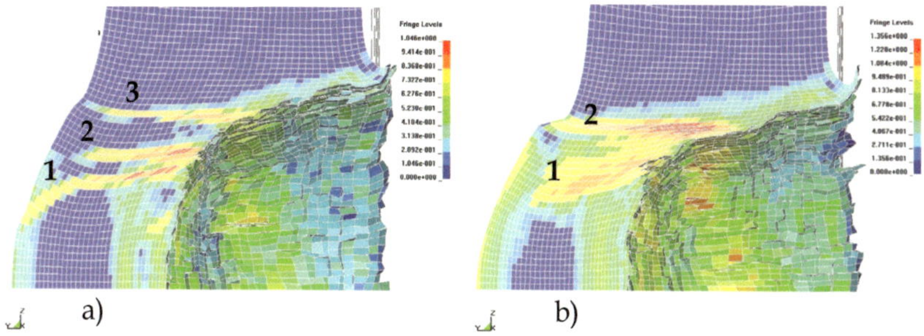

Fig. 7. Influence of the value of the constant k (hardening) of the TEVPD model. Numerical deterioration ($\mathrm{Tr}\tilde{\mathbf{D}}$) map in the configuration with H=2R at the same time for a FSP initial velocity lower than the ballistic limit; a) k=10; b) k=30

deterioration under adiabatic shear banding. To palliate this deficiency in simulation involving the mechanism of localized deformation, the use of Johnson and Cook model necessitates meshing initially very finely the zone in which the band is supposed to propagate, the mesh size being lower than the bandwidth (see e.g. Børvik et al., 2001). This method implies the *a priori* knowledge of the band trajectory because usually it is not envisioned to mesh finely the whole structure. It may lead to favour the deformation localization in the finely meshed zone to the detriment of other potential propagation areas. An alternative method consists in using an adaptive mesh refinement technique (see e.g. Camacho & Ortiz, 1997) which remains nevertheless still costly in term of computation. Supposing this limitation overcome, the phenomenon of adiabatic shear banding generates in the concerned finite elements very high strain rates (10^5-10^6 s^{-1}), in any way much greater than the strain rates involved in the mechanical tests for the model constants identification. In this sense the material behaviour in the ASB affected FE is *de facto* uncorrectly described.

In the methodology proposed in this paper the finite element must contain the band, remind the scale postulate $\ell > \lambda$ put forward in Sect.2 and commented further. In other words, the bandwidth must be lower than the mesh size. Satisfying this condition, a simulation with Johnson and Cook law and a simulation with the TEVPD model for the metal plate have been performed. Corresponding numerical results for a FSP initial velocity lower than the ballistic limit are shown in Fig.8. According to Fig.8a, the simulation with Johnson and Cook model does not show any localization area at the time considered. On the contrary the simulation with the TEVPD model, Fig.8b, reveals at the same time a band of localized deformation which propagates through the thickness of the plate and produces some striction at the plate rear. This is clearly the consequence of the incorporation of ASB induced deterioration together with the specific scale postulate in the TEVPD model.

Influence of the mesh size. The last part of this section deals with the influence of the mesh size which is the restrictive point for numerical simulations in the presence of localization phenomena. One should insist here once more on the scale postulate put forward as the TEVPD modelling premise. Its consequence is that the band must be embedded in the finite element. This point, regarding standard simulation requiring dense meshing (at least locally), does not mean that any mesh size is suitable. The scale postulate comes to be fairly satisfied in practice for a mesh size about 5 times the material bandwidth, i.e. for a steel considered here, for about 500 μm and more. This is the case for the configuration in Fig.9a. The configuration in Fig.9b for a coarse meshing shows an expanded area of deteriorated finite elements. This discrepancy is also induced by a rough treatment of the contact FSP/plate interaction and not only by localization effects.

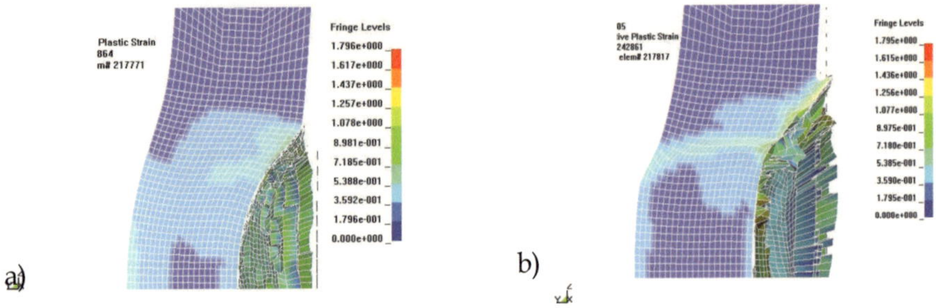

Fig. 8. Plastic deformation (p) map in the configuration with H=R at the same time for a FSP initial velocity lower than the ballistic limit; a) Johnson-Cook model; b) TEVPD model

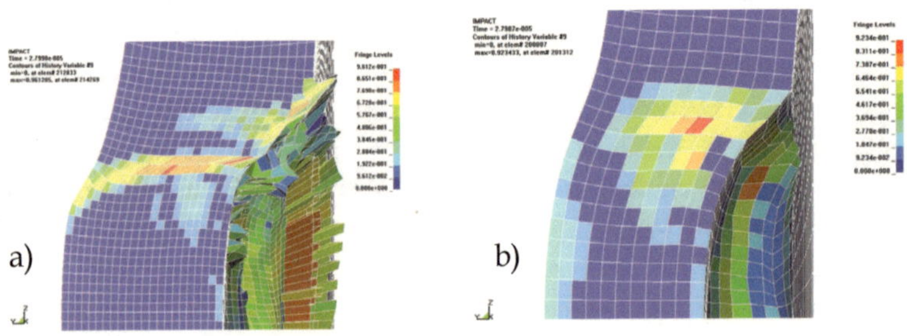

Fig. 9. Numerical deterioration ($\mathrm{Tr}\tilde{\mathbf{D}}$) map in the configuration with H=R at the same time for a FSP initial velocity lower than the ballistic limit; a) a=0.5mm; b) a=1mm

4. Evaluation of the inelastic heat fraction in the context of microstructure-supported dynamic plasticity modelling

4.1 Basic concepts and unified approach

Under dynamic adiabatic conditions the plastic work is known to dissipate into heat and inducing thermal softening. From both theoretical and numerical viewpoints the proportion of effectively dissipated plastic work is commonly evaluated using the so-called Taylor-Quinney coefficient (Taylor & Quinney, 1934) usually assumed to be a constant empirical value. On the other hand experimental investigations have shown its dependence on strain, strain rate and temperature.

A methodology combining dislocation theory in the domain of thermally activated inelastic deformation mechanisms and internal variable approach applied to thermo-elastic/viscoplastic behaviour is developed allowing for obtaining a physically based inelastic heat fraction expression. The latter involves explicitly the combined influence of the parameters mentioned above and highly evolving nature of the inelastic heat fraction.

This section aims at reconciling two main methodologies of modelling, namely the physically based, i.e. dislocation kinetics related formalism and the phenomenological one. In a first sub section the former is briefly applied to plastic deformation mechanisms controlled by thermal activation in the cases of fcc and bcc materials. Afterwards the irreversible thermodynamics related internal variable procedure is considered regarding thermo-elastic/viscoplastic materials. In the last sub section a unified approach is employed in which the dislocation interaction mechanisms based modelling is incorporated in the formalism of standard generalized materials.

Dislocation mechanics based modelling. The following modelling is devoted to metallic materials which deform plastically under dislocation motion and accumulation/ annihilation mechanisms. It refers explicitly to the concept of thermally controlled mechanisms. In the range of strain rate (high enough to consider the deformation mechanisms as thermally activated but low enough to exclude the phonon drag phenomenon) and temperature considered, the resistance to dislocation motion is supposed to be due to two kinds of obstacles: long-range barriers typically formed by grain boundaries and other far-field influent microstructural elements relative to a rate and temperature independent stress (athermal stress), and short-range barriers formed by disoriented dislocations and other point defects relative to a rate and temperature dependent stress (thermal/viscous stress). According to this framework, the flow stress τ may be decomposed into an athermal contribution τ_a and a thermal/viscous contribution τ_{th} as follows:

$$\tau = \tau_a\left(\gamma^P\right) + \tau_{th}\left(\gamma^P, \dot{\gamma}^P, T\right) \tag{32}$$

where γ^P represents the plastic strain, $\dot{\gamma}^P$ the plastic strain rate and T absolute temperature. The athermal stress τ_a reflects the influence of the presence of solute, original dislocation density and grain size (the material state considered here is not the virgin one if the material was submitted to thermo-mechanical treatments) through a constant contribution τ_0 and the accumulation of dislocation through a hardening contribution $\bar{\tau}$. Assuming a bounded dislocation density at large deformation, the hardening stress is supposed to saturate, following Voce's form:

$$\tau_a\left(\gamma^P\right) = \tau_0 + \bar{\tau}\left(\gamma^P\right); \ \bar{\tau}\left(\gamma^P\right) = \tau_\infty\left[1 - \exp\left(-b\gamma^P\right)\right] \tag{33}$$

where τ_∞ represents the maximum hardening stress and b a material constant characterizing the hardening kinetics.

According to Orowan's law in the context of thermally activated inelastic mechanisms, the plastic strain is assumed in the following Arrhenius form, where the constant pre-exponential term $\dot{\gamma}_0$ is notably related to mobile dislocation density and obstacle overcoming frequency, k represents the Boltzmann constant and ΔG the activation energy or energetic barrier needed for dislocation to overcome:

$$\dot{\gamma}^P = \dot{\gamma}_0 \exp\left(-\frac{\Delta G}{kT}\right) \ ; \ \Delta G = G_0\left[1 - \left\langle\frac{\tau_{th}}{\hat{\tau}}\right\rangle^w\right]^q \tag{34}$$

where the total energy G_0 is related to the material strain-rate sensitivity via the activation volume, $\hat{\tau}$ the maximum glide resistance, and w and q express the statistical shape of the obstacle profile. According to (34), one obtains

$$\dot{\gamma}^P = \dot{\gamma}_0 \exp\left\{-\frac{G_0}{kT}\left[1 - \left\langle\frac{\tau_{th}}{\hat{\tau}}\right\rangle^w\right]^q\right\} \ ; \ \tau_{th} = \hat{\tau}\left\{1 - \left[-\frac{kT}{G_0}\ln\left\langle\frac{\dot{\gamma}^P}{\dot{\gamma}_0}\right\rangle\right]^{1/q}\right\}^{1/w} \tag{35}$$

In the case of bcc materials, the maximum glide resistance $\hat{\tau}$ is assumed to be a constant, i.e. $\hat{\tau} = \hat{\tau}_0$, yielding the following form for the total flow stress:

$$\tau = \tau_0 + \tau_\infty\left[1 - \exp\left(-b\gamma^p\right)\right] + \hat{\tau}_0\left\{1 - \left[-\frac{kT}{G_0}\ln\left\langle\frac{\dot{\gamma}^p}{\dot{\gamma}_0}\right\rangle\right]^{1/q}\right\}^{1/w} \tag{36}$$

This expression for the bcc material flow stress reflects experimental observations showing that, for isothermal processes, the apparent strain hardening $d\tau / d\gamma^p$ is neither affected by strain rate at a given initial temperature nor by initial temperature at a given strain rate. This explains the additive decomposition of the flow stress into separated strain hardening contribution and thermal/viscous contribution (see Zerilli & Armstrong, 1987, and Voyiadjis & Abed, 2006).
In the case of fcc materials, the maximum glide resistance is assumed to involve the former athermal stress contribution affected by temperature. Let us consider the following expression corresponding to a simplification of other more complex forms available in literature (see, e.g. Nemat-Nasser & Li, 1998):

$$\hat{\tau} = \left[\tau_0 + \bar{\tau}(\gamma)\right]a(T) \; ; \; a(T) = 1 - \left(\frac{T}{T_m}\right)^2 \tag{37}$$

According to (32), (33), $(35)_2$ and (37) the total flow stress for fcc material is thus given by

$$\tau = \left\{\tau_0 + \tau_\infty\left[1 - \exp\left(-b\gamma^p\right)\right]\right\}\left[1 + \left[1 - \left(\frac{T}{T_m}\right)^2\right]\left\{1 - \left[-\frac{kT}{G_0}\ln\left\langle\frac{\dot{\gamma}^p}{\dot{\gamma}_0}\right\rangle\right]^{1/q}\right\}^{1/w}\right] \tag{38}$$

Contrarily to bcc materials, the flow stress for fcc materials is known to combine multiplicatively the influence of both strain hardening and thermal/viscous contributions (see Zerilli & Armstrong, 1987, and Voyiadjis & Abed, 2005). This feature is respected in expression (38).
Thermodynamic framework. Following irreversible thermodynamics framework detailed in Sect.2.3, the instantaneous state of the material is supposed to be described via the free energy $\tilde{\psi} = \rho\psi$, with $\tilde{\psi}\left(T;\mathbf{e}^e,p\right)$, such that

$$\dot{\tilde{\psi}} = \frac{\partial\tilde{\psi}}{\partial T}\dot{T} + \frac{\partial\tilde{\psi}}{\partial\mathbf{e}^e} : \mathbf{d}^e + \frac{\partial\tilde{\psi}}{\partial p}\dot{p} = -\tilde{s}\dot{T} + \boldsymbol{\sigma} : \mathbf{d}^e + r\dot{p} \; ; \; \tilde{s} = -\frac{\partial\tilde{\psi}}{\partial T} ; \; \boldsymbol{\sigma} = \frac{\partial\tilde{\psi}}{\partial\mathbf{e}^e} \; ; \; r = \frac{\partial\tilde{\psi}}{\partial p} \tag{39}$$

where $\mathbf{d}^e = \overset{\nabla}{\mathbf{e}^e} = \dot{\mathbf{e}}^e - \boldsymbol{\omega}\mathbf{e}^e + \mathbf{e}^e\boldsymbol{\omega}$, ∇ representing the objective Jaumann derivative of a 2nd order tensor and $\boldsymbol{\omega} = \left[\mathbf{L}\right]^{AS}$ the spin. According to the second principle of thermodynamics intrinsic mechanical dissipation is written as

$$D_{int} = \boldsymbol{\sigma} : \mathbf{d}^p - r\dot{p} \geq 0 \tag{40}$$

where $\boldsymbol{\sigma} : \mathbf{d}^p$ represents the plastic part of the mechanical work rate and $r\dot{p}$ the stored energy rate. Combining (39) with the first law of thermodynamics and assuming that r is independent of temperature (see $(44)_2$ below) lead to the following form for the heat equation:

$$\tilde{c}_y \dot{T} + \mathrm{div}\mathbf{Q} - R = T\frac{\partial \boldsymbol{\sigma}}{\partial T} : \mathbf{d}^e + \boldsymbol{\sigma} : \mathbf{d}^p - r\dot{p} \tag{41}$$

where $\tilde{c}_y$ $\left(\tilde{c}_y = -T\partial^2\tilde{\psi} / \partial T^2\right)$ represents the heat capacity per unit mass at fixed y, $y = \left(\mathbf{e}^e, p\right)$, $\mathbf{Q}$ heat flux vector per unit surface and R heat supply per unit volume. The context considered herein concerns loading at high strain rate excluding heat supply and for which conditions can be assumed as adiabatic. Relation (41) above is thus reduced to

$$\tilde{c}_y \dot{T} = T\frac{\partial \boldsymbol{\sigma}}{\partial T} : \mathbf{d}^e + \boldsymbol{\sigma} : \mathbf{d}^p - r\dot{p} = D_{int} + T\frac{\partial \boldsymbol{\sigma}}{\partial T} : \mathbf{d}^e \tag{42}$$

where $T\left(\partial\boldsymbol{\sigma} / \partial T\right) : \mathbf{d}^e$ represents the thermo-elastic coupling contribution. Considering that $D_{int} \geq 0$ and $T\left(\partial\boldsymbol{\sigma} / \partial T\right) : \mathbf{d}^e \leq 0$ for tensile loading (implying cooling) or $T\left(\partial\boldsymbol{\sigma} / \partial T\right) : \mathbf{d}^e \geq 0$ for compressive loading (implying heating), thermo-elastic and thermo-viscoplastic mechanisms act in an opposite or like way regarding temperature rise.
According to the aforementioned assumptions, the free energy $\tilde{\psi}\left(T;\mathbf{e}^e, p\right)$ is now expressed in the following form:

$$\tilde{\psi}\left(T;\mathbf{e}^e,p\right) = \frac{\lambda}{2}\left(\mathrm{Tr}\mathbf{e}^e\right)^2 + \mu\mathbf{e}^e : \mathbf{e}^e - \alpha K \mathrm{Tr}\mathbf{e}^e \vartheta - \tilde{c}_0\left[T\ln\left(\frac{T}{T_0}\right) - \vartheta\right] + h(p) - h(0) \tag{43}$$

where the heat capacity $\tilde{c}_y$ is supposed to have a constant value, i.e. $\tilde{c}_y = \tilde{c}_0$, and where $h(p)$ represents the stored energy of cold work as a function of strain hardening variable. After partial derivation of (43) with respect to state variables, the thermodynamic forces are

$$\boldsymbol{\sigma} = \left(\lambda \mathrm{Tr}\mathbf{e}^e - \alpha K\vartheta\right)\boldsymbol{\delta} + 2\mu\mathbf{e}^e \; ; \; r = h'(p) \; ; \; \tilde{s} = \alpha K \mathrm{Tr}\mathbf{e}^e + \tilde{c}_0 \ln\left(T / T_0\right) \tag{44}$$

The dissipation potential is assumed of the Perzyna's type, i.e. $\phi(\boldsymbol{\sigma}, r) = \phi(\langle F(\boldsymbol{\sigma}, r)\rangle)$. The viscoplastic multiplier Λ^P and the yield function F are assumed as

$$\Lambda^P = \frac{\partial\phi}{\partial F} = H\left(\langle F(\boldsymbol{\sigma}, r)\rangle\right) \geq 0 \; ; \; F(\boldsymbol{\sigma}, r) = J_2(\boldsymbol{\sigma}) - g(r) \; ; \; J_2(\boldsymbol{\sigma}) = \sqrt{\frac{3}{2}\mathbf{s}:\mathbf{s}} \; ; \; \mathbf{s} = \boldsymbol{\sigma} - \frac{\mathrm{Tr}\boldsymbol{\sigma}}{3}\boldsymbol{\delta} \tag{45}$$

where H is a function of the yield surface F. The strain hardening function g(r) in (45) represents the von Mises surface radius. It is assumed in the form

$$g(r) = R_0 + r(p) \tag{46}$$

It includes the first term R_0 independent of strain hardening and the isotropic hardening force r as the second term. The quantity R_0 accounts for residual stresses potentially induced by the previous thermo-mechanical history of the material. Assuming normality rule, evolution laws are expressed by

$$\mathbf{d}^p = \frac{3}{2}\Lambda^p \frac{\mathbf{s}}{J_2(\boldsymbol{\sigma})} \; ; \; \dot{p} = \Lambda^p \tag{47}$$

Inverting $(45)_1$ and using $(45)_2$ and (46) yield

$$J_2 = R_0 + r(p) + \Phi(p,\dot{p},T) \; ; \; \Phi = H^{-1} \tag{48}$$

The rate of plastic work $\boldsymbol{\sigma}:\mathbf{d}^p$ and the dissipation in (40) are thus given by

$$\boldsymbol{\sigma}:\mathbf{d}^p = J_2\dot{p} = \left[R_0 + r(p) + \Phi(p,\dot{p},T)\right]\dot{p} \; ; \; D_{int} = \left[R_0 + \Phi\right]\dot{p} \geq 0 \tag{49}$$

Dislocation mechanics-irreversible thermodynamics unified approach. The concepts of thermally activated processes developed previously are now incorporated in the internal variable procedure formalism (see also Voyiadjis & Abed, 2006). The first step consists in unifying the notations. The corresponding terms are reported in Table 2. The following yield function describing athermal processes is also assumed (see Eqs. (32)(33) and $(45)_2$(46)):

$$F(\tau,\bar{\tau}) = \tau - (\tau_0 + \bar{\tau}) = F(\boldsymbol{\sigma},R) = J_2(\boldsymbol{\sigma}) - (R_0 + r) \tag{50}$$

Noting that $\tau_{th}(\gamma,\dot{\gamma},T) = \tau - \tau_a(\gamma) = F(\tau,\bar{\tau}) \geq 0$ stands for viscoplastic yielding, expression $(35)_1$ is converted into

$$\dot{p} = \dot{p}_0 \exp\left\{-\frac{G_0}{kT}\left[1 - \left\langle\frac{F(\boldsymbol{\sigma},R)}{\hat{\tau}}\right\rangle^w\right]^q\right\} = H\left\langle F(\boldsymbol{\sigma},R)\right\rangle \tag{51}$$

Expression (48) has to be compared to the following one obtained from Eqs. (32) and (33):

$$\tau = \tau_0 + \bar{\tau}(\gamma^p) + \tau_{th}(\gamma^p,\dot{\gamma}^p,T) \tag{52}$$

Dislocation mechanics	Internal variable procedure
γ^p	p
$\dot{\gamma}^p$	$\dot{p}$
τ	J_2
$\tau_a(\gamma^p) = \tau_0 + \bar{\tau}(\gamma^p)$	$g(p) = R_0 + r(p)$
τ_0	R_0
$\bar{\tau}(\gamma^p) = \tau_\infty\left[1 - \exp(-b\gamma^p)\right]$	$r(p) = R_\infty\left[1 - \exp(-bp)\right]$
$\tau_{th}(\gamma,\dot{\gamma},T)$	$\Phi(p,\dot{p},T)$
τ_∞	R_∞

Table 2. Corresponding terms for dislocation mechanics-irreversible thermodynamics unified approach

4.2 Application for fcc and bcc materials: evolving character of the inelastic heat fraction

According to the dislocation mechanics-irreversible thermodynamics unified viscoplasticity approach developed previously, this section aims at showing the influence of the modelling regarding the evolution of the inelastic heat fraction and related temperature rise. Actually it is shown that, from the thermodynamic viewpoint, the inelastic heat fraction rate is strongly dependent on the strain hardening/softening rate. Fcc and bcc materials are modelled and the inelastic heat fraction is deduced in both cases. Its evolution is analysed considering a simple shear loading.

General expression for the inelastic heat fraction. In the following the effects of strain hardening, thermal softening and viscosity on stress/strain behaviour, temperature rise and inelastic heat fraction are studied. Thermo-elastic coupling contribution to temperature rise is actually particularly significant in problems involving very high velocity impact and/or high pressure shock loading. In the context of this work, velocity and pressure are considered moderately high and thermo-elastic coupling is neglected. Heat equation in (42) is thus reduced to

$$\tilde{c}_0 \dot{T} = D_{int} \tag{53}$$

Starting from the definition of the inelastic heat fraction β as $\beta = \tilde{c}_0 \dot{T} / \boldsymbol{\sigma} : \mathbf{d}^p$, the following expression is deduced:

$$\beta = 1 - \frac{r\dot{p}}{\boldsymbol{\sigma} : \mathbf{d}^p} \tag{54}$$

Accounting for Eq. $(49)_1$, relations (53) and (54) become

$$\dot{T} = \frac{1}{\tilde{c}_0}[J_2 - r]\dot{p} = \frac{R_0 + \Phi(p,\dot{p},T)}{\tilde{c}_0}\dot{p} \ ; \ \beta = 1 - \frac{r}{J_2} = 1 - \frac{h'(p)}{R_0 + h'(p) + \Phi(p,\dot{p},T)} \tag{55}$$

Consequently, the inelastic heat fraction β appears explicitly as a function of thermal/athermal hardening/softening and viscosity mechanisms via $\Phi(p,\dot{p},T)$ and $h'(p)$ and of the prior plastic deformation history via R_0. The form $(55)_2$ highlights the evolving nature of β with temperature, strain and strain rate evolution. On this basis further remarks can be made as follows.

Remark 1. Under the modelling assumption, for plastic strain $p_2 > p_1$ close enough to consider that $T_1 \approx T_2 \approx T$, one can write from (55):

$$\beta(p_2,\dot{p},T) - \beta(p_1,\dot{p},T) \approx -[h'(p_2) - h'(p_1)]\frac{1}{R_0 + h'(p) + \Phi(p,\dot{p},T)} \tag{56}$$

Using the notation $\chi = \frac{1}{R_0 + h'(p) + \Phi(p,\dot{p},T)}$, with $\chi \geq 0$, relation (56) is reduced to

$$\frac{\partial \beta}{\partial p} \approx -\chi h''(p) \tag{57}$$

According to (57), it is possible to conclude that for material exhibiting strain hardening ($h''(p) > 0$), the inelastic heat fraction is decreasing with increasing strain, i.e. $\frac{\partial \beta}{\partial p} < 0$. On the contrary, for material exhibiting strain softening ($h''(p) < 0$), the inelastic heat fraction is increasing with increasing strain, i.e. $\frac{\partial \beta}{\partial p} > 0$.

Remark 2. According to $(55)_2$, $\beta(p,\dot{p},T)$ is equal to unity when $h'(p)=0$ which is satisfied for a perfectly plastic material (no strain hardening).

Application to fcc and bcc materials. The unified approach is now applied to fcc and bcc materials in the case of simple shearing such that $L_{ij}=\partial v_i/\partial x_j=0$ except $L_{12}=\partial v_1/\partial x_2=\dot{\Gamma}\neq 0$. Material constants used for numerical simulations have been identified to reproduce Copper type material behaviour (see Voyiadjis & Abed, 2005, for experimental results) and Tantalum type material (see Voyiadjis & Abed, 2006, for experimental results) and are reported in Table 3.

	Copper (fcc)	Tantalum (bcc)
E (GPa)	120	170
ν	0.33	0.34
ρ_0 (kg/m³)	8930	16600
c_0 (J/kg.K)	380	140
T_m (K)	1350	3300
w	1/2	1/2
q	3/2	3/2
k/G_0 (K^{-1})	4.9E-5	8E-5
$\dot{p}_0$ (s^{-1})	1E10	1E9
R_0 (MPa)	100	100
R_∞ (MPa)	300	100
b	10	5
$\hat{\tau}_0$ (MPa)	X	1700

Table 3. Material constants for simple shearing simulation

The numerical evolution of stress invariant J_2, temperature T and inelastic heat fraction β is given versus shear strain $e_{12}=\gamma_{12}/2$ (the strain tensor $\mathbf{e}$ is obtained by time integration of the non objective strain rate tensor $\dot{\mathbf{e}}$, with $\dot{\mathbf{e}}=\mathbf{d}+\boldsymbol{\omega}\mathbf{e}-\mathbf{e}\boldsymbol{\omega}$) for various strain rates and initial temperatures considering Copper behaviour model in Fig.10 and Tantalum behaviour model in Fig.11. Adiabatic conditions are assumed for strain rates higher than 100 s^{-1}.

Figs.10a-11a show the increase of the flow stress with the increase of the strain rate whereas Figs.10d-11d show the increase of the flow stress with the decrease of the initial temperature. Fig.11a shows also the thermal softening induced in the flow stress of Tantalum while thermal softening is not significant in Fig.10a concerning Copper.

Values of numerical temperature in Fig.11b are very similar to those measured by (Kapoor & Nemat-Nasser, 1998) on Ta-2.5%W alloy under dynamic compression.

According to Figs.10c-10f and 11c-11f initial value of β is equal to 1 whatever the strain rate and the initial temperature. At large strain β converges to a value which depends on strain rate and initial temperature with a rate (negative according to remark 1) whose absolute value increases with decreasing strain rate and increasing initial temperature. The value for β at convergence is much smaller for Copper than for Tantalum.

Recent experimental investigations using fast response infrared optical device devoted to the measurement of heating during dynamic loading on Aluminium alloy (fcc) and steel (bcc) have shown that the inelastic heat fraction decreases with increasing strain (see respectively Lerch at al., 2003, and Jovic et al., 2006). Unfortunately, time resolved data obtained with this type of reliable device are missing concerning Copper and Tantalum.

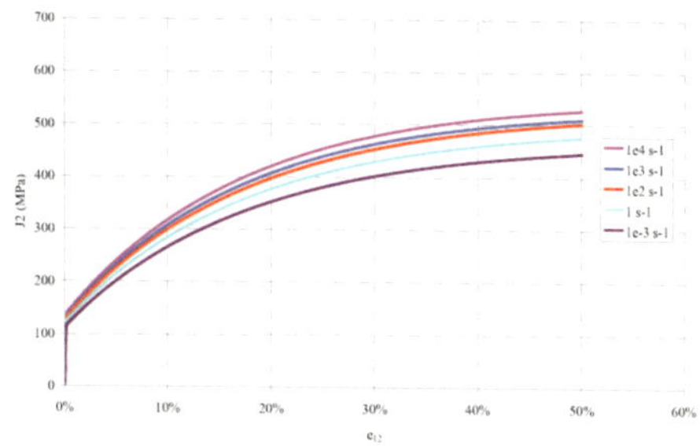

a) Stress invariant J_2 vs. strain e_{12} - T_0=300K

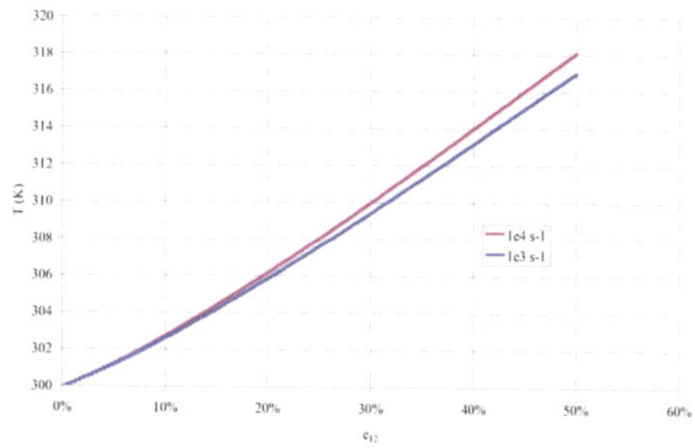

b) Temperature T vs. strain e_{12} - T_0=300K

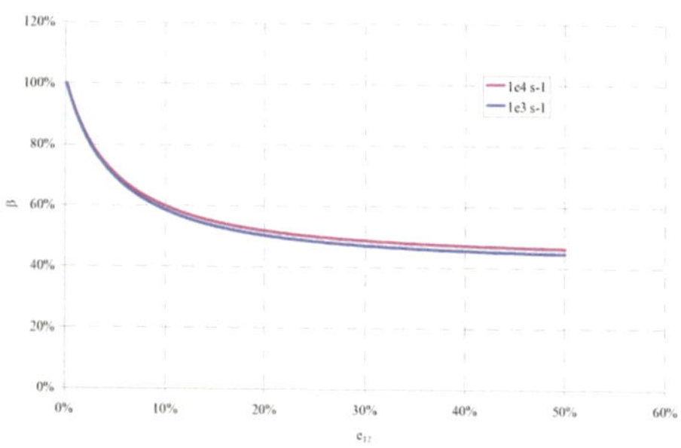

c) Inelastic heat fraction β vs. strain e_{12} - T_0=300K

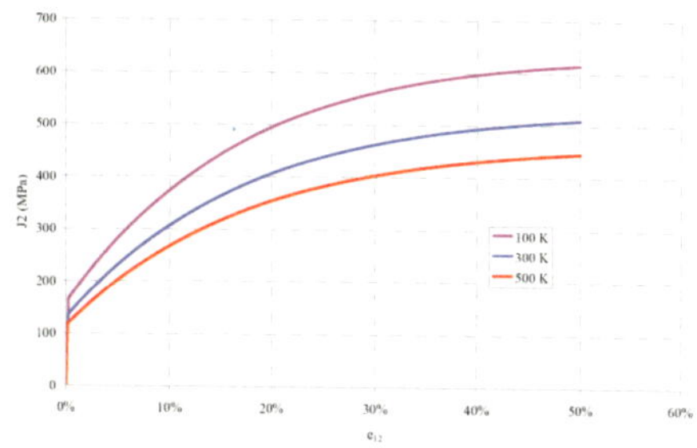

d) Stress invariant J_2 vs. strain e_{12} - $\dot{\Gamma}$ =1000s^{-1}

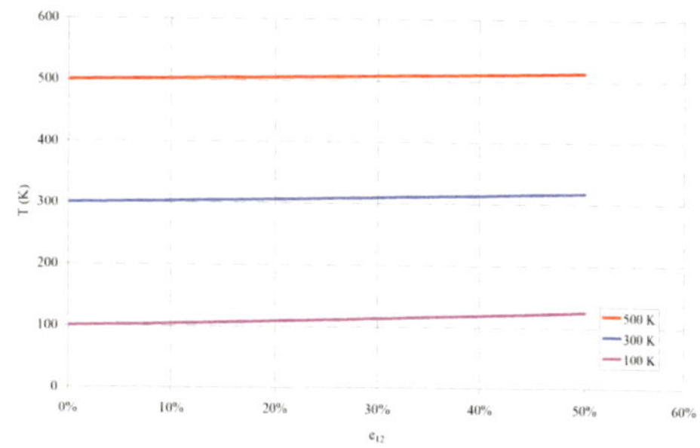

e) Temperature T vs. strain e_{12} - $\dot{\Gamma}$ =1000s^{-1}

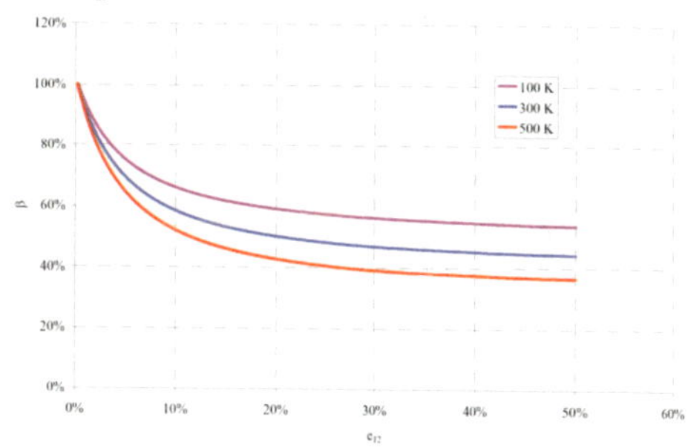

f) Inelastic heat fraction β vs. strain e_{12} - $\dot{\Gamma}$ =1000s^{-1}

Fig. 10. Influence of shear strain rate and initial temperature on stress invariant and inelastic heat fraction. Adiabatic conditions are assumed for strain rates higher than 100 s^{-1}. Copper (fcc material).

5. Concluding remarks

The thermo-elastic/viscoplastic constitutive model, incorporating thermomechanical softening, ASB-induced degradation and anisotropy in the finite deformation framework, has the form favouring its adaptation for a large spectrum of metals and alloys susceptible to develop the ASB-related mechanism of deformation and failure under dynamic loading. As in any purpose-built constitutive model, some simplifications are introduced in the

model presented. They concern notably the strain hardening – limited to the isotropic one –, and the absence of the strain rate memory. However, the approach advanced brings in several novel potentialities. The principal one consists in the manner to account for ASB feedback effects, i.e. additional softening expressed via the strain hardening affinity (thermodynamic force) and furthermore in the manner to account for the ASB-induced plastic anisotropy in the yield function. At the same time, with regard to the absence of consensus concerning large elastic-plastic deformation including induced anisotropy, the particular kinematics developed in the model, based on the analogy between a band cluster and a macrodislocation, constitutes a physically motivated way (for the scale level considered) for a reasonable global description of thermomechanical consequences of ASB.
The model describes indeed most of salient effects while its modelling scale is based on a RVE much larger than the order of magnitude proper for the band's width. The deterioration internal variable introduced herein and its evolution capture principal singular features, notably the singular temperature growth, see also (Longère et al., 2005), where singular heating effects are quantified for a particular shock event. Another advantage concerns the three-dimensional formulation of the model, while many ASB-related studies and models regard fine description mostly limited to one-dimensional insight.
From the numerical standpoint (which is outlined here in the context of the application presented for a particular shock configuration for a ballistic penetration problem), there is no need to know *a priori* the band trajectory neither to refine finite element meshing for areas crossed by bands. For the ballistic penetration problem dealt with, the complex ASB-induced deterioration history is shown via numerical simulations presented. The plugging failure pattern is correctly issued, in accordance with projectile/plate geometry and shock configuration. Prospectively, there is a need to proceed with further numerical simulations for loading cases involving rotating principal stress directions and curved bands as observed, for example, in the experiments of Nesterenko et al. (1998). Thanks to the regularizing effects produced by material scale postulate, the double viscosity (viscoplasticity and viscous ASB-degradation), and an adaptive time step procedure, only slight mesh size dependence is observed in the post-localization (softening dominated) stages.
Regarding inelastic heat fraction study, a unified approach combining both concepts of dislocation mechanisms controlled by thermal activation and internal variable viscoplasticity for macroscopic modelling is considered in the present work. It is applied to strain, strain rate and temperature dependent metallic material behaviour in a range covering low velocity to moderately dynamic loading. Following the internal variable procedure and assuming the existence of thermodynamic potentials (free energy and dissipation potential), a consistent expression for the inelastic heat fraction is obtained. The corresponding form involves explicitly the influence of strain, strain rate and temperature as observed experimentally, and allows concluding that for a strain hardening model the inelastic heat fraction is decreasing with increasing strain. These theoretical results show the influence of the pertinent modelling – in terms of strain hardening/softening, thermal softening and strain rate dependence – on the inelastic heat fraction form and its highly evolving nature, notably for larger strain. Some models are actually intrinsically able to reproduce observed phenomena, pointedly the temperature rise induced by plastic deformation under adiabatic conditions, while others are not. The interest of satisfactory quantification of temperature rise in dynamic plasticity is evident. As shown e.g. by

Klepaczko & Resaig (1996), for adiabatic shear banding involving strain rates of about 10^5 s^{-1}, the increase in temperature for a class of bcc metals is close to the melting point.

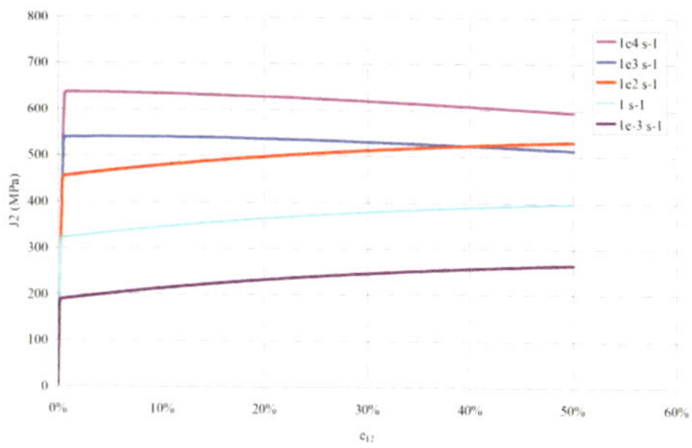

a) Stress invariant J_2 vs. strain e_{12} - T_0=300K

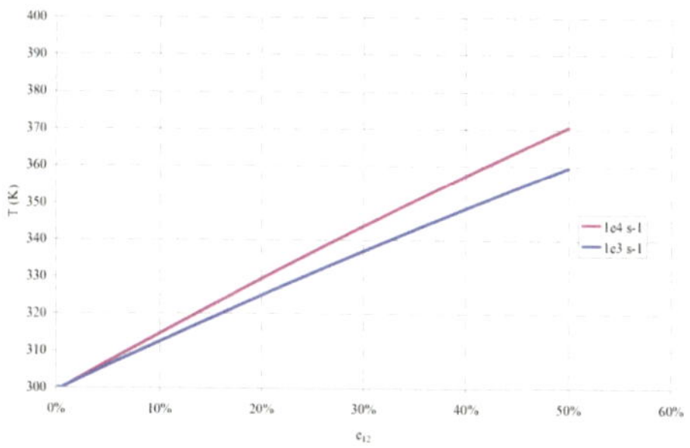

b) Temperature T vs. strain e_{12} - T_0=300K

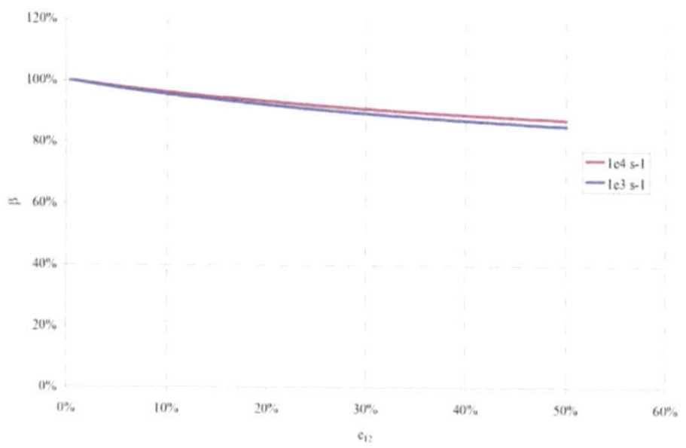

c) Inelastic heat fraction β vs. strain e_{12} - T_0=300 K

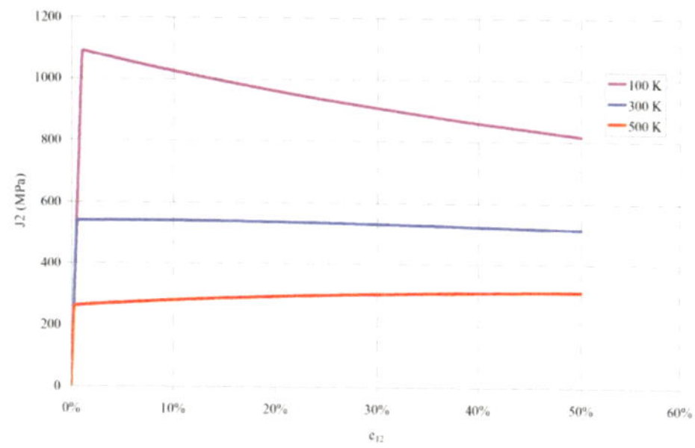

d) Stress invariant J_2 vs. strain e_{12} - $\dot{\Gamma}$ =1000 s^{-1}

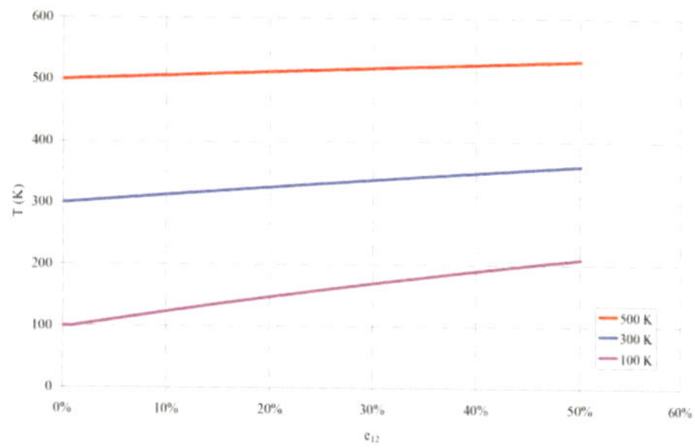

e) Temperature T vs. strain e_{12} - $\dot{\Gamma}$ =1000 s^{-1}

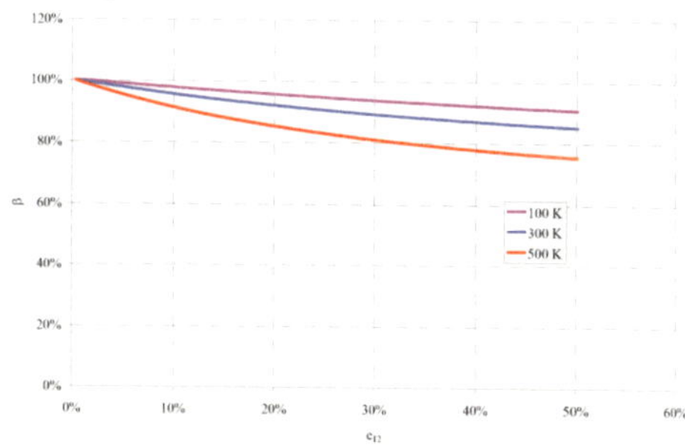

f) Inelastic heat fraction β vs. strain e_{12} - $\dot{\Gamma}$ =1000 s^{-1}

Fig. 11. Influence of shear strain rate and initial temperature on stress invariant and inelastic heat fraction. Adiabatic conditions are assumed for strain rates higher than 100 s^{-1}. Tantalum (bcc material)

6. References

Abu Al-Rub R.K. and Voyiadjis G.Z., 2006, A finite strain plastic-damage model for high velocity impact using combined viscosity and gradient localization limiters: Part I-Theoretical formulation, Int. J. Damage Mech., 15, 4, pp.293-334.

Aravas N., Kim K.S., Leckie F.A., 1990, On the calculations of the stored energy of cold work, J. Eng. Mat. Tech. (ASME), 112, pp.465-470.

Backman M.E. and Goldsmith W., 1978, The mechanics of penetration of projectiles into targets, Int. J. Engng Sci., 16, pp.1-99.

Bai Y.L., 1982, Thermo-plastic instability in simple shear, J. Mech. Phys. Solids, 30, 4, pp.195-207.

Bai Y.L. and Dodd B., 1992,.Adiabatic shear localisation, Oxford : Pergamon Press

Bataille J. and Kestin J., 1975, L'interprétation physique de la thermodynamique rationnelle, J. de Mécanique, 14, 2, pp.365-384.

Batra R.C. and Lear M.H., 2005, Adiabatic shear banding in plane strain tensile deformations of 11 thermoelastoviscoplastic materials with finite thermal wave speed, Int. J. Plast., 21, pp.1521-1545.

Børvik T., Hopperstad O.S., Berstad T. and Langseth M., 2001, Numerical simulation of plugging failure in ballistic penetration, Int. J. Solids Structures, 38, pp. 6241-6264.

Bronkhorst C.A., Cerreta E.K., Xue Q., Maudlin P.J., Mason T.A. and Gray III G.T., 2006, An experimental and numerical study of the localization behavior of tantalum and stainless steel, Int. J. Plast., 22, pp.1304-1335.

Burns T.J. and Davies M.A., 2002, On repeated adiabatic shear band formation during high speed machining, Int. J. Plast., 18, pp.487-506.

Camacho G.T. and Ortiz M., 1997, Adaptive Lagrangian modelling of ballistic penetration of metallic targets, Comput. Methods Appl. Mech. Engng, 142, pp.269-301.

Clifton R.J, Duffy J., Hartley K.A. and Shawki T.G., 1984, On critical conditions for shear band formation at high strain rates, Scripta Met., 18, pp.443-448.

Coleman B.D. and Gurtin M.E., 1967, Thermodynamics with internal state variables, J. Chem.-Phys., 47, pp.597-613.

Couque H., 2003a, A hydrodynamic hat specimen to investigate pressure and strain rate dependence on adiabatic shear band formation, J. Phys. IV, 110, pp.423-428.

Couque H., 2003b, Essais chapeau hydrodynamique d'un acier, GIAT Industries, Technical note DSAM/DT/MCP/3050.13.03C.

DeLuca E., Prifti J., Betheney W. and Chou S.C., 1998, Ballistic impact damage of S 2-glass-reinforced plastic structural armor, Composites Sc. Tech., 58, pp. 1453-1461.

Johnson G.R. and Cook W.H., 1983, A constitutive model and data for metals subjected to large strains, high strain rates and high temperatures, in Proceedings of the Seventh International Symposium on Ballistics, The Hague, The Netherlands, pp.541-547.

Jovic C., Wagner D., Hervé P., Gary G. and Lazzarotto L., 2006, Mechanical behaviour and temperature measurement during dynamic deformation on split Hopkinson bar of 304L stainless steel and 5754 aluminium alloy J. Phys. IV, 134, pp.1279-1285.

Kapoor R. and Nemat-Nasser S., 1998, Determination of temperature rise during high strain rate deformation, Mech. Mat., 27, pp.1-12.

Klepaczko J.R., 1994, Some results and new experimental technique in studies of adiabatic shear bands, Arch. Mech., 46, pp.201-229.

Klepaczko J.R. and Resaig B., 1996, A numerical study of adiabatic shear banding in mild steel by dislocation mechanics based constitutive relations, Mech. Mat., 24, pp.125-139.

Kulkarni M., Belytschko T. and Bayliss A., 1995, Stability and error analysis for time integrators applied to strain-softening materials, Comput. Methods Appl. Mech. Engng, 124, pp.335-363.

Lerch V., Gary G. and Hervé P., 2003, Thermomechanical properties of polycarbonate under dynamic loading, J. Phys. IV, 110, pp.159-164.

Liao S-C. and Duffy J., 1998, Adiabatic shear bands in a Ti-6Al-4V titanium alloy, J. Mech. Phys. Solids, 46, 11, pp.2201-2231.

Lodygowski T. and Perzyna P., 1997, Localized fracture in inelastic polycrystalline solids under dynamic loading processes, Int. J. Damage Mech., 6, pp. 364-407.

Longère P. and Dragon A., 2007, Adiabatic heat evaluation for dynamic plastic localization, J. Theor. Appl. Mech., 45, 2, pp.203-223.

Longère P. and Dragon A., 2008, Plastic work induced heating evaluation under dynamic conditions : critical assessment, Mech. Res. Com., 35, pp.135-141.

Longère P. and Dragon A., 2008, Evaluation of the inelastic heat fraction in the context of microstructure supported dynamic plasticity modelling, Int. J. Impact Eng., 35, 9, pp.992-999

Longère P. and Dragon A., 2009, Inelastic heat fraction evaluation for engineering problems involving dynamic plastic localization phenomena, J. Mech. Mat. Struct., 4, 2, pp.319-349.

Longère P., Dragon A. and Deprince X., 2009, Numerical study of impact penetration shearing employing finite strain viscoplasticity model incorporating adiabatic shear banding, J. Eng. Mat. Tech., ASME, 131, pp.011105.1-14.

Longère P., Dragon A., Trumel H. and Deprince X., 2005, Adiabatic shear banding induced degradation in a thermo-elastic/viscoplastic material under dynamic loading, Int. J. Impact Engng, 32, pp.285-320.

Longère P., Dragon A., Trumel H., de Resseguier T., Deprince X. and Petitpas E., 2003, Modelling adiabatic shear banding via damage mechanics approach, Arch. Mech., 55, pp.3-38.

Mahfuz H., Zhu Y., Haque A., Abutalib A., Vaidya U., Jeelani S., Gama B., Gillespie J. and Fink B., 2000, Investigation of high-velocity impact on integral armor using finite element method, Int. J. Impact Engng, 24, pp.203-217.

Marchand A. and Duffy J., 1988, An experimental study of the formation process of adiabatic shear bands in a structural steel, J. Mech. Phys. Solids, 36, 3, pp.251-283.

Martinez F., Murr L.E., Ramirez A., Lopez M.I. and Gaytan S.M., 2007, Dynamic deformation and adiabatic shear microstructures associated with ballistic plug formation and fracture in Ti-6Al-4V targets, Mat. Sc. Eng. A, 454-455, pp.581-589.

Mason J.J., Rosakis A.J. and Ravichandran G., 1994, On the strain and strain rate dependence of the fraction of plastic work converted to heat: an experimental study using high speed infrared detectors and the Kolsky bar, Mech. Mat., 17, pp.135-145.

Meixner J., 1969, Processes in simple thermodynamic materials, Arch. Rational Mech. Anal., 33, pp.33-53.

Molinari A., 1985, Instabilité thermoviscoplastique en cisaillement simple, J. Méca. Théorique et appliquée, 4, pp.659-684.

Molinari A., 1997, Collective behavior and spacing of adiabatic shear bands, J. Mech. Phys. Solids, 45, pp.1551-1575.

Molinari A. and Clifton R.J., 1987, Analytical characterization of shear localization in thermoviscoplastic materials, J. Appl. Mech., 54, 4, pp.806-812.

Molinari A., Musquar C. and Sutter G., 2002, Adiabatic shear banding in high speed machining of Ti-6Al-4V: experiments and modeling, Int. J. Plast., 18, 4, pp.443-459.

Nemat-Nasser S., LI Y. and Isaacs J.B., 1994, Experimental/computational evaluation of flow stress at high strain rates with application to adiabatic shear banding, Mech. Mat., 17, pp.111-134.

Nemat-Nasser S. and LI Y., 1998, Flow stress of f.c.c. polycrystals with application to OFHC Cu, Acta Mater., 46, 2, pp.565-577.

Nesterenko V.F., Meyers M.A. and Wright T.W., 1998, Self-organization in the initiation of adiabatic shear bands, Acta Mater., 46, 1, pp.327-340.

Pecherski R.B., 1998, Macroscopic effects of micro-shear banding in plasticity of metals, Acta Mech., 131, pp. 203-224.

Perzyna P., 1990, Influence of anisotropic effects on the micro-damage process in dissipative solids, in Yielding, Damage, and Failure of Anisotropic Solids, Ed. by J.P. Boehler, Mech. Engng Pub., pp. 483-507.

Recht R.F., 1964, Catastrophic thermoplastic shear, J. Appl. Mech., 31E, pp.189-193.

Rittel D., 1999, On the conversion of plastic work to heat during high strain rate deformation of glassy polymers, Mech. Mat., 31, pp.131-139.

Rittel D., 2009, Some comments on adiabatic shear localization, in Dynamic Behavior of Materials, Ed. A. Rusinek and P. Chevrier, pp.17-19.

Rittel D., Landau P. and Venkert A., 2008, Dynamic recrystallization as a potential cause for adiabatic shear failure, Phys. Rev. Letters, 101, 16, p.165501.

Rosakis P., Rosakis A.J., Ravichandran G. and Hodowany J., 2000, A thermodynamic internal variable model for the partition of plastic work into heat and stored energy in metals, J. Mech. Phys. Solids, 48, pp.581-607.

Sidoroff F. and Dogui A., 2001, Some issues about anisotropic elastic-plastic models at finite strain, Int. J. Solids Structures, 38, pp. 9569-9578.

Stevens J.B. and Batra R.C., 1998, Adiabatic shear bands in the Taylor impact test for a WHA rod, Int. J. Plast., 14, pp.841-854.

Suffis A., Lubrecht A.A. and Combescure A., 2003, A damage model with delay effect. Analytical and numerical studies of the evolution of the characteristic damage length, Int. J. Solids Structures, 40, pp. 3463-3476.

Taylor G.I. and Quinney H., 1934, The latent energy remaining in a metal after cold working, Proc. Roy. Soc., A413, pp.307-326.

Voyiadjis GZ. and Abed FH., 2005, Microstructural based models for bcc and fcc metals with temperature and strain rate dependency, Mech. Mat., 37, pp.355-378.

Voyiadjis GZ. and Abed FH., 2006, A coupled temperature and strain rate dependent yield function for dynamic deformations of bcc metals, Int. J. Plast., 22, pp.1398-1431.

Woodward R.L., 1990, Material failure at high strain rates, [in:] High velocity impact dynamics, J.A. Zukas [Ed.], John Wiley & Sons, pp.65-125.

Wright, 2002, The physics and mathematics of adiabatic shear bands, Cambridge University Press, Cambridge.

Zehnder A.T., 1991, A model for the heating due to plastic work, Mech. Res. Com., 18, 1, pp.23-28.

Zener C. and Hollomon J.H., 1944, Effect of strain rate upon plastic flow of steel, J. Appl. Phys., 15, pp.22-32.

Zerilli FJ. and Armstrong RW., 1987, Dislocation-mechanics-based constitutive relations for material dynamics calculations, J. Appl. Phys., 61, 5, pp.1816-1825.

14

Influencing the Effect of Treatment of Diseases Related to Bone Remodelling by Dynamic Loading

Václav Klika[1,2], František Maršík[1] and Ivo Mařík[3]
[1]Institute of Thermomechanics, v.v.i., Academy of Sciences of Czech Republic, Dolejškova 5,182 00 Prague
[2]Dept. of Mathematics, FNSPE, Czech Technical University in Prague, Trojanova 13, Prague
[3]Ambulant Centre for Defects of Locomotor Apparatus, Olsanska 7, Prague 3
Czech Republic

1. Introduction

1.1 Physiology of bone

Morphogenesis, growth and modelling of the skeletal system are dynamic processes, and the skeleton, once formed, is managed dynamically through remodelling. *Morphogenesis* begets growth. Morphogenesis is a consummate series of events during embryogenesis, bringing cells together to permit inductive opportunities - the outcome is a three-dimensional structure, such as a bone. The term *growth* embraces processes in endochondrally derived, tubular bones that increase length and girth prior to epiphyseal plate closure. In the cranium, the physis analog is the fontanelle. The process that permits bone growth is *modelling,* an active pageantry of cells embraced in mysterious partnership. Modelling produces functionally purposeful sizes and shapes of bones. Modelling drifts mainly determine outside bone diameter, cortical thickness, and the upper limit of bone strength. The final product of growth and modeling is a skeletal complex of 206 adult bones demanding continuous maintenance, which is accomplished by remodelling. Remodelling sustains structure and patches blemishes in the adult skeleton, while to homeostatic demands to ensure calcium and phosphate balance: "remodelling. . . is replacement of older by newer tissue in a way that need not alter its gross architecture or size"(Lieberman & Friedlaender, 2005).

Remodelling is a fundamental property of bone that permits adaptation to a changing mechanical environment. The skeleton's tissue-level functions and biomechanical influences on them were unknown before 1964 (Frost, 1964). The remodelling of bone tissue and orientation of osteons depends on very complex states of external loading caused by various positions and activities of human body which involve alternating extensions and shortenings of individual regions of bone tissue. Osteon orientation of the diaphysis of the long bones in man was confirmed on archaeological femurs and exactly biomechanically explained by Heřt et al. (Heřt et al., 1994). Rubin and Lanyon (Rubin & Lanyon, 1984; 1985a) proved in their experiments that bone reacts to intermittent strains only in defined range

1000 - 2000-2500 microstrains. Longitudinal strain 1000 microstrain in compression is one that would shorten a bone by 0.1 %. One microstrain is defined as 10^{-6} original lengths at shortening and by 0.5 10^{-6} of original length in tension.

H.M. Frost has defined the minimum effective strain (Frost, 1987c). The alternating strains above that threshold level 2000 - 2500 microstrains (overuse) affect modelling and remodeling activities in ways that change the size and configuration of growing bones (bone formation) to their new mechanical usage and return their strains to the threshold level (i.e. feedback). Vice versa, the alternating strains below 1000 microstrains (disuse) causes bone resorption.

The newer Utah paradigm of bone physiology by H.M. Frost (Frost, 2000; 2004) includes in part the skeleton's tissue-level "nephron equivalents" (the tissue-level multicellular units that provide special skeletal activities and functions, e.g. modelling drifts, remodelling), precursor cells (osteoblasts and osteoclasts in bone), mechanical effects, microdamage physiology, a marrow mediator mechanism, creep physiology (Frost, 1987c), mechanostats, maintenance activities that tend to preserve the mechanical competence of skeletal organs and the related feedback. Nowadays, the most part of authors distinguishes the modelling of bones as a form of sculpting which determines the shape, size and proportions of long bones by locally modifying their directions and speed of growth, from remodelling, signifying a quantised turnover of bone in remodelling packets called "basic multicellular units (BMU)" which couple an initial resorption process to formation processes in the same place of the bone surface (periosteal, Haversian, cortical-endosteal and trabecular). The bone remodelling begins with a resting surface, a resorption cavity (Howship's lacuna) is excavated by ostoeclasts, which osteoblasts then refill with new bone. In a simplified way, modelling of bones can be described like this: packets of bone are removed where the mechanical demand of the skeleton is low and new bone is formed at those sites where mechanical strains are repeatedly detected.

In summary, succinctly according to Frost, "Growth determines size. Modelling molds the growing shape. Remodelling then maintains functional competence (replacement, maintenance and homeostasis)." The processes of macromodelling and minimodelling continue in the adult skeleton, where macromodelling increases the ability of bone to resist bending (by expanding periosteal and endosteal cortices) and minimodelling rearranges trabeculae to best adapt to functional challenges (Frost, 1987b; c; 2000; 2004; Kimmel, 1993).

In the Utah paradigm the biologic mechanisms that determine skeletal health and disorders still need "nonmechanical things" in order to work. "Nonmechanical things (agents)" include sex, age, diet, vitamins, hormones, other humoral agents, genes, cytokines, membrane receptors and ligands, biochemical reactions, apoptosis, pinocytosis, etc. Mechanostat is the combination of biologic mechanisms that adapts skeletal strength and architecture to the needs of voluntary physical activities (Frost, 1987b). In load-bearing skeletal organs mechanical factors guide those mechanisms and cells in time and anatomical space, including their effects on skeletal strength and architecture. Nonmechanical factors can help or modulate that guidance but cannot replace it. E.g., so they cannot normalise skeletal organs in paralysed limbs.

Because of the organic components such as collagen, proteoglycans, elastine and intercellular fluid, *the bone tissue has viscoelastic properties* which are manifested by long-term viscoelastic deformation changes occurring in contradiction of elastic behaviour even under constant loading and after unloading. These long-term strain changes continue much longer than those nearly instantaneous ones and depending on the moment of loading and unloading. Starting from the foregoing facts and considerations, Sobotka and Mařík (Sobotka & Mařík, 1995) arrived at the deformational-rheological theory of remodelling of bone tissue according to which the stimulating mechanical effects depend not only on the amount but also on the duration of deformation changes. The elastic after-effect then involves a relatively long continuation of deformation changes under non-varying loading. In this manner, the existence of remodeling effects even at rest can be explained. These effects are used at ortotic treatment (Culik et al., 2008; Mařík et al., 2003) and physiotherapy for many years.

1.2 Bone metabolism—RANK/RANKL/OPG concept

Remodelling of skeleton is a complex process performed by the coordinated activities of osteoblasts and osteoclasts. Osteoblasts originate from pluripontent mesenchymal stem cells, which also give rise to chondrocytes, muscle cells, adipocytes and stromal bone marrow cells and are the cells responsible for the synthesis of the bone matrix. Osteoclasts are derived from hemopoietic stem cells of the monocyte-macrophage lineage and are the only cells capable of resorbing mineralised bone (Manolagas, 2000). It is generally concluded the osteoclasts resorb bone during growth, modelling and remodelling. The interactions between osteoblasts and osteoclasts, which guarantee a proper balance between bone gain and loss, is known as coupling (Rodan & Martin, 1981). The birth and death of osteoblasts and osteoclasts are controlled by local factors such as cytokines, growth factors and prostaglandins that are produced by skeletal and non-skeletal tissues. The effects of these factors can be mediated through autocrine, paracrine or even endocrine signal pathways, although factors produced by skeletal tissue and stored in bone may have more direct effects (Rucker et al., 2002). Many of these factors not only have redundant effects on bone cells, but can also modulate their own and each other's production in a cascade fashion (Manolagas, 2000). Thus even a small change of concentration of one factor can dramatically affect the concentrations of others.

Terms osteoblast and osteocyte were originally used to define the active and inactive stages, respectively, of the same cell type. Osteocytes play the active role e.g. in the sensing and transmission of mechanical strains. There are stromal cells (marrow-associated and bone associated) that include fibroblastic and reticular cells which constitute and secrete the collagen framework (i.e. the stroma) and bone lining cells that closely resemble osteocytes as regards their ultrastructure. Bone lining cells differ from osteocytes in that they retain their bone-forming potentiality and thus, under appropriate stimuli, can reconvert into osteoblasts (Miller et al., 1989). It should be said that all osteoblasts were found to be in contact with vascular dendrites of mature osteocytes, i.e. dendrites radiating from the osteocyte plasma membrane facing the bone vascular surface. While vascular dendrites continue to elongate, during bone deposition, in order to remain in contact with the osteoblastic lamina, mineral dendrites of the newly formed osteocytes do not seem to grow. Marotti (Marotti, 1996) with co-workers morphologically proved that the cells of the osteogenic lineage form a continuous cytoplasmatic network from the vascular endothelium to the osteocytes, passing through the stromal cells and the cells carpeting the bone surfaces, i.e. osteoblasts or bone lining cells. It appears that the overall system made up of the cells of the osteogenic lineage, including the vascular endothelium, constitutes a functional syncytium. It means that the transmission of signals throughout such a cellular system may occur by means of two mechanisms - wiring transmission (WT) and volume transmission

(VT) similarly like transmission of signals in the central nervous system. The concept of VT in bone simply corresponds to the well-known endocrine, paracrine and autocrine routes to the bone cells followed by hormones, cytokines and growth actors. VT should generally affect wider skeletal regions or even the whole skeleton, whereas WT would seem to participate in the local modulation of bone cells, particularly as far as mechanical stimuli are concerned. Cytoplasmic stress-strain and fluid movement (fluid flow in canalicular extracellular matrix) are possible operational mechanisms securing the osteocyte-osteoblast interaction and may function as a mechanism for the transduction of mechanical strain to osteocytes in bone (Lieberman & Friedlaender, 2005).

The aspects of RANK/RANKL/OPG biology were delineated during the past 13 years that are ushered in a totally new era of understanding of bone resorption. A number of labs using different methods and biological systems uncovered the new molecules (essential cytokines, receptors and ligands) in the Tumour Necrosis Factor family members and their biologic activities involved in the regulation of bone resorption (Martin, 2004).

Several factors have been associated with osteoclast formation, including PTH, 1,25-dihydroxy vitamin D_3, interleukins-1, -6, and -11, tumour necrosis factor (TNF), leukemia inhibitory factor, ciliary neurotropic factor, prostaglandins, macrophage colony-stimulating factor (M-CSF), granulocyte colony-stimulating factor, and RANK (Teitelbaum, 2000).

In response to homeostatic demands, systemic humoral cues for cells of the BMU can include 1,25-dihydroxy vitamin D_3, androgen, calcitonin, estrogen, glucocorticoids, growth hormone (GH), parathormone (PTH) and thyroid hormone. PTH and 1,25-dihydroxy vitamin D_3 stimulate resorption, they are countered by calcitonin, which inhibits resorption. Mechanisms for interactions are still not well known. The key systemic signal for bone is estrogen (Pacifici, 1998): a decrease of this hormone can cause resorption to outstrip formation, bone mass falls, and the diagnosis for this disease is osteoporosis. Advancing age is associated with an increased serum level to PTH and a decrease in estrogen, which may evoke increased cytokine levels of IL-1, IL-6, TNF-α, and probably RANK-L (Eghbali-Fatourechi et al., 2003). Estrogen depletion provokes osteocyte apoptosis, and could cause bone loss (Tomkinson et al., 1997).

Local humoral cues can include BMPs (bone morphogenic proteins), FGF (fibroblast growth factor), IGF (insulin-like growth factor), TGF-β (tumour growth factor beta), PDGF (platelet-derived growth factor), PTHrP for formation and GM-CSF (granulocyte macrophage colony stimulating factor), ILs (interleukins 1,4,6,11,13,18), and M-CSF (macrophage colony-stimulating factor), leading to resorption (Raisz, 1999). TGF-β can promote both resorption and formation.

In addition to local factors, adhesion molecules (proteins expressed on the surface of bone cells and progenitors) also have important regulatory roles by mediating cell-cell and cell-matrix interaction that enable the migration of osteoprogenitors to the remodeling sites; anchor mature osteoblasts unto bone surface; and communicating local, hormonal and mechanical signals (Raisz, 1999). Circulating hormones and mechanical signals exert potent effects on skeletal metabolism by modulating the production and action of these local factors. The molecular and physiological mechanisms of control of osteoclast formation and activity have been explained with the discovery of three protein members of the TNF superfamily which have been proposed as final effectors for many of the local factors and hormones. Receptor activator of NF-κ B ligand (RANKL, also called Tumour Necrosis Factor-Related Activation-Induced Cytokine - TRANCE, osteoprotegerin ligand, or osteoclast differentiating factor) is the type II membrane protein (cytokine) in cells of the osteoblastic lineage (committed preosteoblastic cells) which interacts with its receptor, receptor activator of NF-κB (RANK), on hematopoietic precursors (osteoclast progenitors) to promote osteoclast formation and maintain their viability and activity. RANKL binds to RANK with high affinity and, with the permissive effect of macrophage stimulating factor (M-CSF), this interaction is essential and sufficient for osteoclastogenesis. The process is further negatively regulated by the decoy receptor, the third non-membrane bound protein, osteoprotegerin (OPG), osteoclast inhibitory factor (OCIF) respectively, that is also produced by stromal/osteoblastic cells, and which binds to RANKL to prevent RANKL stimulation of osteoclast formation binding to RANK (Bekker et al., 2001; Simonet et al., 1997; Yasuda et al., 1998). Osteoprotegerin, has been shown to be a potent osteoclast inhibitor in vitro and in vivo studies (Simonet et al., 1997).

The RANK-RANKL-OPG pathway is coupled to the dual action of tumour growth factor beta (TGF-β) on osteoblasts. TGF-β, as well as other growth factors and specific components embedded in the bone matrix, are released by osteoclasts during bone resorption (Bonewald & Dallas, 1994). On one hand, TGF-β has the potential to stimulate osteoblast recruitment, migration and proliferation of osteoblast precursors (responding osteoblasts). On the other, TGF-β inhibits terminal osteoblastic differentiation into active osteoblasts (Alliston & Choy, 2001). TGF-β is also known to induce osteoclast apoptosis.

The evidence of all came from the validation studies in genetically manipulated mice or other rodent models that uncovered physiologic roles for these molecules. Overexpression of OPG resulted in mice with osteopetrosis because of failure to form osteoclasts (Simonet et al., 1997) whereas genetic ablation of OPG led to severe osteoporosis (Bucay et al., 1998; Mizuno et al., 1998). Genetic ablation of RANKL resulted in osteopetrosis because RANKL is necessary for normal osteoclast formation (Kong et al., 1999). Genetic ablation of RANK led to osteopetrosis also because it is the receptor for RANKL (Dougall et al., 1999).

1.3 Human bone diseases related to bone remodelling

Aging. In the healthy young adult skeleton, resorption and formation are balanced so that bone mass is maintained. Starting around the fourth or fifth decade of life, however, bone loss with age happens at all skeletal sites in both sexes and is characterized by a remodeling imbalance, in which resorption exceeds formation. With menopause (or male hypogonadism) the rate of bone loss increases dramatically, a change attributed to cellular mechanisms (Manolagas, 2000). The result is clinical disease osteoporosis. Both estrogen and androgens (perhaps through conversion to estrogen) normally suppress the production of IL-6, TNF and M-CSF, which stimulate the formation of osteoclasts and osteoblasts from the marrow. In addition, estrogen promotes osteoclast apoptosis (probably mediated through TGF-β), while exerting anti-apoptotic effects on osteoblast and osteocytes (Manolagas, 2000). As a result, loss of estrogen increases not only the number of active BMUs, but also the lifespan of osteoclasts while reducing the lifespan of osteoblasts and osteocytes. The increased lifespan of the osteoclasts, in particular, is thought responsible for the deepening of resorption cavities (Eriksen et al., 1999) and trabecular perforation leads to micro-structural weakness of bone and increased fracture risk in women in the early postmenopausal period (Rucker et al., 2002). In contrast to postmenopausal bone loss resulting from osteoclast hyperactivity, the inexorable bone loss seen with senescence in both sexes is thought to be osteoblast mediated. A decrease in osteoblast number decreases bone formation (Manolagas, 2000). Although it is difficult to separate sex-steroid deficiency from aging effects, bone marrow osteoblastogenesis also decreases with age. The decrease in osteoblastogenesis is attributed to an over-expression of genes that redirect mesenchymal stem cells to differentiate into adipocytes rather than osteoblasts, as well as age-related decreases in the pulsatile excretion of growth hormone that result in decreases insulin-like growth factors (IGFs) and their binding proteins (Weinstein & Manolagas, 2000).

There are several other important endocrine factors implicated in age-related bone loss. With increasing age, the ability to absorb calcium from the gut decreases because of decreased levels of the active vitamin D hormone, 1,25-dihydroxy vitamin D, ($1,25(OH)_2D$). Although $1,25(OH)_2D$ itself has potent stimulatory effects on local factors that stimulate osteoclasts and osteoblasts, the major physiologic function of this hormone is to stimulate intestinal calcium absorption. Insufficient $1,25(OH)_2D$ reduces serum calcium that in turn increases synthesis and secretion of parathyroid hormone (PTH). PTH then increases bone remodeling to mobilize calcium from the skeleton. PTH has potent stimulatory effects on the development and activity of osteoblasts and interferes with bone formation at the transcriptional level (Rucker et al., 2002). Pharmacological doses of glucocorticoids also have various harmful effects bone remodeling. Glucocorticoid excess inhibits osteoblastogenesis, increases osteoblast and osteocyte apoptosis, suppresses circulating gonadal steroid production, and decreases calcium absorption (Manolagas, 1998).

The genetic basis of the several human *extremely rare heritable disorders of the RANK/RANKL/OPG pathway* was uncovered following the elucidation of the biological activity and significance of the pathway members (Whyte & Mumm, 2004). These remarkable skeletal disorders were found to reflect gene defects leading to constitutive activation of RANK or to deficiency of OPG. Hughes et al. (Hughes et al., 2000) investigated familial expansile osteolysis (FEO) and identified an activating 18-bp tandem in the gene encoding RANK (TNFRSF11A) in three affected kindred, and similar 27-bp duplication in an unusual, familial form of early-onset Paget disease of bone (PDB) in Japan. Whyte and Hughes (Whyte & Hughes, 2002) reported that a seemingly unique disorder designated expansile skeletal hyperphosphatasia (ESH) was allelic to FEO and involved 15-bp tandem duplication in RANK. Whyte et al. (Whyte et al., 2002) documented homozygous complete deletion of the gene encoding OPG (TNFRSF11B) as the first molecular explanation for idiopathic hyperphosphatasia, called juvenile Paget disease (JPD).

The majority of *human metabolic bone diseases* are caused by excessive extent of bone resorption that exceeds the rate of bone formation, resulting in loss of bone mass. With accumulating evidence of the role of the OPG/RANKL/RANK cytokine system for normal osteoclast biology, it became clear that many clinically relevant metabolic disease in humans, including inflammatory bone diseases (e.g. rheumatoid arthritis), malignant bone tumours (e.g. myeloma or osteolytic metastases) and different forms of osteoporosis are caused by alterations of the OPG/RANKL/RANK system (Teitelbaum, 2000). Skeletal estrogen agonists (including 17 β-estradiol, raloxifene and genistein) induce osteoblastic OPG production through estrogen receptor-α activation in vitro, while immune cells appear to over-express RANKL in estrogen deficiency in vivo. OPG administration can prevent bone loss associated with estrogen deficiency as observed in both animal models and a small clinical study (Bekker et al., 2001). Glucocorticoids and immunosuppressants concurrently up-regulate RANKL and suppress OPG in osteoblastic cells in vitro, and glucocorticoids are among the most powerful drugs to suppress OPG serum levels in vivo. As for hyperparathyroidism, chronic PTH exposure concurrently enhances RANKL production and suppresses OPG secretion through activation of osteoblastic protein kinase A in vitro which would favour increased osteoclastic activity. PTH receptors are largely expressed on the osteoblast surface. While continuous PTH exposure (binding these receptors) stimulates the production of RANKL and inhibits the production of OPG by osteoblasts. This mechanism enhanced the RANKL-to-OPG ratio by up to 25-fold and stimulated osteoclastogenesis. Later was proved that intermittent (pulsatile) PTH administration stimulated IGF-1 mRNA, an anabolic skeletal growth factor. PTH is currently involved in numerous clinical trials as an anabolic agent for the treatment of low bone mass in osteoporosis (Locking et al., 2003; Neer et al., 2001). In sum, RANKL/OPG imbalances is the likely etiology of metabolic bone diseases (Hofbauer et al., 2004).

These data point to the promise that targeted RANKL antagonist therapy could bring to the many clinical settings where excessive bone loss leads directly to increased morbidity and mortality. There is a few years experience with bisphosphonates, raloxifene, teriparatide (parathormone 1-84) and stroncium ranelate in treatment of different forms of osteoporosis (idiopathic postmenopausal and secondary osteoporosis) and heritable disorders of the RANK/RANKL/OPG pathway, too. *In published Czech case of Familial expansile osteolysis (Marik et al., 2006b) the treatment with bisphosphonates was successful and allowed surgical correction of severe shank deformity after normalisation of bone turnover (a note of the author). There are other rare heritable disorders with high bone turnover, e.g., Hajdu-Cheney syndrome (Marik et al., 2006a) and Pachydermoperiostitis (Latos-Bielenska et al., 2007), where treatment with bisphosphonates has a positive influence.*

Safety and efficacy of above mentioned drugs is still studied in clinical trials. At present, the basis for osteoporosis prevention and therapy is supplementation of vitamin D and calcium together with appropriate physical activities with respect to age. At present, clinical trials of osteoporosis with recombinant OPG and anti-RANKL provide additional support for innovative treatment strategy.

1.4 Physical activity and mechanical loading

It is well known that bone adapts to its environment; Galileo was among the first to recognize that body weight and activity were related to bone size (Galileo, 1638). This structure/ function relation was formally described in the late 19th century in what has been designated as Wolff's law (Wolff, 1892). Over time, Wolff's law promulgated into a teleological paradigm that bone is a well-designed engineering structure, adding bone and changing its architecture to minimize strain on the skeleton (McLeod et al., 1998). Frost and others (Frost, 1987a; Lanyon et al., 1982) described the mechanical regulation of bone as a "mechanostat", whereby bone increases its mass with the mechanical loading and, conversely, loses bone mass when there is no little or no mechanical stimulus. Supporting this structural efficiency paradigm is a wealth of observational and experimental evidence, such as loss of bone mass during disuse (Nishimura et al., 1994) or space flight (Morey & Baylink, 1978), and local bone hypertrophy related to mechanical loading (Haapasalo et al., 1994; Kravitz et al., 1985; Rubin & Lanyon, 1985a; Turner et al., 1994).

While the concept that the mechanical environment affects bone is well accepted, it remains unknown exactly what aspects of the mechanical milieu are paramount for osteogenesis. Much of what we do know about functional adaptations at the tissue level comes from well-controlled animal models to assess physical influences on bone formation. The intensity, duration and manner of the loading environment is translated and expressed as mechanical strain (relative deformation of a material) or other related parameters of the strain environment, such as strain frequency, rate and gradients (Zernicke & Judex, 1999). These studies show that only dynamic loads increase bone formation. Furthermore, if the magnitude is high enough, increasing the number of strain cycles beyond a certain point does not increase bone mass (Rubin & Lanyon, 1984). On the other hand, strains need not be large in magnitude if strains are unusual in their distribution (Lanyon, 1996), high in frequency or rate (Turner et al., 1994), or have gradients (Gross et al., 1997; Judex et al., 1997).

It has been shown that exercise-induced bone formation is site-specific (Loitz & Zernicke, 1992) although few of the animal studies have taken this into account. Animal studies that relate the mechanical parameters to morphological changes in bone have demonstrated that the osteogenic stimulus varies with skeletal maturity. Central to elucidating precisely how bone adapts to mechanical stimulus is to know how bone interprets mechanical stimuli at the cellular level. Mechanotransduction is the process of converting mechanical stimuli into a cellular response and occurs in a wide variety of physiologic functions. In bone, mechanotransduction involves the transduction of a mechanical signal into a local signal perceived by cells, and followed by the transduction of this local signal into a biochemical signal to stimulate osteoblasts or osteoclasts to form or remove bone. In theory, all eukaryotic cells are sensitive to their mechanical environments (Ingber, 1997). In bone, osteoclasts, osteoblasts, osteocytes and bone lining cells are sensitive to mechanical stimulation in vitro and in vivo. Osteoblasts, however, make up only 5% of cells in adult bone, and osteoclasts comprise under 1%. Thus, even if all active osteoblasts were directly stimulated, the effect would not significantly increase bone mass (Duncan & Turner, 1995). To facilitate an adaptive modeling/remodeling response, osteoprogenitors must be recruited to the bone surface. Rather than the mechanical signal directly stimulating osteoblasts or osteoclasts directly, it is hypothesized that osteocytes or bone lining cells, which make up approximately 95% of all bone cells (Parfitt, 1994), act as the sensor cells. That hypothesis is a function of the connectivity of these cells: osteocytes are connected to neighboring osteocytes and lining cells on the bone surface by a network of slender long processes linked via gap junctions (Shapiro, 1997). Thus communication is enabled through the bone matrix. Since neither osteocytes nor bone lining cells resorb or form new bone, they signal to "effector" cells (osteoclasts and osteoblasts) to produce bone adaptations (Duncan & Turner, 1995). Mechanical loading can activate osteocytic production of autocrine or paracrine factors, such as prostaglandins, nitric oxide (NO), and IGF (Zaman et al., 1997). Experimental evidence implicates fluid flow as a local signal for stimulating osteocytes (Weinbaum et al., 1994). When bone is loaded, interstitial fluid flows from the medullary canal into the vascular system and lacunar spaces of bone tissue. Fluid flow stimulates osteocytes directly through shear stresses or indirectly by electric fields (streaming potentials) (Otter et al., 1985).

The stimulus for remodeling can come from internal factors (e.g., hormones, cytokines-growth factors) and external factors (e.g., physical activity and mechanical loading). It is widely accepted that physical activity benefits the musculoskeletal system but the mechanisms affecting bone mass and density that are set off by physical activity in general and mechanical loading in particular are still poorly understood. It appears that mechanical strain inhibits RANKL production and up-regulates OPG production in vitro. Hence, lack of mechanical strain during immobilisation (disuse) may favour an enhanced RANKL-to-OPG ratio leading to increase bone loss. Nowadays, it is believed that the static loading is not osteogenic. Instead, the dynamic loading plays the essential role of stimulating the bone remodelling process, which is supported by many experimental and clinical studies. Increasing age, declining levels of sex hormones, or calcium deficiencies produce an imbalance between resorption and formation resulting in bone loss. Physical activity through its mechanical effects on bone can mitigate this bone loss. Optimal mechanical stimuli differ between growing and mature bone, and mature bone is influenced by aging or other systemic factors such as nutrition and hormones. Recently so-called Whole Body Wibration (WBW) has been introduced to improve impaired biomechanical function of the musculoskeletal system in adults. The therapeutic principle is based on the activation of proprioceptive spinal circuits. These reflexes can be induced by upright standing on a vibrating platform. The application of vibrations increased bone formation and the metabolism in skeletal muscles and skin. WBW is characterised to prevent the loss of bone and muscle mass in immobilised adults. WBW improves inter- and intramuscular co-ordination over induction of agonists and antagonists in the neuromuscular system. At present, some clinical trials confirm therapeutic effects of the Cologne Standing-and-Walking-Trainer powered by Galileo on the mobility of children and adolescents affected with diseases characterised by a disease-related sarcopenia due to physical immobilisation such as patients with osteogenesis imperfecta (OI), infantile cerebral palsy and Meningomyelocele (Schönau, 2008). The effect of WBW is also studied in muscular dystrophy patients and children with juvenile idiopathic arthritis with the aim to improve muscular force and motor function.

Greater understanding of how mechanical stimuli interact with systemic factors is central for the development of more effective exercise programs in the prevention of bone loss, as well as enhancing complementary of exercise and pharmacological therapies.

1.5 Available models of bone remodelling

With the development of computer-aided strategies and based on the knowledge of bone geometry, applied forces, and elastic properties of the tissue, it may be possible to calculate the mechanical stress transfer inside the bone (Finite Elements analysis or FE analysis). The change of stresses is followed by a change in internal bone density distribution. This allows to formulate mathematical models that can be used to study functional adaptation quantitatively and furthermore, to create the bone density distribution patterns (Beaupré et al., 1990; Carter, 1987; Weinans et al., 1992). Such mathematical models have been built in the past. Since they calculate just mechanical transmission inside the bone and not considering cell-biologic factors of bone physiology, they just partially correspond to the reality seen in living organisms. Basically, there are essentially two groups of models for bone remodelling. One assumes that the mechanical loading is the dominant effect, almost to the exclusion of other factors, and treatment of biochemical effects are included in parameter with no physical interpretation (Beaupré et al., 1990; Carter, 1987; Doblaré & García, 2002; Huiskes et al., 1987; Ruimerman et al., 2005; Turner et al., 1997). The results or predictions of these models yield the correct density distribution patterns in physiological cases. However, they have a limited ability to simulate disease. The second group, the biochemical models, consider control mechanisms of bone adaptation in great detail, but with limited possibilities for including mechanical effects that are known to be essential (Komarova et al., 2003; Lemaire et al., 2004; Müller, 2005).

We realize that biochemical reactions are initiated and influenced primarily by genetic effects and then by external biomechanical effects (stress changes). Our thermodynamic model enables to combine biological and biomechanical factors (Klika & Maršík, 2009b).

Such a model may also reflect changes in remodelling behaviour resulting from pathological changes to the bone metabolism or from hip joint replacement. However, it is a model and thus it is a great simplification of the complex process of bone remodelling. In this paper, a more detailed description of biochemical control mechanisms will be added to the mentioned model (Klika & Maršík, 2009b) which in turn leads to possibility to study several concrete bone related diseases using this model.

2. Simulation of diseases and their treatment

In our previous work, the influence of mechanical stimulation on (chemical) interactions in general was studied and it was shown how to comprise this effect into a model of studied biochemical processes (Klika & Maršík, 2009a). These findings were used to describe the bone remodelling phenomenon (Klika et al., 2008; Maršík et al., 2009; Maršík et al., 2005). Most actual version of this model with identified parameters which has captured the main features of bone remodelling is currently under revision in Biomechanics and Modelling in Mechanobiology (Klika & Maršík, 2009b)[1]. In this chapter, an extension of the mentioned bone remodelling model (influences of concrete biochemical factors) will be presented where the essential significance of dynamic loading will still be apparent. The approach cannot be so straightforward, actually, bounds of applicability will be searched.

Firstly, fundamental control factors will be mentioned. As was mentioned in the introduction, the RANKL-RANK-OPG pathway is essential in the bone remodelling control. Osteoprotegerin (OPG) inhibits binding of ligand RANKL to receptor RANK and thus prevents osteoclastogenesis. Since osteoclasts are the only resorbing agents in bone, osteoprotegerin "protects bone" (osteo-protege). Further, one of the major problems connected to bone remodeling is a rapid bone loss after menopause that affects a significant portion of women after 50 years of age. Menopause is linked to a rapid decrease in estrogen levels. And because estrogen significantly affects bone density, it would be beneficial to be able to simulate the influence of estrogen levels on the bone remodelling process. Similarly, the parathyriod hormone PTH, tumour growth factor TGF-β_1, and nitric oxide NO play a significant role during the bone adaptation process.

PTH causes a release of calcium from the bone matrix and induces MNOC differentiation from precursor cells, estrogen has complex effects with final outcome in decreasing bone resorption by MNOC, calcitonin decreases levels of blood calcium by inhibiting MNOC function, and osteocalcin inhibits mineralisation (Sikavitsas et al., 2001). The discovery of the RANKL-RANK-OPG pathway enabled a more detailed study of the control mechanisms of bone remodelling. Robling et al. states that all PTH, PGE (prostaglandin), IL (interleukin), and vitamin D are "translated" by corresponding cells (osteoblasts) into RANKL levels (Robling et al., 2006). Further, nitric oxide NO is known to be a strong inhibitor of bone resorption and recently it has been known that it works in part by suppressing the expression of RANKL and, moreover, by promoting the expression of OPG (Robling et al., 2006). Both these effects eventually lead to a decrease of numbers of active osteoclasts MNOC, which in turn causes decrease of bone resorption. Kong et al. mentions that the OPG expression is induced by estrogen (Kong & Penninger, 2000). Boyle et al. add that OPG

---

[1] Please, contact the authors for update about this paper

production by osteoblasts is based on anabolic stimulation from TGF-β or estrogen (Boyle et al., 2003). Martin also deals with the question how hormones and cytokines influence contact-dependent regulation of MNOC by osteoblasts. He summaries results from the carried out experiments (mainly in vitro) that PTH, IL-11, and vitamin D (1.25$(OH)_2D_3$ more precisely) promotes RANKL formation, which in turn increases osteoclastogenesis (Martin, 2004).

RANKL-RANK-OPG pathway mediates many of these above mention biochemical factors. Moreover, RANKL levels also reflect microcrack density. Hence, it is essential to incorporate this pathway into our model. The connection will be enabled through the amount RANKL-RANK bonds that are one of the components of developed model, noted as *RR*, see (Klika & Maršík, 2009b).

2.1 Incorporation of RANKL-RANK-OPG pathway into the bone remodelling model

A new model for RANKL-RANK-OPG chain kinetics will be formulated and added to the mentioned model of bone remodelling (fundamental ideas can be found in (Maršík et al., 2009) and its most recent version is under review in Biomechanics and Modelling in Mechanobiology (Klika & Maršík, 2009b)). RANKL is a ligand molecule and binds to RANK forming a bond, here noted as *RR* and its molar concentration as [RR], between osteoblasts and precursors of osteoclasts. Osteoblasts also secrete a decoy receptor osteoprotegerin OPG[2] that binds with high affinity to RANKL and thus prevents the needed connection between osteoblasts and osteoclastic precursors.

The reaction scheme of interaction of the mentioned molecules can be described as follows:

$$\begin{aligned} RANKL + RANK &\overset{k_{\pm 1}}{\rightleftarrows} RR, \\ RANKL + OPG &\overset{k_{\pm 2}}{\rightleftarrows} RO_{\text{inactive}}, \end{aligned} \tag{1}$$

where RO_{inactive} represents the bond between the decoy OPG and ligand RANKL. Using the law of mass action (Klika & Maršík, 2009a) we may infer kinetics of the above mentioned interactions. Only the simplification, when assuming a relation between forward and backward reaction rates $k_{+i} \gg k_{-i}$, is not applicable here. We get

$$\begin{aligned} \frac{\mathrm{d}n_{RANKL}}{\mathrm{d}\tau} &= -n_{RANKL}(\beta_{\text{RK}}^{\text{RRO}} + n_{RANKL} - n_{OPG}) + \\ &\quad + \delta_{-1}^{\text{RRO}}(\beta_{\text{RR}}^{\text{RRO}} - n_{RANKL} + n_{OPG}) - \\ &\quad - \delta_{+2}^{\text{RRO}} n_{RANKL} n_{OPG} + \delta_{-2}^{\text{RRO}}(\beta_{\text{RO}}^{\text{RRO}} - n_{OPG}), \\ \frac{\mathrm{d}n_{OPG}}{\mathrm{d}\tau} &= -\delta_{+2}^{\text{RRO}} n_{RANKL} n_{OPG} + \delta_{-2}^{\text{RRO}}(\beta_{\text{RO}}^{\text{RRO}} - n_{OPG}), \end{aligned} \tag{2}$$

where

[2] Osteoblasts are not the only producers of OPG - in fact, around 60 % is produced by cells in heart, kidney, and liver (Boyce & Xing, 2008).

$$\delta_{-1}^{\mathrm{RRO}} = \frac{k_{-1}}{k_{+1}[\mathrm{RANKL}_{\mathrm{stand}}]},$$
$$\delta_{-2}^{\mathrm{RRO}} = \frac{k_{-2}}{k_{+1}[\mathrm{RANKL}_{\mathrm{stand}}]},$$
$$\delta_{+2}^{\mathrm{RRO}} = \frac{k_{+2}}{k_{+1}}, \tag{3}$$
$$\beta_{\mathrm{RO}}^{\mathrm{RRO}} = \frac{C_{\mathrm{RO}}}{[\mathrm{RANKL}_{\mathrm{stand}}]} = \frac{[\mathrm{RO}_0]+[\mathrm{OPG}_0]}{[\mathrm{RANKL}_{\mathrm{stand}}]},$$
$$\beta_{\mathrm{RR}}^{\mathrm{RRO}} = \frac{C_{\mathrm{RR}}}{\mathrm{RANKL}_{\mathrm{stand}}} = \frac{[\mathrm{RR}_0]+[\mathrm{RANKL}_0]-[\mathrm{OPG}_0]}{[\mathrm{RANKL}_{\mathrm{stand}}]}.$$

Again $k_{\pm i}$ are reaction rate coefficients, δ_i are interaction rates, and β_j^{RRO} represents the normalized initial molar concentrations of corresponding substances, denoted with index 0 and finally [$\mathrm{RANKL}_{\mathrm{stand}}$] represents standard serum level of RANKL used for normalisation of molar concentrations of substance i, n_i. All the parameters have evidently a physical interpretation and are measurable. However, hardly any such in vivo data for humans is available. Fortunately, the recent progress in the understanding of bone remodelling control enabled in vitro studies of individual factors.

Quinn et al. studied the influence of RANKL and OPG concentration on a number of osteoclasts (more precisely, TRAP positive multinucleated osteoclasts) in a dose-dependent way (Quinn et al., 2001). We would like to use this data to determine the above mentioned parameters of the RANKL-RANK-OPG model. Because the carried out experiments are studying effects of RANKL and OPG separately, the reaction scheme (1) may be splitted into two separate reactions for parameter setting. This is convenient because the kinetics of a single biochemical reaction can be described using a single differential equation (in this case non-linear). Moreover, both normalised differential equations corresponding to these two reactions can be written in the same form:

$$\dot{x} = -Ax^2 - Bx + C, \quad A > 0, C > 0, \tag{4}$$

where $A = 1$, $B = \beta_{\mathrm{RK}} + \delta_{-1}$, $C = \delta_{-1}\beta_{\mathrm{RR}}$ for the RANKL reaction and $A = \delta_{+2}$, $B = \delta_{+2}\beta_{\mathrm{RANKL}} + \delta_{-2}$, $C = \delta_{-2}\beta_{\mathrm{RO}}$ for OPG reaction. The normalised form is also useful because it decreases the number of unknown parameters. The differential equation (4) has the following solution for positive constants A, C and for initial value x_0:

$$x(\tau) = \left[\frac{2A}{\sqrt{B^2+4AC}} \left(1 + \frac{1+\frac{2A}{\sqrt{B^2+4AC}}\left(x_0+\frac{B}{2A}\right)}{1-\frac{2A}{\sqrt{B^2+4AC}}\left(x_0+\frac{B}{2A}\right)} e^{\sqrt{B^2+4AC}\tau} \right) \right]^{-1} \cdot$$
$$\cdot \left[\left(1 - \frac{B}{\sqrt{B^2+4AC}}\right) \frac{1+\frac{2A}{\sqrt{B^2+4AC}}\left(x_0+\frac{B}{2A}\right)}{1-\frac{2A}{\sqrt{B^2+4AC}}\left(x_0+\frac{B}{2A}\right)} e^{\sqrt{B^2+4AC}\tau} - \frac{B}{\sqrt{B^2+4AC}} - 1 \right]. \tag{5}$$

Because we know the analytic form of function describing the kinetics of RANKL (and OPG), we may use the least square method for determination of the unknown parameters according to the carried out experiments. Data from the Quinn et al. in vitro experiment relates RANKL (and OPG) concentration to MNOC concentration (the number of osteoclasts per well). The mentioned reaction scheme (1) of RANKL-RANK-OPG interaction has an output product denoted as *RR*. Thus, to be able to use the mentioned data from Quinn et al., we need to relate RANKL-RANK bonds ([RR]) to the number of osteoclasts ([MNOC]). To get a precise prediction of this relationship from the presented model we would also need to know the analytical solution of the system of ODEs that describe the bone remodelling process (Klika & Maršík, 2009b; Maršík et al., 2009), which is not possible. On the other hand, the interaction that describes the relation between RANKL-RANK bonds and MNOC concentration is the first one in our bone remodelling scheme (Klika & Maršík, 2009b; Maršík et al., 2009) and it will be assumed that the number of formed and active osteoclasts is proportional to the *RR* concentration. It means that it was assumed that in vitro, where no remodellation occurs, the formation of osteoclasts may be described by:

$$RR \rightleftarrows MNOC.$$

This assumption will be used just for purposes of parameter setting and from final results it will be possible to see if this simplification was too great or not.

The next issue we have to deal with is finding a possible relation between in vitro and in vivo data. In vivo ones are more or less unavailable, especially in such a detail that is needed for parameter setting. Further, determination of standard serum levels of OPG and RANKL is needed. The problem is that in most cases in vitro concentrations have to be much higher to reach a similar effect as in vivo. Moreover, no such relation may exist. It will be assumed that there is a correspondence among these two approaches and that it is linear, i.e. in vivo data can be gained from in vitro after appropriate scaling of concentrations.

The search for standard serum levels of osteoprotegerin and RANKL was not simple. Studies differ greatly in the presented values. Kawasaki states that the standard level of osteoprotegerin is 250 $\frac{pg}{\mu l}$ (Kawasaki et al., 2006) and Moschen et al. mention 800 $\frac{pg}{\mu l}$ (Moschen et al., 2005). Further, Eghbali-Fatourechi et al. determined OPG serum levels to be 2.05 $\frac{pmol}{l}$ (Eghbali- Fatourechi et al., 2003). The probable cause of these discrepancies lies in differently used techniques of gaining osteoprotegerin and measuring its concentration. Kawasaki et al. measured the amount of RANKL in gingival crevicular fluid, Moschen et al. performed collonic explant cultures from biopsies and consequently measured RANKL and OPG levels using an ELISA kit, and Eghbali-Fatourechi used a different cell preparation technique followed by measurement with an ELISA kit. One of the manufacturers of the ELISA kit for assessment OPG levels cites several studies on OPG levels in humans and also submits results from their own research (OPG ELISA kit, 2006). At least all these measurements are carried out by the same measurement technique and are comparable. Therefore, we set standard OPG and RANKL levels according to data that are there referred to - $[RANKL_{stand}] = 0.84 \frac{pmol}{l} = 55 \cdot 0.84 \frac{pg}{ml} = 46.2 \frac{pg}{ml}$ and $[OPG_{stand}] = 1.8 \frac{pmol}{l} = 20 \cdot 1.8 \frac{pg}{ml} = 36 \frac{pg}{ml}$ in serum (Kudlacek et al., 2003), where the knowledge of molecular weights $MW_{RANKL} = 55\ 10^3$, $MW_{OPG} = 20\ 10^3$ was used (OPG ELISA kit, 2006; RANKL product data sheet, 2008). Now it is needed to find a reasonable relation with in vitro data from Quinn that will be used for the least squares method for parameter estimation. The following consideration will be used: the physiological range of levels of OPG and RANKL will be found and consequently related to studied effective in vitro range by Quinn. OPG serum levels found in human are 12-138 $\frac{pg}{ml}$ = 0.6–6.9 $\frac{pmol}{l}$ and RANKL serum levels are 0–250 $\frac{pg}{ml}$ = 0–4.55 $\frac{pmol}{l}$ with standard values of 0.84 $\frac{pmol}{l}$ for RANKL and 1.8 $\frac{pmol}{l}$ for OPG, respectively. When we relate these values to the in vitro ranges of RANKL 0–500 $\frac{ng}{ml}$ and of OPG 0–30 $\frac{ng}{ml}$, we get the in vitro equivalents for standard values: $[RANKL_{invitrostand}] = 92.3\ \frac{ng}{ml}$, $[OPG_{invitrostand}] = 7.83\ \frac{ng}{ml}$.

A list of parameters that will be determined by least squares from the RANKL experiment are the following:

$$\delta_{-1}^{\mathrm{RRO}}, \tau_{7\mathrm{days}}^{\mathrm{RRO}}, n_{RK_0}, n_{RR_0},$$

where $\tau_{7\mathrm{days}}^{\mathrm{RRO}}$ is the dimensionless time that corresponds to 7 days. Before the parameter setting by curve fitting (least square method) is carried out, it is reasonable to have at least some estimation of parameter values. Because the normalisation was done by division with term $k_{+1}[RANKL_{stand}]^2$ and from (3), we get:

$$\tau_{7\mathrm{days}}^{\mathrm{RRO}} = tk_{+1}C_{\mathrm{RR}}\,|_{t=7\,days} = 6\,10^5\,10^7\,10^{-12} \doteq 10^0,$$

$$n_{RR_0} \doteq 10^0,$$

$$n_{RK_0} \doteq 10^0,$$

$$\delta_{-1\mathrm{RRO}} = \frac{k_{-1}}{k_{+1}[\mathrm{RANKL}_{\mathrm{stand}}]} \doteq k_{-1}10^5,$$

where the value of k_{+1} was estimated from the parameter setting in the bone remodeling model, standard value of RANKL $[RANKL_{stand}] \doteq 1\ \frac{pmol}{l}$ was mentioned above, and the k_{-1} value may be anywhere in $(0, 10^7)$ but most probably lower than one.

The least square method with the used data from Quinn et al. (Quinn et al., 2001) and the analytic function as described above gives the following estimates:

$$\delta_{-1}^{\mathrm{RRO}} = 4.92\,10^{-6}, \tau_{7\mathrm{days}}^{\mathrm{RRO}} = 4.64, n_{RK_0} = 1.037, n_{RR_0} = 0.0947. \tag{6}$$

If we compare these values with their order estimation above, we see that the values are acceptable and the curve fit is as well, see figure 1a.

Now, we may proceed with OPG parameters. The difference is that if we use only the second reaction of RANKL-RANK-OPG reaction scheme (1), we do not know how initial OPG concentration influences the number of bonds between RANKL and RANK. However, this influence is mediated by a decrease in number of available ligands RANKL by binding with OPG. Because OPG binds with higher affinity to ligand RANKL than this ligand to its

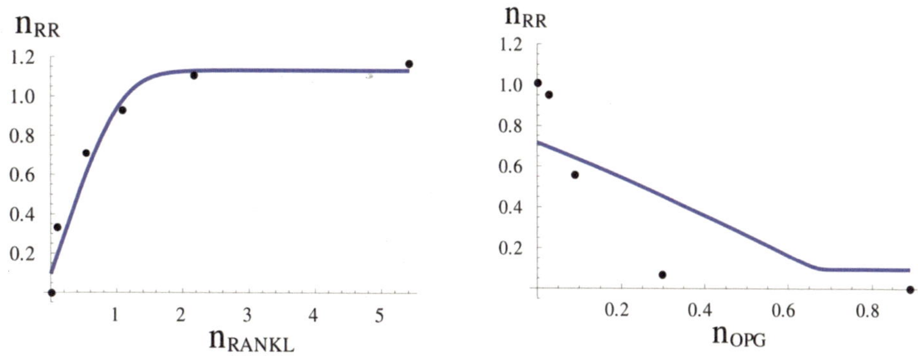

(a) RANKL (b) OPG

Fig. 1. RANKL and OPG fitted solutions (blue curves) by least squares method to data measured (dots) by Quinn et al. (Quinn et al., 2001). Firstly, n_{RR} as a function of n_{RANKL_0} is determined and consequently n_{RR} as a function of n_{OPG_0}, created by embedding dependency of [RANKL] on [OPG] and of [RR] on [RANKL] concentration, was found.

receptor RANK (otherwise the decoy effects of OPG would be very limited), it will be assumed that OPG binds to RANKL more rapidly than the competiting reaction. The reason for this is again in the need of analytic solution of differential equations that govern the kinetics of mentioned processes (we was not able to solve the full system of two differential equations (2) so the mentioned simplification was needed; again, from the results to come it seems reasonable). Thus, the influence of levels of osteoprotegerin on the *RR* concentration may be mediated by an appropriate modification of initial concentration of RANKL which in turn affects the resulting *RR* concentration. Schematically:

$$2^{\text{nd}} \text{ reaction in (1)} \rightarrow [\text{OPG}](t)$$

and consequently $[\text{RANKL}_0] = [\text{OPG}](\tau_{\text{OPG}})$, which is used in

$$1^{\text{st}} \text{ reaction of (1)} \rightarrow [\text{RR}][t_{7\text{days}}]$$

where τ_{OPG} is a time to be determined.

The already determined parameters from the RANKL setting will be used and only the yet unknown will be determined, i.e.

$$\delta_{-2}^{\text{RRO}}, \delta_{+2}^{\text{RRO}}, \tau_{\text{OPG}}^{\text{RRO}}, n_{RO_0},$$

Again, the least squares in the case of OPG give the following estimates (based on data from Quinn and the fact that molecular weight of RANKL is 55 10^3 and of OPG 20 10^3):

$$\delta_{-2}^{\text{RRO}} = 5.86\,10^{-19}, \delta_{+2}^{\text{RRO}} = 12.96, \tau_{\text{OPG}}^{\text{RRO}} = 11.36, n_{RO_0} = 6.135. \qquad (7)$$

Also, the values are admissible and the curve fit as well (the function here is much more complicated because OPG concentration is firstly used to determine an initial RANKL concentration for a consecutive reaction that finally gives [RR] outcome), see figure 1b.

If the mentioned results of parameter estimation are combined, all the needed values of parameters of RANKL-RANK-OPG model (3) may be inferred:

$$
\begin{aligned}
\delta_{-1}^{\mathrm{RRO}} &= \frac{k_{-1}}{k_{+1}[\mathrm{RANKL_{stand}}]} = 4.92\,10^{-6}, \\
\delta_{-2}^{\mathrm{RRO}} &= \frac{k_{-2}}{k_{+1}[\mathrm{RANKL_{stand}}]} = 5.86\,10^{-19}, \\
\delta_{+2}^{\mathrm{RRO}} &= \frac{k_{+2}}{k_{+1}} = 12.96, \\
\beta_{\mathrm{RO}}^{\mathrm{RRO}} &= \frac{C_{\mathrm{RO}}}{[\mathrm{RANKL_{stand}}]} = \frac{[\mathrm{RO_0}]+[\mathrm{OPG_0}]}{[\mathrm{RANKL_{stand}}]} = 6.135 + n_{OPG_0}, \\
\beta_{\mathrm{RR}}^{\mathrm{RRO}} &= \frac{C_{\mathrm{RR}}}{[\mathrm{RANKL_{stand}}]} = \frac{[\mathrm{RR_0}]+[\mathrm{RANKL_0}]-[\mathrm{OPG_0}]}{[\mathrm{RANKL_{stand}}]} = 0.0947 + n_{RANKL_0} - [\mathrm{OPG_0}], \\
\beta_{\mathrm{RK}}^{\mathrm{RRO}} &= \frac{C_{\mathrm{RK}}}{[\mathrm{RANKL_{stand}}]} = \frac{[\mathrm{RK_0}]-[\mathrm{RANKL_0}]+[\mathrm{OPG_0}]}{[\mathrm{RANKL_{stand}}]} = 1.037 - n_{RANKL_0} + n_{OPG_0}, \\
\tau_{7\mathrm{days}}^{\mathrm{RRO}} &= 4.64.
\end{aligned} \tag{8}
$$

Interconnection between this RRO model and bone remodelling model is mediated by [RR]. The concentration of RR influences the value of parameter β_1 in the developed thermodynamic bone remodelling model, see (Klika & Maršík, 2009b). There are different normalizations used in these two mentioned models and we assume that in the case of standard values of RANKL and OPG, the parameter β_1 should have its standard value (corresponding to "healthy" state). Further, the typical normalised concentration of RR in bone remodeling model is $n_{RR} \in (1.35, 1.41)$ in standard state (see (Klika & Maršík, 2009b)). Thus:

$$\beta_1 = 1.41 / 0.79 n_{RR} - 0.81, \tag{9}$$

which gives the value $\beta_1 = 0.6$ for standard values of RANKL and OPG because n_{RR} under these condition equals 0.79 and n_{RR} is a result of the interaction in RANKL-RANK-OPG pathway at time $\tau_{7\mathrm{days}}^{\mathrm{RRO}}$. As can be seen, the value of n_{RR} influences only β_1, i.e. it acts only as a modification of initial conditions of the bone remodelling model. However, it will be seen in the results below that it sufficiently captures the influence of the whole pathway.

The increase in ligand concentration RANKL should lead to an increase in osteoclast formation, and consequently, the decrease of bone tissue density, and conversely, osteoprotegerin OPG prevents osteoclastogenesis. Modelling of this pathway is carried out through solving kinetic equations (2) with the above mentioned parameter values (8). Consequently, the output value of n_{RR} is used as an input variable in the bone adaptation model - (9). Tab. 1 gives an idea of how the added RANKL-RANK-OPG pathway may influence bone density (percentual changes of n_{RR} are more or less in accordance with data found in Quinn et al. (Quinn et al., 2001).

2.2 Incorporation of estradiol effects into the bone remodelling model

Estradiol is a major estrogen hormone in humans. Kong and Penninger mention that osteoprotegerin expression is promoted by estrogen (Kong & Penninger, 2000). Hofbauer et

The predicted effects of RANKL and OPG serum levels on bone density			
[RANKL] $\frac{pmol}{l}$	[OPG] $\frac{pmol}{l}$	n_{RR} [1]	normalised bone density [1]
0.84 (standard)	1.8 (standard)	0.790	100%(0.811)
4.55	1.8	1.132	76.9%(0.624)
0.1	1.8	0.13	**172.6% (1.40)
0.84	6.9	0.276	**152.9% (0.1.24)
0.84	0.6	0.892	92.5% (0.75)

Table 1. The predicted effects of the RANKL-RANK-OPG pathway on bone density. n_{RR} is a result from the RANKL-RANK-OPG pathway model, and consequently, bone density (the number in parentheses in the last column) is predicted from the presented thermodynamic bone remodelling model based on the calculated n_{RR}. The asterisk in the front of values notices that it may be necessary to intermit the treatment after a certain time:
* - after a longer time, ** - after a shorter period. Simulated or predicted data by model that are boxed are in accordance with data found in literature - (Kudlacek et al., 2003).

al. studied in vitro responses of osteoprotegerin production to estradiol levels (Hofbauer et al., 1999). They clearly showed that osteoprotegerin levels are dose-dependent on estradiol concentrations in vitro. We will take advantage of this observation and incorporate estradiol effects into the presented model.
As was mentioned, estradiol promotes osteoprotegerin expression. Thus, we may describe this fact using the following interaction:

$$Estradiol + OPG_{\text{producers}} + Substratum \overset{k_{\pm 1}}{\rightleftarrows} OPG + OPG_{\text{producers}}, \tag{10}$$

where $OPG_{\text{producers}}$ represents the group of cells that are expressing OPG and a mixture of substances needed for osteoprotegerin production is noted as *Substratum*. Similarly, as in case of RANKL-RANK-OPG pathway, a differential equation describing kinetics of estradiol concentration can be derived:

$$\frac{d[\text{Estradiol}]}{d\tau} = -[\text{Estradiol}](\beta^{\text{estr}}_{Substr} + [\text{Estradiol}]) + \delta^{\text{estr}}_{-1}(\beta^{\text{estr}}_{\text{OPG}} - [\text{Estradiol}]), \tag{11}$$

where

$$\begin{aligned} \delta^{\text{estr}}_{-1} &= \frac{k_{-1}}{k_{+1}[\text{RANKL}_{\text{stand}}]}, \\ \beta^{\text{estr}}_{\text{OPG}} &= \frac{C_{\text{OPG}}}{[\text{RANKL}_{\text{stand}}]} = \frac{[\text{OPG}_0] + [\text{Estradiol}_0]}{[\text{RANKL}_{\text{stand}}]}, \\ \beta^{\text{estr}}_{\text{Substr}} &= \frac{C_{\text{Substr}}}{[\text{RANKL}_{\text{stand}}]} = \frac{[\text{Substr}_0] - [\text{Estradiol}_0]}{[\text{RANKL}_{\text{stand}}]}. \end{aligned} \tag{12}$$

Again, this differential equation can be rewritten into (4) where $A = 1$, $B = \beta_{\text{Substr}} + \delta_{-1}$, $C = \delta_{-1}\beta_{\text{OPG}}$. Therefore, we know the analytical function that describes the evolution of estradiol concentration in time from its initial concentration. In vitro data from Hofbauer et al. will be used for estimation of these parameter values. Thus it is needed to know how the initial concentration of estradiol influences osteoprotegerin concentration after 24 hours. For this purpose we will use a relation between OPG and estradiol concentration following from (10):

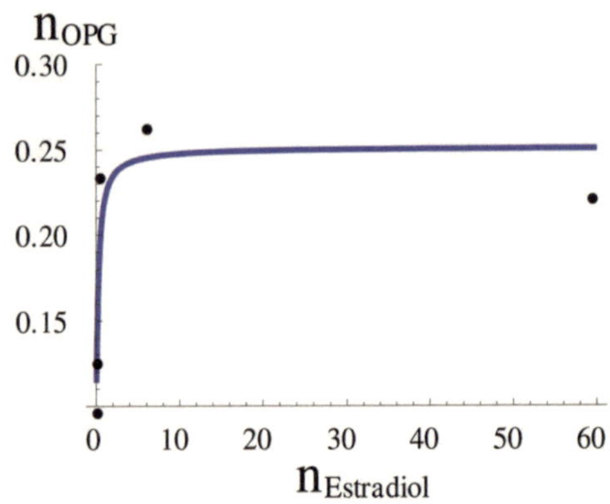

Fig. 2. Estradiol fitted solution (blue curve) by least squares method to data measured (dots) by Hofbauer et al. (Hofbauer et al., 1999).

$$[\mathrm{OPG}] = \beta_{\mathrm{OPG}}^{\mathrm{estr}} - [\mathrm{Estradiol}].$$

Now we may use the data from Hofbauer et al. to estimate all the parameters; a least square method will be used. Firstly, we need to normalise data from the experiment. Normalisation of concentrations and β_i parameters was carried out by [$\mathrm{RANKL}_{\mathrm{Standard}}$] concentration:

$$\frac{10^{-10}\,\mathrm{M}}{[\mathrm{RANKL}_{\mathrm{Standard}}]} = \frac{10^{-10}\,\frac{mol}{l}}{[\mathrm{RANKL}_{\mathrm{invitrostand}}]} = 0.0596.$$

Similarly, the other concentrations may be normalised.
The least square method gives the following values of parameters and the data fit is depicted in figure 2:

$$\delta_{-1}^{\mathrm{estr}} = 0.145,\ \tau_{24\mathrm{h}}^{\mathrm{estr}} = 26.17,\ n_{Substr_0}^{\mathrm{estr}} = 0.018. \tag{13}$$

The studied in vitro concentrations of estradiol most probably differs from serum levels found in human. It is needed to find a relation between in vitro and in vivo data. In other words, the in vitro data is used for gaining a qualitative fit because in vitro experiments enable dose-dependent studies that are needed. Consequently, a suitable scaling is used to obtain in vivo concentration values while the qualitative fit (shape of curve) is kept.
Ettinger et al. describe standard values of estradiol in humans 40–60 $\frac{pg}{ml}$ (Ettinger et al., 1998). Further, from the data mentioned in this study we may observe that there is a significant correlation between estrogen serum levels and bone density. Concretely, the difference in bone density between a group of women with mean estradiol level 10–25 $\frac{pg}{ml}$ and a group with $< 5\ \frac{pg}{ml}$ was +5.7% (higher bone density in the case with higher estradiol levels). From here it follows, that we may define standard estradiol serum level to be 50 $\frac{pg}{ml}$ = 184 $\frac{pmol}{l}$ ($\mathrm{MW}_{\mathrm{Estradiol}}$ = 272.38 (Estradiol analyzing method PV2001, 2001)) and further that a change from 35% of standard level (the average of the first group - 17.5 $\frac{pg}{ml}$) to 2.5% (the average of the second group - 2.5 $\frac{pg}{ml}$) causes a decrease in bone density by 5.7%.

Firstly, linkage of this simple model of estradiol influence on osteoprotegerin production with bone remodelling model is naturally mediated by RANKL-RANK-OPG pathway and thus by the already mentioned model of this control pathway. The predicted value of osteoprotegerin concentration based on estrogen level will be used as an input into RANKL-RANK-OPG model, and consequently, will be translated into appropriate change in number of active osteoclasts (see the previous subsection).

Now the aim is to determine the in vitro equivalent of the standard level of estradiol and to find a linear relation between the predicted normalised value of OPG from this model and of the RANKL-RANK-OPG model that would lead to behaviour as observed in vitro. If these considerations are used, one will find out that the in vitro equivalent of the standard level of estradiol is 10^{-8} M and the searched linear relation is:

$$[\mathrm{OPG}_0]^{\mathrm{RRO}} = k[\mathrm{OPG}]^{\mathrm{estr}}(\tau_{24\mathrm{h}}^{\mathrm{estr}}) + c,$$

where $k = 2$, constant c is opted so that normalised standard values of OPG coincide, $[\mathrm{OPG}_0]^{\mathrm{RRO}}$ represents the input value (initial concentration) of OPG for RANKL-RANK-OPG model, and $[\mathrm{OPG}]^{\mathrm{estr}}(\tau)$ represents the predicted normalised concentration of OPG at time τ based on estradiol level.

The normal range of estradiol serum levels is 40–60 $\frac{pg}{ml}$. It can be seen that predicted bone density is almost constant in this range (variation is 0.2%), see Tab. 2. After menopause, estradiol levels decrease to 10–25 $\frac{pg}{ml}$ in some women (Ettinger et al., 1998), which have almost normal bone density (1% decrease). However, in some women there is a more dramatic drop in estrogen (< 5 $\frac{pg}{ml}$) and bone density is approximately 5.7% lower than in the previously mentioned group (most probably this leads to osteoporosis). The same behaviour is observed here (more precisely the parameters were opted to capture this

The predicted effects of estradiol serum levels on bone density	
[Estradiol] $\frac{pg}{ml}$	normalised bone density [1]
60	100,1% (0.812)
50 (standard)	100%(0.811)
40	99.9%(0.810)
20	99.0% (0.803)
17.5	98.9%(0.802)
10	97.7% (0.792)
2.5	93.1%(0.755)

Table 2. The predicted effects of estradiol serum levels on bone density. Estradiol influences OPG expression, which in turn influences osteoclastogenesis. Consequently, bone density (the number in parentheses in the last column) is predicted from the presented bone remodeling model based on the calculated [RR]. Simulated or predicted data by model that are boxed are in accordance with data found in literature - (Ettinger et al., 1998) - here the observed effect in human is a decrease by 5.7% when the estradiol level is changed from 17.5 to 2.5 $\frac{pg}{ml}$.

effect): 0.755/0.802 = 94.1%. Simulation predicts that the more affected group of women experiences 6.9% decrease in bone density due to estrogen drop. Interestingly, these values and prediction may be valid for men as well, if they experience such changes in estrogen levels, because Hogervorst et al. states that estradiol levels in elderly men is 83.47 $\frac{pmol}{l}$= 22.8 $\frac{pg}{ml}$ which is in considered range of concentrations (Hogervorst et al., 2004). If these values in elderly men and women are compared, it can be seen that there is a considerable difference which may contribute to higher occurrence of osteoporosis in women than in men.

3. Examples of predictions of bone remodelling based on the presented model

We may now simulate the response of bone remodelling to changing environment, both mechanical and biochemical. Similarly, as was described in (Maršík et al., 2009), density distribution patterns may be obtained using FEM. The results from the previous section will be used.

Example - menopause

During menopause, a decline in estradiol levels occur. In some women, the decrease is very dramatic (a drop bellow 5 $\frac{pg}{ml}$ is observed, whereas a standard serum level is 40–60 $\frac{pg}{ml}$) while in some not (serum level remains above 20 $\frac{pg}{ml}$), see section 2.2. Further it was observed that, together with estradiol, there is a decline in nitric oxide levels (van't Hof and Ralston, 2001). An example of a woman who is physically active (correct mechanical stimuli on regular daily basis, i.e. approximately 20000 steps per day) but in a consequence of menopause has decreased serum levels of estradiol is depicted in figure 3. The presented model predicts a decrease of 8% in bone tissue density, which does not seem to be osteoporosis yet. This may be because menopause is accompanied by more effects than these two mentioned (as the mentioned decrease in NO) and also most probably because they are less physically active (may be caused by pain). If we combine the 8% decrease (figure 3) caused by menopause alone with another 9% decline (not yet published results) caused by improper loading, we get a significant drop by almost 20% in the overall bone density of the femur, which can be considered as osteoporotic state. One possible treatment of bone loss connected with menopause is treated with hormone therapy (HRT). Simulation of such a treatment that increased estradiol serum levels to 20 $\frac{pg}{ml}$ is given in figure 3. Again, the importance of mechanical stimulation shown when increased physical activity (running 30 minutes every other day) increases bone density in similar fashion as HRT treatment (the same figure). And best results are reached when both effects are combined and even the original bone tissue density can be restored - figure 3.

4. Conclusion

A natural goal of the modelling of a process in the human body is to help in understanding its mechanisms and ideally to help in the treatment of diseases related to this phenomenon. For this reason, more detailed influences of various biochemical factors were added.

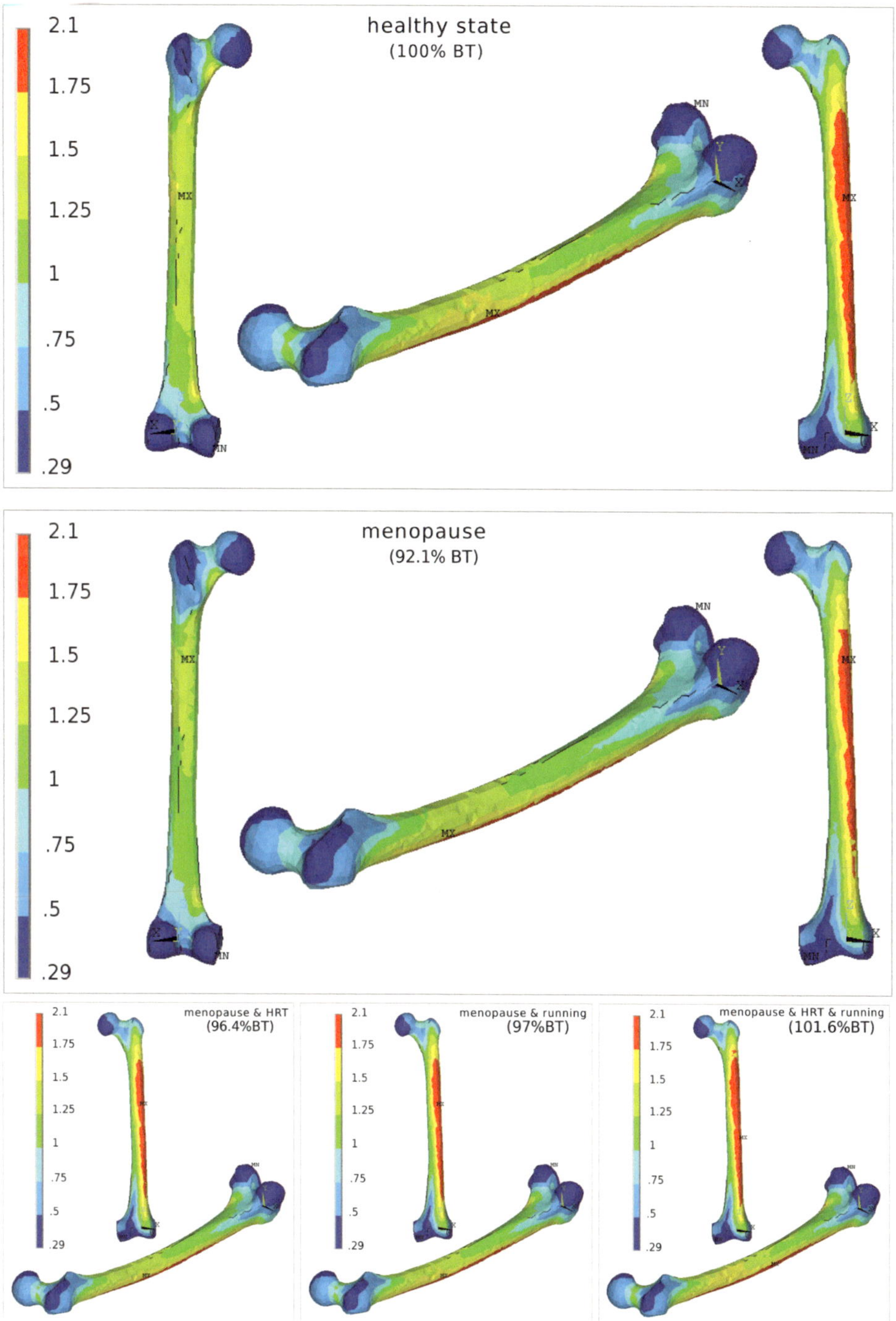

Fig. 3. Prediction of the menopause effect on bone quality (estradiol levels decreased to 2.5 $\frac{pg}{ml}$ l), treatment proposal, and its simulation - hormonal treatment (HRT), running (30 minutes every other day). Notice the change of bone mass (BM) of the whole femur.

Nowadays, the RANKL-RANK-OPG chain is deemed to be one of the most important biochemical controls of the bone remodelling process. The direct cellular contact of osteoclast precursor with stromal cells is needed for osteoclastogenesis. This contact is mediated by the receptor on osteoclasts and their precursor, RANK, and ligand RANKL on osteoblasts. Osteoprotegerin binds with higher affinity to RANK which inhibits the receptor-ligand interaction and as a result, it reduces osteoclastogenesis. Thus, the raise in OPG concentration results in a smaller number of resorbing osteoclasts, which leads to higher bone tissue density. The results discussed in the presented work have exactly the same behaviour. Similarly, the effects of RANKL, RANK, and estradiol were added to the mentioned model. Consequently, a disease, menopause, and its possible treatment were simulated. These results were partially validated by clinical studies found in literature.
However, the impression that the presented model is able to simulate the bone remodeling process in the whole complexity is not correct. It has limitations, as mentioned below, in the spatial precision of the results (i.e. actual structure of bone tissue) and also some control mechanisms cannot be included (e.g. TGF-βeffects). But still, the model can be at least considered as a summary of known important factors, comprising much of the currently known knowledge of the bone remodelling phenomenon, with some predictive capabilities and encouraging predictive simulations.
Since the presented model is a concentration model, it cannot be used arbitrarily. The limitation is, of course, in the spatial precision of results. The minimal volume unit (finite element) should be sufficiently large to contain enough of all the substances entering the reaction schemes, namely osteoclasts and osteoblasts. It surely cannot be used on the length scales of BMU where it is no longer guaranteed that any osteoclast is present. There are approximately 10^7 BMU in a human skeleton present at any moment (Klika & Maršík, 2009b) and, because bones have a total volume of 1.75l, there is 1 BMU per 0.175 mm^3 on average at any moment. In other words, the presented model cannot be used for length scales smaller than $\sqrt[3]{0.175\,mm^3}$ and we recommend that it is not used at length scales below $\sqrt[3]{0.5\,mm^3} \doteq 0.8\,mm$.
Ongoing applications of the model include simulations of the 3D geometries of the femur and vertebrae (FE models) under various conditions (both biochemical and mechanical). The preliminary results are encouraging and show the correct density distribution. Currently, we are working on bone modelling (change of shape of bone) model that would add the possibility to adapt bone shape to its mechanical environment as it is observed in vivo. Further, we would like to have a more detailed description of the inner structure of bone as an outcome of the model. Most probably, a homogenisation technique will be used for addressing this goal.

5. Acknowledgement

This research has been supported by the Czech Science Foundation project no. 106/08/0557, by Research Plan No. AV0Z20760514 of the Institute of Thermomechanics AS CR, and by Research Plan MSM 6840770010 'Applied Mathematics in Technical and Physical Sciences' of the Ministry of Education, Youth and Sports of the Czech Republic.

6. References

Alliston, T. and Choy, L. (2001). Tgf-beta-induced repression of cbfa 1 by smad3 decreases cbfa 1 and osteocalcin expression and inhibits osteoblast differentiation., *Embo J* 20(9): 2254–2272.

Beaupré, G. S., Orr, T. E. and Carter, D. R. (1990). An approach for time-dependent bone modeling and remodeling-application: a preliminary remodeling simulation, *Journal of Orthopaedic Research* 8: 662–670.

Bekker, P. J., Holloway, D. and Nakanishi, A. (2001). The effect of a single dose of osteoprotegerin in postmenopausal women., *J Bone Miner Res* 16: 348–360.

Bonewald, L. F. and Dallas, S. L. (1994). Role of active and latent transforming growth factor beta in bone formation., *J Cell Biochem* 55(3): 350–357.

Boyce, B. F. and Xing, L. (2008). Functions of rankl/rank/opg in bone modeling and remodeling, *Archives of Biochemistry and Biophysics* 473: 139–146.

Boyle, W. J., Simonet, W. S. and Lacey, D. L. (2003). Osteoclast differentiation and activation, *Nature* 423(3): 337–342.

Bucay, N., Sarosi, I. and Dunstan, C. R. (1998). Osteoprotegerin-deficient mice develop early onset osteoporosis and arterial calcification., *Genes Dev* 12: 1260–1268.

Carter, D. R. (1987). Mechanical loading history and skeletal biology, *Journal of Biomechanics* 20: 1095–1109.

Culik, J., Marik, I. and Cerny, P. (2008). Biomechanics of leg deformity treatment, *J Musculskelet Neuronal Interact* 8(1): 58–63.

Doblaré, M. and García, J. M. (2002). Anisotropic bone remodelling model based on a continuum damage-repair theory, *Journal of Biomechanics* 35(1): 1–17.

Dougall, W. C., Glaccum, M., Charrier, K. et al. (1999). Rank is essential for osteoclast and lymph node development., *Genes Dev* 13: 2412–2424.

Duncan, R. L. and Turner, C. H. (1995). Mechanotransduction and the functional response of bone to mechanical strain., *Calcif Tissue Int* 57: 344–358.

Eghbali-Fatourechi, G. et al. (2003). Role of rank ligand in mediating increased bone resorption in early postmenopausal women., *Journal of Clinical Investigation* 111: 1221–1230.

Eriksen, E. F. et al. (1999). Hormone replacement therapy prevents osteoclastic hyperactivity: A histomorphometric study in early postmenopausal women., *J Bone Miner Res* 14(7): 1217–21.

Estradiol analyzing method PV2001 (2001). Method number PV2001,Methods Development Team, Industrial Hygiene Chemistry Division,OSHA Salt Lake Technical Center, Salt Lake City UT 84115-1802. [online] http://www.osha.gov/dts/sltc/methods/partial/pv2001/2001.pdf.

Ettinger, B., Pressman, A., Sklarin, P. et al. (1998). Associations between low levels of serum estradiol, bone density, and fractures among elderly women: The study of osteoporotic fractures, *Journal of Clinical Endocrinology and Metabolism* 83(7): 2239–2243.

Frost, H. M. (1964). *The laws of bone structure*, C.C. Thomas, Springfield, Illinois.

Frost, H. M. (1987a). Bone "mass" and the "mechanostat": A proposal, *Anat Rec* 219: 1–9.

Frost, H. M. (1987b). The mechanostat: a proposed pathogenetic mechanism of osteoporoses and the bone mass effects of mechanical and nonmechanical agents, *Bone and mineral* (2): 73–85.

Frost, H. M. (1987c). Osteogenesis imperfecta. the set point proposal (a possible causative mechanism)., *Clinical orthopaedics* (216): 280–296.

Frost, H. M. (2000). The utah paradigm of skeletal physiology: an overview of its insights for bone, cartilage and collagenous tissue organs., *Journal of Bone and Mineral Metabolism* (18): 305–316.

Frost, H. M. (2004). *The Utah paradigm of skeletal physiology*, Vol. first, first edn, ISMNI, Greece.

Galileo, G. (1638). *Discorsi e dimostrazioni matematiche, intorno a due nuove scienze attinente all meccanica e i movimenti.*, University of Wisconsin Press, Madison, WI.

Gross, T. S., Edwards, J. L., McLeod, K. J. and Rubin, C. T. (1997). Strain gradients correlate with sites of periosteal bone formation., *J Bone Miner Res* 12(6): 982–8.

Haapasalo, H., Kannus, P., Sievanen, H., Pasanen, M., Uusi-Rasi, K., Heinonen, A. et al. (1994). Long-term unilateral loading activity on bone mineral density and content in female squash players., *Calcif Tissue Int* 54: 249–255.

Heřt, J., Fiala, P. and Petrtýl, M. (1994). Osteon orientation of the diaphysis of the long bones in man., *Bone* 15: 269–277.

Hofbauer, L. C., Khosla, S., Dunstan, C. R., Lacey, D. L., Spelsberg, T. C. and Riggs, B. L. (1999). Estrogen stimulates gene expression and protein production of osteoprotegerin in human osteoblastic cells, *Endocrinology* 140(9): 4367–4370.

Hofbauer, L. C., Kuhne, C. A. and Viereck, V. (2004). The opg/rankl/rank system in metabolic bone diseases., *J Musculoskel Neuron Interact* 4(3): 268–275.

Hogervorst, E., De Jager, C., Budge, M. and Smith, A. D. (2004). Serum levels of estradiol and testosterone and performance in different cognitive domains in healthy elderly men and women, *Psychoneuroendocrinology* 29: 405–421.

Hughes, A. E., Ralston, S. H., Marken, J. et al. (2000). Mutations in tnfrsf11a, affecting the signal peptide of rank, cause familial expansile osteolysis., *Nat Genet* 24: 45–48.

Huiskes, R.,Weinans, H., Grootenboer, H., Dalstra, M., Fudala, B. and Slooff, T. (1987). Adaptive bone-remodeling theory applied to prosthetic-design analysis., *Journal of Biomechanics* 20(11): 1135–1150. doi:10.1016/0021-9290(87)90030-3.

Ingber, D. E. (1997). Tensegrity: The architectural basis of cellular mechanotransduction., *Ann Rev Physiol* 59: 575–99.

Judex, S., Gross, T. S. and Zernicke, R. F. (1997). Strain gradients correlate with sites of exerciseinduced bone-forming surfaces in the adult skeleton., *J Bone Miner Res* 12(10): 1737– 45.

Kawasaki, K., Takahashi, T., Yamaguchi, M. and Kasai, K. (2006). Effects of aging on rankl and opg levels in gingival crevicular fluid during orthodontic tooth movement, *Orthodontics and Craniofacial Research* 9: 137–142.

Kimmel, D. (1993). A paradigm for skeletal strength homestasis., *J. Bone Joint Miner. Res.* 8(2): 515–522.

Klika, V. and Maršík, F. (2009a). Coupling effect between mechanical loading and chemical reactions, *Journal of Physical Chemistry B* 113: 14689–14697.

Klika, V. and Maršík, F. (2009b). A thermodynamic model of bone remodelling: the influence of dynamic loading together with biochemical control, *submitted to Biomechanics and Modelling in Mechanobiology* contact the authors for update.

Klika, V., Maršík, F. and Landor, I. (2008). Longterm prediction of bone remodelling effect around implant., *XXII International Congress of Theoretical and Applied Mechanics,*

Adelaide, Astralia, Abstracts book, Edited by J. Denier, M. Finn and T. Mattner. CD-ROM proceedings, Australia, ISBN 978-0-9805142-1-6, http://ictam2008.adelaide.edu.au.

Komarova, S. V., Smith, R. J., Dixon, S. J., Sims, S. M. and Wahlb, L. M. (2003). Mathematical model predicts a critical role for osteoclast autocrine regulation in the control of bone remodeling, *Bone* 33: 206–215.

Kong, Y.-Y. and Penninger, J. M. (2000). Molecular control of bone remodeling and osteoporosis, *Experimental Gerontology* 35: 947–956.

Kong, Y. Y., Yoshida, H., Sarosi, I. et al. (1999). Opg is a key regulator of osteoclastogenesis, lymphocyte development and lymph-node organogenesis., *Nature* 397: 315–323.

Kravitz, S. R., Fink, K. L., Huber, S., Bohanske, L. and Ciciloni, S. (1985). Osseous changes in the second ray of classical ballet dancers., *J Am Podiatr Med Assoc* pp. 346–348.

Kudlacek, S., Schneider, B., Woloszczuk, W., Pietschmann, P. and Willvonsedera, R. (2003). Serum levels of osteoprotegerin increase with age in a healthy adult population, *Bone* 32: 681–686.

Lanyon, L. E. (1996). Using functional loading to influence bone mass and architecture: Objectives, mechanisms, and relationship with estrogen of the mechanical process in bone., *Bone* 18: 37S–43S.

Lanyon, L. E., Goodship, A. E., Pye, C. J. and MacFie, J. H. (1982). Mechanically adaptive bone remodelling., *J Biomech* 15(3): 141–54.

Latos-Bielenska, A., Marik, I., Kuklik, M., Materna-Kiryluk, A., Povysil, C. and Kozlowski, K. (2007). Pachydermoperiostitis - critical analysis with report of five unusual cases., *Eur J Pediatr* 166: 1237–1243.

Lemaire, V., Tobin, F., Greller, L., Cho, C. and Suva, L. (2004). Modeling the interactions between osteoblast and osteoclast activities in bone remodeling., *Journal of Theoretical Biology* (229): 293–309. doi:10.1016/j.jtbi.2004.03.023.

Lieberman, J. R. and Friedlaender, G. E. (2005). *Bone Regneration and Repair.*, Humana Press Inc., Totowa, New Jersey.

Locking, R. M., Khosla, S., Turner, R. T. and Riggs, B. L. (2003). Mediators of the biphasic responses of bone to intermittent and continuously administered parathyroid hormone., *J Cell Biochem* 89: 180–190.

Loitz, B. J. and Zernicke, R. F. (1992). Strenuous exercise-induced remodelling of mature bone: Relationships between in vivo strains and bone biomechanics., *J Exp Biol* 170: 1–18.

Manolagas, S. C. (1998). Cellular and molecular mechanisms of osteoporosis., *Aging (Milano)* 10(3): 182–190.

Manolagas, S. C. (2000). Birth and death of bone cells: Basic regulatory mechanisms and implications for the pathogenesis and treatment of osteoporosis., *Endocr Rev* 21(2): 115– 137.

Mařík, I. et al. (2003). New limb orthoses with high bending pre-stressing, *Orthopadie-Technik Quarterly* English edition III: 7–122.

Marik, I., Kuklik, M., Zemkova, D. and Kozlowski, K. (2006a). Hajdu-cheney syndrome: Report of a family and a short literature review., *Australasian Radiology* 50: 534–538.

Marik, I., Marikova, A., Hyankova, E. and Kozlowski, K. (2006b). Familial expansile osteolysis- not exclusively an adult disorder., *Skeletal Radiol* 35: 872–875.

Marotti, G. (1996). The structure of bone tissues and the cellular control of their deposition., *Ital J Anat Embryol* 101(4): 25–79.

Maršík, F., Klika, V. and Chlup, H. (2009). Remodelling of living bone induced by dynamic loading and drug delivery - numerical modelling and clinical treatment, *Mathematics and Computers in Simulation*. doi:10.1016/j.matcom.2009.02.014.

Maršík, F., Mařík, I. and Klika, V. (2005). Chemistry of bone remodeling processes., *Locomotor System* 12(1+2): 51-61. [online] http://www.pojivo.cz/pu/PU_12_2005.pdf.

Martin, T. J. (2004). Paracrine regulation of osteoclast formation and activity: Milestones in discovery, *Journal of Musculoskeletal and Neuronal Interactions* 4(3): 243–253.

McLeod, K. J., Clinton, C. T., Otter, M. W. and Qin, Y. (1998). Skeletal cell stresses and bone adaptation., *Am J Med Sci* 316: 176–183.

Miller, S. C., de Saint-Georges, L., Bowman, B. M. and Jee, W. S. S. (1989). Bone lining cells: structure and function., *Scanning microscopy* 3: 953–961.

Mizuno, A., Amizuka, N. and Irie, K. (1998). Severe osteoporosis in mice lacking osteoclastogenesis inhibitory factor/osteoprotegerin, *Biochem Biophys Res Commun* 247: 610-615.

Morey, E. R. and Baylink, D. J. (1978). Inhibition of bone formation during space flight., *Science* 201(4361): 1138–41.

Moschen, A. R., Kaser, A., Enrich, B., Ludwiczek, O., Gabriel, M., Obrist, P., Wolf, A. M. and Tilg, H. (2005). The rankl/opg system is activated in inflammatory bowel disease and relates to the state of bone loss, *Gut* 54: 479–487.

Müller, R. (2005). Long-term prediction of three-dimensional bone architecture in simulations of pre-, peri- and post-menopausal microstructural bone remodeling, *Osteoporosis International* 16: S25–S35.

Neer, R. M., Arnaud, C. D. et al. (2001). Effect of parathyroid hormone (1 – 34) on fractures and bone mineral density in postmenopausal women with osteoporosis., *N Engl J Med* 344(19): 1434–1441.

Nishimura, Y., Fukuoka, H., Kiriyama, M., Suzuki, Y., Oyama, K., Ikawa, S. et al. (1994). Bone turnover and calcium metabolism during 20 days bed rest in young healthy males and females., *Acta Physiol Scand Suppl* 616: 27–35.

OPG ELISA kit (2006). BIOMEDICA OSTEOPROTEGERIN ELISA (BI-20402) FAQ. [online] http://www.bmgrp.com/fileadmin/user_upload/immunoassays/ BI-20402_OPG_FAQ_060717.pdf.

Otter, M. W., Shoenung, J. and Williams, W. S. (1985). Evidence for different sources of stress-generated potentials in wet and dry bone., *J Orthop Res* 3: 321–324.

Pacifici, R. (1998). Cytokins, estrogen, and postmenopausal osteoporosis - the second decade., *Endocrinology* 135: 971–976.

Parfitt, A. (1994). Osteonal and hemi-osteonal remodeling: the spatial and temporal framework for signal traffic in adult human bone., *Journal of cellular biochemistry* (55): 273- 286.

Quinn, J. M. W., Itoh, K., Udagawa, N., Hausler, K., Yasuda, H. et al. (2001). Transforming growth factor beta affects osteoclast differentiation via direct and indirect actions, *Journal of Bone and Mineral Research* 16(10): 1787–1794.

Raisz, L. (1999). Physiology nad pathophysiology of bone remodeling., *Clin. Chem.* 45(8B): 1353–1358.

RANKL product data sheet (2008). Product data sheet alx-522-131: Fc (human):rankl, soluble (mouse) (rec.), enzo life sciences. [online] http://www.enzolifesciences.com/fileadmin/reports/Fc_humanRANKL_Soluble_mouse_rec_rep_ Xcq55b.pdf.

Robling, A. G., Castillo, A. B. and Turner, C. H. (2006). Biomechanical and molecular regulation of bone remodeling, *Annual Review of Biomedical Engineering* 8: 455–498.

Rodan, G. A. and Martin, T. J. (1981). Role of osteoblasts in hormonal control of bone resorption - a hypothesis., *Calc Tissue Int* 33(4): 349–351.

Rubin, C. T. and Lanyon, L. E. (1984). Regulation of bone formation by applied dynamic loads., *J Bone Joint Surg* (66-A): 395–402.

Rubin, C. T. and Lanyon, L. E. (1985a). Regulation of bone mass by mechanical strain magnitude., *Calcif Tissue Int* (37): 411–422.

Rucker, D., Hanley, D. and Zernicke, R. (2002). Response of bone to exercise and aging., *Locomotor System* 9(1+2): 6–22.

Ruimerman, R. et al. (2005). A theoretical framework for strain-related trabecular bone maintenance and adaptation., *Journal of Biomechanics* (38): 931–941.

Schönau, E. (2008). New treatment strategy on neuro-musculo-skeletal diseases in childhood and adolescent., *Pohybové ústrojí* 15(3-4): 244–245.

Shapiro, F. (1997). Variable conformation of gap junctions linking bone cells: A transmission electron microscopic study of linear, stacked linear, curvilinear, oval, and annular junctions., *Calcif Tissue Int* 61(4): 285–93.

Sikavitsas, V. I., Temenoff, J. S. and Mikos, A. G. (2001). Biomaterials and bone mechanotransduction, *Biomaterials* 22: 2581–2593.

Simonet,W. S., Lacey, D. L., Dunstan, C. R., Kelley, M., Chang, M.-S., Luthy, R., Nguyen, H. Q., Wooden, S., Bennett, L. and et. al. (1997). Osteoprotegerin: A novel secreted protein involved in the regulation of bone density, *Cell* 89: 309–319.

Sobotka, Z. and Maˇrík, I. (1995). Remodelation and regeneration of bone tissue at some bone dysplasias., *Locomotor System* 2(1): 15–24.

Teitelbaum, S. L. (2000). Bone resorption by osteoclasts., *Science* 289: 1504–1508.

Tomkinson, A. et al. (1997). The death of osteocytes via apoptosis accompanies estrogen withdrawal in human bone., *J. Clin. Endocrinol. Metab.* 82: 3128–3135.

Turner, C. H., Anne, V. and Pidaparti, R. M. V. (1997). A uniform strain criterion for trabecular bone adaptation: Do continuum-level strain gradients drive adaptation?, *Journal of Biomechanics* 30(6): 555–563. doi:10.1016/S0021-9290(97)84505-8.

Turner, C. H., Forwood, M. R., Rho, J.-Y. and Yoshikawa, T. (1994). Mechanical loading thresholds for lamellar and woven bone formation., *J Bone Miner Res* 9: 87–97.

van't Hof, R. J. and Ralston, S. H. (2001). Nitric oxide and bone, *Immunology* 103: 255–261.

Weinans, H., Huiskes, R. and Grootenboer, H. (1992). The behaviour of adaptive bone-remodeling simulation models., *Journal of Biomechanics* (25): 1425–1441.

Weinbaum, S., Cowin, S. C. and Zeng, Y. (1994). A model for the excitation of osteocytes by mechanical loading-induced bone fluid shear stresses., *J Biomech* 27(3): 339–360.

Weinstein, R. S. and Manolagas, S. C. (2000). Apoptosis and osteoporosis., *Am J Med* 108(1): 153–64.

Whyte, M. P. and Hughes, A. E. (2002). Expansile skeletal hyperphosphatasia is caused by a 15-base pair tandem duplication in tnfrsf11a encoding rank and is allelic to familial expansile osteolysis., *J Bone Miner Res* 17: 26–29.